DEAD WOMAN WALKING

This book is dedicated to the memory of:

Louise Masset

Ada Williams

Amelia Sach

Annie Walters

Emily Swann

Leslie James

Edith Thompson

Louie Calvert

Ethel Major

Dorothea Waddingham

Charlotte Bryant

Margaret Allen

Louisa Merrifield

Styllou Christofi

Ruth Ellis

Dead Woman Walking

Executed women in England and Wales 1900-1955

ANETTE BALLINGER

Ashgate

DARTMOUTH

Aldershot • Burlington USA • Singapore • Sydney

Published by
Dartmouth Publishing Company Limited
Ashgate Publishing Ltd
Gower House
Croft Road
Aldershot
Hants GU11 3HR
England

Ashgate Publishing Company
131 Main Street
Burlington
Vermont 05401
USA

Ashgate website: http://www.ashgate.com

British Library Cataloguing in Publication Data
Ballinger, Anette
    Dead woman walking : executed women in England and Wales,
    1900-1955
    1.Women murderers - England 2.Women murderers - Wales
    3.Executions and executioners - England - History - 20th
    century 4.Executions and executioners - Wales - History -
    20th century 5.Capital punishment - Sex differences
    I.Title
    364.6'6'082'0942

Library of Congress Control Number: 00-134020

ISBN 1 84014 789 X

Printed in Great Britain by
Antony Rowe Ltd, Chippenham, Wiltshire

Contents

Preface

During interviews for academic posts and while seeking a publisher for this book this research was repeatedly referred to as falling outside the 'mainstream', 'unusual' and 'off the beaten track'. One established publishing company informed me that 'we don't do history'; another was of the opinion that there would not be enough demand for a book on such an 'obscure' subject.

In view of the fact that the research for this book indicated two miscarriages of justice (both of which are still on-going) and a third possible miscarriage of justice, it is difficult to accept that the subject matter is either 'obscure' or 'unusual'. Revelations concerning miscarriages of justice have become increasing common-place during the past 15 years, for example in the form of the Birmingham Six, the Guildford Four, the Bridgewater Three and Judith Ward. Individuals such as Eddie Browning have also been released as a result of his conviction being judged unsafe. If 'unsafe' convictions were the focal point of this book, we could easily challenge several of the other convictions apart from the three cases of possible miscarriages of justice. Bearing this in mind we are therefore entitled to ask why the cases of the women in this book are not perceived as deserving the same kind of scrutiny and the same kind of publicity? These cases all took place during the 20th century too, why then are they regarded as 'obscure' and 'outside the mainstream' of academic research subjects?

In an era where postmodernism in general and postmodern feminism in particular receive plenty of attention feminist academics and activists may wish to pause for a moment and consider not only what feminism has achieved during the 20th century but also the obstacles we still face - for example - why is it still necessary to justify the relevance of a book such as this?

However, the focus of this book is neither miscarriages of justice nor unsafe convictions (although these are important issues which are discussed where appropriate). Instead it is concerned with the punishment of women. This is a subject which affects over half the world's population and which - as far as Britain is concerned - usually captures the public imagination more than any other subject - for example in the form of the cases of Myra Hindley and Rosemary West. Historically too, this subject has received plenty of attention (and rightly so) - as can be seen, for example by the amount of research which has been carried out on the witch-hunts. Once again therefore, we are entitled to ask why it is that the punishment and death of women within living memory is judged to be 'obscure'?

While we no longer implement the death penalty in Britain the histories of executed women of the 20th century provide the immediate history to women serving current life-sentences in British prisons. Cases such as those of Sara Thornton, Kiranjit Ahluwalia and Emma Humphreys demonstrate just how important it is to 'do history'. Within a decade of the original trials - sometimes less - the same evidence resulted in very different outcomes for these women (and in other, less known cases) as a result of feminist challenges and campaigns.

The Ruth Ellis case is scheduled to be heard by the Criminal Cases Review Commission this year and will hopefully provide another example of the same evidence being interpreted very differently - only in this case the outcome will always remain the same whatever the Commission's findings, for the execution of Ruth Ellis is not reversible. Conversely, women do not need to be officially condemned to death to suffer the ultimate punishment as the case of Emma Humphreys demonstrates.

Cases such as these remind us that there is a close relationship between modern history and the present, that the fact the death penalty is no longer implemented does not make the history of executed women 'obscure' or outside the 'mainstream' - instead their lives, trials and deaths are crucial to our creation and understanding of the history of the present.

Acknowledgements

I would like to thank Ashgate Publishing Limited for having displayed confidence in this book from the very beginning. Also many thanks to the various members of staff whom it has been my good fortune to come into contact with, and who dealt patiently with my queries and provided helpful comments and suggestions.

Many individuals have offered valuable practical support, as well as intellectual stimulation during the research for and preparation of this book. My thanks therefore to Emily Atherton, Kim Atherton, Tony Baker, Alana Barton, Lillian Bloodworth, Tony Bunyan, Roy Coleman, Mary Corcoran, Frank Cotterell-Boyce, Paul Gilroy, Gillian Hall, Tina Hall, Paddy Hillyard, Peter Linebaugh, Stephen Mason, Susan O'Malley, Marion Price, Mick Ryan, Ann Singleton, Phil Thomas, Steve Tombs, Rod Tyrer, Tony Ward, Vron Ware, Anne Marie Webster.

My thanks also to the staff at Crookesmoor Library at the University of Sheffield and the Harold Cohen Medical Library at the University of Liverpool. Many thanks to the staff at the Public Record Offices in Chancery Lane and Kew, who were always extremely courteous and helpful. Silvester Manu and Tom O'Shea showed me great hospitality during my visits to The Royal Courts of Justice and the Lord Chancellor's Department, and Richard Kirby - also of the Lord Chancellor's Department - dealt patiently and efficiently with my various enquiries when I was establishing the research.

I am especially indebted to Tony Jefferson - who in his capacity as supervisor of my Ph.D. - provided valuable suggestions and critical comments on the original draft, and to Betsy Stanko and Anne Worrall for their support and encouragement in developing my thesis into a book.

I am grateful to Liz James and Dave Whyte whose technical expertise was crucial to the camera ready copy of this script. They both gave up precious personal time to help with the preparation of the script and offered support and advice which made this otherwise daunting task manageable.

Tia Ballinger's sense of humour and late night phone-calls was exactly what was needed after a hard day at the computer. Her view of the world added to the perspective of this book.

A special thank you to Kristi Ballinger for the many ways in which she has encouraged me. They are too numerous to list.

Finally, it has been my good fortune to have enjoyed and benefited from the intellectual insights and unerring encouragement of Joe Sim. From the conception of the research topic to the final draft of this book, his technical and practical support - always offered graciously and generously - has been invaluable.

*I was transfixed with horror, and over me there swept the sudden
conviction that hanging was a mistake - worse, a crime.
It was my awakening to one of the most terrible facts of life -
that justice and judgment lie often a world apart.*

(Emmeline Pankhurst, *My Own Story* 1914).

*Stupid men - you who believe in laws which punish murder by murder
and who express vengeance in calumny and defamation!*

(George Sand, *Intimate Journal* 1837).

The above quotations are cited in Partnow, E. (compiler and editor)
(1978) *The Quotable Woman* Anchor Books, New York p.101; p.11.

1 Introduction

> Do you not know that each of you is Eve? The sentence of God on
> this sex of yours lives in this age: the guilt must of necessity live too.
> *You* are the Devil's gateway. *You* are the unsealer of the forbidden
> tree. *You* are the first deserter of the divine law. *You* are she who
> persuaded him whom the Devil was not valiant enough to attack. *You*
> destroyed so easily God's image man. On account of your desert, that
> is death, even the Son of God had to die.[1]

Between 1900 and 1950 130 women were sentenced to death for murder in
England and Wales.[2] Only 12 of these women were executed. Thus, 91% of
women murderers had their sentence commuted. Of these 130 women, 102
had killed a child, nearly always their own, most of whom were under one
year old.[3] Two of the 130 condemned women were certified insane and one
had her conviction quashed by the Court of Criminal Appeal. That only 9%
of the total number of women sentenced to death were eventually executed
clearly illustrates that women stood a very high chance of having their
sentence commuted - usually to life imprisonment.

If we examine the corresponding figures for men, we find that during
the same period, 1,080 men were sentenced to death, 45 of whom were
certified insane, "22 had their convictions quashed on appeal, and 2 died
while under sentence of death."[4] In the remaining 1,011 cases 390 or 39%
had their sentence commuted,[5] leaving a total of 621 men who were
executed.[6] Thus, at first glance it would appear that state servants working
within the criminal justice system were far more reluctant to hang women

---

[1] Tertullian, 'Du cultu feminarum' 1.1. quoted in Noddings, N. (1989) *Women and
Evil*, University of California Press, Berkeley, p.52.
[2] *Royal Commission on Capital Punishment 1949-1953 Report* (1953), Her Majesty's
Stationery Office, London p.326.
[3] No woman has been executed for the murder of her own child under the age of one
since 1849. Following the enactment of the Infanticide Act of 1922 such cases did not
usually result in a murder charge being brought forward; instead the charge was
likely to be infanticide. Even in cases where a mother murdered her own children
older than one it was often assumed that she was psychologically unbalanced, and
there has been no case of a mother being executed for the murder of her own child,
regardless of age, since 1899. (*Royal Commission on Capital Punishment 1949-53
Report* 1953:11; Huggett, R. & Berry, P. (1956) *Daughters of Cain*, Allen & Unwin,
London, p.241).
[4] *Royal Commission on Capital Punishment 1949-1953 Report* 1953:326.
[5] *Royal Commission on Capital Punishment 1949-1953 Report* 1953:326.
[6] *Royal Commission on Capital Punishment 1949-1953 Report* 1953:301.

than men. But a closer examination of this apparent discrepancy reveals it to be a misconception which has come about as a result of the above statistics regarding infanticide. That is to say - unlike men - the vast majority of women murderers have killed their own child/children.[7] Once this is taken into account we find that women who had murdered an adult had less hope of a reprieve than men.[8] Thus, the large proportion of women murderers as killers of their own children has created a false impression of how female murderers fared inside the criminal justice system.[9]

Moreover, even if we accept that there was a "'natural reluctance' to carry out the death sentence on a woman" as the *Royal Commission on Capital Punishment 1949-1953 Report* argued,[10] that still leaves us with a total of 15 women who *were* executed during the 20th century in England and Wales. What was it then about these 15 women that caused the criminal justice system to overcome this 'natural reluctance'? Why were they not regarded as deserving of a reprieve from death? What were the discourses that a member of the public gallery activated, when, after the Ruth Ellis trial in 1955, he commented that she was "a typical West End tart"?[11] Or in 1953 when the trial judge in the Louisa Merrifield case in his summing up speech called her "a vulgar, stupid woman with a dirty mind"?[12] Similarly, at the trial of Edith Thompson in 1922, the judge saw fit to interrupt the closing speech for the defence with these words to the jury:

> ... you should not forget that you are in a Court of justice trying a vulgar and common crime. You are not listening to a play from the stalls of a theatre.[13]

---

[7]For example, in the years between 1900-1949 a total of 19 men were convicted of murdering children under one year, while 58 women were convicted of the same offence. These figures however, are more than reversed when considering the murder of older children in connection with sexual assault, where during the same period 31 men and no women were convicted (*Royal Commission on Capital Punishment 1949-1953 Report* 1953:304).

[8]Huggett & Berry 1956:240.

[9]Of the 130 women who were sentenced to death during the first half of the 20th century, 100 had been found guilty of murdering their children. This figure does not include the 512 women who were convicted of infanticide between 1923 and 1948 (1922 being the year when The Infanticide Act was introduced) *Royal Commission on Capital Punishment 1949-1953 Report* 1953:58.

[10]*Royal Commission on Capital Punishment 1949-1953 Report* 1953:12.

[11]Marks, L. & Van Den Bergh, T. (1990) *Ruth Ellis: A Case of Diminished Responsibility?* Penguin, Harmondsworth p.148.

[12]HO 29/229 XC2573, Court of Criminal Appeal Judgement p.17, Public Record Office, Kew, Richmond, Surrey TW9 4DU.

[13]Young, F. (ed) (1923) *The Trial of Frederick Bywaters and Edith Thompson* William Hodge & Co Ltd, Edinburgh and London p.119.

Questions and issues such as these have provided the motivation for initiating this research project; they form the backbone of this work and will be dealt with throughout the book.

The centrality of women's conduct and sexuality within our culture, and how women who step outside patriarchal definitions of acceptable female behaviour come to be regarded as 'dangerous' women - threatening patriarchal hegemony - has been well documented by several writers.[14] Women's behaviour, both in the private and public sphere, has been and still is regulated, disciplined and controlled by a pervasive system of male definitions of what constitutes a 'normal' woman. The constraints which women experience as a consequence of these definitions take both a material and ideological form and restrict their lives in a variety of ways. Thus, women's material reality is affected by child care and family responsibilities; limited financial resources; the threat and fear of male violence as well as actual violence. At an ideological level, discourses around sexuality, respectability, domesticity and pathology are crucial to the regulation and self-policing of women's behaviour.[15]

While the lives of all women are affected by these discourses, they become particularly visible when criminal women face the courts. For example, research carried out by Pat Carlen has shown that "single women, divorced women and women with children in Care ... [are] more likely to receive custodial sentences than women who, at the time of their court appearances, are living at home with their husbands and children."[16] Similarly, barrister Helena Kennedy has observed that a woman appearing in court in "bovver boots and a spiky hair-do" is likely to be judged more severely than a woman "in a broderie anglaise blouse and M&S skirt." In other words it is very important for a female defendant to "'soften' herself to conform with the judge's stereotype of appropriate womanhood by presenting an image of docility."[17] The mere fact that a woman has broken the law ensures that she will be regarded as someone who has failed to fulfil gender role expectations, and if this is overlaid by a refusal to demonstrate her commitment to conventional female roles in her personal life, especially in the areas around sexuality, respectability, domesticity and motherhood, she can expect to find herself at the receiving end of the full force of what Carlen has termed 'judicial misogyny'.[18] In this book I argue that every one of the women in my 15 case-studies fell well short of gender role expectations and, through a series of complex and sometimes contradictory processes, fell victim to cultural misogyny in general and judicial misogyny in particular.

---

[14]See for example Heidensohn, F. (1986) *Women & Crime* Macmillan, Basingstoke; Carlen, P. (ed) (1985) *Criminal Women* Polity, Cambridge; Jones, A. (1991) *Women Who Kill* Gollancz, London.

[15]See for example Hutter, B. & Williams G. (1981) *Controlling Women* Croom Helm, London.

[16]Carlen, P. (ed) (1985) *Criminal Women* Polity, Cambridge p.11.

[17]Helena Kennedy quoted in *The Guardian* 12th March 1991.

[18]Carlen 1985:10.

How certain perceptions of female murderers are produced and how these perceptions come to be regarded and accepted as *true* at the expense of other versions of 'the truth' about these women and their crimes, is a crucial issue if we are to understand why 15 women were legitimately killed by the British state in the name of its people. In her book *Offending Women* Anne Worrall addresses two central questions: "Under what conditions do certain people claim to possess knowledge about female law-breakers?" and "What is the process whereby such claims are translated into practices which have particular consequences for female law-breakers?"[19] Following Worrall, I intend to apply these questions to my case-studies. My aim is to create a bridge of understanding between the reality experienced by these 15 women at one end, and, at the other, a different version of that reality which was created as a result of the wealth of professional discourses surrounding them as their cases were processed through the criminal justice system. In the words of Worrall "members of muted groups, if they wish to communicate, must do so in terms of the dominant modes of expression."[20] If they cannot accomplish this, defendants become disqualified as speakers - their accounts become muted.[21] It is my intention to expose, explore and analyse the differences between how these women viewed themselves and the circumstances which led up to their crimes, as opposed to how, after their accounts had been mediated and 'translated' into the legal and medical discourses of the courtroom, they were viewed by state-servants, the media and the public.

No-one can ever claim to 'know' the reality of these women's lives or exactly how they felt - before, during and after the crimes of which they were accused and at their subsequent trials. As Maureen Cain states:

> ... anyone producing knowledge occupies a relational and historical site in the social world which is likely to shape and set limits to the knowledge formulations produced.[22]

Yet, by employing a feminist standpoint epistemology which argues for research that is located in and proceeding from "the grounded analysis of women's material realities"[23], it is possible to present alternative accounts to those put forward by judicial or medical personnel - accounts which I maintain are closer to these women's experiences than those which were to become official versions of 'the truth'. My examination of these 14 cases (one

---

[19]Worrall, A. (1990) *Offending Women* Routledge, London p.5.
[20]Worrall 1990:11.
[21]Worrall 1990:21.
[22]Cain, M. (1993) 'Foucault, feminism and feeling: What Foucault can and cannot contribute to feminist epistemology' in Ramazanoglu, C. (ed) (1993) *Up Against Foucault* Routledge, London p.88.
[23]Stanley, L. & Wise, S. (1990) 'Method, methodology and epistemology in feminist research processes' in Stanley, L. (ed) (1990) *Feminist Praxis* Routledge, London p.25.

was a case involving two women, hence 15 women, 14 cases), indicates that medical and legal discourses emphasised the 'wickedness' of the women's actions while minimising and marginalising their personal circumstances. The starting point of my account therefore will be to locate these women within the structural categories of social class, gender and sexuality and the material and ideological impact of these structures on their everyday lived experiences - their life histories. Moreover, these life histories can only begin to be understood after social processes such as poverty, education, domestic violence, motherhood, domesticity and respectability become part of the analysis. These are issues which, in varying degrees, had great bearing upon the lives of the 15 women in this study, and thus played a part in providing the context within which their crimes were committed and can best be understood. At the same time I shall show how difficult it was for the women to argue their cases on this terrain. This is because the wealth of feminist discourses around the different aspects of women's oppression within patriarchal society developed over the last three decades were not yet available in the first half of the 20th century and could therefore not be articulated. In stating this I do not wish to undermine or ignore the important achievements of first wave feminism. First wave feminist campaigners were successful in achieving the implementation of several pieces of important legislation culminating in equal voting rights for women in 1928.[24] The work of first wave feminists was both crucial and essential in establishing legal rights for women and in working towards the goal of legal equality between the sexes. Yet women of later generations were soon to realise that legal equality does not ensure substantive equality, nor does it bring an end to the predominance of patriarchal ideologies and discourses. First wave feminists can thus be seen to have laid the foundations on which second wave feminists can - and indeed already have built. This involves identifying all the discourses which play a part in the oppression of women, a process which is

---

[24]Frances Power Cobbe for example, in *Wife Torture in England* published in 1878, identified issues within domestic violence which are still relevant today such as "under-reporting, non-intervention, drink, blaming the victim, provocation and nagging" (Dobash R.E. & Dobash R. (1979) *Violence Against Wives* Open Books, Shepton Mallet p.73). *Wife Torture in England* is reproduced in Radford, J. & Russell, D.E.H. (eds) (1992) *Femicide* OU Press, Buckingham pp. 46-52). She also understood that men's assumption that they owned their wives was used to legitimise their ill treatment of them. In doing so Cobbe conceptualised domestic violence as a social rather than an individual problem, and her campaign for women's right to leave violent husbands played an important part in the implementation of the *Matrimonial Causes Act* in 1878. This Act meant that a woman could be legally maintained and separated from a husband who had been convicted of assaulting her. Similarly, Caroline Norton campaigned for over a decade for what in 1857 became *The Reform of the Marriage and Divorce Laws* and which, after several reforms, became *The Married Woman's Property Act* in 1882. Another example is that of Josephine Butler whose tireless campaign eventually resulted in the repeal of the Contagious Diseases Acts in 1883 (Forster, M. (1984) *Significant Sisters* Penguin, Harmondsworth p.48; p.171).

by no means complete.[25] But as we identify the many relationships which have bound us down we can apply our new-found knowledge retrospectively - to women of the past. This is what I intend to develop in my analysis of executed women. These women had similar experiences to contemporary women in terms of domestic violence, social powerlessness, poverty and economic marginalisation, but they either failed in their struggle to express their experiences because they had no language in which to do so; or, if they did succeed in expressing their reality, they were not 'heard' because they did not communicate within the boundaries of "the dominant modes of expression."[26] Nonetheless, all the above-mentioned structural categories - as well as the feelings and experiences which accompany them - existed before they were identified in feminist discourse and one of the great achievements of feminist theorists is their invention of "a place in which they can legitimately claim to have discovered relationships which no one 'knew' about, to have identified relations which pre-existed their identification."[27]

Thus, following Cain, I shall address the issue of how experience can become discourse - that is how some relationships bind women down and "are not yet available to politics because they are not yet available to anyone's knowledge" - hence they have not yet become discourses through which women can speak.[28] I shall argue that these 15 women's lives and personal accounts have been muted and their personal knowledges repressed or disqualified. The feminist task of building and creating "discourses and practices which are not yet there"[29] came too late to save the lives of these women, but there is still time to employ such discourses for the purpose of unlocking and releasing the biographies and knowledges which each woman held, and that is the task I have set myself.

Agency, Rationality and Violence

Unpacking and analysing the various legal and medical discourses as well as the sexist and misogynist ideologies which surround criminal women is essential if we are to restore a sense of rationality to the actions of female murderers. Throughout history women who kill have been portrayed as 'mad' - they did not know what they were doing - or 'bad', their evilness making them an aberration and setting them apart from 'true' feminine behaviour.[30] By denying the rationality behind women's murderous acts, traditional ideas around women's nature - their "supposed passivity, submissiveness,

---

[25]Cain 1993:84.
[26]Worrall 1990:11.
[27]Cain 1993:83.
[28]Cain 1993:84.
[29]Cain 1993:89.
[30]See for example Morris, A. & Wilczynski, A. (1993) 'Rocking the cradle: Mothers who kill their children' in Birch, H. (ed) (1993) *Moving Targets* Virago, London p.199.

asexuality and gentleness"[31] are allowed to remain unchallenged - such women are not 'real' women after all. This denial of rationality thus involves the "perpetrator's abnormal character" becoming the focus of attention while the social and personal circumstances which led up to the crime are largely ignored.[32] Feminism itself has shown reluctance to deal with female violence, perhaps concerned the subject will harm the feminist cause. Yet to deny that women are capable of violence and of experiencing the full range of human emotion is to argue on the same terrain as men who have perpetuated sexist myths regarding women's 'nature' throughout history.[33] When feminists have addressed the issue of violent women they are often portrayed as either victimised individuals reacting to a particular set of circumstances, or, resisting and challenging dominant ideologies around female behaviour.[34] Both these portrayals are valid and relevant and I draw from them in my own case-study analysis. Yet - undeniably - there is 'something else', another ingredient within women's violence which we find difficult to articulate because of the limited language available in which to express ourselves in this area. For example, in her discussion of Myra Hindley, Helen Birch writes:

> The mythology of Myra Hindley reveals, above all, that we do not have a language to represent female killing, and that a case like this disrupts the very terms which hold gender in place.[35]

The Hindley case is an extreme example of how difficult it is to discuss female killers without placing them in the 'mad or bad' category. Such labelling provides no insight into or understanding of the violent behaviour of women who kill. What is lacking here is an understanding that *all* human beings - including 'ordinary' women - have the capacity to suspend 'moral vigilance'[36], to put our own interests first and to harm others in pursuit of our goal. Therefore, when women act aggressively, whether such acts arise from feelings of revenge, a need for control or sheer powerlessness, it cannot automatically be assumed they are either 'mad' or 'bad'. Thus, in the following quote concerning an incident where Myra Hindley was assaulted and beaten by another female inmate, rationalising a case of serious female violence does not present a problem:

> '... two prisoner [sic] officers gave me a copy of the *News of the World* in which there was an article about the whole of the case.

31Morris & Wilczynski 1993:199.
32Campbell, B. (1991) 'Foreword' in Jones, A. (1991) *Women Who Kill* Gollancz, London p.xi.
33See for example Kirsta, A. (1994) *Deadlier than the Male* HarperCollins, London pp.5-8.
34Morris & Wilczynski 1993:199-200.
35Birch, H. (1993) 'If looks could kill: Myra Hindley and the iconography of evil' in Birch 1993:61.
36Kirsta 1994:169.

That did it. What I read, all about the tortures and the tapes, made me shake with horror and fury so much they had to take me for a walk to calm me down ... A few days later, when she passed me during recess, I snapped and just went for her. I battered her and battered her, I punched and kicked and head-butted her, I cracked her head off the railings and wall. I broke her fingers stamping on her hands trying to make her let go of the floors so she'd fall off down to the bottom and be killed. I wanted to kill her. I saw bone show through her face when I bashed her. When I'd finished with her, her teeth were all loosened at the front, her nose crossed to the left side of her face, two black eyes, split lip, ear, knees. She had to eat through a straw for the next six weeks and needed cosmetic surgery.' Expecting severe punishment, Josie was treated like a hero by the staff. The incident, she then realized, had been set up ... 'I heard one officer say to another: "I've been waiting twelve years for someone to do that."'[37]

The perpetrator of this severe level of violence is not considered mentally abnormal because she is responding to stimuli which is considered *normal* for women to be angry about. That is to say, her behaviour is classed as operating within the ideological norms of the female psyche - someone who loves children, will do anything to defend them and seeks revenge upon those who harm them. Hindley's violence, on the other hand, cannot be rationalised because it disrupts and "unhinges our assumptions about women."[38] In short, women's violence can only be rationalised and understood when it can be analysed within the framework of existing sexist assumptions regarding appropriate female behaviour. My case-studies however, include several cases where women's violence falls outside this criterion, hence I have set myself the task of avoiding the 'mad or bad categories', thereby restoring agency and rationality to their actions and in doing so, adding to the language which represents women who kill.

To assist me in achieving the above aims this book will be organised in the following order: Chapter Two consists of a social history of capital punishment, with a focus on women who were executed prior to the 20th century. The purpose of this chapter is twofold: first, to situate my case-studies in a wider historical and theoretical context which will indicate that throughout history, themes around sexuality and conduct have been applied to criminal women, and have mobilised discourses which ultimately contributed towards the final outcome of their trials and punishments. Second, I intend to illustrate that historically, as presently, the reasons why women kill cannot usually be traced to pathological causes - that is - the majority of these women are neither mad nor bad. Instead, "the story of women who kill is the story of women. Women who kill suffer from the same problems as the rest

---

[37]Kirsta 1994:109.
[38]Birch 1993:61.

of us, only worse."[39] This chapter therefore sets the tone for one of the major themes which is addressed throughout the book: that the starting point for our understanding of female murderers must be the social and political context rather than one which problematises individual psychology.

Chapter Three provides a specific feminist critique of traditional and well-established theories of punishment - the classical perspective, as well as Marxist, Foucauldian and cultural perspectives. I then discuss how feminists have challenged these masculinist perspectives by developing our own theories of women's punishment. A feminist theoretical perspective shifts the focus away from pathological explanations of women's actions to an examination of the wider mechanisms of social regulation, discipline and control which affect all women within patriarchal society. Here my aim is to illustrate how women are judged differentially according to their reputation, respectability, conduct and sexuality, and how this has particular implications for criminal women on trial in a court of law. Feminist theorists have made substantial inroads into the task of developing gendered analyses of women's criminality and their treatment within the criminal justice system. It is also due to the diligent work of feminist writers that we today are able to study detailed accounts of women who were criminalised and of crimes committed against them several centuries ago such as the witch trials and burnings. Yet within this area some territories have remained relatively uncharted by feminists - one of them is that of women who have been executed during the 20th century. It is my aim to fill this gap, hence Chapter Three is also where I outline a feminist theoretical framework which I argue can be applied to the women in my case studies.

Chapters Four, Five and Six consist of my 15 case studies. Here the individual women are situated within their particular historical moment, their lives are examined within the context of their sex, gender and class, their personal and social circumstances are explored. As each case is reviewed it will be analysed according to the principles of the feminist theoretical framework outlined in Chapter Three. For the purpose of clarity my case studies will be organised in the following manner: Chapter Four consists of an analysis of women who were executed as a result of killing children. In Chapter Five I examine the cases of executed women whose crime had been the murder of another woman. Finally, in Chapter Six I analyse the cases of women who were hanged as a consequence of having been found guilty of murdering their partners/husbands. Organising my case studies in this way allows me to both take account of the differences between individual cases within the same category as well as pointing to similarities between cases from the different categories.

Chapter Seven concludes this book by providing a summary of the central arguments raised throughout my case-studies. In this chapter I also bring these arguments up to date by analysing contemporary cases of women who kill as well as the legal changes which have taken place since the execution in 1955 of Ruth Ellis, the last woman to be hanged.

---

[39] Jones 1991:xvii.

It should be noted that the difference in the sizes of the case-studies reflects the unequal size of the files examined. Unsurprisingly, controversial cases generated larger volumes of documentation. Conversely, prisoners who had nobody to protest on their behalf, and/or whose execution did not attract a public outcry, have left little trace of their existence behind, a point which emphasises their muted state.

2 From Antiquity to Modernity: A Social History of Capital Punishment and Gender

The earliest records of capital punishment taking place in England stem from 450 BC when it was custom to throw the condemned into a quagmire.[1] Other early recorded executions include one from the year AD 695 for theft, its purpose being to set an example and discourage others.[2] From Anglo-Saxon times onwards the most common method of execution was hanging. The King reserved the right to choose specific forms of death and in addition to the gallows, beheading, burning, drowning, stoning and casting from rocks were also implemented. The Middle Ages saw a steady increase in the numbers of executions carried out each year, with torture accompanying the punishment in the majority of cases. Capital offences included "murder, manslaughter, arson, highway robbery, burglary and larceny," and in 1382 "the death penalty was extended to heretics under the writ *de heretico comburendo*..."[3] The cheapness of human life is illustrated by a case during the reign of Edward I, when the mayor and the porter of Exeter were executed for failing to shut the city gate in time to prevent the escape of a murderer.[4] The sheer numbers put to death is also noteworthy. During the 38-year reign of Henry VIII it has been estimated that 72,000 people were executed.[5] Accounting for its larger population this is equivalent to 20,000 people being executed per year in 20th-century Britain.[6]

---

[1] Laurence, J. (1932) *A History of Capital Punishment* Kennikat Press, N.Y./London p.2.
[2] Potter, H. (1993) *Hanging in Judgment* SCM Press, London, p.2.
[3] Laurence 1932:5.
[4] Laurence 1932:6.
[5] Holinshed, quoting Romilly, House of Commons Debate, 9th February 1810 in Calvert, E.R. (1927) *Capital Punishment in the Twentieth Century* C.P. Putnam's Sons, London, p.4. This estimate was originally made by David Hume in his *History of England* and is quoted in *Select Committee on Capital Punishment Report 1931* His Majesty's Stationery Office, London p.vii.
[6] Byrne, R. (1992) *Prisons and Punishments of London* Grafton, London, p.185; Potter 1993:3. Sharpe argues that a figure of 70,000 must be "a gross exaggeration, but it might well represent some folk-memory of what had been a real increase in judicial severity against convicted felons." (Sharpe, J.A. (1990) *Judicial Punishment in England* Faber & Faber, London p.29. Conversely, Gatrell estimates that in the century 1530-1630, 75,000 people were executed - the highest number ever (Gatrell,V.A.C. (1994) *The Hanging Tree* Oxford University Press, Oxford p.7.

While men were hanged, drawn and quartered for high treason, women were burned for this crime. Some writers have argued this was done to protect women's modesty: "For as decency due to the sex forbids the exposing and publicly mangling their bodies, their sentence is to be drawn to the gallows, and there to be burnt alive."[7] Others maintained that:

> Such judicial ferocity was directed wholly against women offenders. Many complex sociological motives were involved in this inhuman bias, which ... was influenced ... by the conception of woman as a vessel of sin.[8]

O'Donnell's scepticism over the issue of decency may be well founded if the case of Mary Blandy - hanged for the murder of her father in 1752 - is representative of women's treatment following execution. As she climbed the scaffold-ladder Mary said: "Gentlemen, don't hang me high for the sake of decency."[9] Her plea was to no avail:

> In about half an hour the body was cut down, and carried thro' the croud [sic] upon the shoulders of a man with her legs exposed very indecently, for two or three hundred yards, to a neighbouring house, where it was put into a coffin ...[10]

Social class as well as gender ensured differentiation in punishment. Beheading was considered "an honourable mode of death", hence reserved for higher classes from the 13th century onwards, where the axe was "for gentlemen and the rope for the common herd."[11] While the vast majority of those burned at the stake were women, ideological and religious offences were punishable by burning for both sexes.

From 1350 when the statute *Pro Clero* was implemented, until the 16th century, men who succeeded in pleading 'benefit of clergy' could avoid death altogether. This statute benefited the educated class since a defendant's ability to read was 'proof' he was a clerk of holy orders and usually ensured a commutation of the death sentence with a one year prison sentence, "in the custody of the local bishop rather than in a common gaol."[12] The benefit of the clergy plea became available to women in 1623 in a very limited form. Another 70 years were to pass before women could plead on equal footing with men. By this time (1692) the plea had been withdrawn in cases of serious offences, hence excluded most capital cases anyway. Therefore the

---

[7]Laurence 1932:9.

[8]O'Donnell, B. (1956) *Should Women Hang?* W.H. Allen, London, p.23.

[9]Gonda, C. (1992) '"Exactly Them Words": Histories of a Murderous Daughter' in Gonda, C. (ed) (1992) *Tea & Leg-Irons*, Open Letters, London, p.79; MacNalty, A.S. (1929) *A Book of Crimes* Elkin Mathews & Marrot Ltd, London p.197.

[10]Gonda 1992:80.

[11]Laurence 1932:6.

[12]Byrne, 1992:187.

'benefit of clergy' plea played a minimum role in saving women from the gallows.[13]

Both men and women suffered extraordinary cruel deaths, often for acts which are no longer criminalised. Margaret Clitheroe, for example, was charged with harbouring priests in 1586. She "preferred to remain 'mute'" (refused to plead), accordingly her punishment was to lie down on the cell floor with her arms and legs tied to posts and a heavy door laid over her:

> After this they laid weight upon her which when she first felt she said, 'Jesu! Jesu! Jesu! have mercy upon me!' which were the last words she was heard to speak. She was dying in one quarter of an hour. A sharp stone, as much as a man's fist, was put under her back: upon her was laid to the quantity of seven or eight hundred weight at the least, which, breaking her ribs, caused them to burst forth of the skin.[14]

Even when the punishment was death by hanging the sheer incompetence of those carrying out the sentence could give rise to scenes of extraordinary cruelty at the gallows. Ann Green from Oxford, was sentenced to death for infanticide in 1650, but miraculously survived her treatment on the scaffold:

> She was turned off the ladder hanging by the neck for the space of almost half an houre [sic], some of her friends meantime thumping on her breasts, others hanging with all their weight upon her legs, sometimes lifting her up and then pulling her doune [sic] again with a sudden jerk, thereby the sooner to dispatch her out of her pain: insomuch that the Under Sheriff fearing lest thereby they should break the rope forbad [sic] them to do so any longer.

Assuming she was dead, Ann's friends then placed her in a coffin and proceeded to the funeral destination at which point Ann again began to show signs of life:

> A lusty fellow that stood by (thinking to do an act of charitie [sic] in ridding her of the reliques of a painful life) stamped several times on her breast and stomach with all the force he could.[15]

---

[13]Beattie, J.M. (1986)*Crime and the Courts in England 1660-1800*, Clarendon Press, Oxford, p.142; p.451.

[14]Ancient document quoted in O'Donnell 1956:17-18. Some prisoners refused to plead in order to prevent the confiscation of their estates. Pressing prisoners slowly to death was often employed as a means of forcing them to plead (Calvert 1927:4-5).

[15]'News From The Dead, or a true and exact narration of the miraculous deliverance of Ann Green, who, being executed at Oxford, December 14 1650, afterwards revived, and by the care of certain Physitians [sic] there, is now perfectly recovered'

Women were burned at the stake until 1783.[16] The equivalent punishment for men - being hanged, drawn and quartered - was legal until 1814 when it was reduced to hanging with decapitation after death. This punishment remained legal until 1870, although decapitation did not occur after 1820.[17]

The fact that literate defendants could avoid the noose by pleading 'benefit of clergy' contributed towards ensuring impoverished and powerless people formed the vast majority of those executed. The real possibility of an untimely death for criminals within this social stratum must therefore have loomed large in their minds. Yet the evidence does not suggest disagreement within society about capital punishment itself.[18] Rather, it was justified on both utilitarian and religious grounds. Society had a right and duty to eliminate dangerous individuals and capital punishment was an expedient way of achieving this. Moreover, religious authority occupied a central part of pre-industrial culture, with biblical commands being utilised to authorise "capital punishment for offences against the law of nature that were universally condemned, such as murder."[19] This authority was epitomised in the pivotal role which the ordinary, and later, the prison chaplain played in proceedings prior to executions. Put at its simplest the ordinary could withhold sacrament if a prisoner refused to confess.[20] Confessions were important for two reasons. First, "the 'main business of the Ordinary [was] to break the spirits of capital convicts, so that they make no physical resistance to the hangman.'"[21] More importantly, however, the state was acutely aware of the role confessions played in lending legitimacy to executions, hence the chaplain's role in securing a confession was a crucial part of public proceedings leading up to the hanging:

'the processional to the gallows and the execution itself were supposed to be a carefully stage-managed theatre of guilt in which the offender and the parson acted out a drama of exhortation, confession and repentance before an awed and approving crowd.' The scaffold was both an altar and a stage.[22]

(1651) quoted in O'Donnell 1956:13-4. Thankfully, Ann was allowed her freedom after her ordeal.

[16]Laurence 1932:9.

[17]Byrne 1992:185.

[18]See for example Sharpe 1990:18 where he writes that issues around crime and punishment did not become a matter for public debate until the middle of the 18th century.

[19]Beattie, 1986:453.

[20]Linebaugh, P. (1977) The Ordinary of Newgate and His Account' in Cockburn, J.S. (ed) (1977) *Crime in England 1550-1800* Methuen, London p.260.

[21]Potter 1993:18.

[22]Ignatieff 1978:21 quoted in Potter 1993:20.

In this way public executions served a double purpose: individuals considered to be particularly wicked or dangerous were disposed of; at the same time they also "demonstrated to the broad ranks of the laboring poor the ultimate consequences of disobedience and immoral habits and law breaking."[23] Thus, while chaplains were supposedly servants of God whose job it was to attend to the spiritual needs of prisoners, men of the cloth who colluded in and encouraged what often appeared to be stage-managed 'confessions' and exhortations, also served a second master, the state.[24] In short, through the "varied means of caring for the condemned the interests of state and church coincided exactly."[25] However, public executions were not "an unchanging, static phenomenon" throughout the centuries and felons were not expected to make dramatic 'dying speeches' prior to the 16th century.[26] But throughout the 17th century the 'last dying speech' became an important ritual through which the condemned were expected to make public their state of penitence and contrition, declaring the fairness of the legal system and their willingness to die, freely acknowledging they deserved their punishment.[27] The majority of prisoners appear to have fully cooperated in this ceremony which in some cases began long before the actual execution. Elizabeth Caldwell, for example, "awaiting execution in Chester gaol, saw up to three hundred visitors a day and ... she gave them good admonitions, wishing that her fall might be an example unto them".[28]

Such speeches were of great benefit to the State, legitimising both capital punishment and the nature of 17th century secular and religious authority. That the state was anxious that even the most lowly and poor criminals demonstrate their support for and obedience to the established authority, indicates an acute concern about the social order. A state without a police force and therefore with very limited powers of physical coercion had to rely heavily on ideological control:

> Civil order depended, to a much greater extent than in the bureaucratized societies of a later age, on the effective internalization of obedience, the external sanctions being so often unreliable.[29]

This was particularly true of the 17th century, an era where the concept of 'absolute obedience to the King' was being questioned and Church authority over common people was weakening. It is within this context that Sharpe regards the public execution as the state's principal method of exercising power:

---

[23]Beattie 1986:455.
[24]Potter 1993:21-22.
[25]Potter 1993:29.
[26]Sharpe, J.A. (1985) '"Last Dying Speeches": Religion, Ideology and Public Execution in Seventeenth-Century England', in *Past and Present* 107, 1985, p.165.
[27]Sharpe 1985:152.
[28]Quoted in Sharpe 1985:152.
[29]Mervyn James (1978) quoted in Sharpe 1985:158-9.

public executions were not merely displays of brutality, but rather attempts by the authorities to exert ideological control, to reassert certain values of obedience and conformity. [30]

State and Church authorities however, could not count on cooperation from every condemned prisoner. For example, Hannah Blay - a prostitute hanged in 1668 - refused to conform:

> When urged to repent by the clergymen who visited her in prison, "she would laugh at them, and reply in some such language as she had learned in the devil's school, with which she was well stored". Her defiance continued to the gallows, where, we are told, "she ended her wicked life by a shameful death, without the least signs of repentance for her abominable whoredomes and wickedness."[31]

In the main however, the condemned accepted the set norms and values of their culture which included notions of 'dying good' and dying bravely, as well as acceptance of a "doctrine of absolute obedience." This acceptance crossed class boundaries, for in pre-industrial England it was not uncommon for members of the ruling elite to be executed, usually as a result of treason charges.[32] As England entered the 18th century with its accompanying 'Bloody Code' the anxiety over sinfulness, disobedience and disorder had been replaced by an overwhelming concern for the defence of property, and while the clergyman was still an important figure at the foot of the scaffold, the public execution itself "was becoming more of an embodiment of the secular power."[33]

Gender-Specific Crimes in Pre-Industrial England and Wales

Certain crimes in English pre-industrial society were gender-specific and applied to women only. Scolding, for instance, although not a capital offence, illustrates how the behaviour of both sexes was circumscribed.[34] Scolding was treated as a criminal offence, tried in a court of law until the mid-18th century and involved a "woman who criticized her husband, who bossed him, who insulted him, or who in any way showed her rejection of his authority."[35] Her punishment would take the form of public humiliation such as being locked into the pillory, being lashed, chained and/or whipped in public, wearing the 'scold's bridle', "a metal apparatus which fit (sic) over the

---

[30]Sharpe 1985:158.
[31]Quoted in Sharpe 1985:155.
[32]Sharpe 1985:163.
[33]Sharpe 1985:165.
[34]Faith, K. (1993) *Unruly Women: The Politics of Confinement & Resistance*, Press Gang Publishers, Vancouver p.32.
[35]Faith 1993:29.

head and into the mouth, with sharp points that cut into the woman's tongue if she attempted to speak." At the same time, the husband had failed to fulfil his gender role - being unsuccessful in enforcing his authority over her - ensuring she be a submissive and dutiful wife, obeying him at all times. Hence, he too could expect to suffer public humiliation and ridicule such as mocking and taunting, indicating that "just as women were being trained to be passive so were men being trained to be authoritarian."[36]

In 1650 adultery became a capital offence for women only.[37] If a woman killed her husband she was guilty of *petit treason* for she had committed the treasonous act of killing her lord and master:

> To premeditate the murder of one's husband was an aggravated form of homicide, an affront to hierarchical male authority as the foundation of the state and social order. The guilty woman was a traitor to gendered power relations and thus a threat to the male-dominant status quo.[38]

The burning of women at the stake was outlawed in 1790, while the *petit treason* charge was repealed in 1828.[39]

Convictions of infanticide were relatively rare prior to the 16th century, although this may indicate that only prosecutions, not infanticide itself, were rare, thus suggesting social attitudes to this crime were more relaxed than was the case at the beginning of the 17th century.[40] This period saw the authorities grow "increasingly fearful of the sexual immorality and criminal tendencies of the increasingly numerous wandering poor."[41] Within this context new legislation was passed in 1624, aimed solely at unmarried mothers which made concealment of birth a capital offence. Moreover, the prosecution no longer had to prove that a mother had killed her baby, instead the burden of proof that a child, the birth of whom she had concealed, was stillborn, fell upon the mother.[42] This legislation was not motivated by a desire to preserve the lives of new-born infants but was aimed "against lewd whores, who ... to avoid their shame, and the charge of a bastard ... privately destroy the infant."[43] In reality however, this legislation served to control and regulate the sexuality of a most vulnerable group, for the vast majority of women to whom this law applied, were not 'lewd whores' but domestic

---

[36]Faith 1993:29-30; 30.

[37]According to Faith (1993:30) the year was 1650; O'Donnell however, states the year was 1630 (1956:11).

[38]Faith 1993:32.

[39]Faith, 1993:33.

[40]Hoffer, P. & Hull N.E.H. (1984) *Murdering Mothers: Infanticide in England and New England 1558-1803*, New York University Press, New York pp.5-6.

[41]Hoffer & Hull 1984:12.

[42]Beattie 186:113; Smart, C. (1992) 'Introduction' in Smart, C. (ed) (1992) *Regulating Womanhood*, Routledge, London p.16.

[43]17th century commentator quoted in Beattie 1986:113-14.

servants.[44] Women servants could be pressurised to have sex by fellow servants and by masters who were in a position of power should they refuse to comply. Yet they would not be allowed to keep their position if pregnant. Infanticide was therefore usually a desperate act, committed by 'respectable' women in an attempt to maintain their good character. After all, if a woman was already considered to be a 'lewd whore', an illegitimate child could hardly damage her image further, as was recognised at the time:

> Common whores, whom all the world knows to be such, hardly ever destroy their children ... because they have lost their modesty to a greater degree, and the fear of shame makes hardly an impression on them.[45]

The fact that married women were excluded from this law confirms it was not concerned with the protection of infant life, but instead "sought to discourage fornication by making it more difficult for unmarried women to escape the results of their immorality."[46] At another level, there was a reluctance to acknowledge married women could be guilty of infanticide, hence they were rarely convicted of this crime.[47] In cases where the evidence was indisputable the mother would usually be acquitted on the grounds of insanity.[48] The idea of a married woman wishing to rid herself of a legitimate child was threatening and unacceptable to the patriarchal legal establishment, it was therefore quietly denied or ignored.

In sum, concealment of birth, like adultery and petit treason, was a gender-specific capital offence; moreover, it was a crime which in almost all cases affected powerless impoverished women who had no hope of supporting themselves or their infants, instead an illegitimate child meant stigmatisation for life, with little chance of future employment or marriage.[49] While there were plenty of 'guide' books available instructing female servants in how to avoid intimate contact with male servants and masters, there was no attempt by the legal establishment to hold the fathers of the dead infants responsible for 'immoral behaviour'. As the century drew to a close, the sheer injustice of the 1624 Concealment Act increasingly resulted in juries refusing to convict women and gradually it became necessary for the prosecution to prove a woman had intended to kill her child.[50] The law was finally repealed in 1803.[51]

---

[44]Malcolmson, R.W. (1977) 'Infanticide in the Eighteenth Century' in Cockburn, J.S. (ed) (1977) *Crime in England 1550-1800*, Methuen & Co Ltd, London p.192; Beattie 1986:114.
[45]Mandeville, quoted in Beattie 1986:114.
[46]Beattie 1986:113; Smart 1992:17.
[47]Hoffer & Hull 1984:107.
[48]Hoffer & Hull 1984: Ch.4.; Beattie 1986:121.
[49]Malcolmson 1977:192-3.
[50]Beattie 1986:120.
[51]Malcolmson 1977:197.

The Witch Hunts

> If all the harm that women have done
> Were put in a bundle and rolled into one,
> Earth would not hold it
> It could not be lighted nor warmed by the sun.
> Such masses of evil
> Would puzzle the devil
> And keep him in fuel while Time's wheels run.
> But if all the harm that's done by men
> Were doubled and doubled again,
> And melted and fused into vapour and then
> Were squared and raised to the power of ten,
> There wouldn't be nearly enough not near
> To keep a small girl for the tenth of a year.[52]

Although not a gender-specific crime it has been estimated that of the 9 million who were executed for witchcraft offences during the 15th, 16th and early 17th century, 85-90% were women.[53] Again, certain groups of women were targeted - in this case poor, illiterate peasant women, a considerable number of whom were over 40 years old.[54] Furthermore, over 50% of women found guilty of witchcraft were either widowed or single.[55] Thus, many of the accused enjoyed relative economic independence, either because they had inherited their husband's craft, trade, property or land,[56] or because they possessed healing skills and knowledge of herbs and poisons in an era without an organised medical profession.[57] Such skills and knowledge earned them respect and standing within their community, and together with their status as single women, they enjoyed a degree of independence in many areas of their lives - physically, intellectually, spiritually, as well as at an economic and moral level. Daly argues it was as a result of this independence - and hence this *alternative* lifestyle - that these women came to be regarded

---

[52]Stephen, J.K. "A Thought" in Noddings, N. (1989) *Women and Evil*, University of California Press, Berkeley, p.35.

[53]Hester, M. (1992) *Lewd Women & Wicked Witches*, Routledge, London, p.161. Hester's research of the Assize Court records for Essex revealed that in this county "at least 90% of those formally accused of using witchcraft were women" (p.161). See also Goode, E. & Ben-Yehuda, N. (1994) *Moral Panics* Blackwell, Oxford, p.157; Morgan, R. (1989) *The Demon Lover*, Methuen, London, p.78; Dworkin, A. (1982) *Our Blood*, The Women's Press, London, p.17 for estimates of the numbers of women killed as a result of the witchcraze.

[54]Hester 1992:161.

[55]Hester 1992:161.

[56]Hester 1992:161.

[57]Miles, R. (1989) *Women's History of the World* Paladin, London, p.136; English, D. & Ehrenreich, B. (1979) *For Her Own Good* Pluto, London, Ch.2.

as dangerous.[58] They presented "an option of 'eccentricity'"[59] - their *conduct* was both "anomalous and non-conformist"[60] - hence, they posed an active and profound threat to male monopoly in every sphere of daily life.[61] As Ussher notes:

> The juxtaposition of the witch and the spinster is in reality a continuation of the discourse wherein the woman outside of the controls of a relationship with a man is deemed a threat.[62]

Detailed historical accounts and feminist analyses of the witch-hunts have been uncovered and developed by several authors elsewhere[63] and it is not the purpose here to review this literature. However, no book on executed women can be complete without considering what Szasz has likened to the persecution of the Jews by Nazis in the 20th century[64], and Anderson and Zinsser have called "the most hideous example of misogyny in European history."[65] While it is too simplistic to attribute the witch-hunts to a single cause, a familiar set of themes are as clearly identifiable in connection with these hunts as they are in other areas of women's punishment - including 20th century execution. I have already discussed the theme of transgression; the second theme is that of female sexuality and the third theme is the structural forces which influenced the socio-political culture during this period.

The Catholic theology text *Malleus Maleficarum* - written in 1486 - was highly influential at the time of the witchcraze.[66] It reinforced existing misogynist ideologies and beliefs and provided numerous examples of the male terror of female sexuality. The authors explain witchcraft as a woman's

---

[58]Support for this thesis is offered in the theological text *Malleus Maleficarum (The Hammer of Witches)* (1486) written by two monks, Henry Sprenger & James Kramer where, in their chapter 'Concerning Witches', they write "no-one does more harm to the catholic faith than midwives", and, "midwives ... surpass all others in wickedness." (Naish, C. (1991) *Death Comes to the Maiden* Routledge p.29; p.26).

[59]Daly M. (1979) *Gyn/Ecology* The Women's Press London, p.186.

[60]Miles 1989:137.

[61]Daly 1979:184.

[62]Ussher, J. (1991) *Women's Madness* Harvester Wheatsheaf, London, p.47.

[63]See for example Hester, M. (1992) *Lewd Women & Wicked Witches* Routledge, London; Barstow, A.L. (1994) *Witchcraze* Pandora, London; Purkiss, D. (1996) *The Witch in History* Routledge, London.

[64]Szasz, T.S. (1971) *The Manufacture of Madness* RKP, London, p.95.

[65]Anderson, B.S. & Zinsser, J.P. (1988) *A History of Their Own* Vol I, Harper & Row, New York, p.172.

[66]As noted above, the authors were two Dominican Inquisitors, Kramer & Sprenger. Given that printing was in its infancy in 1486, it must have been quite an achievement for *Malleus Malificarum* to have reached its 32nd edition by 1660 with translations in both German and French (Anderson, B.S. & Zinsser, J.P. 1988:166). Over five centuries after its first publication the book is still in print and was published by Bracken Books (London) in 1996.

crime because she is "more vulnerable to Satan's enticements", a woman is "more carnal than a man, as is clear from her many carnal abominations", and "all witchcraft comes from carnal lust, which is in women insatiable."[67] As Naish points out, such statements reveal more about the psychology of the authors than of women's role in witchcraft. Indeed, the highly "exotic sexual confessions characteristic of witches tried by the Inquisition occur *only* in those trials." It therefore seems reasonable to assume they are the "creations of the scholastic Inquisition" - not the vocabulary of poor, illiterate peasant women.[68] At the same time, this sexual construction of womanhood served to justify and legitimate men's control over women - "women were in a general sense seen as naturally deviant in relation to men and the male-dominated society, and were perceived to be especially prone to the ultimate deviance of siding with the Devil."[69] Their sexual unruliness *required* them to be kept under control.[70]

This intensified concern about 'unruly' women and the perceived need to control them can best be understood within the wider social, political and cultural framework of a society going through a protracted move from medievalism to modernity which created an atmosphere of uncertainty:

> Learned men sensed impending chaos. All of the traditional means of establishing order seemed discredited and useless. Religious reformers and prosletyzers questioned the Catholic faith and its rituals. Protestant sects condemned everything from the authority of the Pope to everyday practices like the saying of the rosary. Printing presses carried the doubts and attacks all over Europe. Religious and civil wars in Germany, France, and Scotland with one prince replaced by another, one faith by another, called all princes and all beliefs into question. Locally controlled markets and trade gradually had given way to great trading centers and monopolies protected by the regulations of dynastic rulers, leaving town elders - the guildsmen and the wealthy entrepreneurial families - without the familiar economic system that had guaranteed them their livelihood and hegemony.[71]

Goode and Ben-Yehuda also place the witch-hunts within the context of a period traumatised by upheaval:

> [It] was a time of great enterprise, bold thought, innovation, as well as one of deep confusion and anomie, a feeling that society had lost

---

[67]Dworkin, A. (1982) *Our Blood* The Women's Press, London. p.17.
[68]Naish 1991:29.
[69]Hester 1992:144.
[70]Hester 1992:148.
[71]Anderson & Zinsser 1988:162.

its norms and boundaries and that the uncontrollable forces of change were destroying all order and moral tradition.[72]

Questions and doubts about issues hitherto taken for granted about the world in turn led to an environment of "social intolerance and a search for scapegoats,"[73] and for a time women identified as witches appeared to represent all that was wrong with the world. The witch-hunts - "embellished with all of the oldest misogynist mythology" - can be seen as an expression of this social intolerance.[74] The witches, with their unconventional lifestyle, appeared to be successful in their efforts at self-determination and this, together with their support of the powerless, seemed to narrow the gap between ruler and ruled.[75] The witches themselves thus became part of the perceived disorder and uncertainty of the era. "By persecuting witches, this society, led by the church, attempted to redefine its moral boundaries."[76] Church and secular elites worked to restore "order through definition and conformity." Hence, both Church and State claimed to offer an end to uncertainty and misfortune through the elimination of witches:

> If peasant women and men, townswomen and men, would identify the cunning folk, officials of Church and state with all the paraphernalia of legal procedures and scientific rules of evidence would try and execute them. Thus rich and poor, powerful and powerless, Protestant and Catholic tacitly and actively participated in the persecution and murder of thousands of illiterate peasant women.[77]

Because witches were mainly older, illiterate peasant women, they proved to be a particularly easy target for the inquisitors since they had "no organized or identifiable successors;" there was "no group to protect their good name."[78] Meanwhile, the witch-trials themselves provide further evidence of the extraordinary contradictions inherent in an era which was both rational and irrational, where law and science were in their infancy, divine intervention was questioned, yet a new order and structure was not in place - "the law was not yet just" and "science not yet scientific."[79] Once a new order and structure were in place - that is to say - once Protestantism had succeeded in redefining patriarchy by replacing the image of the evil woman with that of the proper wife in religious literature, it was no longer necessary

---

[72]Goode & Ben-Yehuda 1994:168.
[73]Szasz 1971:112; Goode & Ben-Yehuda 1994:168.
[74]Anderson & Zinsser 1988:164.
[75]Szasz 1971:89.
[76]Goode & Ben-Yehuda 1994:169.
[77]Anderson & Zinsser 1988:164.
[78]Szasz 1971:106.
[79]Anderson & Zinsser 1988:169.

to ensure women's conformity by brute force such as torture and burning at the stake.[80]

The Protestant Reformation transformed patriarchal discourses by rejecting notions of women's inherent evilness and emphasising the concept of spiritual equality between the sexes. Women should be regarded as helpmates and companions to their husbands - couples "should be as two sweet friends, bred under one constellation ..."[81] Each family was to become a "little church and a little state"[82] - keeping itself in a state of purity. It was within this context that a redefinition of marriage, sexuality and adultery became necessary. This redefinition appeared to elevate the status of women, however, in reality women remained subordinate to men who were now "the spiritual leaders of their families."[83] 'Spiritual equality' was not to be extended into the material reality of women's lives, instead Luther, Calvin and Knox all insisted that women should "be obedient to their husbands, keep silent in public, and busy themselves with their households."[84] Moreover, the demand by these Protestant leaders that convents should be abolished, closed the one option which had hitherto been open to women who did not relish the prospect of marriage and countless pregnancies which invariably followed in an era without reliable contraception. Therefore the Reformation brought with it a more restricted and closely defined role for women than in previous eras - a role almost entirely confined to the private sphere - that of domesticity and motherhood.[85] By replacing the twin evils of women and sex with a doctrine of the good wife and mother, the Reformation had successfully redefined patriarchy. From then onwards, 'the cult of domesticity'[86] rather than women as 'apostles of the devil'[87] would play the dominant role in regulating female behaviour.

The Bloody Code

The witchcraze reached its peak in the 16th century, although the Statutes were not repealed until 1736, and as late as 1716 children were being executed as in the case of Elizabeth Hicks, aged 11, hanged with her mother Mary "for having, on their own confession, sold their souls to the devil and obliged their neighbours to perform this painful miracle."[88] The tail end of

---

[80]Hamilton 1978:73.

[81]Hamilton 1978:65.

[82]Quoted in Hamilton 1978:55.

[83]Hamilton 1978:68.

[84]French, M. (1986) *Beyond Power: On Women, Men & Morals*, Abacus, London, p.171.

[85]French 1986:171; Hamilton 1976:68.

[86]O'Donovan, K. (1985) *Sexual Divisions in Law*, Weidenfeld & Nicolson, London, pp.53-57.

[87]Hamilton 1978:64.

[88]Hibbert, 1968:31.

the witchcraze therefore overlapped with the era in which the English system of law was known as the 'Bloody Code' - the years between 1688 and 1815. Thus, apart from the Witchcraft Statute introduced in 1542, there was a general intensification in the power of law to punish with an increasing number of statutes carrying the death penalty during the 16th century.[89] This increase followed a period where numbers of executions appear to have been relatively low[90] and - as argued above - were part of wider political, social and economic changes within the nation as a whole. In the words of McLynn:

> ... the Bloody Code was an organic process of adaptation by a society concerned to protect new forms of property and to restrict the benefits of a huge increase in wealth ... In functional terms the Bloody Code was the response of a society where capital enterprise was releasing new forms of wealth which could not be adequately protected without a regular police force.[91]

During this period capital statutes rose from approximately 50 to 200, of which the vast majority was concerned with offences against property. No longer was the interest of Divine Will or the state paramount. "Property had swallowed them all" - hence Locke wrote that "Government has no other end but the preservation of property."[92]

By the mid-18th century capital offences included stealing a horse or sheep; "to pickpocket more than a shilling; to steal more than forty shillings in a dwelling place or five shillings in a shop; to purloin linen from a bleaching ground or woollen cloth from a tenter ground; to cut down trees in a garden or orchard; to break the border of a fishpond so as to allow the fish to escape;"[93] and robbing a rabbit warren.[94] This multitude of capital statutes did not however, result in an increase in executions, for the point of the Bloody Code was not that *every* individual committing such offences would automatically be executed, but that this punishment should be applied *selectively*.[95] If every petty criminal was executed the law would not be able to maintain credibility. Capital punishment was therefore designed to be exemplary rather than efficient in nature. In a society with no professional police force even the most minor crimes carried the death penalty because of what was believed to be its *deterrent* value. As expressed by Paley: "The

---

[89]Sharpe 1990:27.

[90]Sharpe, 1990:28. For example, in the 20-year period between 1377 and 1397 only 13 were hanged in Warwickshire (p.29).

[91]McLynn 1991:ix-x; ix.

[92]Hay, D. (1977) 'Property, authority and the criminal law' in Hay, D., Linebaugh, P., Rule, J., Thompson, E.P. & Winslow, C. (eds) (1977) *Albion's Fatal Tree* Penguin, Harmondsworth p.18.

[93]McLynn 1991:x.

[94]Calvert 1927:4.

[95]Sharpe 1990:38; McLynn 1991:xiii.

proper end of human punishment is not the satisfaction of justice, but the prevention of crimes."[96]

Mary Jones was to feel the full brunt of this philosophy. Having no means of supporting herself and her two children after her husband was press-ganged into the navy, she stole some "coarse linen from a shop counter" in a desperate effort to feed her starving children. For this crime she was executed in 1771. As she was taken to Tyburn in an unsprung cart "the youngest baby suckled at her breast but she never saw her other child who had been handed over to the Poor Law authorities. In the closing minutes of her life Mary fondled the child she loved so dearly and prayed ..." One witness commented: "Mary Jones met her death with amazing fortitude."[97] Mary was 19 years old.[98] She had committed her crime at a time when shoplifting was perceived as a major problem in the Ludgate area, therefore she must be made an example of - sending the message to would-be shoplifters that this crime would not be tolerated. The haphazard nature of this system of punishment is well illustrated by two cases which took place around the time of Mary's execution. Judge Hardinge tried two young women for the crime of housebreaking. One was reprieved, while the other was hanged. Mary Robert "was to die 'to enforce a law, which aimed not at [*her*] death, but at the *death* of her *crime*.'"[99] This system of punishment was therefore based on the principles of deterrence and retribution rather than justice and reform. As Potter observes: "Punishment was to serve a utilitarian purpose; it was no longer linked to justice."[100] Indeed it was recognised at the time that there would inevitably be instances where the innocent would be executed.[101] They however, could die happy, knowing they had died for England:

> He who falls by mistaken sentence may be considered as falling for his country, whilst he suffers under the operation of those rules, by the general effect and tendency of which the welfare of the community is maintained and upheld.[102]

Sarah Lloyd who was executed in Bury St Edmunds suffered this fate. Sarah, an illiterate servant-girl, who had not even "been taught the Lord's Prayer" - had fallen victim to seduction by a man of "low repute" - Joseph Clarke.[103] Making false promises of marriage, Clarke induced Sarah to steal from her mistress before setting fire to the house. Yet Sarah was

---

[96]William Paley quoted in Potter 1993:13.
[97]O'Donnell 1956:27; Bailey 1989:35.
[98]Potter 1993:10.
[99]George Hardinge (1818) quoted in Potter 1993:10. Emphasis in the original.
[100]Potter 1993:13.
[101]For example by Archdeacon William Paley, author of *Principles of Moral and Political Philosophy* (1819).
[102]Paley quoted in Potter 1993:14.
[103]Gatrell 1994:341.

sentenced to death while Clarke escaped punishment altogether. The Revd Drummond, who petitioned for a reprieve, recognised Sarah was a "poor, unfortunate deluded girl [who] was Clarke's helpless instrument."[104] But the judge ruled "that for example's sake" she should be executed. Sarah had betrayed the all important relationship of trust between servant and mistress - a crime which could not go unpunished. Her crime reminded masters and mistresses of the importance "of watching the conduct" and "improving the morals" of servants. The importance of "sobriety, chastity, fidelity, honesty, obedience" particularly in female servants, could not be over-emphasised.[105] Sarah had lost these virtues, hence both the trial judge and the Home Secretary agreed she must also lose her life as an example to other servants:

> There is a superior mercy due to all inhabitants of houses, and masters of families, with which the pardon or even respite of this unfortunate woman's sentence seems to me incompatible. Such is my abhorrence and idea of her crime as it affects the publick [sic], that if Clarke or any other accomplice had been convicted I [should still be] of opinion that for example's sake her life ought not to have been spared.[106]

> 'The great object of punishment is example' ... and this case 'must be one of those which calls the loudest for being marked and branded with the most rigorous hand of the law as a warning and terror to misdeeds of a similar tendency.'[107]

In accordance with this philosophy and despite honourable efforts by individuals of high social standing such as Capel Lofft and Revd Drummond to save Sarah's life, all pleas for mercy were ignored and she was executed on 23rd April 1800, in front of a large crowd many of whom wept at the injustice of her misfortune.[108]

The executions of Mary Jones, Mary Robert and Sarah Lloyd provide a fair representation of the *kind* of person most likely to be executed, for when Paley and his contemporaries talked of punishment, they were referring almost exclusively to punishment of the poor. In the past when treason had been the main concern of the ruling elite, even kings and queens were occasionally executed. In the 18th century, however, when concern over the protection of property replaced the fear of treason, capital punishment was reserved almost exclusively for the poor[109] - "the very lowest and worst of the people ... the scum both of the city and the country", according to

---

[104]Gatrell 1994:343.
[105]Gatrell 1994:342.
[106]Sir Nash Grose, Judge in the Sarah Lloyd case, quoted in Gatrell 1994:342.
[107]The Duke of Portland, Home Secretary, quoted in Gatrell 1994:347.
[108]Gatrell 1994:348.
[109]Potter 1993:14; McLynn 1991:ix-xvi.

Elizabeth Fry.[110] Women living alone in cities were particularly likely to suffer severe poverty and hardship, since much of their work was casual, menial and seasonal with wages a mere fraction of men's. Consequently they often found themselves in an even more precarious position than men, and many offences against property were committed out of sheer economic necessity.[111] Despite these factors women committed far less crime than men. For example, in the county of Surrey between 1660-1800 a total of 3,938 men were found guilty of property offences, while the figure for women was 1,228. During the same period 233 murders were committed by men, while only 19 women were found guilty of this crime.[112] 1,130 men were convicted of capital offences, 481 of whom were executed, the corresponding figures for women were 149 and 37. Women therefore stood a higher chance of being reprieved (75.2%) than men (57.4%).[113] It should be borne in mind, however, that this figure included women who were reprieved due to being pregnant as well as those who had killed their own children. Moreover, a higher proportion of women than men, were discharged by juries, and they had charges against them reduced to non-capital offences more frequently.[114] As discussed in Chapter One, great caution should be exercised when analysing such statistics since they do not indicate the specific *types* of women who were executed compared to those who were reprieved. However, these figures suggest the majority of criminal women did not pose the same kind of threat to the social order as men; that indeed it might have been counter-productive if all impoverished female petty criminals were harshly dealt with since this might invoke pity and empathy for defendants and thus question the legitimacy of the criminal justice system. In short, it was not necessary, or even desirable, for large numbers of women to receive public punishment. "The broader purposes of the law and of the administration of justice could be served by the very occasional example of a woman harshly dealt with."[115] The state had good reason to be concerned with the legitimacy of punishment, for, as noted above, the execution of women such as Sarah Lloyd did not pass without opposition, from both the general population as well as individual members of the ruling elite. Similarly, when Mary Jones was sentenced to death, public sentiment was aroused and a petition for her reprieve was organised which emphasised that until the time of her offence Mary "had led a decent and respectable life and that she should be allowed to return and care for her young children."[116] As in the case of Sarah Lloyd, individual members of the ruling elite were prepared to publicly state their outrage at the brutality of the law, and six

---

110Quoted in Gatrell 1994:8.
111Beattie 1986:242-243.
112Beattie 1986:437.
113Beattie 1986:437-8.
114Beattie 1986:438.
115Beattie 1986:439; see also McLynn 1991:128-9.
116O'Donnell 1956:26-7.

years after Mary's execution her case was still remembered by Sir William Meredith who told Parliament:

> I do not believe that a fouler murder was committed against the law than the murder of this woman by the law.[117]

It was also common for juries to resist the harshness of the law by deliberately downgrading the crime of the accused. For example, as noted above, it was a capital offence to steal goods valued at five shillings or more, subsequently juries deliberately under-valued stolen goods when they believed the accused did not deserve to hang.[118] Yet, in keeping with the importance placed upon the protection of "the new system of paper credit and exchange", forgery, counterfeiting and coining were crimes for which a felon would almost certainly hang - male or female.[119] Coining was treated as high treason and women found guilty of this offence were burned at the stake as in the case of 17-year-old Barbara Spencer in 1721.[120]

While some women murderers were shown mercy and escaped the gallows, those found guilty of murder by poisoning were never reprieved. Poisoning by a woman was regarded as a particularly loathsome and odious crime for several reasons. First, it was impossible to regard this act as a *crime passionnel* - a poisoner was not a hysterical woman overcome by the intensity of her emotions - instead, by definition, poisoning could only be a premeditated crime. Second, the woman poisoner had transgressed "the fundamental laws of nature" - that is - poisoning was perceived as "a distortion of a traditional female role: the preparation of food."[121] Moreover, poisoning was difficult to detect. Taken together, these aspects of poisoning "tapped a profound male fear of female deviousness; it was the ultimate horror even to conceive of the possibility that the polite yet secretive female might harbour dark homicidal urges under the mask of gentility."[122] The discourses surrounding women poisoners will be further explored in the following chapters, where cases from the 20th century are analysed.

In sum, the Bloody Code represents an era in which the beliefs of the Divine Will of God and the Divine Right of Kings and Queens had lost much of their authority. A new ideology was therefore needed to compel the deference of the common people. The ideology of justice attempted to fill that gap. The law appeared both terrifying and mysterious. On the one hand it had the power to execute anybody found guilty of the most petty crime - *if*

---

[117] Sir William Meredith MP for Wigan 1754-61 and Liverpool 1761-80, quoted in Potter 1993:31; see also O'Donnell 1956:27; McLynn 1991:125.

[118] See for example McLynn 1991:125.

[119] McLynn 1991:xiii.

[120] O'Donnell 1956:20. There are many documented cases of women who suffered this fate, for example Isabella Condon in 1779, Phoebe Harris in 1786 and Christiane Murphy in 1789 (O'Donnell 1956:23; McLynn 1991:123).

[121] McLynn 1991:119.

[122] McLynn 1991:119.

it so chose - on the other hand, pardons increased at almost the same rate as capital statutes, and the actual numbers executed each year remained fairly stable because only a certain number of public punishments were necessary to teach "lessons in justice and power":

> The law made enough examples to inculcate fear, but not so many as to harden or repel a populace that had to assent, in some measure at least, to the rule of property.[123]

From the perspective of the powerless the capriciousness and unpredictability of executions and pardons ensured the maintenance of the "mystery and majesty of the law."[124] From the perspective of the powerful, the delivery of justice was perfectly predictable: it was the labouring poor as a class category who were the target for punishment. As illustrated above, although statistically, a larger proportion of women than men were discharged by the grand jury and those who were convicted stood a better chance of a reprieve, many felt the full brunt of the Bloody Code and paid for their crimes with their lives. Moreover, women who "broke the unspoken rules of gender and sex roles and acted 'mannishly', aggressively, or without due deference" stood almost no chance of being pardoned.[125] The complex relationship between such discourses, gender and punishment is a central theme in this book and will be analysed throughout the remaining chapters.

Reforming the Penal Code

The number of people who were executed under the Bloody Code should not be underestimated, in London for example, 348 persons were hanged between 1783 and 1787, "97 in 1785 alone."[126] Yet these statistics must be regarded in the context of those of clemency. For example, between 1791 and 1795, "5,592 persons were discharged before trial, while 2,962 were acquitted after trial."[127] These figures illustrate the reluctance of both juries and judges to convict and condemn the vast majority of criminals to the gallows even though they had the power to do so. The contradictions of this policy of terror therefore became increasingly obvious - in pragmatic terms it simply did not work and by the last quarter of the 18th century, Enlightenment ideas were influencing the minds of philosophers and legal reformers such as Bentham and Romilly. These reformers were well aware of the "acute crisis in the administration of criminal justice", which had come about as a result of the disintegration of the old social order. The political challenges brought

---

[123]Hay 1977:57.

[124]Hay 1977:59.

[125]McLynn 1991:129.

[126]Ignatieff, M. (1978) *A Just Measure of Pain* Macmillan, London p.87.

[127]McLynn 1991:xii. Moreover, Gatrell has estimated that between 1770 and 1830, 35,000 were sentenced to death, 7,000 of whom were executed (Gatrell 1994:7).

about by rapid and far-reaching industrial and economic changes meant old mechanisms of social control could no longer function. Hence the reformers sought to create a more *rational* and *exact* legal system designed to regain a legitimacy amongst the rapidly increasing industrial working class, which they felt had been either lost or "jeopardized by the excessive severities and gratuitous abuses of the Bloody Code."[128]

Reform therefore became the means whereby the public, especially the poor, would learn to respect the law. They must be made to understand that punishment was 'for their own good' - not merely a tool employed by the ruling elite to safeguard its own interests.[129] Punishment, according to Bentham, was no longer to be "'an act of wrath or vengeance,' but an act of calculation, disciplined by considerations of the social good and the offenders' needs."[130] Rather than simply eliminating criminals, their behaviour could be corrected; by acknowledging their guilt they could become reformed characters. To achieve this goal, it was necessary to make punishment rational, impersonal and humane.

Those in favour of reforming the penal code initially found themselves in a small minority whose ideas were met with strong opposition. William Eden's *Principles of Penal Law* (1771) for example, did not go as far as to suggest abolition of capital punishment, merely a "thorough revision of capital statutes" yet, was responded to by pamphlets such as *Hanging Not Punishment Enough* which proposed increased levels of torture prior to execution.[131]   Nonetheless, despite sharp opposition from influential individuals such as the Rev Martin Madan and Archdeacon William Paley, who ensured their views were heard through publications,[132] Romilly, the Solicitor-General, began a parliamentary campaign in 1810 to reform the penal code. The spirit of reform had taken root two years earlier with the formation of *The Society for the Diffusion of Knowledge upon the Punishment of Death and the Improvement of Prison Discipline* - the first abolitionist organisation in England.[133] The Quakers were the driving force behind this movement, and it was they who organised petitions against capital punishment. The pressure for reform had become a force which could no longer be ignored, and in 1819 a Commons' Select Committee on Criminal Law recommended "the abrogation of the death penalty ... in many crimes" especially "of all statutes authorising capital punishment which had fallen into disuse."[134] This did not end the barbarity of the Bloody Code, courts could still issue death sentences for crimes other than murder if considered appropriate. In 1831, for example, a nine-year-old boy was executed in

---

[128]Ignatieff 1978:79.
[129]Ignatieff 1978:75; McLynn 1991:xv.
[130]Ignatieff 1978:75.
[131]Hibbert, 1968:57-8.
[132]Madan, M. (1785); *Thoughts on Executive Justice;* Paley, W. (1819) *The Principles of Moral and Political Philosophy.*
[133]Tuttle 1961:4; Potter 1993:33.
[134]Tuttle 1961:6.

Chelmsford for arson.[135] In the main, however, the tide of reform was still ongoing. Gibbeting was abolished in 1834; the pillory in 1837. In 1831, only 52 of the 1,601 sentenced to death, were executed, and by 1838, only 14 statutes carried the death penalty, largely as a result of the recommendations of a Royal Commission on Criminal Law, established in 1833, which advocated "'certainty of punishment' [be] substituted for 'severity of punishment.'"[136] Thus, after 1838 only murderers were executed during peace time.[137] The first Parliamentary motion to abolish capital punishment was introduced in 1840 by William Ewart and received over 90 votes. Ewart subsequently formed the *Society for the Abolition of Capital Punishment* whose members campaigned nationally for total abolition. By 1861 only four capital statutes remained: "murder, treason, piracy with violence, and arson in government dockyards and arsenals."[138]

Capital Punishment: The Move from the Public to the Private

For many decades Samuel Johnson's view that "executions are intended to draw spectators. If they do not draw spectators; they don't answer their purpose",[139] had been widely accepted. However, the Victorian era, with its concern over decorum and morality, gave rise to an increasing anxiety around the public nature of hangings.[140] Rather than viewing public hangings as "moral, judicial, and religious dramas", it was now suggested that such spectacles were in bad taste, vulgar in nature and more likely to brutalise and corrupt the minds of the audience, especially "the vicious, the uneducated, and all those most open to evil impressions."[141] During a Parliamentary debate in 1849, Ewart, who argued in favour of abolition, voiced his concerns over the spectacle of public executions:

> What can be more appalling than the sight of half-a-dozen men dragging a woman of 18 or 20 years of age - a woman untrained, most ignorant, to some extent partly imbecile - dragging her to a public execution, and clergymen coaxing or exhorting her to walk

---

[135]Christoph, J. B. (1962) *Capital Punishment and British Politics* Allen & Unwin, London p.15.

[136]Tuttle 1961:11.

[137]Tuttle 1961:13; Potter 1993:42; Hibbert 1968:68.

[138]Christoph 1962:17; Potter 1993:43.

[139]Samuel Johnson quoted in Potter 1993:64.

[140]For an in-depth discussion of the Victorian 'polite classes' see Gatrell 1994:225-228. Literary figures such as Thackeray and Dickens also helped to draw attention to the issue of public hanging - Thackeray by publishing 'Going to See a Man Hanged' in *Fraser's Magazine* in 1849; and Dickens by writing numerous letters to newspapers from 1841 onwards, the most famous being one published in *The Times* 1st February 1849.

[141]Parliamentary Debates, 23rd June 1840, quoted in Potter 1993:68.

quietly to the scaffold. Now, what could be the effect upon the multitude assembled to witness that execution? I do not believe there is a single Member of this House who can be of opinion that the effect of that execution upon any human being who witnessed it would be otherwise than most unfavourable for the very purpose for which these executions are assumed to take place.[142]

The scenes in Horsemonger Lane on the eve of the double execution of Mr and Mrs Manning in November 1849 did nothing to alleviate the fears and concerns of the polite classes:

the dregs and offscourings of the population of London, the different elements that composed the disorderly rabble crew being mingled together in wild and unsightly disorder, the 'navvy' and Irish labourer smoking clay pipes and muzzy with beer, pickpockets plying their light-fingered art, little ragged boys climbing up posts, and standing on some dangerous elevation, or tumbling down again, and disappearing among the sea of heads.[143]

For, while the Victorian middle class became preoccupied with refinement and respectability, increasingly it was the labouring poor and "the most abandoned, debauched, and dissolute characters"[144] who made up the crowd which could number as many as 40,000.[145] Thus, while "men of right-thinking minds and virtuous habits" could watch executions without danger of giving in to moral debasement, it was a different matter for the lower classes, who treated such occasions as 'open-air' entertainment - dancing and singing, drinking and screaming, uttering blasphemies and obscene jokes.[146]

The maintenance of public order was therefore becoming an increasing concern, especially after a disaster in 1807, when during a double execution at Newgate, almost one hundred people were trampled to death.[147] Apart from concerns over morality and disorder, there was evidence that public hanging did not achieve its aim, since the very people who needed to be deterred - habitual criminals - were the most regular attenders. Thus, Cope, a prison governor, claimed that during 15 years of service at Newgate,

---

[142] Parliamentary Debates, House of Commons vol civ, 1st May 1849, col 1076.

[143] *The Times* quoted in Borowitz, A. (1989) *The Bermondsey Horror* Robson, London, p.249.

[144] Potter 1993:68.

[145] Hibbert 1968:70.

[146] Sir Fitzroy Kelly MP quoted in Potter 1993:68. While members of the 'respectable' classes did not usually mingle with the 'roughs' at the foot of the gallows, they were still present and just as eager to witness hangings. They however, could afford to hire rooms, rooftops or even just a window overlooking the gallows, so they could watch in comfort - using opera-glasses to see better, and consuming champagne and cigars (Borowitz 1989:265; Gatrell 1994:67-8).

[147] Hibbert 1968:70.

he had never hanged someone who had not witnessed an execution, and of the 40 men Dr Lyford saw hanged at Winchester Gaol, 38 had attended an execution. At Bristol Prison, chaplain John Roberts noted that of the 167 death sentence prisoners he had attended, only three had never been to a public hanging.[148] Such statistics suggested the very class of people - the labouring poor - who were meant to be deterred by public executions, were instead corrupted by them. Moreover, there was concern over the vast numbers of women in the audience who would 'shriek' with excitement or hiss and boo if they felt particular animosity towards the prisoner as in 1829, when Esther Hibner was executed for starving a workhouse child to death.[149] Similarly, when Greenacre was hanged in 1837 for the particularly vicious murder of Jane Jones, the women in the audience "were, if possible, more ruthless than the men."[150]

There were other aspects associated with public hanging which the new refined and respectable Victorian middle class found disturbing. One was the detection of sexual titillation within the spectacle of female executions. The articulation of such erotic fascination is easily discernible in the writing of Thomas Hardy who witnessed several executions, including that of Elizabeth Martha Brown in 1856. "He never forgot the rustle of the thin black gown the woman was wearing as she was led forth by the warders ... He was so close that he could actually see her features through the rain-damp cloth over her face."[151] When Hardy was in his eighties he wrote of Martha Brown "what a fine figure she showed against the sky as she hung in the misty rain, and how the tight black silk gown set off her shape as she wheeled half-round and back."[152] Although Hardy was born more than a century after the execution of Mary Channing in 1705, he made detailed notes on the horrifying circumstances of her dying moments, where, after being strangled, "the burning of her body revived her; she 'writhed and shrieked', and one of the constables, seeking to stop her cries, 'thrust a swab into her mouth ... & the milk from her bosoms (she had recently given birth to a child) squirted out in their faces and made 'em jump back.'"[153] Similarly, "the disgusting eagerness of the people to witness the execution of Manning and his wife"[154] in 1849, would, at least in part, have arisen from the pleasure of watching a beautiful woman sent to her death:

---

[148]Potter 1993:69.

[149]Gatrell 1994:68.

[150]Weekly Chronicle, 7th May 1837, quoted in Gatrell 1994:69.

[151]Quoted in Gittings, R. (1975) *Young Thomas Hardy* Heinemans' Educational Books, London p.34; p.33. Gittings wrote "The rustle of a woman's dress had enormous sexual meaning for Hardy" after this event.

[152]Quoted in Gittings 1975:33.

[153]Quoted in Orel, H. (1987) *The Unknown Thomas Hardy* Harvester Press, p.129.

[154]Quoted in Potter 1993:76.

... the woman's [body], a fine shape, so elaborately corseted and artfully dressed, that it was quite unchanged in its trim appearance as it slowly swung from side to side.[155]

Such voyeurism was even more pronounced in the letters of John Forster, Dickens' companion at the execution:

She was *beautifully dressed*, every part of her noble figure finely and fully expressed by close fitting black satin, spotless white collar round her neck loose enough to allow the rope without its removal, and gloves on her manicured hands ... she called the surgeon, who had led her (blindfold) up the scaffold, and said these words, the last she spoke on this earth. "I am poorly, at present; I trust to you that it shall not be made known." It was true - and she had obtained a clean napkin not ten minutes before she ascended the drop. A sensitive cleanliness of body seems to have been her passion - and the doctor who examined the bodies after death, and who said he had never seen so beautiful a figure, compared her feet to those of a marble statue.[156]

Observations such as these remind us it was not just the 'roughs' who were corrupted by public executions - Sir Fitzroy Kelly was quite wrong when he maintained that men from the polite classes could watch executions without becoming morally debased.

By 1856 individuals such as Samuel Wilberforce, the Bishop of Oxford, was concerned that such gratuitous spectacles had given rise to 'squeamishness' amongst Home Secretaries, who seemed increasingly reluctant to send women to the gallows, "however heinous their crimes."[157] This concern was echoed in the House of Lords that year when Lord St Leonards asked whether the Government intended to abolish the death penalty for women. His question was prompted by two recent cases where women had been pardoned despite having "been convicted for most atrocious murders of their own illegitimate offspring."[158] Lord St Leonards therefore wished to know if the commuting of these sentences was due to "any supposed feeling as to the indecency of executing women in public." If this was the case, "it would be better to execute women in private than to let it be understood that they were not to be executed at all."[159] After all, if the execution of women ceased, it was inconceivable that men should continue to be hanged. Rather than risking the abolitionists gaining ground in abolishing

---

[155]Charles Dickens, quoted in Gatrell 1994:605.

[156]Letter from John Forster to Sir Edward Bulwer Lytton, quoted in Borowitz, A. (1989) *The Bermondsey Horror* Robson, London p.264. Emphasis in the original.

[157]Gatrell 1994:596.

[158]Parliamentary Debates, House of Commons, 3rd Series, vol 142, 6th May to 27th June 1856 col 1056.

[159]Parliamentary Debates, House of Commons, 3rd Series, vol 142, 6th May to 27th June 1856 col 1057.

the death penalty altogether, Wilberforce established a Select Committee to examine the issue of public executions. The Committee recommended their abolition and the introduction of private executions accompanied by:

> black flags, bells tolling, church services ... with prayers for the criminal and improving sermons. The day should be a day of humiliation not merriment. 'A certain mystery and uncertainty about the actual extinction of life creates greater solemnity upon the mind than public witnessing of the act.'[160]

Yet neither the Conservatives nor the radical abolitionists supported these recommendations: The Conservatives because of the belief that private executions would eradicate its deterrent effect and hence hasten total abolition. The abolitionists, on the other hand, believed that if the terror of executions was removed from public view, the demand for total abolition would be diminished. Individuals such as Thomas Beggs also believed - prophetically - as I shall illustrate in Chapter Six, that private executions would not prevent salacious and titillating details of the event "'with all their ghastly accompaniments'" from finding their way into the broadsheets.[161]

Yet the Select Committee Report marked a change in attitude to the death penalty. The reformist notion that punishment should be motivated by justice and decorum rather than vengeance had taken a firm hold within the educated and polite classes some of whom believed private executions might act as a more powerful deterrent than public ones:

> 'the very imagination of death inflicted upon the criminal in the privacy of a prison, in absolute isolation from all his fellows, - the awe and mystery which would be associated with that terrible and silent scene' would more powerfully effect the populace than 'the heterogeneous reminiscences of a public execution'.[162]

A motion, proposing the abolition of public execution in 1864 was defeated, but in July that year a Royal Commission was given the task of investigating issues around capital punishment. Two years later it had recommended the abolition of public executions, and following extensive debate in the House of Commons the Capital Punishment Amendment Act was finally passed in 1868 abolishing public executions.[163] As the abolitionists had feared, this almost destroyed their movement and the *Society for the Abolition of Capital Punishment* was dissolved. The newly formed

---

[160] Quoted in Potter 1993:84.

[161] Quoted in Potter 1993:86.

[162] Quoted in Potter 1993:87.

[163] Tuttle 1961:16-20; Potter 1993:94. The last woman to be executed in public in England was Frances Kidder, hanged in Maidstone 2nd April 1868, for the murder of her husband's illegitimate daughter, Louisa (Wilson, P. (1971) *Murderess* Michael Joseph Ltd, London p.154).

Howard Society, although supporting the abolition of capital punishment, worked from a much broader agenda, its main interest being "in the sphere of prison reform."[164]

Executions had finally been moved from public view to the private sphere behind the prison walls, and with this move, the nature of punishment had changed fundamentally:

> It was the beginning of a dramatic change in the procedure of hanging. From being a painful, agonizing, demeaning, and slow death, in the full gaze of a deriding public, it was to become a highly formalized, technically exact, and wonderfully speedy extinction, attended only by a handful of witnesses.[165]

This move from public to private execution in the latter half of the 19th century marked an important point in the social history of capital punishment. In particular, it signified the introduction of the modern and more 'discreet' style of execution endured by the 15 women who were executed in the 20th century, and whose cases are examined in Chapters Four, Five and Six. Before that however, I provide an overview of the feminist theoretical framework which will be applied to these case-studies.

[164]Ryan, M. (1978)*The Acceptable Pressure Group* Saxon House, Farnborough p.28.
[165]Potter 1993:86-7.

3 Beyond Traditional and Revisionist Theory: Feminist Theory and the Power to Punish

> Where is the account of the disciplinary practices that engender the "docile bodies" of women, bodies more docile than the bodies of men?[1]

> Developing feminist perspectives in criminology is *a project under construction* ... The task is one of re-vision - of taking into account women's and men's experiences, transforming existing knowledge foundations, transgressing traditional knowledge formations, taking tentative steps towards theory-building and creating new methodologies.[2]

My aim in this chapter is to demonstrate that the fate of the 15 women executed during the 20th century can best be understood by employing a specific feminist theoretical framework. This is because the traditional and well-established theoretical perspectives on punishment - classicism, Marxism, Foucauldian and cultural perspectives are androcentric and hence either omit gender altogether in their analysis or fail to recognise that as a result of women's subordination the process of punishment will be experienced differently by women compared to men.

Thus, Enlightenment thinkers supported their classical theories by referring to a 'rational, scientific truth', which carried great moral force due to its "image of uncompromising disinterestedness and objectivity ... serv[ing] no special interests, no class or privileged group."[3] But a feminist analysis reveals that this supposed 'objectivity' is in fact men's subjectivity, it is

---

[1]Bartky, S. L. (1988) 'Foucault, Femininity, and the Modernization of Patriarchal Power' in Diamond, I. & Quinby, L. (eds) (1988) *Feminism & Foucault*, Northeastern University Press, Boston, pp.63-4.
[2]Gelsthorpe, L. & Morris, A. (1990) 'Introduction: transforming and transgressing criminology' in Gelsthorpe, L. & Morris, A. (eds) (1990) *Feminist Perspectives in Criminology* Open University Press, Milton Keynes p.4. Emphasis in the original.
[3]Ehrenreich, B. & English, D. (1979) *For Her Own Good,* Pluto, London, p.77. For elaboration of Enlightenment philosophy see for example Hamilton, P. (1992) 'The Enlightenment and the Birth of Social Science' in Hall, S. & Gieben, B. (eds) (1992) *Formations of Modernity*, Polity, Cambridge.

therefore neither objective nor value-free.[4] This failure to recognise its own bias - together with its gender-blindness - ensures that classical theory is incapable of providing an adequate theory of the punishment of women.

This is also true of Marxism due to its insistence that issues of social class must take prominence over gender in the struggle towards an egalitarian society.[5] This insistence means there is no recognition by orthodox Marxists that women's subordination will result in them having different and separate interests to those of men. Thus, although individual historical materialists have included specific chapters on women's punishment,[6] this 'adding' of women to already established revisionist theoretical frameworks has done little to challenge the fundamentally androcentric nature of existing knowledge. Therefore, in order to understand the process of punishment as experienced *differentially* according to gender, a feminist perspective which puts gender-sensitivity at the forefront of analysis is needed,[7] which involves "the deconstruction of the categories of masculinity and femininity."[8]

Similarly, although Foucault's *Discipline and Punish* added a new and original dimension to theories of punishment which have subsequently become highly influential, Foucault was quite indifferent to gender.[9] As observed by McNay, "sexual difference simply does not play a role in the Foucauldian universe ..."[10] For feminists the gender-neutral, de-sexualised 'human' subject featured in Foucault's work, ensures the continuation of the long history of gender-blindness and sexism within socio-political theories.[11] There is no recognition that the disciplinary techniques utilised to produce 'docile bodies' as described in *Discipline and Punish*, are not always and necessarily the same for men and women. Women's bodies are regulated, controlled and disciplined according to specific discourses embedded within the construction of femininity such as those of physical appearance, sexual conduct, respectability and domesticity. This "disciplinary regime of femininity"[12] ensures Foucault's 'disciplinary society' is experienced quite differently from women's viewpoint, and to deny or "overlook the forms of subjection that engender the feminine body is to perpetuate the silence and

---

[4]See for example Jane Rendall quoted in Johnson (1993) 'Feminism and the Enlightenment' in *Radical Philosophy* 63, Spring 1993 p.10.
[5]Hartmann, H. 'The Unhappy Marriage of Marxism and Feminism' in Sargent, L. (1981) *The Unhappy Marriage of Marxism and Feminism*, Pluto, London p.31. An example of this gender-blindness within Marxism can be found in Rusche, G. & Kirchheimer, O. (1939) *Punishment and Social Structure*, Columbia University Press, New York.
[6]See for example McLynn, F. (1991) *Crime & Punishment*, Oxford University Press, Oxford; Gatrell, V.A.C. (1994) *The Hanging Tree,* Oxford University Press, Oxford.
[7]Howe, A. (1994) *Punish and Critique*, Routledge, London, p. 140.
[8]Bartky 1988:79.
[9]Foucault, M. (1979) *Discipline and Punish*, Peregrine Books, Harmondsworth.
[10]McNay, L. (1992) *Foucault and Feminism*, Polity, Cambridge, p.11.
[11]McNay 1992:11-12.
[12]Bartky quoted in NcNay 1992:33.

powerlessness of those upon whom these disciplines have been imposed."[13] Feminist theorists wishing to utilise the Foucauldian perspective have therefore had to invent 'Foucauldian feminism'. As such, Foucauldian feminists have added their analysis to the multitude of feminist voices who have over the past three decades demonstrated how women's subordination manifests itself through the experience of social control in a multitude of areas of their lives. The areas included here have been selected because of their relevance to the lives and deaths of 20th century executed women as I shall demonstrate in the following chapters.

The above criticisms of the Foucauldian perspective are also applicable to the cultural perspective - developed by theorists such as Elias and Spierenburg[14] and, very importantly, all four perspectives share a major inadequacy in that they only concern themselves with punishment in the public sphere, whilst ignoring the serious impact that informal punishment within the private sphere has on women. It is particularly noteworthy that while both Foucault and Spierenburg paid specific attention to the controlling aspect of punishment, they nonetheless ignored men's punishment of women as a mechanism of control. While culturalists discuss the impact of the 'civilising process' on manners - for example by removing meat-carving from the animal carcass from public view[15] - and while *public* tolerance to issues such as wife-beating may have decreased by the end of the 18th century[16] - just as the removal of meat-carving from the public arena did not cause any change to the actual *process* of carving - so the dwindling level of acceptance of wife-beating did not result in the *elimination* of that act. Thus, while Spierenburg makes references to the way in which activities such as sex, violence and bodily functions were removed from the public to the private sphere, his analysis does not attempt to address associated gender implications. The cultural perspective therefore does nothing to explain the 'continuity' of male 'manners' and behaviour such as violence against and punishment of women in the private sphere. Yet such informal punishment has consequences for all women in general and criminal women in particular - and as such - provides another example of gender-differentiated experiences of punishment. Furthermore, while those working within both Marxist and Foucauldian perspectives have been concerned with uncovering ideologies and discourses which illustrate the difference between "what-is and what-appears",[17] they have neglected to apply this analysis to gender. While Marxist theorists have illustrated how ideologies around the law serve to give

---

[13]Bartky 1988:64.

[14]See for example Elias, N. (1978) *The History of Manners*, Oxford; Spierenburg, P. (1984) *The Spectacle of Suffering*, Cambridge.

[15]Elias, N. (1939) quoted in Garland, D. (1993) *Punishment and Modern Society* The University of Chicago Press, Chicago, p.224.

[16]Clark, A. (1992) 'Humanity or justice? Wife beating and the law in the eighteenth and nineteenth centuries' in Smart, C. (ed) (1992) *Regulating Womanhood*, Routledge, London, pp.187-206.

[17]Bartky 1988:76.

the *appearance* of equal treatment for everybody, but in reality serve the interests of the powerful, and thus help to control the poor; and Foucauldian theorists have described how the supposed benefits of the Enlightenment such as more humanitarianism and less violence and cruelty, have in reality resulted in more discipline and tighter control of the 'human subject', none have attempted to explain how the numerous ideologies and discourses surrounding women's sexuality, in reality serve patriarchal interests. For feminists this is a serious omission because:

> ... it is necessary to explore how meanings, particularly representations of gender, are mobilized within the operations of power to produce asymmetrical relations amongst subjects.[18]

The following pages deal with such an exploration. For the purposes of clarity the organisation of this literature has a chronological component with early feminist studies in social control preceding the more recently developed Foucauldian feminist perspective.

Women and Social Control: Early Theoretical Explanations

> The social control of women assumes many forms, it may be internal or external, implicit or explicit, private or public, ideological or repressive.[19]

> Although men provide more menace to the basis of a society, it is women who are instructed in how to behave ... Only women are instructed every week, in case they should possibly ever forget, in how to *be* women ...[20]

We cannot fully understand the circumstances surrounding the crimes, trials and executions of the 15 women discussed in the following chapters without first examining the control-mechanisms and discourses which surround and regulate the conduct and behaviour of *all* women. As Worrall has argued:

> ... the conditions and processes that over-determine the fate of ... [a] group of deviant women are intrinsically no different from those within which 'conventional' women are also controlled.[21]

---

[18]McNay 1992:35.
[19]Smart, C. & Smart, B. (1978) 'Women and social control: An introduction' in Smart, C & Smart, B. (eds) (1978) *Women, Sexuality and Social Control*, Routledge, Kegan Paul, London, p.2.
[20]Heidensohn, F. (1986) *Women & Crime* Macmillan, London, p.106. Emphasis in the original.
[21]Worrall, A. (1990) *Offending Women* Routledge, London, p.4.

Similarly, Smart maintains:

"the strategy of inflicting harsh punishment on the few ... [can be] translated into modes of discipline and surveillance of the many."[22]

These statements exemplify powerful feminist challenges to the androcentric theories discussed above. During the 1970s and early 1980s these challenges focused on exposing the various ways in which all women experience 'social control' within patriarchal society, which in turn has specific implications for deviant and criminal women. Below I focus on these social control theories before examining the impact Foucauldian theory has had on feminism during the 1990s. Before embarking upon this task, it is important to clarify that the concept 'social control' does not refer to a crude or conspiratorial model of oppression in which women are helpless victims of patriarchy. Feminists recognise that "in a class-divided society *both* women and men are subject to material, repressive and ideological forms of social control ..."[23] Women, however, are affected differentially and specifically, within the private sphere where they are economically, legally and ideologically subordinate to men. Additionally, Smart and Smart have identified four main areas within which women alone experience social control. These are the reproductive cycle; a double standard of morality; a subordinate social and legal status (vis-a-vis men) in the family, as well as "the separation of 'home' and 'work' and the ideology of woman's place."[24] Therefore, the meaning of the concept 'social control' here is that identified by Green, Hebron and Woodward who define "social control ... as an ongoing process, one element in the struggle to maintain male hegemony which sets the limits of appropriate feminine behaviour."[25]

Social Control and the Private Sphere

The behaviour of all women - within the public and private sphere - is regulated, disciplined and controlled by a pervasive system of male definitions of what constitutes a so-called 'normal' woman. The constraints and restrictions which women experience as a consequence of these definitions take both material and ideological forms. As a result of women's subordinate position within patriarchal society, their material reality is restricted in a variety of ways, most notably by child-care and family responsibilities; limited financial resources; the threat and fear of male

---

[22]Smart, C. (1992) 'The Woman of Legal Discourse' in *Social & Legal Studies* vol 1, No 1, March 1992, Sage, London, p.38.
[23]Smart & Smart 1978:3. My emphasis.
[24]Smart & Smart 1978:3.
[25]Green, E., Hebron, S. & Woodward, D. (1987) 'Women, Leisure and Social Control' in Hanmer, J. & Maynard, M. (eds) (1987) *Women, Violence and Social Control,* Macmillan, London, p.79.

violence as well as actual violence. In Chapter Two I examined the mechanisms through which Protestantism successfully redefined notions of womanhood and family life. The Reformation transformed patriarchy by confining women to a more restricted and closely defined role within the private sphere - 'the cult of domesticity.' This split between the public and the private, and hence of 'work' and home, which took place in tandem with - and became a crucial aspect of - the development of the capitalist mode of production and the rise of industrialism, had a major impact upon the status of women - giving rise to the notion of a 'woman's place' being in the home, while simultaneously downgrading unpaid domestic work, thus increasing their financial dependence on men.[26] The unwaged and invisible nature of domestic work, coupled with the physical and emotional isolation experienced by women working within the private sphere, create conditions which are conducive to feelings of powerlessness, lack of confidence and self-esteem. Women are thus locked into a systemic social control apparatus reinforced by "lack of mobility, cash and free time."[27]

Running parallel with this material oppression we find a highly developed ideological social control apparatus regulating behaviour within the private sphere. Ideologies around marriage, motherhood, domesticity and respectability play key roles in ensuring women's compliance with expected domestic and moral standards. The 'normal' woman possesses a 'maternal instinct' and happily sacrifices her own interests in favour of those of her family,[28] "whereas 'bad' mothers are 'selfish' in their quest for a career"[29]:

> Putting the baby first is perhaps the primary definition of normal motherhood in modern industrialised society ... normal mothers are essentially altruistic, the servers of others' needs rather than their own ... mothers who consider their own needs are bad mothers.[30]

This "ideology of motherhood"[31] has real consequences for women in terms of limiting or controlling their access to independent lives, and together with notions of the maternal instinct, can be extended to include "sick or helpless adults."[32] Thus, a 'good' woman considers it her *duty* to care for elderly relatives, rather than placing them in institutions.[33] Statistically

---

[26]Smart & Smart 1978:6.

[27]Dahl, T. & Snare, A. (1978) 'The coercion of privacy: A feminist perspective' in Smart, C. & Smart, B. 1978:22.

[28]Green, Hebron & Woodward in Hanmer & Maynard 1987:84, referring to the work of Anne Oakley.

[29]Williams & Hutter 1981:23.

[30]Oakley, A. (1981) 'Normal Motherhood: An Exercise in Self-Control?' in Williams & Hutter 1981:84; 83-84.

[31]Smart, C. (1984) *The Ties That Bind* RKP, London, p.124.

[32]Smart (1978) *Women, Crime and Criminology* RKP, London, p.39.

[33]Williams & Hutter 1981:23; see also Philipson, C. (1981) 'Women in Later Life: Patterns of Control and Subordination' in Williams & Hutter 1981:185-201.

daughters are three times more likely to be called upon to care for ageing relatives than are sons.[34] Even when married sons have relatives living with them the majority of care work will be carried out by daughters-in-law. Under these circumstances the day-to-day experiences of middle-aged women carers mirror their earlier lives when they cared for young children, including the restrictions and sacrifices this entailed.[35] That women should be expected to make such sacrifices, is explained and justified by ideologies around womanhood based on assumptions that caring for others and 'putting herself last' are 'natural' and normal aspects of femininity. In reality however, these are moral assumptions and expectations imposed on women which, together with their over-representation within the voluntary sector, prevent them from leading a financially independent life. It is difficult to challenge these assumptions since gender role definitions are supported "by the full weight of patriarchal ideology"[36] which acts as a powerful mechanism for invoking guilt when women perceive themselves to have slackened in their responsibilities.

Women's lack of financial and social independence ensures the relationship between husband and wife is deferential and hierarchical in nature, and, because "it appears both natural and immutable", has achieved the status of a 'moral order'.[37] When this 'moral order' breaks down - that is - when ideologies alone fail to ensure acceptance of gender roles, a more overt control mechanism may come into play within the private sphere, that of physical violence or 'wife-battering'. Violence against women who fail to recognise male authority is legitimated by husbands who perceive themselves to have not only the right but the *obligation* to discipline an 'uppity' wife, thereby "putting her in her place."[38] Thus, while women's fear of violent attack in the public sphere is constantly fuelled by sensational media reporting - they are in fact much more likely to experience violence within the domestic setting:

> ... for a woman to be brutally or systematically assaulted she must usually enter our most sacred institution, the family. It is within marriage that a woman is most likely to be slapped and shoved about, severely assaulted, killed, or raped.[39]

Dobash and Dobash support this statement with statistical evidence from their 1979 study which revealed that 77% of the women interviewed had not experienced violence before marriage, yet within the first three years of

---

[34]Philipson, C. (1981) 'Women in Later Life: Patterns of Control and Subordination' in Williams & Hutter 1981:189.

[35]Philipson 1981:190.

[36]Green, Hebron & Woodward in Hanmer & Maynard 1987:85.

[37]Bell & Newby quoted in Heidensohn 1986:179; see also Dobash, R.E. & Dobash R. (1979) *Violence Against Wives*, Open Books, p.93.

[38]Dobash & Dobash 1979:93.

[39]Dobash & Dobash 1979:75.

marriage 84% had been hit.[40]   More recent studies by Hanmer and Maynard[41] and Edwards[42] confirm that wife-battering is both prevalent and widespread - a normal part of many women's everyday lives.[43] In short, "many women are clearly disciplined and dominated in the home by domestic violence in ways which enormously constrain and confine what they can do."[44]

Social Control and the Public Sphere

Catherine Macaulay Graham wrote in 1720 that while men "continue ... to use their natural freedom with impunity ... women, having been considered as the mere property of ... men ... ha[ve] no right to dispose of their own persons."[45] Graham had thus identified early strands of what was to become 'the cult of domesticity' by the late 18th century, involving the construction of distinctive and separate gender identities for men and women. Men's 'natural' environment became the public sphere where they were free to move around and participate in public activities.[46] In contrast, women became associated with the private sphere "as domestic beings, 'naturally' suited to duties in the home and with children." A woman's respectability depended on her moral and sexual purity which in turn "guaranteed the home as a ... source of social stability."[47] Respectability involved displaying the traits of dependency, delicacy and fragility - to indicate a desire for independence was considered 'unnatural'. It was men's duty to venerate and protect respectable women and to treat them "with decorum, respect and propriety."[48]

  While today's women *theoretically* have equal access to the public sphere, and *officially* do not require chaperoning to qualify as 'respectable', it is nonetheless the case that both access to, and movement within the public sphere remain problematic for many women. Green et al write that "access to

---

[40]Dobash & Dobash 1979:94.

[41]Hanmer, J. & Maynard, M. (eds) (1987) *Women, Violence and Social Control* Macmillan, London.

[42]Edwards, S. (1989) *Policing 'Domestic' Violence* Sage, London.

[43]Research carried out by Channel Four's 'Battered Britain' team between June and September 1995 indicated that over half of the women murdered each year in Britain are killed by their male partners. Furthermore, police statistics reveal that they receive over a million calls annually from women assaulted by husbands or boyfriends. (*To Death Us Do Part* Channel 4, *The Guardian* 13th September 1995).

[44]Heidensohn 1986:176.

[45]Catherine Macaulay Graham, from Letters on Education, 1790 in Jones, V. (ed) (1990) *Women in the Eighteenth Century* Routledge, London.

[46]Nead, L. (1990) *Myths of Sexuality*, Blackwell, Oxford, p.32.

[47]Nead 1990:33-34.

[48]Nead 1990:29. 'Respectable' women usually meant middle-class women. Working-class women by contrast, were taken to be robust, self-sufficient and suited for physical labour, hence in no need of male protection. (Nead pp.29-31).

any social life outside the home is ... a 'charged' area" to the degree that many women forego an independent social life, simply to avoid conflict.[49] This is because many men still see themselves as keepers of their partner's sexuality, emphasising her status as 'respectable' and using this as a justification for enforcing restrictions on her movements.

For single women access to the public sphere is restricted by the powerful notion of "keeping your reputation."[50] Young girls and older women alike have to tread the thin line between being sexually desirable without appearing provocative or too sexually experienced since they will then qualify for insulting and derogatory labels such as 'slut', 'tart', 'scrubber' and 'slag' - terms which have no male equivalent.[51] The fear of losing one's reputation thus operates as a mechanism for controlling women's behaviour in public places. Furthermore, women can be made to police themselves since they know that "to deviate from women's allotted space is to run the risk of attack by men."[52] Such attacks may take the verbal form described above, or involve various degrees of antagonism, objectification and harassment in public places generally, and in public houses and clubs in particular, where women without male escorts are assumed to be 'available' and hence legitimate targets for sexual advances.[53] Most serious of all, such attacks may take the form of physical violence, rape and/or murder, attacks for which the victim may be held partly or wholly responsible, depending on a number of factors such as where and what time it took place, how she was dressed, how she behaved, what she said or did not say. In short, a woman's conduct plays an important role in determining the extent of her culpability in the crime committed against her. Being scantily clad, being out alone late at night or hitchhiking all qualify as precipitating factors towards the crime as can be seen from headlines such as "Raped hiker impudent." This headline referred to a case where a judge ruled the attacker's "responsibility was 'diminished' by the fact that the girl had, in effect, solicited him by getting into his car."[54] Such victim-blaming sends a clear message:

---

[49]Green, E., Hebron, S. & Woodward, D. (1987) 'Women, Leisure and Social Control' in Hanmer & Maynard 1987:87.

[50]Heidensohn 1986:183.

[51]Mills, J. (1991) *Womanwords* Virago, London p.xx. Mills writes that "the sheer number of slang terms which define woman as sexually promiscuous ... (comparatively few for men) meant that I had to draw an arbitrary line less *Womanwords* turned into a dictionary of slang." See also Greer, G. (1973) *The Female Eunuch* Paladin, St Albans pp.263-72.

[52]Heidensohn 1986:183.

[53]Green, Hebron & Woodward 1987:86.

[54]*The Guardian* 15th April 1976, quoted in Smart, C. & Smart, B. 'Accounting for rape' in Smart, C. & Smart, B. (eds) (1978) *Women, Sexuality and Social Control* p.101.

Women in general are not free to come and go as they please. If they attempt to do so they can be labelled as irresponsible and 'asking for trouble'.[55]

The media play a crucial role in placing responsibility for women's safety on *their* conduct rather than on the men carrying out the attacks:

The accumulative effect of press reports of rape is to remind women of their vulnerability, to create an atmosphere of fear and to suggest, as a solution, that women should withdraw to the traditional shelter of the domestic sphere and the protection of *their* men.[56]

Police officers whose responsibility it is to detect and arrest violent criminals also regard the restriction and control of women's movements within the public sphere as the solution to women's safety problems, as was exemplified by their advice during the 'Yorkshire Ripper' hunt. In doing so, official spokes-persons reaffirm that only those who conduct themselves 'improperly' risk being attacked.[57] More recently, following the murder of backpacker Johanne Masheder, *The Daily Mail* asked: "Why do young girls risk their lives on the back-pack trail?" (Masheder was not a 'girl' but a 23-year-old qualified solicitor). *The Guardian* added that her death "highlights the vulnerability of women abroad."[58] Yet, as discussed earlier, it is within the private sphere women are most likely to experience violence. Nonetheless, the fear and the real possibility of being attacked in a public place, coupled with media amplification of this issue and the negation of private violence, together act as 'controlling agents' on all women's behaviour. Moreover, it may well be due to women's own self-policing and regulation of their behaviour and movements that statistics concerning public attacks remain relatively low.[59]

---

[55]Green, Hebron & Woodward 1987:91.

[56]Smart & Smart 1978:102. Emphasis in the original.

[57]See for example Bland, L. (1984) 'The Case of the Yorkshire Ripper: Mad, Bad, Beast or Male?' in Scraton, P. & Gordon, P. (eds) (1984) *Causes for Concern* pp.185-209.

[58]Natasha Walter in *The Guardian* 18th January 1996. Walter added that of the 43 Britons murdered abroad in 1995, only eight were women. Yet no-one asked "why young boys risk their lives on the tourist trail or told us that ... [their] death[s] highlighted the vulnerability of men abroad."

[59]Heidensohn 1986:182. See also Stanko, E. (1990) 'When precaution is normal: a feminist critique of crime prevention' in Gelsthorpe, L. & Morris, A. (eds) (1990) *Feminist Perspectives in Criminology* Open University Press, Milton Keynes, where she states that "most women don't simply walk down the street at night ... [but instead] negotiate and manage situations to avoid those which they feel are potentially dangerous" (p.176).

Punishing Female Deviancy

Taken together, the extensive network of informal and institutional social control of women described above - regardless of age, class or race - plays a major role in defining and limiting women's conduct and behaviour. Yet, despite such pressure to conform women resist both ideological and material control mechanisms continuously. That resistance takes many forms ranging from instigating divorce, becoming single parents, leaving their children, refusing to 'moderate' their appearance and/or behaviour when in public places without male escorts, drunkenness, prostitution and various forms of criminal behaviour. The engagement in such activities does not necessarily imply a conscious and deliberate political challenge to dominant ideologies.[60] The ideological dominance of the 'normative' standard around female conduct may be different from what is common practice; however, it has the effect of creating "the impression that the conventional sex role is the majority case, and that departures from it are socially marginal." Casting those who engage in behaviour which stands outside the 'normative standard' as individual deviants helps to eliminate "the element of power from gender relations. It also eliminates the elements of resistance to power and social pressure, the fact of social struggle - open or covert - going on around definitions of sexuality and gender."[61] Such behaviour is nonetheless greeted with anxiety in a male dominated society where female deviancy poses a threat and a challenge to patriarchal hegemony. Deviant women become 'dangerous' women - "a source of disorder in patriarchal society" - and therefore cause for concern.[62] The double standard of morality means that women's deviance is never considered to be 'just horseplay'; thus behaviour considered acceptable - even normal - in men such as drunkenness and promiscuity is classified as deviant when found in women.[63] Otto, in her study 'Women, Alcohol and Social Control' found that while heavy drinking in men was considered "in some way natural" or even glamorous, drunken women were met with no such tolerance, but were instead considered to be overly promiscuous and

---

[60]For example many prostitutes would argue sheer economic necessity drove them into prostitution (see for example Roberts, N. (1992) *Whores in History* Grafton, London, pp.341-2). Conversely, women like Dolores French who resigned from her full-time job to pursue her "chosen career" and who has never regretted "becoming that glamorous, self-confident, financially independent woman who entertained men for money", reminds us of the incomplete nature of dominant ideologies and the struggle which takes place around them. French writes about her decision to become a prostitute: "I was about to turn a corner. I was going to charge for sex, and I was already thinking about how I would spend the money. After tomorrow, I thought, no one will ever be able to use the word *whore* against me. After tomorrow, it will no longer be the worst curse someone could throw at me, it will simply be a statement of fact. (French, D. (1991) *Working* Victor Gollancz, London, p.19).
[61]Connell, R.W. (1987) *Gender & Power* Polity, Cambridge, p. 52.
[62]Larner quoted in Heidensohn 1986:92.
[63]Smart & Smart 1978:4-5.

'disgusting'.[64] A woman's role as wife and mother is not compatible with the loss of self-control associated with drunkenness:

> Because the role of women has been equated with the stabilising functions of wife and mother, the drunken woman has seemed to be a special threat: no one likes to believe that the hand that rocks the cradle might be a shaky one.[65]

Accordingly, women alcoholics in the public sphere "are much more likely to be apprehended, arrested and convicted" than male alcoholics, hence are regulated more severely and formally than their male counterparts who may simply be portrayed as a bit of a rogue or a 'noble-savage'.[66] In contrast, a woman alcoholic is regarded as having lost "respectability in all areas, especially the sexual ones", thus is "devoid of gender and personality characteristics" - a non-entity.[67]

Such double standards of morality also become visible when women reject moral regulation of their sexuality and fail to 'keep their reputation' in terms of their sexual conduct. Promiscuous women are greeted with anxiety since they indicate rejection of and "rebellion against their *natural* feminine roles which stresses passivity and conformity."[68] While promiscuity in young men is not only tolerated but positively encouraged,[69] it is condemned and punished, both informally and formally in young women. As discussed above, informal punishment of sexual deviancy involves being labelled with insulting and derogatory terms and being treated disrespectfully. At a more formal level, courts and social welfare agencies may treat sexually active female delinquents differentially which suggests "one of the latent functions of the juvenile court ... [is] the reinforcement of the conventional female sex role":

> it was often doubtful whether supervision orders made upon some girls, were imposed on them as a result of the offence which had been committed as is the case with boys, or whether the orders were made because of deviations from the expected form of feminine behaviour.[70]

---

[64]Otto, S. (1981) 'Women, Alcohol and Social Control' in Hutter & Williams 1981:154, 155, 156.

[65]Curlee quoted in Otto 1981:155.

[66]Otto 1981:164; 163.

[67]Otto 1981:156; 162.

[68]Smith, L.S. (1978) 'Sexist assumptions and female delinquency' in Smart & Smart 1978:75. Emphasis in the original.

[69]Smart, C. & Smart, B. (1978) 'Women and social control: An introduction' in Smart & Smart 1978:4.

[70]Wilson, D. (1978) 'Sexual codes and conduct' in Smart & Smart 1978:72. See also Hudson, B. (1985) 'Sugar and Spice and all things nice' in *Community Care* 4th April 1985.

Given these attitudes it is unsurprising that prostitute women are the target of persistent and harsh punishment at both informal and formal levels. The excessive stigmatisation associated with prostitutes reflects the moral double standards applied to women in general while the sexual conduct of men remains relatively unscrutinised. Prostitutes are perceived as threatening and dangerous because their presence signals a challenge to ideologies around family life, motherhood, domesticity and respectability. In selling sex for money prostitutes appear to have rejected all notions of respectability, morality and other 'natural' female inclinations. Instead "their whole identity bec[o]me[s] 'whore'" - they are nothing but "disgusting moral nonentities"[71] whose mere presence signals their ability to "deprave and corrupt",[72] and who, as a result of their sexual conduct, have forfeited the right to be treated with respect and dignity. They can therefore expect to receive harsh treatment and rough justice when confronted with the legal and criminal justice system.[73] Feminist research has consistently revealed evidence of informal punishment in the form of police harassment of prostitutes "as a matter of course" which, in some cases, "amounts to positive brutality."[74] Such research has also identified "'respectability' as a significant factor influencing the sentencing decision of the court." Thus, at a formal level, 'disreputable' women may be awarded a harsher sentence for a first time offence than a 'respectable' woman with a criminal record.[75] The informal disciplining of prostitutes may take a 'negative' form - that is - ignoring their pleas for help. For example, when 'disreputable' women complain to police about rape or assault they may not be believed, nor is their complaint necessarily investigated.[76] Prostitutes are considered to 'provoke their own demise' because of their lack of sexual conformity and are therefore less deserving of sympathy, even when it is recognised a crime has been

---

[71]Wilson, E. (1983) *What Is To Be Done About Violence Against Women?* p.112, 110.

[72]Smart, C. (1981) 'Law and the Control of Women's Sexuality' in Hutter & Williams 1981:50.

[73]Edwards, for example, writes that "the regulation and control of prostitution has been a major policing preoccupation" with prosecution figures for prostitution reaching an all time high of 10,674 in 1982. "No similar war was waged against procurers, pimps and ponces, or against male violence to women." However, she also notes that there are signs of a change in attitude as police have become "more aware of the violence frequently inflicted on prostitute women." (Edwards, S. (1989) *Policing 'Domestic' Violence* Sage, London p.34; p.35). Similarly Lord Chief Justice Bingham's decision to increase the sentence of a man who had raped prostitute women from four to six years in the Court of Appeal in January 1997 can be seen to reflect this change in attitude. (*The Guardian* 22nd January 1997).

[74]Naffine, N. (1990) *Law & The Sexes* Allen & Unwin, London p.144.

[75]Naffine 1990:144.

[76]Edwards, S. (1987) '"Provoking Her Own Demise": From Common Assault to Homicide' in Hanmer & Maynard 1987:153. See also Morris, A. (1987) *Women, Crime and Criminal Justice* Blackwell, Oxford, p.81.

committed against them. This became apparent during the so-called 'Yorkshire Ripper' hunt when Assistant Police Chief Constable Jim Hobson stated:

> He has made it clear that he hates prostitutes. Many people do. We, as a police force, will continue to arrest prostitutes. But the Ripper is now killing innocent girls. *This indicates your mental state and you are in urgent need of medical attention.*[77]

For Caputi, this statement indicates Sutcliffe's violent crimes "only become socially problematic when he turns to 'innocent girls'."[78] In short, victims who have deviated from their appropriate gender role cannot expect equal treatment to 'respectable' or 'innocent' victims.[79]

Punishing Criminal Women

While female drunkenness, promiscuity and prostitution are not criminal offences they nevertheless fit under the heading 'deviant female conduct', and how women who engage in such activities are treated has important implications for the ultimate deviant woman - the female criminal. Feminist theorists have analysed the treatment of criminal women by the criminal justice system in considerable detail over the last two decades. In particular, they have responded to debates around 'chivalry' versus unduly harsh punishment. The issue here is whether women are the beneficiaries of chivalrous attitudes when facing the bench or whether on the contrary, they receive more severe punishment than men who have committed similar offences.[80] While bearing in mind consistency in sentencing does not prevail for either sex,[81] different studies have nonetheless indicated that what is at issue is the *type* of woman being judged since "different types of women

---

[77]Quoted in Caputi, J. (1987) *The Age of Sex Crime* The Women's Press, London pp.93-4. My emphasis.

[78]Caputi 1987:94. See also Morris 1987:81.

[79]Edwards 1987:153.

[80]The 'chivalry' thesis put forward by writers such as Pollak, maintains that, as a result of paternalistic and chivalrous attitudes (male) police officers are reluctant to arrest women, and "judges, prosecutors, and juries do not like to assist in convicting them" (Leonard, E.B. (1982) *Women Crime & Society* Longman, London, p.4. See also Pollak, O. (1950) *The Criminality of Women* University of Pennsylvania Press, Philadelphia). This view stands in contrast to those who maintain that women are treated more harshly than men when facing the bench (See for example Casburn quoted in Heidensohn 1986:43). For a fuller discussion and critique of the chivalry thesis see Klein, D. (1973 'The etiology of female crime' in Muncie, J., McLaughlin, E. and Langan, M. (1996) *Criminological Perspectives* Sage, London, pp.161-86.

[81]Heidensohn 1990:43.

receive different treatment."[82]   Thus, the ideologies around motherhood, domesticity, respectability and conduct discussed above in relation to *all* women, play a powerful role in the way criminal women are treated. For example:

> Females whose offence pattern is more consistent with sex role expectations seem to experience less harsh outcomes than females whose offence pattern is less traditional.[83]

What counts is whether the defendant is a 'good' woman - "loyal and loving, compliant and altruistic" - who abandons her own interests in favour of those of her family, and "is a faithful wife and mother whose sphere is the home, not the competitive arena of the marketplace." These findings are confirmed in Carlen's study of women's imprisonment:

> *when the sheriffs ... are faced with a sentencing dilemma in a case where the offender is female, they mainly decide their sentence on the basis of their assessment of the woman as mother.*[84]

Thus, one of the sheriffs Carlen interviewed stated that "if she's a good mother, we don't want to take her away. If she's not a good mother, it doesn't really matter." A magistrate participating in the study offered further insight into sentencing policy:

> If upon inquiry you discover that a woman has no children then it clears the way to send her to prison. If she has children but they are in care then I take the view that she is footloose and fancy-free and I treat her as a single woman.[85]

This statement bears out Naffine's view that "those who are deemed to be too free in their behaviour, who are therefore unfeminine may be treated more punitively than men."[86]   It also confirms that 'the ideology of motherhood' continues to play a crucial role in how women are regarded *after* they have entered the criminal justice system.

Kruttschnitt's 1982 study confirmed that the Victorian ideologies around dependency discussed above continue to be taken into account when women defendants are sentenced:

> For most offence categories, the economic dependency of the defendant emerged as the primary factor determining the severity of

---

[82]Naffine 1990:138.
[83]Nagel quoted in Heidensohn 1986:44.
[84]Carlen, P. (1983) *Women's Imprisonment* RKP, London, p.63. Emphasis in the original.
[85]Carlen 1983:67.
[86]Naffine 1990:137, 138.

the sentence. From the comments of probation officers, it transpired that dependent women were regarded as safer bets because their family was thought to exert a degree of control over their behaviour and guide them into better ways.[87]

These findings are confirmed by Farrington and Morris:

Divorced and separated women received relatively severe sentences, as did women coming from a deviant family background. These may be the kind of women whom magistrates, especially female magistrates, disapprove of: they are women who do not conform to notions of 'respectable' women.[88]

Respectability is a constant theme in different studies and is repeatedly identified as an influencing factor in sentencing policies:

The more 'respectable' a woman was, the more lenient her sentence ... Regardless of the offence, the lower a woman's respectability the greater the likelihood that she would receive a severe sentence and that women with previous convictions who were respectable were given more lenient sentences than women viewed as disreputable who had no criminal record.[89]

Finally, Worrall found that while the offence was the most important consideration when sentencing men, for women personal conduct was significantly more important:

Provided the woman act her part (modest, humble, remorseful) and references can be made to her previous good character or competence in the home, she is not seen as 'criminal' ... But once a woman has a criminal record or does not conform to these expectations, she is not viewed as a woman at all; she can no longer claim to be 'out of place'.[90]

In short, women criminals who not only commit crime but also fail to measure up to 'appropriate' standards where motherhood, domesticity, respectability and conduct are concerned, are 'doubly bad' women. In failing to conduct themselves with decorum they "have abandoned their femininity and hence their right to be given the law's protection or favour. Where a good woman may attract the sympathies of the court, a positively censorious

---

[87]Naffine referring to the work of Kruttschnitt cited in Naffine 1990:139.

[88]Morris, 1987:89-90.

[89]Morris 1987:90 referring to the work of Kruttschnitt (1982) 'Respectable women and the law' in *The Sociological Quarterly* 23, 2, p.221.

[90] Morris 1987:91 referring to the work of Worrall, A. (1981) 'Out of Place: Female Offenders in Court' in *Probation Journal* 28, 1981, p.90.

approach may be taken to women who are thought to be bad."[91]   Overall, then, feminist social control theorists are united in maintaining that female defendants are not simply judged according to their crimes but also according to their conduct and behaviour as *women* - especially in the areas of motherhood, domesticity respectability and sexuality:

> The majority of women who go to prison are sentenced not according to the seriousness of their crimes but primarily according to the courts' assessment of them as wives, mothers and daughters.[92]

Indeed a woman's conduct may come under *closer* scrutiny than her criminality, and in turn play an important part in determining the severity of her sentence.[93] Those studying the social control of women are therefore not surprised to find that women who received the harshest punishment of all during the 20th century - death by execution - had stepped far beyond the boundary of acceptable female conduct and behaviour. In the following chapters I test this hypothesis.

Foucault and Feminism: A Politics of Difference

Before embarking on an analysis of my case-studies I shall consider feminist theoretical developments during the 1990s. This decade has seen a challenge to the social control theories discussed above from theorists employing a Foucauldian post-structuralist perspective. These theorists have responded to criticisms that concepts such as 'patriarchy' and 'social control of women' are monolithic and construct universal explanations of women's oppression, hence are incapable of explaining the differential nature of women's experience of subordination:

> An insistence on women as passive victims of male oppression oversimplifies the complexities of women's subordination by placing too great a stress both on the universal nature of oppression and the common undifferentiated enemy of patriarchy.[94]

Adapting Foucault's gender-neutral conception of power to one which places gender at the centre of analysis, feminists have argued that power is not simply 'held' by a particular group (men) for the purpose of oppressing another group (women). For Foucault "power emanates from not one source

---

[91]Naffine 1990:142. See also Worrall 1981:92 where she writes: "The machinery for processing female offenders is built on the myth that 'real' women cannot commit 'real' crime."
[92]Carlen, P. (1988) *Women, Crime and Poverty* Open University Press, Milton Keynes, p.10.
[93]See for example Naffine 1990:144; Morris 1987:91; Heidensohn 1986:43-4.
[94]McNay 1992:64.

but everywhere", and analyses of power relations reveal "that their actual effects are often very different from their intended effects."[95] Furthermore, "power is not an attribute of individuals, is not something which is possessed", the exercise of power is therefore not just associated with "a narrow class of outcomes such as winning and losing in situations of conflict."[96] Consequently, Foucauldian conceptions of power do not accept "an all-encompassing division between the 'rulers' and the 'ruled'"[97] as implied in social control theories. Instead Foucauldian feminists recognise the existence of power differences between women themselves according to factors such as race, class, heterosexuality, age and ethnicity. Gender is therefore "not the only determining influence on women's lives." If anything, McNay argues, it is only a minority of white, privileged, Western women for whom "sexism is the main form of oppression." Other women will experience different forms of oppression according to their specific histories which may be rooted in experiences related "to slavery, forced labour, enforced migration, plantation, colonialism, imperialism, etc."[98]

Foucauldian feminism therefore rejects the notion of a pre-given subject and hence, by implication, cannot accept a unitary category of 'Woman'. Instead it concerns itself with analysing how subjects come into being via discourses - the 'discursive construction of the subject'. The categories discussed earlier such as prostitutes, bad mothers or women alcoholics therefore do not "exist in an a priori state, waiting for institutions to act upon them ... [but] are being continually constituted and ... also constitute themselves through language/discourse."[99] In short, a Foucauldian feminism recognises that multiple factors and discourses all play their part in constructing and determining the particular course of an individual's life. These multiple determinants which sometimes interact, sometimes conflict with each other, will always, inevitably produce *differential* results and effects which, in turn, are compounded by the use individuals make of them:

> ... against this background of multiple determinants, individuals act upon themselves and order their own lives in numerous and variable ways.[100]

---

[95]Cousins, M. & Hussain, A. (1985) *Michel Foucault* Macmillan, Basingstoke, p.230.

[96]Cousins & Hussain 1985:230-1.

[97]Cousins & Hussain 1985:235.

[98]McNay 1992:64. Moreover, Colin Sumner writes: "The dominant gender norm within disciplinary power practices is that of the hegemonic masculinity, which censures *both* the feminine and alternative masculinities." In other words, just as we can no longer accept a universal category of 'woman' so we cannot accept the category of 'man' as a universal oppressor either. (Sumner, C. (1990) 'Foucault, gender and the censure of deviance' in Gelsthorpe & Morris 1990:38. My emphasis.

[99]Smart, C. (1995) *Law, Crime and Sexuality* Sage, London, p.8.

[100]McNay 1992:65.

Moreover, this theoretical framework poses an important challenge to the Enlightenment notion of an absolute 'truth'. For example, while legal and medical personnel can draw on powerful discourses due to their position within "the hierarchy of knowledges and ... [their] power to subjugate other discourses",[101] subordinate and marginalised groups can de-stabilise such official truths by constructing 'alternative truths'. While these alternative truths articulated from below do not have a greater claim to 'reality', they do "have a resistant or progressive function in so far as they hinder the 'domination of truth' by those who govern."[102] Occasionally the space which is created as a result of this challenge to official truth is stable long enough to allow a redefinition of official truth, as for example when rape within marriage became recognised as a criminal offence. Thus, just as Foucault did not recognise a pre-given subject, he did not concern himself with a pre-given truth, but concentrated instead on its construction and deconstruction.

During the last two decades feminist theorists have become increasingly involved in articulating and applying a Foucauldian perspective to feminist politics. In particular a body of academic literature has been developed around women's 'docile bodies'. Foucault's thesis that punishment has - since the 18th century - moved from the body to the mind, hence changed from a reliance on brute force to a network of discipline, surveillance and regulation designed to produce a 'self-controlled' body, has been developed by feminists. For Foucault, 'subjects' who internalise commands - "who habitually do ... what is required without need of further external force" - become 'docile' bodies within a disciplinary society.[103] Within this context Bartky asks: "Where is the account of the disciplinary practices that engender the 'docile bodies' of women?" noted at the beginning of this chapter.[104] She explains how, through a series of disciplinary practices directed at women's appearance, behaviour and gestures, a female body is produced which is inscribed with an inferior status.[105] The disciplines imposed on the female body include: dieting - 'the tyranny of slenderness'; specific forms of exercise designed not to strengthen the body but to re-sculpture it to conform to the current desired model; make-up; skin-care; hair-care and removal of body-hair which, taken together, constitute a 'feminine body discipline', designed to produce a fragile, immature, infantilised body.[106] Moreover, the typical body-language of a woman is one of "relative tension and constriction" signalling her "subordinate status in a hierarchy of gender." Thus, where social control theorists describe sexual harassment as a power held by men and exercised over women, Bartky writes:

---

[101]Smart 1995:8.
[102]McNay 1992:137.
[103]Garland 1993:137.
[104]Bartky 1988:63-4.
[105]Bartky 1988:71.
[106]Bartky 1988:73.

> Higher status individuals may touch their subordinates more than they themselves get touched ... What is announced in the comportment of superiors is confidence and ease, especially ease of access to the Other.[107]

Similarly, where social control theorists point to the double standard of morality, a Foucauldian analysis maintains that women's faces and bodies "are trained to the expression of deference":

> Woman's space is not a field in which her bodily intentionality can be freely realized but an enclosure in which she feels herself positioned and by which she is confined. The 'loose woman' violates these norms: her looseness is manifest not only in her morals, but in her manner of speech and quite literally in the free and easy way she moves ... The 'nice' girl learns to avoid the bold and unfettered staring of the 'loose' woman who looks at whatever and whomever she pleases.[108]

Women are not *forced* to diet or remove body-hair, these disciplinary practices are self-imposed, which for Bartky illustrates that discipline is not necessarily institutionally *bound* but may also be institutionally *unbound*. The disciplinary power which "inscribes femininity in the female body" is not held by men or within formal institutions, it "is everywhere and nowhere, the disciplinarian is everyone, and yet no one in particular."[109] It therefore has the quality of anonymity, which effectively disguises the extent to which the interests of domination are served by disciplinary practices. It also has the effect of making such practices appear voluntary or natural. Yet the heterosexual woman knows that failure to impose these practices may result in the loss of male patronage, they must therefore be understood "as aspects of a far larger discipline, an oppressive and inegalitarian system of sexual subordination":

> This system aims at turning women into the docile and compliant companions of men just as surely as the army aims to turn its raw recruits into soldiers.[110]

A woman internalises disciplinary practices by incorporating them into the very structure of her sense of 'self' which means they become part of her self-identity. She therefore has a stake in the perpetuation of disciplinary skills, since to do otherwise "threatens her with de-sexualization, if not outright annihilation."[111]

---

[107] Bartky 1988:74.
[108] Bartky 1988:66; 67.
[109] Bartky 1988:74.
[110] Bartky 1988:75.
[111] Bartky 1988:78.

Bartky's Foucauldian feminist analysis of women's oppression allows us to explain how this oppression has changed historically. Previously I noted Foucault's insistence that following the Enlightenment, punishment moved from the body to the mind. In Chapter Two I pointed to the various forms of physical punishments inflicted on women who had broken the codes around female conduct and behaviour in earlier centuries. These punishments included the use of implements such as the ducking-stool, the pillory, and the 'scold's bridle' - all designed to inflict pain upon the body. The power to punish lay with husbands, fathers and men of the church and was thus easily identifiable:

> In the days when civil and ecclesiastical authority were still conjoined, individuals formally invested with power were charged with the correction of recalcitrant women whom the family had somehow failed to constrain.[112]

By contrast, while contemporary Western women enjoy more freedom, both economically and sexually, than in any other previous era, and while they need not fear violent sanctions such as the pillory or ducking-stool if disobedient, the invasion of disciplinary power into the female body is nonetheless "well-nigh total":

> The female body enters "a machinery of power that explores it, breaks it down and rearranges it." The disciplinary techniques through which the "docile bodies" of women are constructed aim at a regulation that is perpetual and exhaustive - a regulation of the body's size and contours, its appetite, posture, gestures and general comportment in space, and the appearance of each of its visible parts.[113]

As women gain increasing political, sexual and economic "self-determination, they fall ever more completely under the dominating gaze of patriarchy."[114] Hence, there is no longer a need for the ducking-stool or a chaperone to control and regulate the female body, for women themselves have now learned to practice these disciplinary measures against their own bodies. This self-surveillance constitutes not only a "form of obedience to patriarchy" but also the modernization of patriarchal power.[115]

From a Foucauldian perspective women cannot effect change simply by refusing to inflict disciplinary practices upon their bodies. While this form of resistance to patriarchy may result in the erosion of existent forms of domination, "new forms arise, spread and become consolidated" as Bartky's

---

[112]Bartky 1988:80.
[113]Bartky 1988:80.
[114]Bartky 1988:82-3.
[115]Bartky 1988:81.

historical analysis of patriarchy illustrates.[116]   Instead it is necessary to deconstruct the actual category of femininity (and by implication that of masculinity) to allow the construction of a new, radical "and as yet unimagined" meaning of what it is to be female.[117]

Other Foucauldian feminists have applied similar analyses to specific aspects of feminist politics.   Woodhull for example, provides a post-structuralist analysis of rape in which she argues:

> If we are seriously to come to terms with rape, we must explain how the vagina comes to be coded ... as a place of emptiness and vulnerability, the penis as a weapon, and intercourse as violation.[118]

For Woodhull, the view that rape "is nothing more or less than a conscious process of intimidation by which *all men* keep *all women* in a state of fear" as articulated by Brownmiller, merely reinforces male power and female powerlessness.[119]   Therefore she does not consider the feminist demand that rape be defined "as a crime of power, not of sex" to be an adequate solution:

> Instead of sidestepping the problem of sex's relation to power by divorcing one from the other in our minds, we need to analyse the social mechanisms, including language and conceptual structures, that bind the two together in our culture.[120]

Hence, it is necessary to deconstruct "the cultural codes that inform human sexuality in order to understand the role they play in engendering and consolidating power relations of a given society."   Once again, this implies the necessity for a deconstruction of the categories of femininity and masculinity.

Social control theories and deconstructionist theories should not necessarily be regarded as being in direct opposition to each other.   While Foucault's micro perspective of the operation of power has proved useful in illustrating *how* power relationships are maintained and resisted through discursive practices, several feminist theorists have attempted to sustain a relationship between deconstruction theory and the macro perspectives of social control which address questions of *why* and *in whose interests* power operates.   This relationship is evident in Bartky's essay, where her exploration of discursive practices on the female body is followed by a recognition that ultimately such practices constitute an obedience to "the *patriarchal*

---

[116]Bartky 1988:81.

[117]Bartky 1988:79.

[118]Woodhull W. (1988) 'Sexuality, Power and the Question of Rape' in Diamond & Quinby 1988:171.

[119]Brownmiller, S. (1976) *Against Our Will* Bantam Books, New York p.15.

[120]Woodhull, 1988:171.

construction of the female body."[121] Similarly, while Woodhull maintains that a full understanding of rape must involve the deconstruction of cultural codes around sexuality and their connection to power, she is aware that:

> In the course of a typical rape trial it becomes clear that women are regarded as criminals and are punished accordingly - albeit not by legal means - merely for presuming to circulate in public without men's protection, or for daring to articulate what it means to them to be in control of their bodies ... by deciding where, when, with whom and under what circumstances they will participate in a sexual act.[122]

In her book *Losing Out* Sue Lees has applied a Foucauldian analysis to the important relationship between female sexuality and the construction of language. At the same time she has included some overarching concepts articulated by social control theorists whom she echoes when she writes:

> It is regarded as natural for girls ... to enjoy domesticity and to want to get married and have children, but unnatural to want a career that would conflict with marriage ... Most of all a girl is expected to put others before herself and to be caring and unselfish.[123]

Moreover, unlike men, women never acquire a *non-gendered* identity, but are always defined according to their marital status - as wives, mothers or spinsters - or sexual status - as virgins or whores.[124] We lack a language which describes the sexually active woman in *positive* terms. Instead, as discussed above, an entire vocabulary is available for describing such women in derogatory and negative terms such as 'slag', 'scrubber' and 'tart'. Meanwhile, male promiscuity, is a source of pride - something to be admired. However, rather than analysing this double standard of morality in terms of patriarchal ideology which implies the masking of what *'really'* takes place within relationships between men and women, Lees employs discourse analysis. This is because calling someone a 'slag', or regarding rape victims as being culpable in the crimes committed against them *is* "the practice of the language of sexual power, not a reflection of some other process hidden from view."[125] This practice cannot simply be explained as instances of men exercising power over women. Females themselves carry this power with them "which penetrates their lives and recreation."[126] Again we note that rather than conceptualising power as being *held* by men, deconstruction theory relies on discourses to explain how power circulates within a given society:

---

[121]Bartky 1988:77. My emphasis.
[122]Woodhull 1988:172.
[123]Lees, S. (1986) *Losing Out* Hutchinson, London, p.17.
[124]Lees 1986:156.
[125]Lees 1986:159-60.
[126]Lees 1986:82.

The language of slag is not exercised by boys over girls, rather both sexes inhabit a world structured by the language quite irrespective of who speaks to or about whom.[127]

This is not to deny women's oppression and subordination. But, rather than explaining this in terms of women's position as mothers, carers or prostitutes, Lees analyses female subordination through discourses of sexuality which she regards "as a field of force in which boys and girls are equally trapped ..."[128] The implications for punishment are not however, equally distributed between the sexes, for ultimately only females are punished through the language of sexual reputation. As will become apparent in the following chapters, this language played an important role in the distribution of punishment for many women who faced the death penalty in the first half of the 20th century.

A subject which is related to language - that of authority (or lack thereof) and women's speech - also has great relevance to the case-studies as will become apparent. Dorothy Smith has noted the difficulties women have in asserting authority for themselves and for other women.[129] She, however, does not question the concept itself, merely women's deprivation of it, unlike Kathleen Jones whose deconstruction of authority reveals that "the segregation of women and the feminine from authority is internally connected to the concept of authority itself."[130] The dominant discourses associated with authority ensure women's exclusion from it by silencing "those forms of expression linked metaphorically and symbolically to 'female' speech", especially those around "emotive connectedness or compassion" which stand in sharp contrast to the "disciplinary, commanding gaze" of authority.[131] It is precisely by rejecting discourses of compassion and emphasising those of the disciplinary, commanding gaze that authority achieves its power, and in the process, renders discourses of compassion non-authoritative. Instead they become nothing but "marginal pleadings for mercy - gestures of the subordinate."[132]

Deconstructing authority thus exposes "the ways that a particular conceptual framework restricts our knowledge of it."[133] At the same time, our willingness to grant authority to male characteristics of speech like self-

---

[127]Lees 1986:160. For Foucault, "one doesn't have here a power which is wholly in the hands of one person who can exercise it alone and totally over others. It's a machine in which everyone is caught, those who exercise power just as much as those over whom it is exercised." (Ramazanoglu & Holland 1993:247).

[128]Lees 1986:166-7.

[129]Smith, D.E. (1987) *The Everyday World As Problematic* Open University Press, Milton Keynes, pp.17-43.

[130]Jones, K.B. (1987) 'On Authority: Or, Why Women Are Not Entitled to Speak' in Diamond & Quinby 1988:120.

[131]Jones 1988:120.

[132]Jones 1988:121.

[133]Jones 1988:121.

assuredness and self-assertiveness devalues and derogates speech patterns associated with women such as those of hesitancy and uncertainty. In so doing, authority is deprived of humanity and ambiguity.[134] However, this lack of authority in women's speech serves as a reminder of "what has been hidden by the ordered discourse of authority."[135]

This deconstruction of authority is not incompatible with an understanding that the rules governing authority ultimately serve as "a system of rules for social control within the context of social hierarchies."[136] Jones's essay thus provides another example of a gender-specific Foucauldian analysis which has contributed to feminist politics by casting issues of women's oppression in a new light.

Conclusion

Modernist humanistic thinking is deeply rooted in the Enlightenment discourses of reason, rationality, progress, science and individualism which have created a conception of individuals as rational agents in control of their own destiny who formulate their own meanings and values within society. Above all else Enlightenment philosophy has taught us to assume "that the speaker or writer is unified and coherent, the origin of what is spoken and written."[137] Foucault challenged this insistence on an "autonomous, self-determining subject" and instead maintained "that 'subjects' are created in and through discourses and discursive practices."[138] Consequently, his goal was not to discover who *holds* power but to excavate "the patterns of the exercise of power."[139] Foucauldian theory therefore appears attractive to those who are concerned about the plurality of factors which underpin women's oppression. The pluralism of discourse theory means that women no longer need to be regarded as a fixed and unitary category, instead differences between them are problematised . Indeed, as I shall illustrate, it would be foolish to ignore or deny the real differences between the women in my study. Yet this de-stabilising of 'woman' as a category has created its own theoretical problems for it is equally undeniable that women as a *category* share certain experiences as an oppressed group, both within the informal domestic setting and the formal setting of the courtroom. And while second wave pre-Foucault feminism has itself been accused of taking its cue from Enlightenment philosophy, its emphasis upon identifying the oppressor in order to resist it, and thereby empowering women, has had identifiable,

---

[134]Jones 1988:122
[135]Jones 1988:131.
[136]Jones 1988:121.
[137]Ransom, J. (1993) 'Feminism, difference and discourse: The limits of discursive analysis for feminism' in Ramazanoglu, C. (ed) (1993) *Up Against Foucault* Routledge, London, p.123.
[138]McNeil, M. (1993) 'Dancing with Foucault' in Ramazanoglu 1993:154, 155.
[139]McNeil 1993:149.

materialist results, for example in the form of rape-crisis centres and refuges for battered women.[140] In Foucault's universe, however, the emphasis upon 'what is said' rather than 'who speaks' means that he repeatedly ignores the asymmetry of what is said by men as opposed to what is said by women. It is not enough to claim that 'where there is power there is resistance' and that women can challenge dominant discourses of motherhood by refusing to have children or by "doing an evening course in roofing."[141] Men and women do not exist in a moral vacuum or a neutral universe in which they have equal access to the creation of dominant discourses.[142] Women share a need to understand how particular (male) versions of reality become privileged over other (female) versions. Feminist theory is imbued, not with 'neutrality' but with alternative visions and versions of reason where women enjoy moral, sexual and social justice. We therefore need not only a recognition of the plurality of discourses and variety of struggles but also the articulation of "their different levels and moments. We need ... a theory that can grasp that the gender of the social agent determines an asymmetry in relationship to the categories in which 'sex' is presented to us."[143] Foucault's restoration of "a genuine notion of difference, variation, diversity, nonreductionism" is an important one, but it is not adequate by itself.[144] What also needs to be included is a *hierarchy* of power forms if we are to provide adequate explanations of social transformation.[145] Foucault's discourse theory pays almost no attention to the mode of production which gives rise to a much more contradictory social reality than his theory allows for. Instead he emphasises the way "everybody has everybody else locked into power in some ways, as well as being the object of power" in what at times appear to be almost equal proportions.[146] This is why discourse theory is unable to explain the difference between an affluent woman who has easy access to cheap tea and an impoverished woman who has to work long hours for a minimum wage to produce it. This example illustrates that although we must not underestimate the importance of differences between women, it is equally crucial "to retain the capacity to identify the structural contradictions of our differences."[147] Stuart Hall has suggested how these two strands of power can be incorporated into analysis rather than separated out. While he agrees

---

[140]See for example Dobash, R.E. & Dobash, R.P. (1992) *Women, Violence & Social Change* Routledge, London.

[141]Ransom 1993:134.

[142]See for example Ramazanoglu and Holland's discussion in 'Women's sexuality and men's appropriation of desire' in Ramazanoglu 1993:258.

[143]Ransom 1993:140.

[144]Hall, S. (1988) 'The Toad in the Garden: Thatcherism among the Theorists' in Nelson, C. & Grossberg, L. (eds) (1988) *Marxism and the Interpretation of Culture* Macmillan, London p.70.

[145]de Sousa Santos, B. (1985) 'On Modes of Production of Law and Social Power' in *International Journal of the Sociology of Law* 1985, 13, p.325.

[146]Hall 1988:71.

[147]Ransom 1993:144.

with Foucault that power does not simply radiate from one source but is multidimensional, he also maintains "there *are* centres that operate directly on the formation and constitution of discourse."[148] Hall identifies two such centres, the media and political parties. I shall add a different type of centre - that of gender. This notion of power allows an analysis which on the one hand, recognises differences between women such as that of the tea-grower and tea-buyer, and on the other hand, recognises the tea-grower and tea-buyer have some experiences in common as a result of their gender, for example domestic violence or sexual harassment.[149] In this way we incorporate aspects of Foucault's concept of power into our analysis, while refusing his absolute dispersion of it by recognising that while power circulates between centres rather than emanating from one centre, that circulation takes place "between constituted points of condensation."[150] In turn, this has tangible and observable consequences for women as a social group and the issue of punishment. For example, while Lees is right to point out that men and women share a world which is structured by sexually abusive language against women and derogatory terms for female sexuality, it is only one sex - women - whose sexuality is policed in this way, and who are punished through this discourse, for any perceived transgression of that sexuality.[151] Indeed Lees herself notes how labels such as 'slag' function to control girls' sexuality by steering them "towards a married existence as the only legitimate form of sexuality."[152] Females who make no effort to curtail or legitimate their sexuality must bear the punitive consequences at both an informal and formal level. We have thus come full circle from the early social control theories - via Foucauldian feminist theory - to a point where we can articulate and justify the need to place - not only a woman's criminality but also her sexuality and the moral censures surrounding it which play a pivotal role in constituting the gendered subjectivity of the female - at the very centre of theories of punishment.[153] A failure to do so means "ignoring this fundamental and near universal discourse" of sexuality through "which girls are constituted and in large part constitute themselves."[154] This type of theoretical framework is able to expose and challenge taken-for-granted assumptions and 'knowledge' about women, which in turn creates the possibility of women conceptualising themselves in alternative ways. In

---

[148]Hall 1988:71. Emphasis in the original.

[149]For example, Sue Lees argues derogatory terms such as 'slag' operate "as a form of generalised social control, along the lines of gender rather than class." In other words, while social class will create differences amongst women, at times discourses around gender will override those around class. (Lees, S. (1989) 'Learning to Love' in Cain, M. (ed) (1989) *Growing Up Good* Sage, London, p.21.

[150]Hall 1988:71.

[151]See for example Maureen Cain's discussion of Lees' work in Cain, M. (1989) 'Feminists transgress criminology' in Cain 1989:7.

[152]Lees 1986:165.

[153]Howe, A. (1994) *Punish and Critique* Routledge, London, p.140.

[154]Cain 1989:4.

doing so, it is inevitable that barriers between criminal and non-criminal women will be broken down, since, as I have shown in this chapter, these moral censures as well as the disqualification of women to speak with authority and state their own case, straddle both categories. Criminal and non-criminal women are further linked by their shared experience of informal punishment. Yet criminal women are also separated from the majority of women for whom non-penal and non-legal constraints are so powerful as to render formal punishment unnecessary. Thus, in studying executed women it is my aim, not only to restore these women to their rightful place in history, but also to create new spaces in which we can begin to conceptualise both their biographies and crimes in ways which challenge taken for granted knowledge about the 'good' as well as the 'bad' woman. In the following three chapters I set out to achieve this by situating my 15 case-studies of executed women in a revised 'social control' theoretical framework which is sensitive to Foucault's contribution to feminist theory, but which aims to avoid the pitfalls associated with discourse theory: the lack of emphasis upon personal empowerment; the negation of "the importance of personal and group definition and affirmation" and hence collective action as a strategy for social and political change; the general lack of theorisation of agency and the scant attention paid to the subject's own "understanding of her conditions of oppression."[155] It is also a framework which, rather than dismissing the currently unfashionable body of feminist literature known as 'social control' theory, sets out to refine it, by being mindful of its initial tendency to globalise and generalise complex issues of women's oppression, a tendency which at times has marginalised or ignored the uniqueness of and differences between individual women. It is my contention that unlike Foucauldian theory, this revised theoretical framework is able to illustrate how many aspects of men's sexual and social freedom is directly linked to women's 'unfreedom' in those same areas. Above all else, applying this theoretical framework to events surrounding the violent yet legal deaths of fifteen 20th century women will bring Foucault's false dichotomy of power versus violence to an end.[156]

---

[155]Deveaux, M. (1994) 'Feminism and Empowerment: A Critical Reading of Foucault' in *Feminist Studies* Vol 20, No 2 Summer 1994, p.240; 241.

[156]See Deveaux's discussion on this dichotomy as well as her points relating to men's freedom versus women's unfreedom in Deveaux 1994:236.

4 Women as Child-Killers: Four Case-Studies

Part I: Introduction

In the previous chapter I emphasised the importance of recognising differences between women, it is therefore not my intention here to present the five women executed for child-murder as a unitary category who necessarily have more in common with each other than with women executed for other types of killing. Indeed comparisons will be made between categories as the case-studies unfold. At the same time, recognising the unique set of circumstances of each case within this category does not of course, rule out the existence of certain similarities as I shall demonstrate throughout my analysis. For example, four of the five child-killers executed in the 20th century had in common their means of livelihood - so-called 'baby-farming'.

The Baby-Farmers: Women who Killed other Women's Children

> One of the amazing things about certain forms of female crime is the complete absence in the criminals of the maternal instinct ... It is altogether a baffling mystery. It applies particularly to the class of criminals known as 'baby-farmers.'[1]

It is no coincidence that all the 'baby-farming' cases occurred within the first decade of the 20th century. Baby-farming as a profession was both despised and stigmatised, since its existence emphasised the contradictions between dominant images of idealised motherhood, and its reality for those women whose circumstances did not fit this image. Thus, baby-farming could only exist within a culture that stigmatised illegitimate children, and which almost totally excluded the single mother from the necessary means to support herself and her child. Within this context there was always a demand for baby-farmers willing to adopt unplanned babies for a price on the understanding that they would 're-sell' the baby to suitable adoptive parents. Baby-farmers were usually uneducated and poor themselves, hence unlikely to have access to suitable adoptive parents. Some of them would therefore simply accept the baby and the agreed fee, usually between £7 and £30, kill the child and keep the money. The prevalence of baby-farming and the cheapness of a child's life can be gathered from a newspaper report published in 1899:

---

[1] Adam, H.L. (1911) *Women and Crime* T. Werner Laurie, London p.176.

A very large trade is done in adopting children, and so quickly do they pass from hand to hand that it becomes almost an impossible task to trace a child to its original adopter or to discover the identity of the parents. Week by week the bodies of children, from the recently born babe to a child even five and six years of age, are found in various parts of London generally in a nude state, wrapped in brown paper or some old piece of linen that offers not the slightest clue, whilst the verdict of "Murder against some persons unknown" has ceased to extort even a paragraph in the highly sensational evening newspapers which make a startling contents bill out of nothing.[2]

One of the most notorious baby-farmers was Amelia Dyer whom O'Donnell describes as a "diminutive slayer ... almost a dwarf, only four feet in height, and the more repellent because she pretended to be a woman of deep religious convictions to whom murder was abhorrent."[3] Adam considered Dyer to be "one of the greatest hypocrites that ever lived ... one of the most colossal petticoated atrocities that ever blackened the fair name of womanhood."[4] Mrs Dyer refused to reveal how many babies she had thrown into the Thames with these words: "You'll know all mine by the tape round their necks."[5] She was found guilty of murder in March 1896 and executed on the 10th June of that year. In the following section I examine the case of the first baby-farmer to be executed in the 20th century.

The Case of Ada Chard Williams

Ada Chard Williams and her husband William stood trial for murder at the Old Bailey on 16th February 1900. While William was discharged after the joint two-day trial, Ada was sentenced to death for the murder of 19-month-old Selina Jones. The murder was considered "a cruel one, committed from the basest motive - for money."[6] The autopsy suggested the baby had been grasped by her legs while her head was banged against a wall.[7] The subsequent head injury would have rendered her unconscious, and while in this condition "a white linen bag with tape strings had been pulled over its

---

[2]*The Weekly Dispatch* 1st October 1899 p.11. Adverts in newspapers for child-adoption could be found next to adverts such as "cast-off clothing bought for cash" and "Cob or Horse wanted hire" (*The Herald* 8th August 1899), which, arguably, suggest an extraordinary casual attitude towards young children.
[3]O'Donnell, B. (1956) *Should Women Hang?* W.H. Allen, London, p.142.
[4]Adam 1911:189. See also Ward, A. (1996) *Psychiatry and Criminal Responsibility in England 1843-1939* Unpublished Ph.D. thesis, De Montford University 1996.
[5]Wilson, P. (1971) *Murderess* Michael Joseph, London, p.240, 241; Segrave, K. (1992) *Women Serial and Mass Murderers* McFarland & Co, London, pp.98-101.
[6]HO144/280 XC17335 Public Record Office, Kew, Richmond, Surrey TW9 4DU.
[7]O'Donnell 1956:144. See also HO 144/280/A61654.

head and it had been strangled by means of those tape strings."[8] After being "trussed" the body was wrapped into a parcel and string was tied round it ending with three specific and unusual types of knots: Fishermen's bend, half hitch and reef knots which were to play an important role in the prosecution's case.[9] Moreover, the specificity of these knots ensured the couple were suspected of having murdered other children whose bodies had been 'parcelled' with string and identical knots. This was never proved in court but the *Weekly Dispatch* reported that during the six months they had lived in Barnes "no less than six children can be traced to her [Ada], and curiously enough, six children were subsequently tied up in a similar manner to the child Jones."[10] The couple used false names and moved frequently.[11] Each move coincided with another baby being discovered in the Thames, and the police eventually traced more than 25 children to the Williams's.[12] Yet, had it not been for the action of Ada Williams herself, it is unlikely their crimes would ever have been discovered. In December 1899 Ada wrote to Scotland Yard, apparently in response to a newspaper article linking her to the death of Selina Jones. At first glance the letter appears to have been written for the purpose of defending herself:

> The accusation [of murder] is positively false. ... I have, it is true, been carrying on a sort of baby farm, that is to say, I have adopted babies + then advertised + got them re-adopted for about half the amount I had previously received. I have had five in this way, two died while in my care but I can prove that every attention + kindness was shown them, no money was grudged over their illness, I can prove this by the people with whom we lodged + also from the doctors who attended them.[13]

Ada further stated that Selina had been re-adopted to a "Mrs Smith" whose address she could not remember. The two children referred to had indeed been issued with death certificates from doctors despite the fact that in at least one of the cases the doctor had found the child to be suffering from neglect two days prior to its death and "considered the case unsatisfactory but

---

[8]*The Times* 16th February 1900.
[9]HO144/280/A61654. "Trussed" was described as "heels drawn on each side of the head close by the ears - left arm thrust between left leg and body, right squeezed between body and leg and secured by the cord."
[10]*The Weekly Dispatch* 4th March 1900.
[11]HO 144/280 XC17335. For example, in the two years prior to their arrest they had occupied at least nine different homes.
[12]*The Weekly Dispatch* 4th March 1900.
[13]Quoted from original letter dated 5th December 1899, in CRIM 1/59/4 XC7025, Public Record Office, Chancery Lane, London WC2A 1LR. Underlining in the original.

certified it as a death from bronchitis."[14] It was this letter which made it possible for Scotland Yard to trace the Williams's.

Ada Williams and the Construction of 'Truth'

Ada had been an 18-year-old country girl from Sussex when she married William in 1893. William was double her age and had been a scholar at Cambridge, hence he was perceived as being "socially and intellectually considerably above his wife,"[15] and "a vastly different person from his wife."[16] Despite this supposed superiority, Adam, an observer at the trial, offered the opinion that it was "quite clear that he was completely under the control of his wife":

> This became apparent as they sat in the dock. Mrs Williams, although looking so modest and demure, was in fact a woman of invincible will-power and irresistible resolution. She was also extremely callous and cruel. This was indicated by her thin and firmly-compressed lips. She sat facing the jury, whom it was obvious she had set herself the task of favourably impressing. She had designedly assumed an air of demureness and inoffensiveness for that purpose. She has so placed her chair in the dock as to bring her face to face with the jurymen, because in the ordinary course of things a prisoner faces the bench, the dock being at right-angles to the jury-box. Mrs Williams was one of those women who exercise great influence over men, and who are thoroughly alive to the extent of their power. As she had ruled her husband through the medium of this same influence, so she set herself to win over the jury by similar means.[17]

Adam's judgement of Ada's character was by most accounts a fair assessment of contemporary public opinion. O'Donnell for example, placed her in the same category as Amelia Dyer: "She was a hatchet-faced woman of vile temper ... [with] a mind as evil as ever woman possessed."[18] The mobilisation of this antagonistic and hostile response to Ada's personality therefore must be examined. In Chapter One I discussed how women's violence is denied rationality by classifying the perpetrators as mad or bad. I noted how rationality is denied by focusing on the perpetrator's abnormal character rather than on social and personal circumstances leading up to the crime. The case of Ada Williams provides a prime example of these processes at work. Even a perfunctory deconstruction of the above quotation indicates that Ada was categorised as a 'bad' rather than 'mad' woman. The

---

[14]HO 144/280 XC17335.
[15]Adam 1911:199.
[16]O'Donnell 1956:145.
[17]Adam 1911:199-200.
[18]O'Donnell 1956:144.

description of Ada's power over men is reminiscent of the attitudes towards women expressed in the 15th-century theology text *Malleus Maleficarum* discussed in Chapter Two. The overall image presented is of a manipulative, cunning and deceitful woman whose power over men makes her highly dangerous. The discourses mobilised to create this image of an 'evil' woman centred on Ada's conduct and behaviour as both a wife and mother as I shall now illustrate.

First, Ada's position within her marriage is that usually reserved for the male - she is the dominant partner while her husband's attitude towards her is one "of dog-like devotion."[19] As a result she is regarded as an unruly and 'uppity' woman, someone who does not 'know her place' and who does not show appropriate deference to her husband. For example, during the trial William sat facing Ada, continually directing glances in her direction as well as speaking to her on several occasions, but Ada allegedly ignored him.[20] Furthermore, as I shall illustrate later, Ada, on at least one occasion, had been overheard to threaten William with physical violence. She was therefore not a submissive or deferential wife who obeyed her husband or recognised his authority. Instead her demeanour within the courtroom disturbed and disrupted the ideal image of passive and self-effacing femininity, and as such her presence came to represent a threat to patriarchal hegemony.

Second, discourses around motherhood - both at a structural and individual level - played an important role in this case. Rose has commented that while infanticide reached its peak in the 1860s and had long been in decline by 1900, the fact that four baby-farmers were executed between 1900 and 1907 "probably indicates a greater police vigilance and a lower public tolerance of infant disposal."[21] While this view may form one aspect of the explanation for the execution of these four women, it is necessary to examine broader social, cultural, political and economic issues in order to make sense of the prejudice and hostility towards baby-farmers at this historical moment. In particular, we need to be aware of the state's role in the construction of the discourse 'dangerous womanhood'. In chapter Two I discussed how draconian legislation passed in 1623 against those suspected of infanticide or concealment was aimed solely at unmarried mothers, and had little to do with the preservation of the lives of infants. Instead such drastic measures were motivated by a desire to control and regulate the sexuality of a vulnerable group of women by making it more difficult to escape the consequences of immoral conduct.[22] Although resistance to this legislation from juries was so great that it eventually had to be modified, women's 'unruly bodies' nevertheless continued to cause anxiety. Consequently:

---

[19]Adam 1911:201.

[20]Adam 1911:201.

[21]Rose, L. (1986) *The Massacre of the Innocents: Infanticide 1800-1939* RKP, London.

[22]It will be remembered from Chapter Two that a large proportion of illegitimate children were not the product of "immoral conduct" by women, but of female servants being raped or seduced by their masters.

This specific focus on illegitimate children and hence unmarried mothers remained a feature of legislation dealing with concealment of birth until 1828 and with infanticide until 1861.[23]

Concern over infanticide intensified between 1860-65 when it increasingly became associated with moral decline and 'un-British' conduct and as such presented "a threat to the social order and civilised values."[24] It is within this context that a moral panic had developed by 1870 about some of the practices associated with baby-farming. Baby-farmers were nearly always working-class women, so impoverished that even when they did not kill their charges intentionally, many died anyway from neglect and malnutrition as baby-farmers did not possess the means or skills necessary to care adequately for the infants. By 1871 a House of Lords Select Committee was established to consider issues and problems associated with baby-farming. Unsurprisingly, the Committee found that women resorted to baby-farmers for the same reasons they resorted to infanticide or abortion: shame of their unmarried status, poverty so severe that keeping the baby was not an option, and lack of support, financial or otherwise, from the father.[25] These findings resulted in the creation of the *Protection of Infant Life Act* in 1872, which stipulated minimum standards of care of infants and demanded the licensing of baby-farmers. Yet, as Smart notes, the Committee remained "entirely silent on the central problem facing working-class women of how to earn a living and look after children."[26] The licensing and regulation of baby-farmers therefore did nothing to enhance the chances of infant survival, but did much to ensure an increase in prosecutions of poor working-class women whose financial position remained unchanged. In effect legal discourse had defined 'dangerous motherhood' in class terms, containing this form of 'unruly womanhood' within the working-class "or the immoral classes."[27] Together, these discourses around baby-farming made up the framework through which Ada's case was heard.

With specific reference to Ada's case, the quality of mothering which she provided fell well short of acceptable standards. As discussed in Chapter Three, the ideology of motherhood can be extended to female carers as both roles have similar moral assumptions and expectations attached to them. Women's caring role is regarded as innate and 'natural'. A 'normal' woman and a good carer/mother happily makes personal sacrifices and puts the

---

[23]Smart, C. (1992) 'Disruptive bodies and unruly sex' in Smart, C. (ed) *Regulating Womanhood* Routledge, London, p.16.
[24]Smart 1992:16-17.
[25]Smart 1992:22. See also Clark, A. (1987) *Women's Silence Men's Violence* Pandora, London p.74 where she writes: "The bastardy clauses of the New Poor Law exonerated fathers of illegitimate children from any responsibility for their maintenance, placing the moral blame and financial burden on the shoulders of impoverished and unmarried mothers."
[26]Smart 1992:23.
[27]Smart 1992:24.

interests of her family/charge before her own. In Ada's case the distinction between mother and carer was particularly blurred as baby-farmers were expected to replace the biological mother, thus fulfilling both roles. Yet doctors had found her previous charges to be suffering from malnutrition and neglect. Furthermore, Mrs Loughborough, a witness for the prosecution and neighbour of the Williams's while a young girl, Lily, had been in their charge, testified that:

> She [Ada] put it in the corner & gave it a smack, when I went there to tea. ... She told me afterwards that she had beating [sic] the child with a stick. Mr objected & she said you mind your own game or I'll serve you the same ... She told me Lily had dirted [sic] on the floor & she had beat [sic] her with stick for doing so & left her laying [sic] in it. ... I said "Poor little thing." She said "Serve it right." A day or two after I went again. I saw her back had "wails" weals on it about as thick as my finger. She showed me the marks & said Look what I've done. I said what wd [sic] the mother say. She said I don't care what the mother says.[28]

When Lily was no longer part of the Williams household, Mrs Loughborough asked Ada what had happened to the child:

> her mother came & took her home ... A damned good job it has gone. Now I feel in heaven.

Mrs Loughborough's description of Ada's child-rearing methods is not an attractive one. Ada is portrayed as a cruel, callous and heartless mother, bad tempered and lacking in compassion. Because the skills associated with mothering are considered to be innate in women, and not skills that have to be learnt as in other areas of the world of work, Ada's shortcomings are taken to be 'unnatural' - implemented by her as a deliberate policy. In that sense a particular type of rationality which focuses on individual wickedness is imposed on her behaviour. But categorising her as 'bad' ignores Ada's emotional depletion, impoverishment, lack of choice and control over her life and lack of experience in child-rearing practices, features which could all be traced to Ada's social circumstances rather than to her individual psyche.

Ada's image as a callous and evil mother/woman was reinforced by other aspects of her behaviour. For example, the fact she exchanged Lily's clothes for "an art flower pot" with a neighbour, came to signify a whimsical selfishness, as well as a cold and unsentimental attitude towards the absent child. This unsentimentality and lack of commitment to mothering was further reinforced by a Home Office memorandum which, referring to various adverts Ada had placed in newspapers in an attempt to 'sub-farm' children, stated:

---

[28]Mrs Loughborough's statement from deposition file HO 144/280/A61654.

It might be that if prisoner could get rid of the child on advantageous i.e. cheap terms + no enquiry she would prefer that to cruelty or violence - but failing that - she would not hesitate at more criminal courses - or they may have been a mere blind.[29]

Here Ada is being constructed at best, as a woman who half-heartedly attempts to find homes for the children, but if not immediately successful, the child is simply murdered. At worst, it is suggested that despite the couples' grinding poverty, adverts were paid for as 'a mere blind' to hide what in this scenario could only be gratuitous violence and murder.

In sum, Ada's conduct as a wife was considered to be that of a domineering, hysterical and bad-tempered 'battle-axe', while William was regarded as a besotted but ineffectual 'hen-pecked' husband.[30] Ada appeared to have no commitment to the mother/carer role but was judged to be cruel, selfish, callous and whimsical in her dealings with children while William "did his best to care for the foster children ... He saw that they were fed and washed and no father could have been kinder."[31] Once this interpretive schema had established Ada as a 'bad' woman, her conduct and behaviour was read accordingly regardless of the plausibility of this interpretation. Below I suggest a different interpretation of the same evidence, my aim being to construct an alternative 'truth' about Ada which can be understood outside the 'mad/bad' framework.

An Alternative Truth about Ada Williams

The role that male partners played as accomplices to the crimes of executed women is a theme which will recur in other case-studies; the case of the Williams's provides the first example. As noted above, at 36 William had been double Ada's age when the couple married and as a former Cambridge scholar, he enjoyed considerably higher social status than Ada, an uneducated country girl. While the image of William as downtrodden, in awe of his wife and tenderly protecting and caring for his foster children, was accepted by the Court, Home Office communications indicate that power relationships within the marriage did not operate in such simplistic terms. William was described as having "led a wild and roving life ever since he left Cambridge. Indeed his relatives had to advertise for him when his step-father died leaving him £100."[32] William invested this money in a news-agent shop but he was an unsuccessful business-person and soon penniless again. He was unable to

---

29HO 144/280/A61654.

30Indeed William himself appeared to share this representation of their relationship because he wrote in a petition to the Home Secretary that given his age and knowledge of the world he "ought to have exercised a more wholesome influence over her moral nature." (HO 144/280/A61654).

31O'Donnell 1956:145.

32HO 144/280/61654. Home Office Document initialled K.G.D. 23rd February 1900.

work as a scholar due to deafness, it was therefore entirely Ada's responsibility to earn enough money for them both:

> for the first few years of her married life the prisoner submitted to every hardship, worked at laborious toil, and kept herself honestly and respectably - ... there seemed no prospect of a change for the better in her lot - ... it was only during the last 2 years of her life she ever entered into the "kind of baby-farming" to which she so pathetically admitted in her letter to Scotland Yard.[33]

The 'letter' is the same as referred to earlier and it contains several features which challenge the image of Ada as a domineering woman and William as a downtrodden husband, doing his wife's bidding. First, the letter was perfectly constructed, obviously written (or dictated) by an articulate and well-educated person. Even Home Office personnel acknowledged this was not the letter of a 'farmer's daughter': "It is hardly a letter which the woman could have written alone."[34]

Second, the letter was designed to exonerate William from any involvement in Ada's baby-farming activities:

> In conclusion I must tell you that my husband is not to blame in any way whatever, he has always looked upon the whole matter from the first with the greatest abhorrence but only gave way to me because he was, through illness, not of employment, he never, however, once touched any of the money I made by these means.[35]

Third, the letter was the only piece of evidence linking the Williams's to the murder and it was acknowledged that without it they may never have been identified.[36] It is therefore extremely difficult to discern Ada's motive for sending it, although in view of the above quoted passage, it is easy to understand William's motive. Taken together, the above factors - William's age, education and experience of the world compared to Ada's, along with the letter which bore all the signs of him having dictated it to her - could equally lead to the exact opposite conclusion to the one actually drawn: namely that it was *William* who manipulated *Ada* and that she was in awe of him as a result of his higher status to the extent where he, arguably, demanded or forced her to write a letter to Scotland Yard, exonerating him from all blame. The exact nature of the couple's relationship can only remain a matter for speculation, but it is difficult to ignore the possibility that William was aware of the likely

---

[33]"A Statement of the Defence which was not submitted to the Court, at the time of her Trial" HO 144/280/A61654. Underlining in the original.
[34]HO 144/280/A61654.
[35]CRIM 1/59/4. Original letter from Ada Williams to Scotland Yard.
[36]Wilson 1971:253.

outcome if Ada alone became associated with the dead infant found in the river.[37]

Even the prosecution could not ignore the conflicting nature of the evidence and conceded that William must have been involved in the murderous activities for which Ada alone was soon to be executed. The judge's notes also expressed concern over William's involvement.[38] Sir Kenelm Digby, the Permanent Under-Secretary of State, suggested the following points should be considered before determining the safety of Ada's conviction[39]:

> it is difficult to believe that this was done by the prisoner unaided and alone. Taken in connection with their previous history it appears to me that there is a very grave case of suspicion ... that the husband as well as the wife was concerned in this wicked work. Then there is the evidence connecting him with the murder. He makes the arrangement to receive the letters [responses to Ada's baby-farming advert] ... and calls for them. He is present when the arrangements for the rooms ... is made [where Selina Jones's mother handed her baby over to Ada]. He is 'about daily' at ... [the Williams home]. The letter of Dec. 5 is probably his composition ... On the whole, except the instance of his interference when the woman was beating the child, *there seems very little to distinguish between the two cases.* The jury might in my opinion have nearly as much justification for drawing an unfavourable view in his case as in his wife's.[40]

Another Home Office memo echoes Sir Kenelm's views:

> The letter read as if it were the composition of <u>her husband</u> an educated man rather than hers. There is not a little evidence to show by whose hand the child met its death whether by the man or woman.[41]

A third memo went further:

> I am in doubt ... whether the hands were those of the husband or of the wife, and I confess it seems to me the more closely I examine the

---

[37]It is unlikely that William was ignorant of legal matters as "he was a near relation of the late Judge Williams" (Adam 1911:199) and "was at Cambridge with Mr Avory who refused brief in consequence" (HO 144/280/A61654).

[38]Judge's Notes p.10, referred to in Sir Kenelm Digby's minutes dated 23rd February 1900 in HO 144/280/A61654.

[39]The Criminal Appeal Act did not come into effect until 1907.

[40]HO 144/280/A61654. My emphasis.

[41]HO 144/280/A61654. Underlining in the original.

exhibits now before me as I write, *that the work is more probably that of the man than of the woman.*[42]

Such was the concern over the safety of Ada's conviction and William's discharge that the Home Secretary was advised to change her sentence to penal servitude for life, especially as "the letters of the husband to his wife in prison look as if it is possible that he may yet make some further disclosure."[43]

Legal experts and state servants were thus well aware the evidence (or lack thereof) opened up the possibility of a challenge to the dominant 'truth' about Ada as the tyrannical wife and callous and cruel mother, and William, the meek, powerless, ineffectual husband who showed his wife 'dog-like' devotion, and who remained a caring and devoted father protecting his children from her cruelty. Ultimately, however, they did not pursue this challenge because, like others who observed and commented upon the case, they too were caught up in discourses and ideologies concerning the 'good' wife and mother and appropriate female conduct and behaviour. The lack of these qualities within Ada's repertoire ensured she became a prime candidate for the experience of judicial misogyny. There were neither eye-witnesses nor forensic evidence which indicated that Ada was the killer rather than William. Instead judgements were made through an interpretive schema based on what was already 'known' about her:

> From what H.O. has heard from outside sources (Governor of Prison &c.) it would appear that the woman is hot-tempered, violent and hysterical; the man meek and small, and so *the probabilities* are in favour of the murder having been committed by the woman, while the tying up knots &c. were probably done by the man.[44]

Probabilities are of course not evidence, and Home Office personnel recognised the potential problems associated with treating them as such:

> Can it be fairly said that it is more than a probability that this is the true explanation; and would it be safe to hang the woman when *we are absolutely in the dark* as to whether it was her hand that actually committed murder, and when possibly at the last minute the husband might come forward and say "I did it", and it would be impossible to prove that he was not speaking the truth.[45]

By the 6th March 1900, the day Ada was hanged, nothing had occurred to resolve the concern and disquiet surrounding the case. Yet the execution proceeded because those in a position to decide her fate ultimately

---

[42]HO 144/280/A61654. My emphasis.
[43]HO 144/280/A61654.
[44]HO 144/280/A61654. Home Office Document, 2nd March 1900. My emphasis.
[45]HO 144/280/A61654. Home Office Document, 2nd March 1900. My emphasis.

chose to ignore the challenge to the dominant version of truth whilst simultaneously emphasising the importance of the state - through the criminal justice system - *being seen* to punish a thoroughly 'bad' woman:

> I regret very much that I am unable to take this view [of altering Ada's sentence to penal servitude]. I think the woman was clearly proved to have been guilty of the murder and though it is quite possible and even probable that the husband was jointly and equally guilty, the verdict of the jury with which the Judge concurred was to the effect that he was not. Nothing since the trial has weakened the verdict. To respite a woman proved guilty of such an atrocious crime, even on the above grounds, would seem to me to be likely to give a false impression + to weaken the deterrent effect of the sentence.[46]

This quotation provides a clear illustration of the contradictions which lay at the heart of Ada's conviction. On the one hand it is openly admitted William was probably "equally guilty", on the other, legitimacy for carrying out the death sentence on Ada only is sought by referring to the verdict of the jury. There is no doubt about the all male jury's conviction that William had been involved in Selina's murder. As I shall illustrate, they did in fact decide that William was "guilty of being an accessory after the fact" although ultimately he was discharged and left court a free man.[47]

Thus, only Ada was sentenced to death despite the evidence being stacked equally against both defendants even by the prosecution's own reasoning. In order to explain this judgement I shall draw on feminist critiques of the law. While law is imbued with contradictions and cannot simply be reduced to "a vehicle for men's oppression of women ... [or] an embodiment of the values of ... male culture", it nevertheless treats women defendants differentially by defining, supporting, preserving and upholding a traditional view of women's role:

> It does this by slotting people into household units, constituted through marriage, with a breadwinning husband-father at the head, and a subordinate woman performing the unpaid offices of wife and mother, sustaining the traditional 'family values'. Indeed the woman's place is vital to the peace, good order and stability of the patriarchal order: 'She can prevent delinquency by staying at home to look after the children, she can reduce unemployment by staying at home and freeing jobs for the men, she can recreate a stable family unit by becoming totally dependent on her husband so that she cannot leave him. *She* is the answer'.[48]

---

[46]HO 144/280/A61654. Comments by Home Secretary.
[47]*The Times* 19th February 1900.
[48]Naffine, N. (1990) *Law & the Sexes* Allen & Unwin London p.13; p.16 referring to Smart, C. (1984) *The Ties That Bind* 1984:136. Emphasis in the original.

Women who do not fulfil this role become problematised - they are seen as unruly and in need of restraint and control. For Smart the problematised and unruly female body is caught in a double bind. In the first instance women's bodies "are constituted as the archetypal site of irrationality." Within legal discourse the female body has failed to adhere to the principles of reason and rationality which have become subordinate to irrationality and emotionality. However, the second instance illustrates that women cannot escape the sexism of legal discourse by becoming rational since the 'rational' woman appears to be lacking appropriate feminine attributes. For Smart, the dominant notion is "that economic rationality is the highest form of rationality."[49] Hence women applying an economic rationality to services they should provide for free - for example surrogate motherhood or prostitution - become 'monstrous' and 'heinous'.[50] To this we can add the practice of baby-farming, which as described earlier, was considered an unsavoury practice and hence heavily stigmatised. I also drew attention to the view of Home Office personnel that the murder was "a cruel one, committed from the basest motive - for money." While this view is not necessarily incorrect the underlying assumption is that the murder was motivated by financial greed rather than economic need. In that sense Ada as an individual within legal discourse became the problematised body and the unruly woman, while at the same time little or no attention was paid to her personal and social circumstances. I have also illustrated that Ada fell well short of fulfilling the role of the dependent wife and subordinate woman - maintaining family values, creating peace, stability and harmony within the home. The fact she had no choice but to become the breadwinner due to William's disability, is not discussed or even mentioned by those with the power to decide her fate. Only the Defence Statement discussed earlier and her mother drew attention to Ada's financial desperation:

> Her poverty has been very great since her marriage + she has worked very hard - especially since the death of her Father a small tenant farmer as since my widowhood I could not afford to help her.[51]

Thus, the discourses mobilised around Ada as a deviant wife and mother, and hence as an unruly body, culminated in judicial misogyny which impacted on everyone within the courtroom, including the all male jury. This mobilisation ensured a disregard for the structural circumstances which contributed not only to Ada becoming a criminal, but also to ensuring her place within the interpretive schema of a woman in need of restraint and control. Ultimately these discourses filled the gap left by the lack of evidence and allowed the jury to conclude *without* that evidence, "that the woman actually committed the murder and the man disposed or helped to dispose of

---

[49]Smart, C. (1995) *Law, Crime and Sexuality* Sage, London p.227.
[50]Smart 1995:227.
[51]Adelaide Street's plea for mercy towards her daughter Ada, to the Home Secretary, dated 3rd March 1900; HO 144/280/A61654.

the body."[52] That such a verdict could be reached - despite the fact that even the prosecution recognised the evidence could not differentiate or distinguish between Ada's and William's involvement in the murder - is a testimony both to the importance of ideologies around women's conduct and behaviour generally, and the power of discourses around the 'unruly woman' within the courtroom in particular.

The purpose of constructing an 'alternative truth' about Ada Williams's crime and about her as a human being , has not been to suggest she was innocent of the crime for which she was hanged. Rather, it has been an attempt to understand her actions as stemming from other than human greed and cruelty which so far has been the only language in which her story has been told. Similarly, the attempt to reach an understanding of her violent conduct which is closer to the experience of her reality is not meant to be an excuse or apology for her behaviour, but is based on a desire to grant women's violence a rationality which is not necessarily linked to the mad/bad categories.

Moreover, my intention has been to illustrate how Ada was treated *differentially,* not as a result of different evidence but as a result of different gender expectations. In other words, as I noted above, this differentiation was not based on forensic evidence or eyewitnesses' accounts, but in how she was perceived as a woman generally, and, more specifically, as a wife and mother.

Until the very end Ada was perceived as a duplicitous, hysterical female beyond control:

> Throughout the trial she had managed to keep up an appearance of demure innocence, but as soon as she realised what her fate was to be she dropped the mask and revealed herself. She stormed and raged and fought with the wardresses in the dock and, in profane language, boasted that two other children had died while in her charge.[53]

Adam's personal observation of Ada supported this description of her alleged hypocritical behaviour:

> the true character of Mrs Williams asserted itself after she was convicted and when she knew that dissimulation would no longer avail her. When she was brought back to the dock to hear the verdict she was looking extremely pallid and was much agitated. The verdict having been given, she was asked whether she had anything to say. She was so agitated, however that she was unable to speak. The sentence was then pronounced. She was again asked whether she wished to say anything and having by a supreme effort obtained partial control over herself, she said in a studied voice of bravado, "Thank you, my lord." ... As she was descending the steps she suddenly struck out at the attendants, at the same time shrieking out,

---

[52]Home Office communication dated 23rd February 1900, HO 144/280/A61654.
[53]O'Donnell 1956:145.

"let me alone, or it'll be the worse for you!" It was the savage side of her nature asserting itself.[54]

In contrast, *The Times* presented a rather different version of Ada's last moments in court:

The female prisoner, who had preserved perfect composure, said "Thank you, my Lord." Being asked whether she had anything to say in stay of execution, she replied, "I have nothing to say."[55]

Further support for an alternative truth about Ada came from Edward Milman, the Governor of Newgate prison:

The execution of the prisoner took place at 9am - and went off satisfactorily. Death was instantaneous. She was remarkably brave to the last - but made no confession - probably with the idea that she might implicate her husband.[56]

In declining to make a final statement Ada ensured her personal account of Selina's murder would remain muted for ever. Confessions were considered extremely desirous by the Home Office as will become apparent in later case-studies, because they provided a firm basis of legitimacy for a judicial killing. In Ada's case the lack of a confession is explained by referring to the "fear of implicating her husband", thus ensuring that her last moments on this earth would be recorded as contradictory, since such concern would not automatically be attributed to a woman who in life had stood accused of domineering and manipulating her husband. Moreover, a confession from Ada was logically more likely to *exonerate* her husband than to implicate him. Taken together, these accounts (and lack thereof) illustrate, that while the exact 'truth' about Ada Williams can only ever remain a matter for speculation, her character was far more complex than that presented by what were to become dominant accounts of her as an evil and callous 'hatchet-faced hypocrite'.

The Quality of Ada Williams's Defence

As illustrated above, contemporary accounts of Ada Williams's case proved to be a rich source of personal criticism against her. During the course of this research I was unable to locate a single account which criticised William's personal conduct despite the fact that immediately upon being discharged he was re-arrested and charged with fraud, an unrelated crime for which he subsequently received a prison sentence.[57] Neither was I able to locate

---

[54]Adam 1911:203-4.
[55]*The Times* 19th February 1900.
[56]HO 144/280 XC 17335 A61654 Notice to Home Office dated 6th March 1900.
[57]HO 144/280/A61654.

accounts which questioned or challenged the nature of the Williams's defence. Neither newspaper articles nor observers of the trial or Home Office communications questioned the fact that no witnesses were called for the defence in a murder trial which could potentially have concluded with a double execution.

In an attempt to save Ada from the gallows William sent a petition to the Home Secretary Sir Matthew Ridley. It was accompanied by a hand-written 20-page document entitled 'A Statement of the Defence which was not submitted to the Court, at the time of her Trial'. This document included details of six potential character witnesses who had at different times been Ada's employers - "disinterested people" - whose evidence would have proved that "she has all her brief life earned the esteem and regard of every one who has known her."[58] A seventh employer "declared he would be always willing to give prisoner a good character."[59] None of them were called to give evidence. Other potential witnesses which the defence failed to call included Mrs Goacher, the prisoner's sister, whose illegitimate daughter, Ada had looked after for several months before returning the child to her mother, and who was still "alive and could have been produced at the trial"[60]; Dr Richards, Dr Gray and Dr Lauder Hills who had attended the two children who died in 1897 and 1898. All three had sent letters to Ada's solicitor as had a nurse attending Leslie, the second child to die, and the Williams's landlady. Finally, Mrs Meeklenburgh, who had adopted a child from Ada in January 1899 and with whom she kept in touch "several times after she parted with the child," was not called.[61] The reason that none of these witnesses gave evidence was that the "prisoner was unable to pay the expenses of the witnesses for her Defence."[62]

The document also expressed concern over "the respectability, character, or antecedents of ... Mrs Loughborough", the only witness produced by the prosecution to testify Ada was guilty of child cruelty. In particular, it was concerned that "where the life of a human being is at stake the single evidence of only one witness should be received with some caution and reserve."[63] Once again the defendants were unable to have this witness investigated on their behalf because they were "too poor"[64]:

> It is humbly and urgently pointed out that the Prisoners were very poor and friendless and utterly unable to carry out or cause to be carried out any investigations on their behalf. That on the other hand

---

[58]'A Statement of the Defence which was not submitted to the Court, at the time of her Trial' HO 144/280/A61654 p.2.
[59]'A Statement of Defence ...' HO 144/280/A61654 p.2.
[60]'The Humble Petition of William Chard Williams' HO 144/280/A61654.
[61]'The Humble Petition of William Chard Williams' HO 144/280/A61654.
[62]HO 144/280/A61654.
[63]'A Statement of Defence ...' HO 144/280/A61654 p.6. Underlining in the original.
[64]'A Statement of Defence ...' HO 144/280/A61654 p.13.

the Prisoner had opposed to her the whole machinery of Scotland Yard.[65]

Finally, although not a direct criticism of the defence, but rather a comment upon the manner in which the entire case was conducted, it should be noted that William's discharge came about, not as a result of persuasive arguments put forward by Mr Wild or Mr MacMahon-Mahon defending the couple, but as a result of a misunderstanding on the part of the jury. Judge Ridley's summing up and guidance to the jury regarding acceptable verdicts no longer exist, consequently it is impossible to discern how this misunderstanding came about. However, after the jury had found William not guilty of murder, but an accessory after the fact, they were told this verdict was unacceptable. As he had not been charged with this crime William would be entitled to a new trial and in Mr Justice Ridley's opinion not "much good would be gained by [another prosecution] ... in view of what had happened, it was not necessary to ask for a verdict against the male prisoner ... the male prisoner was not the real offender, and if a verdict were returned against him he could not pass severe punishment."[66]

In Chapter One I emphasised the importance of bearing two questions in mind when analysing criminal women. They were "under what conditions do certain people claim to possess knowledge about female criminals" and "what are the processes which result in such claims being translated into practices which have particular consequences for criminal women".[67] The case of Ada and William Williams exemplifies the failure of the criminal justice system to live up to its own rhetoric of due process. The verdict was not arrived at after listening to conclusive evidence within an impartial courtroom. Instead knowledge about Ada - 'the truth' about Ada - had been created by mobilising *discourses* around female conduct and behaviour. By utilising such discourses - speaking through them - those who concerned themselves with the case were able to construct her as an unsympathetic character - the archetypical 'bad' woman. The fact that Home Office personnel, prosecution and judge were united in their recognition that Ada and William were equally likely to have committed the murder, yet simultaneously accept her execution while William left court a free man, reminds us never to underestimate the power of such discourses.

A Double Execution - the Case of Amelia Sach and Annie Walters

The two women, beyond words as wicked a pair as ever stepped in shoe leather, were what is known as 'Baby Farmers.' This does not mean that either of them were babies and even less that they were farmers. *They were wholesale baby murderers* ... In the dock Amelia

---

[65]'A Statement of Defence ...' HO 144/280/A61654 p.15.
[66]*The Times* 19th February 1900.
[67]As outlined in Worrall, A. (1990) *Offending Women* Routledge, London p.5.

Sacks [sic], her face deadly pale ... looked strangely like the prints of Charlotte Corday. She was a handsome woman with well-cut features and a gentleness about her that made the terrible nature of her crimes all the more unbelievable. In direct contrast to this slim and almost elegant creature Emily Waters [sic], at her side, might have been the maiden sister of Quilp ... Small, spare, and motherly-looking in appearance, with her hair parted in the centre and drawn tightly over her ears, her face was lined and creased, and looked like a russet apple of a previous season. She seemed incapable of anything but the greatest kindness, and yet the hands clasped in front of her had been laid across the mouth of many a helpless little creature ...[68]

Three years after Ada Williams's execution attitudes towards baby-farmers remained unchanged. For example, when commenting on the case of Amelia Sach and Annie Walters, *The Lancet* did not question the circumstances which left some women no choice but to seek the services of baby-farmers. Instead it reserved its criticisms solely for the baby-farmers who, as indicated above, were usually as destitute and impoverished as their clients:

The people who relieve ... parents of their offspring act from sordid and not from benevolent motives. The baby-farmer's profits by honestly carrying out the trust undertaken are likely to be but small, and they can be increased only at the expense of the adopted infant, whose death, when a single and final payment has been made, is the most lucrative issue for which the baby-farmer can hope.[69]

The above quotation illustrates how wider social issues around baby-farming could be removed by ignoring the fact that 'parents' were inevitably unmarried mothers without the means to support the child and 'people' were inevitably women with little prospect of supporting themselves by other means. However, just as William Williams was an exception to this pattern so too was Amelia Sach whose motive for criminal involvement was never revealed. Annie Walters however, followed the usual pattern of an uneducated and destitute woman desperate for some means of survival:

Mrs Sach was an attractive and brainy young woman of twenty-nine, but her partner in crime was of low intelligence, illiterate and a pervert with ruthless instincts.[70]

Amelia ran what appeared to be a respectable nursing home for women about to deliver their babies. She obtained clients by advertising in

---

[68]Hicks, S. (1939) *Not Guilty, M'Lord* Cassell and Co Ltd, London pp. 27-28; 29-30. Emphasis in the original.
[69]*The Lancet* 24th January 1903 p.251 (vol I).
[70]O'Donnell 1956:146.

newspapers and she ensured that a large percentage of that clientele would be mothers of illegitimate babies by including the sentence "Baby can remain."[71] Once a baby was born Amelia would offer to find adoptive parents for it in exchange for a £30 fee. But rather than fulfilling her part of the agreement she would pass the baby on to Annie who disposed of it. As had been the case with Ada Williams, Annie and Amelia stood trial for one murder only, that of Miss Galley's baby, but were suspected of being responsible for the deaths of other infants. Indeed another infant had died in Annie's care only days before the death of the Galley baby, but this death had been accepted as accidental by her landlord, Mr Seal, a police officer. However, he became suspicious when she brought a second baby home only days later and his superior arranged for her to be kept under surveillance. She was subsequently arrested with the dead baby still in her arms.

Apart from being considered a "pervert" and "of low intelligence" Annie was also described as "a short, plebeian, stubby, plain-faced woman, shabbily attired ... [who] looked as though her occupation in life was 'charing'."[72] The statement which she produced following her arrest may well have been at least partly responsible for these condemnatory and negative opinions:

> i ment the Lady she was in a Brougham she said you have come i said yes i am could get in give me the baby i gave it to her she sad on tye the parcell i on tied it then the on dress the baby and gave me the closes and drest it in fine Lace Robes and a boutfull cloke and Lace Vale she said it will be a lovly baby i said it a good little sole it never cry and i said i dont think my lanlady as herd it at hall.[73]

Not even Annie's defence counsel was persuaded by this statement and subsequently made no attempt to trace this adoptive parent, but argued instead that evidence relating to babies other than the one she was accused of murdering should be rendered inadmissible. His argument was rejected.[74] Other commentators cited the fact that she killed babies inside a police officer's home, as well as her claim that one of the missing babies had been adopted by a coastguard in Kensington well away from coastal waters, as evidence that "she was not too bright."[75] Hence it became widely accepted Amelia was the 'head' while Annie provided the 'hands' within this criminal partnership.[76] Other aspects of Annie's life did nothing to endear her to those

---

[71]Original advert in *Dalton's Weekly House & Apartment Advertiser* 5th June 1902 in CRIM 1/83/2 Public Record Office, Chancery Lane London WC2A 1LR.
[72]Adam 1911:194. See also Segrave 1992:254 who describes Annie as "'bedraggled' or 'squat and ugly.'"
[73]CRIM 1/83/2. From original statement by Annie Walters.
[74]HO 144/690/104226 XC2622 Public Record Office, Kew, Richmond, Surrey TW9 4DU.
[75]Adam 1911:191-2; O'Donnell 1956:147.
[76]Adam 1911:194.

who were soon to judge her. She had been a heavy drinker who occasionally lived with men during an era when marriage was considered the only form of respectable cohabitation between couples.[77] She was therefore a woman who deviated from conventional domestic and moral standards. This deviance extended to her demeanour inside the courtroom where her conduct was considered inappropriate:

> Walters ... maintained a stolid, almost indifferent aspect towards the proceedings ... Once or twice she smiled faintly at something that was said in court.[78]

Here Annie's behaviour is interpreted through the dominant knowledge constructs around appropriate feminine conduct and manners and judged accordingly. However, what Adam interpreted as a deliberate display of insolence towards court proceedings may equally well have sprung from ignorance - a lack of knowledge about appropriate behaviour for the occasion. Annie's background and lack of education ensured she did not possess the necessary skills to re-encode her conduct and behaviour into a model approved of by judicial personnel and commentators like Adam. In short, she failed to communicate through dominant modes of expression.

Considering the various aspects of Annie's life it is easy to understand how she became involved in a murderous form of baby-farming. She was a semi-literate, naive and lonely 54-year-old woman with no skills to sell, no means of support, financial or otherwise, and as part of what Victorians had termed the 'residuum', she had no hope or prospect of changing these circumstances.[79] Letters written from prison to her nieces suggest a personality easily influenced by those who showed her even a fleeting interest, coupled with a desire to please and to be liked.[80] Under those circumstances Annie's murderous deed can be understood as the rational action of someone with few choices available in her daily struggle for

---

[77]Upon her arrest Walters claimed that she was merely waiting for night to fall so she could "do away" with herself "through a man" (CRIM/1/83/2).

[78]Adam 1911:194.

[79]Annie Walters spent over two months in Holloway prison, including the entire Christmas and New Year period, without any letters or visits (Stated in a letter Annie wrote to a relative dated 26th January 1903 and reproduced in Adam 1911:195-6). There are many examples of Annie's naiveté, for example Amelia paid her only "a few shillings" for her part in the crime while Amelia charged the mothers a fee of £25-30 (Judge's Notes p.51 HO 144/690/104226 XC2622).

[80]For example, her letters aquired an increasingly religious fervour during her 10-week prison incarceration, suggesting the influence of the prison chaplain whom Annie wrote, she longed to see each day (letters reproduced in Adam 1911:196-7). Similarly her letters are filled with profuse terms of endearment which appear out of proportion to her actual relationship with the correspondents who had neither written nor visited her until the week before the execution.

survival rather than the simplistic and unproblematic evil-doing of a "pervert" with a "ruthless instinct" "butchering unwanted babies."[81]

Amelia's circumstances were very different. She was a qualified midwife and did not appear to be short of clients. She was also a wife and mother who - according to her husband's petition - was a loved and valued family member.[82] Moreover, police discovered a letter in Amelia's home from someone wishing to adopt a baby from her nursing home which indicates that she could have earned her extra income by legal means.[83] Adam described Amelia thus:

> Sach was tall, fashionably dressed, very attractive, and carrying herself with an air of refinement ... [she] presented the appearance of having just returned from the theatre, with a fashionable cloak thrown over her shoulders.[84]

In short, neither her personal circumstances nor her appearance fitted the image usually associated with baby-farmers: single, poor, friendless, downtrodden lower-class women. Her motive and personality are destined to remain an enigma forever as Amelia did not give evidence at her trial, nor offered any explanation or a single written statement after her arrest.[85] However, a letter written while awaiting trial reveals an excessive concern about her finances. Given the seriousness of her position it is noteworthy that apart from requesting clean underwear, the only other issue discussed is money:

> Dear I left you in charge of the House so will you ask Mrs Galley + Mrs Pardoe to pay you at once + bring the money to me Wednesday morning. Mrs Galley £7.70 on Wednesday Nov 26th Mrs Pardoe £7.70 today Nov 24th from then one Guinea per week note dear be sure to do that.[86]

Moreover, Amelia's personal bank book revealed she had saved £963, a substantial sum in 1902.[87] Her husband was employed as a builders' foreman and they had only one child to support.[88] Taken together, these personal details add ambiguity to Amelia's motivation rather than clarification.

---

[81]O'Donnell 1956:146.

[82]HO 144/690/104226 XC2622. Jeff Sach's Memorial.

[83]Original letter from Laura Bracey dated 22nd November in CRIM/1/83/2. See also *The Times* 15th January 1903.

[84]Adam 1911:194. Adam attended the trial.

[85]Wilson 1971:258.

[86]CRIM 1/83/2, (Exhibit 15). Letter dated 24th November 1902 from Amelia Sach to Mrs Ball.

[87]CRIM 1/83/2. Post Office Savings Bank book dated 15th March 1902

[88]HO 144/690/104226. Jeff Sach's Memorial.

While contemporary commentators all agreed that Amelia was highly intelligent, physically attractive and a member of the 'respectable' class, none drew the conclusion that these attributes made excuses for her murderous conduct more problematic than was the case with Annie. Nor was she considered to be a 'ruthless pervert'. Moreover, her demeanour inside the courtroom fell within the expectations of appropriate female conduct and as such was more acceptable to observers than Annie's:

> ... her face denoted considerable mental suffering ... The look on the face of Mrs Sach was one of deep dejection mingled with almost uncontrollable agitation.[89]

Thus, in contrast to Annie, Amelia's conduct and physical appearance generated sympathy and pity:

> ... in spite of the detestable and brutal character of the crimes attributed to Mrs Sach ... I could not help feeling somewhat sorry for her. Odious as the crimes themselves were, they were not so brutal as those committed by Mrs Dyer.[90]

Adam's personal opinion raises an important issue - that as a result of Amelia's physical appearance, demeanour and 'respectability', we can detect the first signs of her portrayal as a 'victim' as well as a perpetrator. Unlike Amelia Dyer or Ada Williams before her, or her co-accused, Amelia Sach had redeeming 'lady-like' qualities which for some were so convincing that they were prepared to challenge the dominant truth of Amelia being the 'brains' and Annie the 'hands' within their criminal partnership. Miss Woodley for example, wrote to the Home Secretary:

> I beg to suggest that the unfortunate Mrs Sach under the influence of a strong and evil minded woman many years her senior, imbued and degenerate through long association with evil ways, may have easily succumbed by such force to acquiescence to a deed which possibly was revolting to her own nature. Is not this the true situation and would not an act of Grace in her particular case be also an act of true justice?[91]

Like Adam and O'Donnell above, Woodley is revealing a strong class bias, associating ignorance and lack of privilege with wickedness and degeneracy, while simultaneously refusing to accept that such characteristics

---

[89]Adam 1911:194. It should be noted that as the death sentence was passed the two women's demeanour was reversed with Annie weeping while Amelia "heard the sentence unmoved." (*The Times* 16th January 1903).

[90]Adam 1911:194-5.

[91]HO 144/690/104226. Letter to Home Secretary from Miss Woodley dated 26th January 1903.

may also be associated with a 'respectable' woman. Yet the circumstantial evidence against Amelia remained so strong that even her husband, Jeffery, did not plead her innocence in his Memorial to the Home Office which was considered so weak and ineffectual that civil servants commented "that it hardly seems necessary to trouble the Judge with such a poor representation."[92] Ultimately, therefore, her social class, good looks and pleasing demeanour could not override the hostility felt towards baby-farming:

> Sach was the moving spirit who proposed the mock adoption to the unfortunate mothers, telegraphed to Walters, reclaimed the baby clothes and absorbed the lion's share of the adoption fee.[93]

Above all other issues, the two women - like Ada Williams before them - had abused and failed in their roles as mothers/carers, an offence which had to be *seen* to be punished as a deterrent to others:

> ... their crime is of the most dastardly + sordid nature - murder for money. They made a trade of murder, and their dealings seem as extensive or more so than the celebrated cases of Margaret Walters ... and Amelia Dyer ... both of whom suffered the extreme penalty of the law.[94]

Once again we are reminded of Smart's observation that women who apply an economic rationality to services they should be providing for free become 'monstrous' and 'heinous' and must be dealt with accordingly. In Amelia's case, the discourses around dangerous womanhood - the mother/carer as the cold-hearted, brutal child-killer - overrode discourses of social class. Indeed, Amelia's class location arguably exacerbated her dangerousness since her criminal activities stood in sharp contrast to her otherwise 'respectable' status, thus emphasising an 'unpredictable' and 'unknowable' element within her femininity.[95] In that sense her femininity can be understood as more dangerous and more unruly than Annie's whose criminality only confirmed what many Victorians already believed to be the case: that the residuum and the criminal classes were synonymous. These discourses also overrode the state's reluctance to execute women as discussed

---

[92]HO 144/690/104226. Home Office response to Memorial dated 27th January 1903. Circumstantial evidence against Amelia included the discovery of 300 articles of baby clothing which had belonged to various missing and dead babies including the Galley baby.

[93]Home Office minutes by Sir Kenelm Digby dated 26th January 1903, HO 144/690/104226 PRO Kew.

[94]HO 144/690/104226. Home Office Minutes dated 21st January 1903.

[95]As can be seen from Miss Woodley's letter above, some individuals found the possibility of an otherwise refined 'lady' too much to bear and chose to neutralise Amelia's dangerousness by denying her guilt.

in Chapter One. If anything, the reverse was the case - precisely because they were women and had sinned against the very essence of womanhood - the 'maternal instinct' and a woman's 'natural' desire to care - baby-farming offences were almost always guaranteed to result in execution. Thus, Justice Darling, after issuing the death sentence, warned Amelia and Annie not to expect mercy just because they were women.[96] He had the full support of the Home Office:

> These women had murdered defenceless babies in a wholesale way and from the worst motive. The sentence must be carried out.[97]

Public opinion appeared to be in agreement for there was no outcry, protest or petition in support of the women.

Earlier I pointed to the problematic nature of the evidence against Ada Williams and the Home Office's concern about the safety of her conviction. In Annie and Amelia's case the Home Office also recognised that "the evidence in the case charged was weak and that convictions could only be secured if evidence relating to other missing children whose murder the prisoners had not been charged with, was admitted."[98] Sir Kenelm Digby stated that without such evidence "it would have been difficult to disprove Walter's assertion that the child's death might have been due to misadventure. As against Sach there would really have been no case at all."[99] Moreover, a positive identification of the Galley baby was not possible as it had been removed immediately after its birth. However, the marks on its head caused by a forceps delivery, led to the assumption that it was Miss Galley's baby.[100] Mr Stephenson defending Annie, consequently argued the prosecution's case was built on "surmises and conjectures" and by admitting evidence which amounted to nothing more than speculation about other missing babies, the jury would find the defendants guilty as a result of suspicion rather than proof.[101] He therefore argued such evidence should not be admissible. He was overruled and the jury took only 40 minutes to decide the fate of Annie and Amelia.[102] They subsequently became the first two women to hang at Holloway prison on 3rd February 1903.

The case of Amelia Sach and Annie Walters provides testimony to the ease with which criminal women can become members of a muted group. As I have indicated, a variety of factors contributed towards the silencing of

---

[96]*The Times* 16th January 1903. Home Office Minutes written by Sir Kenelm Digby supports Judge Darling's opinion: "... I do not think that their sex affords reason enough for commutation of the sentence in the case of either of these women" (dated 26th January 1903 HO/144/690/104226 XC 2622).
[97]HO 144/690/104226. Home Office Minutes 27th January 1903.
[98]FO371/29537 XC 17007.
[99]HO/144/690/104226 XC 2622. Home Office Minutes 26th January 1903.
[100]HO 144/690/104226. Judge's Notes.
[101]*The Times* 16th January 1903.
[102]*The Times* 16th January 1903.

the women's experiences and their subsequent disappearance from history, including Amelia's self-imposed silence. The limited size of this case-study, despite the fact that it involved two women, is a direct consequence of this silencing since Home Office files concerned with this case are extremely slim. This in turn reflects the almost total lack of controversy around the case which ensured it could be processed with great expediency. Miss Woodley's letter discussed above, was the only communication from a member of the public that attempted to speak on behalf of the two women and thus establish an alternative 'truth' about their crimes, however detrimental this version was to Annie. Similarly, the only petition submitted was from Jeff Sach, Amelia's husband. No family member and no member of the public spoke in favour of Annie. Except for Miss Woodley and Jeff Sach, the impending deaths of Amelia and Annie appeared to be of no interest or consequence to anyone.

The Case of Rhoda Willis alias Leslie James

> I was attracted and fascinated by her blaze of yellow hair, and as she left her cell and walked in the procession to the scaffold the sunlight caused her hair to gleam like molten gold. I had hanged women before but never one so beautiful ...[103]

Rhoda Willis, hanged on her 40th birthday - 14th August 1907 - was the only woman to be executed in Wales during the 20th century.[104] Rhoda was from Sunderland but had moved to Cardiff in 1893 with her husband Thomas and daughter Emma. Following the death of Thomas in 1896 Rhoda changed her name to Leslie James, and I shall henceforth call her by her chosen name.

Leslie was officially the house-keeper of David Evans a shoe-maker, unofficially they were cohabiting as a couple. Her attempts to establish herself as a baby-farmer were never successful. She was known to have taken possession of three babies in exchange for money, the first being the baby of Mrs Stroud, which, on 7th May, was found on the steps of the Salvation Army home in Cardiff. It was taken to the workhouse where it died of diarrhoea a week later.[105] The second baby was the illegitimate child of Stanley Rees, whom Leslie received on 8th May, and re-adopted to her landlady Mrs Wilson. The baby was eventually returned to its biological mother. The third child was the baby of Maud Treasure whom Leslie received on 3rd June in Hengoed and whom she was found guilty of suffocating during the return journey to Cardiff.

---

[103]Harry Pierrepoint, the hangman responsible for hanging Leslie James, quoted in Bailey, B. (1989) *Hangmen of England* W.H.Allen, London p.195.
[104]*The Times* 15th August 1907 states it was Rhoda's 44th birthday, however official documentation available for inspection in the PRO gives her age as 39 at the time of her arrest.
[105]HO 144/861 FO371/29537 XC 17007.

Leslie James and the Construction of 'Truth'

Like Ada Williams before her, Leslie was condemned for her baby-farming activities:

> ... it stands, I think, as a bad murder. Whatever considerations might be addressed in extenuation ... of the case, it is in my judgement impossible to disassociate it from the baby farming habit which the prisoner was forming ... It is in this wider aspect that the case will be regarded by the public.[106]

Similarly, in his concluding remarks to the jury, prosecutor Sir Brynmor Jones reinforced existing condemnatory discourses around baby-farming by emphasising its economic rationale:

> ... prisoner's plan was to make money. She accepted money, spent the money, and then got rid of the various children one after the other, as best she could.[107]

Also like Ada, Leslie was quickly identified as a 'bad' rather than 'mad' woman:

> ... this was not one of those cases in which a mother, more or less insane, actuated by shame and dishonour, destroyed her own offspring ...[108]

The Secretary of State agreed:

> the prisoner is evidently a thoroughly bad woman. She has a previous conviction for theft, + this baby was clearly murdered for money.[109]

Head Constable McKenzie of Cardiff Police added that "she was a woman of drunken habits and low moral character."[110] Witnesses gave evidence in support of this assessment of Leslie's character, for example Mrs Wilson, her landlady, testified that "prisoner was helplessly drunk"[111] and had to be helped into bed the night before the discovery of the dead infant, and David Evans, Leslie's cohabitant, stated she was drunk by midday on

---

[106]HO 144/861/155396. Comments by the Secretary of State.

[107]*Western Mail* 25th July 1907.

[108]Sir David Brynmor Jones opening the case for the prosecution, reproduced in *South Wales Daily News* 24th July 1907.

[109]HO 144/861/155396. Home Office Minutes dated 1st August 1907.

[110]HO 144/861/155396. Home Office communication dated 31st July 1907.

[111]*Western Mail* 24th July 1907.

23rd May when he went to meet her.[112] Rose Smith, another lodger of Mrs Smith's, also testified that "they were both the worse for liquor" the day after Leslie was accused of having suffocated the baby.[113] Mrs Wilson's evidence allowed the prosecution to allege that Leslie's intention had been to dispose of the infant on the day she received it, "but she went out that day and got too drunk to carry out her design."[114] Leslie's sexual reputation was equally tarnished as can be seen from police inquiries about her past which revealed that while still a married woman she began cohabiting with Stewart MacPherson. This relationship produced three illegitimate children. However, in 1901 Leslie left Stewart to live with his brother Gregor MacPherson.[115] In 1903 she was living with Robert Carew, a blacksmith.[116] By 1906 "she had sunk to prostitution"[117] as well as theft for which she was sentenced to one month's imprisonment on 17th July.[118]

Leslie James had thus failed to conform to acceptable standards of female conduct and behaviour in nearly all the areas discussed in Chapter Three. As had been the case with Ada Williams seven years earlier, Leslie failed to convince the all male jury she was capable of satisfactorily fulfilling the mother/carer role. Not only did she rid herself of young babies by whatever means available when the responsibility of caring for them became too much, but there was no sign of the two surviving children Dorothy and Bessie from her relationship with Stewart MacPherson who would have been 7 and 10 years of age.[119] Furthermore, following the death of the Treasure baby she left the corpse in her bed, while she took the Rees baby out. She returned in an advanced drunken stupor, "carrying the baby up-side down."[120] Rather than possessing a maternal instinct, Leslie seemed at best, highly irresponsible in her dealings with children, at worst, cruel, callous, neglectful. She did not put the needs of babies before her own, she was not naturally altruistic, instead she was 'unnatural' and 'abnormal' in her dealings with the most vulnerable part of the population, young babies. It will be remembered from the previous chapter, that as a result of the stabilising functions associated with the mother role, drunken mothers are regarded as a special threat. In short, Leslie was the epitome of 'dangerous motherhood'.

---

[112]ASSI 72/33/1-4 XC 7025.

[113]*South Wales Daily News* 24th July 1907.

[114]*South Wales Daily News* 25th July 1907.

[115]HO 144/861/155396. Communication to the Home Office from Head Constable McKenzie of Cardiff City Police dated 8th August 1907.

[116]HO144/861/155396. Communication to Home Office from Head Constable McKenzie dated 31st July 1907.

[117]Wilson 1971:264.

[118]HO 144/861/155396. Leslie James's previous convictions sheet. She had stolen a medal from the home of a previous employer.

[119]A son, Stuart, had died. HO 144/861 FO371/29537 XC 17007. Communication from Head Constable McKenzie.

[120]HO 144/861/155396.

Leslie's conduct within the courtroom did not help her case. Her composure was repeatedly commented upon, for example, she was described as "quite composed" and "carefully scanning the jurors as each was sworn."[121] When the trial resumed on the second day the prisoner showed "the same calm and determined mien ... Nothing in the evidence appeared to ruffle her."[122] Even during the summing up the prisoner "listened to the proceedings as calmly as at any previous stage of the trial." Finally, while the judge's voice was "breaking with emotion" as he announced the death sentence, Leslie remained unmoved:

> The prisoner maintained an absolutely rigid control of her feelings to the end. She stood up perfectly erect, and looked at the judge immediately on the pronouncement of sentence. There was not the slightest movement or swaying of the body, and her heavy under-jaw was as rigidly fixed as during the whole course of her case.[123]

The South Wales Daily News had the final word, stating that after leaving the courtroom "she put on a callous smile ..."[124] These reports of Leslie's personal conduct and attitude did not denote remorse, regret or sorrow. Instead they reinforced her already established image of an 'unnatural' cold-hearted child-killer.

The jury took just 12 minutes to find Leslie guilty of wilful murder:

> there was practically no public excitement over the death sentence, which appeared to have been generally expected and the scene was remarkably free from any element of sensation.[125]

The judge, Commissioner Shee stated that he concurred with the verdict and warned the prisoner not to expect mercy.[126] It was normal practice to execute prisoners three weeks after sentence had been passed and as far as Commissioner Shee, senior civil servants and the jury were concerned, there were no extenuating circumstances justifying a commutation to life imprisonment.[127] Shee noted the witnesses had been "respectable and truthful" persons[128] who presented their "evidence very well indeed" unlike the prisoner, who had "kept up much false pretence" concerning the dead baby.[129] He was referring to the fact that Leslie had not told anyone she was

---

[121]*South Wales Daily News* 24th July 1907.

[122]*Western Mail* 25th July 1907.

[123]*Western Mail* 25th July 1907.

[124]*South Wales Daily News* 25th July 1907.

[125]*Western Mail* 25th July 1907.

[126]*South Wales Daily News* 25th July 1907.

[127]HO 144/861/155396. Home Secretary's Minutes.

[128]HO 144/861/155396. Home Office Minutes.

[129]HO 144/861/155396. Letter from Commissioner Shee to Mr Gladstone dated 4th July 1907.

about to collect a baby, but instead lied about her trip, stating she was going to visit the father of the baby Mrs Wilson had adopted. The murder of the Treasure baby was therefore interpreted as being premeditated, her lies indicating she had never intended to keep the child. For Shee therefore, the death sentence could not be commuted as this "wd [sic] imply that capital punishment should be abolished for women."[130]

At the same time, those entrusted to decide Leslie's fate acknowledged the preservation of infant life was a secondary consideration in deciding her punishment:

> ... it was the murder of a child which had not reached the stage of conscious existence. *It is a crime more against society* than against the murdered individual.[131]

The Home Secretary fully supported this view:

> I agree that the consequences of the murder of an infant are not so ... painful as they usually are in the murder of an adult.[132]

Despite this lack of deference towards infant life Leslie's life could not be spared because there were "none of the extenuating circumstances attending the common forms of infanticide."[133] The implication here is that it was impossible to pathologise her crime - the available evidence did not warrant a re-classification from the 'bad' to the 'mad' category. Instead she deliberately and wilfully committed 'a crime against society' by betraying 'natural' female instincts that guarantee love and nurture to a helpless infant - "a small life which especially called for protection + care."[134] The economic rationality behind the crime has thus been replaced by a rationality based on unnatural wickedness. As argued by Smart "acts such as infanticide, abortion, contraception and baby-farming are rational responses to severe legal and material penalties consequent upon unmarried motherhood at times of virtual persecution."[135] However, as argued above, it was precisely the financial motive behind these killings which was severely condemned. Baby-farming crimes thus encapsulated the conflict between on the one hand, denying the validity of a financial motive, and on the other, drawing attention to that motive as a justification for issuing severe punishment. The judge, prosecution and defence were united in considering baby-farming an immoral practice, yet none of them were prepared to confront the financial reality of unmarried mothers or the immorality of chastising and persecuting the very

---

[130]HO 144/861/155396. Home Office Minutes dated 9th August 1907.
[131]HO 144/861 FO 371/29537 XC 17007. Home Office Minutes dated 9th August 1907. My emphasis.
[132]HO 144/861 FO 371/29537 XC 17007. Home Secretary Minutes.
[133]HO 144/861/155396. Home Secretary Minutes.
[134]HO 144/861/155396. Letter from Secretary of State dated 9th August 1907.
[135]Smart 1992:24.

members of the community least able to support and defend themselves. It will be remembered from Chapter Two, that the State's failure to distinguish between immorality and economic necessity where unmarried mothers were concerned has a history spanning several centuries. Ultimately then, the practice of baby-farming also encapsulated the conflict between deeply held moral values around women, motherhood and individual families, versus the material reality and cost of motherhood for *single* women living in a culture whose definition of morality excluded a notion of collective or social responsibility for unplanned babies. It was a conflict which was easily won by moral defenders, who, rather than considering and alleviating the material reality of baby-farmers and unmarried mothers, exacerbated that reality by identifying these women as the ultimate propagators of dangerous motherhood. It was within this context that those speaking on behalf of the State judged Leslie's crime:

> Having regard to the widespread laxity which exists as regards infant life, the extent to which the abominable system of baby farming prevails, and the difficulty which usually exists in proving an intention to kill, it appears to me of the utmost importance to do nothing to weaken Home Office practice in connection with baby farming practices. I think remission in this case would tend to weaken that practice. Under all the circumstances I must report that I find myself unable to interfere with the course of the law.[136]

Those involved in Leslie James's trial could not have wished for a better conclusion to the case when Leslie reportedly made an unusually detailed and specific confession:

> It is satisfying to be able to recall that the convict confessed to her crime and fully admitted the justice of the sentence passed upon her by making the following statement voluntarily to her solicitor for the satisfaction of the authorities namely: that she would like to tell W. Lloyd that the sentence passed upon her was a just one - ... "I killed the child in the train. I meant to do it before I left the station. I would like those who tried me, particularly the judge, to know this. I would not like them to have anything in their minds or to think that they had made a mistake."[137]

An Alternative Truth about Leslie James

Leslie had not always been part of the 'immoral' classes. She was born Rhoda Lascelles, the daughter of a respectable hotelier and attended an exclusive

---

[136]HO 144/861/155396. Secretary of State Home Department Memo 9th August 1907.
[137]HO 144/861/155396. Letter from Prison Governor of Cardiff prison to Secretary of State dated 14th August 1907.

boarding school during her formative years.[138] While details about her early life are limited, police investigations established that at the age of 19, she had married a marine engineer, Thomas Willis, whose work caused him to spend long periods at sea. The marriage consequently broke up and Thomas died shortly afterwards. While Leslie maintained contact with her daughter Emma from her marriage to Thomas, his relatives "for some reason which is not known ..., took away the two younger children."[139] This marked the end of her 'respectability' as her life followed a path of gradual decline into alcoholism, a series of cohabitations, the birth of illegitimate children, prostitution and crime.

Two weeks after Leslie commenced working as David Evans's housekeeper she "burst out crying" after receiving a letter.[140] The reason was that only three weeks previously she had given birth to a baby which had been adopted by a Mrs Carruthers who now wanted to return it. David claimed he gave permission for the baby to join them. It was not however, returned. Leslie subsequently wanted to adopt a baby with a premium:

> She said that she would look after it and that she was making her home with me and she could be like a mother to it.[141]

This discussion marked the beginning of Leslie's unsuccessful attempts at baby-farming. Medical reports are absent from her files, and as there is no reference to her mental or physical well-being in the trial extracts we must consider the possibility that a medical examination was never conducted. However, the profuse terms of endearment and figures of speech employed in her correspondence with the biological parents of her charges-to-be suggest a highly charged emotional state of mind inappropriate for what was ultimately a business deal.[142] Thus, while it is unclear whether she ever underwent a medical examination it is certain that no medical expert gave evidence for the defence.

Upon her arrest Leslie insisted she had been part of a conspiracy to murder the baby: "I am not going to stand all the blame, some one else is in it as well as me."[143] While on remand she wrote to David:

---

[138]Wilson 1972:263.

[139]HO 144/861/1155396 Report by Head Constable McKenzie dated 31st July 1907.

[140]ASSI/72/33/1-4 Public Record Office, Chancery Lane, London WC2A 1LA. Statement of David Evans (undated).

[141]ASSI/72/33/1-4 Statement of David Evans (undated).

[142]For example Leslie wrote to Mrs Stroud "your little darling will have everything done for its comfort that loving hearts can do. We are so anxious to have it and are pleased to have it entirely as our own" (ASSI 72/33/1-4 undated). To Mrs English Leslie wrote "you can rest assured that I will be a true friend to you and keep my word" (ASSI 77/33/1-4 dated 2nd June).

[143]HO 144/861/155396 'The Case of Mrs Leslie James' 30th July 1907.

I am in terrible trouble through that woman and her mother that came to see me while I was in your employ. I am almost out of my mind. I don't seem to realise my position. Mrs Wilson told an awful lot of untruths in Court but I am going to have a good solicitor.[144]

While awaiting execution Leslie filed a petition to the Home Office in which she wrote: "I was completely in the hands of unscrupulous people however much the circumstances appeared against me."[145] The Home Secretary felt concerned enough about these statements to write to the trial judge:

> while Leslie James's character was bad, is it not likely that there was something wrong on the part of Mrs English and that the crime committed under the influence of drink was not designed in cold blood? ... It is a reasonable supposition that when she was given the baby she was plied with liquor, under the influence of which she committed the crime?[146]

While the judge remained unmoved, Leslie now implicated David:

> There are some statements that I omitted in my petition that I have thought of since, my mind being so confused ... The witness David Evans swore that I was the one to propose to advertise for a child, but, he proposed it himself saying he had tried to get a baby to adopt for the sake of the money before I knew him, that man was the instigator of my awful position.[147]

Unsurprisingly, David's version of events was very different:

> I told her I would have nothing to do with such a thing ... I would rather work day & night before I would go in for such a thing as it will lead us both into trouble ... [But] at last I was foolish enough to agree to advertise.[148]

The case-files do not provide adequate evidence about the exact nature of her relationship with David, but letters still in existence illustrate they were on intimate terms until the trial had taken place. Moreover, David himself provided a tantalising clue that perhaps his statement was less than truthful:

---

[144] ASSI 72/33/1-4. Letter to David Evans dated June 1907.

[145] HO 144/861/155396 Petition dated 30th July 1907.

[146] HO 144/861/155396 Letter from Gladstone to Commissioner Shee 2nd August 1907.

[147] HO 144/861/155396 Second petition to Home Office from Leslie James dated 7th August 1907.

[148] ASSI 72/33/1-4 and HO 144/861/155396, two statements by David Evans.

Please write a nice long loving letter back and don't show this to anyone, because so false these days [sic], people are so 2 faced now. You can't trust no-one.[149]

As I indicate below, and as Leslie herself repeatedly pointed out, apart from David she was quite alone in the world and terrified of losing him as a result of her alcoholic binges:

Do write and tell me you forgive me [for being drunk]. I am so miserable so I beg of you to forgive me and I will never leave you again but do all I can for you. Oh my love you don't know the mind I have. I hate myself, but it was not my fault and you know that very well. Do forgive me and don't make me more troubled than I am.[150]

Leslie however, came to feel utterly betrayed by David, both as a result of the way he distanced himself from her while she was awaiting trial, and through his evidence in the Coroner's Court:

What a misconstruction I put on the word friend when I addressed that word to you. My only friend is my own money and I have got that to receive when I am out of this trouble.[151]

By the time Leslie wrote her petition she was well aware of her perilous position and while the Victorian period had ended earlier in the decade, she acted in a manner citizens of that era had been taught to approve of - recognising the error of her ways and, as a 'fallen' woman, showing repentance and pleading for forgiveness:

... I am a widow + entirely alone in the world, I am truly repentant for breaking the law, + I beg of you Gentlemen to consider my terrible position in which the awful anguish of my mind I can scarcely realise + I fear to contemplate the unknown future therefore Gentlemen I beg to implore you to extend your leniency to me + mercifully spare my life.[152]

In sum, evidence existed at the time of Leslie's trial which indicated there was more to her life than her status as a 'bad' woman of 'low moral character', and that her crime may not have been the 'open and shut' case it first seemed: a callous, brutal killer acting alone in murdering innocent babies for insignificant financial gain. That evidence also problematised the justification of her execution for many contemporary observers, some of

---

[149] ASSI 72/33/1-4. Letter from David Evans to Leslie James dated 4th June 1907.

[150] ASSI 72/33/1-4. Letter from Leslie James to David Evans received 25th May 1907.

[151] ASSI 72/33/1-4 Letter from Leslie James to David Evans dated 29th June 1907.

[152] HO 144/861/155396 Petition of Leslie James dated 31st July 1907.

whom had been directly involved in her case. This issue forms the final part of my analysis.

The Quality of Leslie James's Defence

In contrast to the three women already discussed, Leslie James was perceived by many as a pathetic, unstable, lonely creature whose decline from respectability was an unfortunate result of her alcoholism, and who therefore deserved pity. Her statement that she was "truly repentant for breaking the law" was immediately seized upon by Home Office personnel as an admission of guilt and was repeated whenever the need arose to justify their non-interference with the course of the law. Despite this, many of those who had been involved in the case remained deeply sceptical about her guilt and 'confession' and believed the baby's death had been accidental. Some considered Leslie to be guilty of no more than gross neglect brought about as a result of her drunkenness. Indeed the Inquest Jury had returned a verdict of manslaughter. When the Coroner learned she had been sentenced to death he felt concerned enough to write to the Home Secretary:

> I cannot help feeling very doubtful whether she actually murdered the child ... It was only a few hours old, and it appears to me quite possible, that it may have been suffocated while in the woman's arms ... The marks of pressure on the body of so young an infant, may probably have been caused by its being wrapped up rather too tightly ... I think it right to let you know the impression that the case made upon me, so that ... you may communicate with the Judge on the matter.[153]

Furthermore, a member of the Coroner's Jury felt motivated to write to Leslie's solicitor suggesting that:

> in order to keep the neighbours in ignorance the cries of the child were stifled to that extent that it was either wholly or partially suffocated before Mrs James received it, and when she did receive it the child was wrapped up so closely so that its cries should not be heard on leaving the house + neighbourhood ... If ever a condemned person was entitled to the benefit of the doubt Mrs James is + I sincerely hope that the Home Secretary may see his way to recommend her reprieve.[154]

Apart from the question of Leslie's guilt observers were also concerned about the quality of her defence. She had been represented by

---

[153]HO 144/861/155396. Letter to Home Secretary from Coroner Bernard Reece 29th July 1907.
[154]HO 144/861/155396. Letter to Leslie's solicitor Harold Lloyd from Joseph Stewart 7th August 1907.

solicitors "throughout the proceedings before the Magistrates", yet, despite the seriousness of the charge, they "were obliged to abandon her defence" before her case reached the trial stage "due to her lack of funds."[155] Subsequently Leslie's trial was allowed to commence without *any* representation:

> It was only DURING THE TRIAL that counsel was instructed for Mrs James, and only as the case proceeded could he learn of the nature of the crime alleged.[156]

The counsel referred to, Ivor Bowen, felt "very anxious about the case"[157] and was so concerned about the fact that Leslie did not have a single person to speak on her behalf that he intervened himself by stating her case to the Home Secretary:

> I most respectfully submit ... that the course of public justice would be sufficiently upheld if a reprieve were granted in this extraordinary and difficult case.[158]

Bowen listed several reasons for a reprieve. First, only one doctor provided medical evidence at the trial, and he had only seen the child two days after its death. Second, the medical evidence provided by this doctor, was not generally recognised within the medical profession as being conclusive evidence of suffocation. Third, the child's death could equally well have been accidental. Fourth, the jury was unfairly influenced by allowing evidence to be heard which related to Leslie's other baby-farming activities even though there had been no evidence of prior criminal intent. Fifth, the prosecution never proved there had been intent to commit murder. Finally, "the prisoner had no means of securing any medical evidence to set up against the evidence of the prosecution."[159]

Leslie's poverty and her subsequent lack of representation became important focal points for those who fought to secure a reprieve. For example MP Llewelyn Williams helped to construct a petition arguing "the woman is

---

[155]HO 144/861/155396. Letter to Home Secretary from Solicitors Harold Lloyd & Cross 30th July 1907.

[156]HO 144/861/155396. Letter to Home Secretary from solicitor Tudor Rees 13th August 1907. Capital letters in the original.

[157]HO 144/861/155396 Letter to W.P. Byrne from Ivor Bowen 28th July 1907. Mr Byrne may have been a member of the legal profession for Mr Bowen asked him to "look into it - All I should like is that the poor wretch shall not be hanged. I really believe it would be safer not to hang her."

[158]HO 144/861/155396. Letter to Home Secretary from Ivor Bowen 29th July 1907.

[159]HO 144/861/155396. Letter to Home Secretary from Ivor Bowen 29th July 1907. Bowen justified his intervention into this case by pointing out that he "was not retained to defend the prisoner."

poor ... she was not represented by a solicitor at the trial ... [and] she had no money to organise a petition."[160]

A solicitor unconnected with the case wrote to the Home Office, expressing the view "that the capital sentence is not vouched by public opinion" and added that Leslie did not have a fair trial because "she was not asked whether she would give evidence on her own behalf and did not ... In cases when convictions have been imposed without informing the prisoner of his right to give evidence under the provision of the Criminal Evidence Act 1899 have been quashed a fortiori a case [sic] of murder."[161]

With only days left before the execution Leslie's sentence became increasingly contentious. At this point the Cardiff City Council became involved, and while some councillors opposed the Lord Mayor's suggestion that council members unite in making a representation for a reprieve, the vast majority signed.[162]

Finally, Leslie's solicitor Tudor Rees presented a dramatic and emotional appeal to the Home Secretary arguing:

> Wales stands staggered at your decision that Mrs Leslie James ... is to pay the last penalty of the law ... [and if this had been known earlier] the petition would have been signed, not by 2,000 but by 20,000 ... Wales throbs with a mighty sympathy for this friendless, heart-broken woman; and I am voicing the feelings of all my fellow-countrymen when I beg of you, humbly ... to reconsider the decision which, if unaltered, will send a (probably innocent) woman to an awful doom.[163]

Displaying passionate support for a reprieve Rees's six-page letter focused on the unfairness of her trial. He wrote that while the case for the prosecution "was diligently prepared by a firm of first-class solicitors, and eloquently put to the jury by two eminent counsel (one of whom was a K.C. and one-time judge) ... no solicitor worked up the case of the unfortunate prisoner."[164] Referring to the Judge's instructions to Bowen to represent Leslie *after the trial had begun*, with no prior knowledge of the case and no time to prepare a defence, Rees argued:

> in such a case as this, whose evidence was purely circumstantial and whose nature was such as to admit of several strong probabilities of

---

[160]HO 144/861/155396. Letter to Home Secretary from Llewelyn Williams MP 8th August 1907.

[161]HO 144/861/155396. Letter to Home Secretary from Thomas Philips 12th August 1907.

[162]*Evening Express* 12th August 1907.

[163]HO 144/861/155396. Letter to Home Secretary from J. Tudor Rees 13th August 1907.

[164]HO 144/861/155396. Letter to Home Secretary from J. Tudor Rees 13th Agust 1907.

innocence, had a solicitor carefully prepared the prisoner's defence, and duly briefed counsel in ample time before the trial, a very different verdict would have followed.[165]

In arguing the baby had died accidentally Rees emphasised that "THE DOCTOR SAID AT THE TRIAL THAT THE DISCOLOURATION ON THE CHILD'S FACE WAS NOT INCONSISTENT WITH ACCIDENTAL SUFFOCATION."[166] Moreover, given Leslie's unfortunate "intemperate habits", and her intoxicated state upon reaching home, "is it not reasonable to suppose that the woman ... leant clumsily, but accidentally, on her charge, and so suffocated it unintentionally ... Generally, the evidence is wholly circumstantial, and extremely unsatisfactory."[167]

Thus, unlike the previous three women discussed, there was a sizeable opposition to the execution of Leslie James. Contrary to the *Evening Express's* insistence that "the wretched woman's habits were horrible" and "accordingly, the entire bulk of medical and medico-legal sentiment throughout the town and country has been in favour of letting the law take its course",[168] there was in fact plenty of evidence indicating the professional classes' discomfort and opposition to Leslie's execution. Thus, the support for her by legal personnel such as Bowen, Rees and Reece, can be understood as a challenge to judicial misogyny.

In the previous chapter I argued that women who engage in promiscuity, prostitution and drunkenness and hence have made no effort to 'keep their reputation' are likely to be treated more harshly by the criminal justice system than 'respectable' women. In other words, women are not judged solely according to their crimes but also according to their conduct and behaviour as women. In this case-study I have argued that Leslie James failed to conform to acceptable standards of female conduct in all three of these areas as well as that of carer/motherhood. Yet the sympathy and support she received during her last days illustrate the complexities involved in criminal women's differential treatment when they face the bench. It also warns us not to regard women's oppression in universal terms, but to be sensitive to differences between women, even within the 'bad' category. In Foucauldian terms, 'bad' women - prostitutes, bad mothers, alcoholics - do not represent a unitary category, but are constructed according to discourses - examples of the 'discursive construction of the subject'.

In Leslie's case the mobilisation of the discourses around the 'fallen woman' helps us understand why - unlike the other three baby-farming cases - her case generated considerable sympathy. The term 'fallen woman' activated very different connotations to that of the 'common prostitute'. It was a class-

---

[165]HO 144/861/155396. Letter to Home Secretary from J. Tudor Rees 13th August 1907.
[166]Capital letters in the original.
[167]HO 144/861/155396. Letter to Home Secretary from J. Tudor Rees 13th August 1907.
[168]*Evening Express* 12th August 1907.

specific term, implying the woman had been respectable in the past but had 'fallen' out of respectable society, perhaps as a result of a betrayal or a seduction.[169] The 'fallen' woman was thus partly perceived as a victim - someone to be pitied rather than condemned. Unlike the common prostitute she was allowed to retain her femininity by remaining "powerless and dependent."[170] The common prostitute however, was a much more threatening figure:

> The combined associations of cash and the public sphere rendered the prostitute powerful and independent - qualities which were the unique privilege of the white, middle-class male.[171]

Moreover, whereas the 'fallen woman' was a term almost exclusively applied to middle-class women, the prostitute was inevitably defined as being a member of the residuum which added to her dangerousness and unacceptability. The construction of Leslie James as a subject can thus be seen to be made up of conflicting discourses - on the one hand she appears to fit the stereotypical image of the 'bad' woman with regard to her criminal record, drunkenness, promiscuity, lack of respectability and inadequate mothering skills. On the other hand, her demeanour in terms of her humble, remorseful and modest plea for her life stood in sharp contrast to her transgressions. As noted above, in her petition Leslie claimed to be truly sorry for her crime, begged forgiveness and repented for her wrong-doing. This attitude ensured she was not *only* perceived as a criminal but also as a helpless and unfortunate victim which in turn allowed much of her femininity to be retained.

Leslie's attitude also stood in stark opposition to that of Ada Williams who was constructed as an 'uppity' women who did not know her place, displayed strength and independence, and refused to be deferential to her husband. It too was very different from Annie Walters whose conduct was constructed as evidence of her dumb ignorance and perverted deviance. Lastly, it was different from Amelia Sach who made no attempt to excuse or justify her behaviour but instead maintained an 'unfeminine' stony silence until the end of her life. None of these three women made a confession and none of them could therefore beg for forgiveness. Instead they remained deviant women to the very end of their lives. There appeared to be no contradiction between their criminal activities and their subsequent conduct. Leslie James's conduct however, did give rise to such contradiction. In Chapter Three - following Smart - I argued that categories such as prostitutes, bad mothers and female alcoholics do not "exist in an a priori state, waiting for institutions to act upon them" but are instead agents who play an active role in constituting themselves through language and discourse. Like Foucauldian feminists, Smart thus reminds us to take account of the multiple

---

[169]Nead, L. (1988) *Myths of Sexuality* Blackwell, Oxford p.95.
[170]Nead 1988:96.
[171]Nead 1988:95.

factors that play a role in constructing the individual. At the same time it is important to be aware that available spaces for subject construction are limited by existing discourses. Thus, as Leslie appeared to be quite sane and therefore could not claim to be 'mad', constructing herself as a passive, helpless and dependent victim was arguably her only alternative. In turn, conforming to acceptable standards of female conduct in terms of her modesty, humbleness and deferential demeanour resulted in a brief destabilisation of powerful legal and medical discourses. For a moment in history the official 'truth' that Leslie was a thoroughly 'bad' person who deserved no mercy, was challenged by an alternative 'truth' which maintained she was a victim as well as a criminal - a 'fallen' woman whose remorsefulness indicated she was not beyond redemption but instead deserved a measure of sympathy. However, as had been the case during Leslie's trial, her challenge to the official truth did not take place in a battle between equals - ultimately she was no match for those who had traditionally exercised the power to define 'truth' - hence the space created as a result of her challenge did not remain open long enough for an alternative truth to become established. Nonetheless, this embryonic 'alternative truth' - shaped by the various responses from those who pleaded Leslie's case - was successful in hindering a total domination of official 'truth', and while her life was not spared, she was the last woman in England and Wales to be executed for child-murder.

Part II: Biological Motherhood on Trial

The Case of Louise Masset

> There is no human creature in this country ... so defenceless as an illegitimate child ... Rarely, except in the first almost irresponsible burst of shame and despair at its birth ... does the great maternal instinct fail. But if that makes default, all is, indeed, lost for the child. For the unnatural mother who beat in her little boy's forehead with a brick, strangled and stripped him, and went her way all unmoved to meet her paramour at Brighton the law will have no mercy. Hanging is almost too good for such a murderous monster as Louise Masset.[172]

> What is ... apparent is the extent to which marriage as a formal legal status, locates women inside or outside certain categories of dangerousness. The unmarried mother was the most dangerous of all, not only to her infant but also to the social order.[173]

---

[172]*Pall Mall Gazette* 19th December 1899.
[173]Smart, C. (1992) 'Disruptive bodies and unruly sex' in Smart, C. (ed) *Regulating Womanhood* Routledge, London p.24.

> Was Louise Masset sent to the gallows because her demeanour failed
> to match the all-male jury's vision of an innocent woman?[174]

While several of the 15 convictions analysed in this book can justifiably be
considered 'unsafe' due to the unsatisfactory nature of the evidence, this does
not necessarily mean the women in question were innocent of the crime for
which they were executed. However, in two of the 15 cases I shall argue not
only that the convictions were unsafe but also that the two women concerned
may have been innocent of the crime for which they were hanged. Louise
Masset, convicted of the murder of her three-year-old son Manfred - and the
first woman to be executed in the 20th century - was one of them.

Several aspects of Louise Masset's lifestyle had more in common
with that of women today than her late Victorian contemporaries. In 1899
she was a single parent and professional woman who supported herself and
her son financially. Half French by birth, Louise gave individual tuition in
French and music to the children of wealthy Victorian Londoners. Louise
herself was from a respectable and educated middle-class background,
arguably the social class which found it most difficult to accept or tolerate
illegitimacy. Consequently, although Louise's family was aware of Manfred's
existence, he was not acknowledged outside the family home. Instead he was
a 'nurse-child' - that is - since the age of three weeks he had been cared for by
a 'nurse' in her home for a weekly fee. This arrangement was quite different
from the baby-farming transactions discussed above, for Louise had no
intention of parting permanently with Manfred, but was considered a "kind
and loving mother" who visited her son every week - bringing him presents
and taking him out.[175]

Despite being 36 years old Louise showed no inclination towards
marriage, but instead enjoyed a pleasant social life which included weekends
away with her 19-year-old lover Eudore Lucas, who was French. Thus,
unlike the poverty-stricken and powerless biological mothers of the child-
victims in the baby-farming cases discussed above, and despite repressive
Victorian values, Louise appeared to have the best of all worlds: she had not
been forced to give up her illegitimate child but could enjoy motherhood
when it suited her; she was free to enjoy the sexual pleasures of a
relationship without having to fulfil the obligations attached to marriage; and
she enjoyed a fulfilling professional life which gave her financial
independence within an already financially secure background. In short, her
lifestyle was highly privileged compared to the drudgery of many of her
contemporaries. I return to these issues below where I argue that the fact

---

[174]Mackay, F. (1993) 'French Leave' in A Granada TV publication introduced by
Woodward, E. *In Suspicious Circumstances* Boxtree, London p.171.

[175]CRIM 1/58/5 Public Record Office, Chancery Lane, London WC2A 1LR.
Deposition of Miss Gentle, Manfred's nurse, dated 25th December 1899. It is clear
from her letters to Manfred's father that she had no intention of ever giving her son up
for adoption (HO 144/1540/A61535 Letter dated 6th October 1899).

Louise was considered never to have paid a price for what was regarded as gross immoral conduct, played a considerable role in the final outcome of her trial.

Louise Masset's 'Truth' versus the Crown's 'Truth'

While all the child-murder cases discussed in this chapter were based on circumstantial evidence, the case against Louise Masset rested on what may have been no more than a few coincidences, and while she could not prove her innocence, the Crown could not provide evidence which conclusively proved her guilt. Louise is the only woman in this chapter who gave evidence on her own behalf, and ultimately therefore, her conviction would partly have been based upon how believable her story sounded to the all-male jury. However, it was impossible to present her story without also revealing her immoral conduct, as I shall now illustrate.

Louise claimed she had been concerned about Manfred's education for some time, a claim which her sister with whom she was living, verified. Manfred's nurse Miss Gentle, was working-class and Louise did not approve of speech patterns such as 'aint' and 'look at them pins' which Manfred was now emulating.[176] On her weekly outings with her son to Tottenham Green Louise claimed to have met and befriended two "perfect" and "respectable" women who were related and both called Mrs Browning.[177] The Brownings were about to start a boarding school and suggested Manfred become their pupil. After discussions with the Brownings during a three-week period Louise agreed. However, Miss Gentle was a kind and loving nurse who was fond of Manfred and to spare her feelings and any implied criticism, Louise lied about her plans stating Manfred was to go to France to be brought up with a cousin of his father's.[178] She told the same lie to her sister and brother-in-law and explained that she would embark upon a two-day journey to France with Manfred on 27th October. This lie was necessary in order to account for her absence between 27-29th October, because she had in fact arranged to spend that weekend with Eudore in Brighton. Manfred was to be handed over to the Brownings on the 27th at 2pm before Louise boarded the 4 o'clock train to Brighton. Although the Brownings were severely delayed, she claimed the hand-over had occurred in time for her to catch the 4 o'clock train. Manfred was found murdered two hours later in the women's toilet at Dalston Junction.

Louise returned from Brighton Sunday evening and on Monday 30th she was teaching her pupils as usual. As she entered Dalston Junction that evening she noticed a placard and a newspaper with the head-line: "Dalston Murder. Identification of the Poor Little Victim. Child of a French woman,

---

176See for example report in *The Telegraph* 16th December 1899.
177*The Telegraph* 16th December 1899; *The Daily News* 19th December 1899.
178CRIM 1/58/5. Exhibit A - original letter from Louise to Mrs Norris (Miss Gentle's mother) dated 16th October 1899.

who took him away from his nurse on the day of the murder."[179] According to Louise's evidence, this was the first she knew of Manfred's murder. She subsequently travelled to Croydon where her second sister lived to seek the advice of her brother-in-law "because he was English."[180] Louise went to the police voluntarily later that night and gave a statement in the presence of her brother-in-law.

The prosecution maintained that Louise had invented the Brownings in much the same way as she - by her own admission - had invented going to France, and that in reality, she had murdered Manfred before catching a later train to Brighton. In support of this claim, the prosecution presented three pieces of circumstantial evidence which, apart from one eyewitness account, was the *only* evidence against her. First, a clinker brick was found by Manfred's body which had been used to stun him before strangulation had taken place. This brick was similar to bricks found in the garden of Louise's home. However, countless gardens contained identical bricks, and the prosecution conceded "that no trace remained in the garden of any brick having been removed therefrom ... nor were there any traces of a single spot of dirt or mould from such a brick in the prisoner's bag or her clothing."[181] Moreover, the *prosecution*, in its opening statement stated that "the brick [found by the body] was somewhat *heavier*" than those in the garden of Louise's home.[182]

Second, Manfred's body was wrapped in a shawl, which the prosecution claimed Louise had purchased some days earlier from Maud Clifford, a draper's assistant, who picked her out from an identity parade. However, on the stand Miss Clifford stated: "I wont [sic] swear positively she is the woman."[183] Moreover, porter Joseph Standing who was called when the body was found gave evidence that: "I should not call it a new shawl at all." The doctor who inspected the body at Dalston agreed: "I do not think it was a new one."[184] Judge Bruce in his summing up added to the ambiguity of this piece of 'evidence':

> Miss Maud Clifford says that she sold *a* shawl - not *the* shawl, because it is a black one, but one like that - on the 24th October ... To whom was it sold? Miss Clifford says "I am *nearly* certain that prisoner was the woman." ... It is always difficult to judge of the

---

[179]HO 144/1540/A61535 Public Record Office, Kew, Richmond, Surrey TW9 4DU. Newspaper article from the *Evening News* quoted in Judge Bruce's Summing Up p.40.

[180]HO 144/1540/A61535. From Louise's statement quoted in Judge's Summing Up p.42.

[181]HO 144/1540/A61535. Petition from Louise Masset's family presented to the Home Secretary.

[182]HO 144/1540/A61535. My emphasis.

[183]CRIM 1/58/5. Evidence of Maud Clifford dated 25th December 1899.

[184]CRIM 1/58/5. Evidence of Joseph Standing and Dr James Fennell dated 25th December 1899.

accuracy of the evidence of witnesses simply by the expression she uses ... Miss Clifford says she is nearly certain. You may judge of the accuracy of her evidence not merely by the expression but more by her conduct. "Would you know the woman?" She is taken on the 4th November ten days after she sold the shawl, and there she is shown fourteen women, and ... she does pick out the person and she says "That is the woman." Of course for all matters of identification it is important that the test should be fairly applied, that there should be no help from the police, but there is this to be said about the various questions put about the help in identification. Mrs Worley was called in. She was unable to identify the prisoner. Although the police were fair in all events in the way in which they conducted the test Mrs Worley was not able to identify the prisoner. Miss Clifford says she did identify the prisoner and she said she is the woman to whom she sold the shawl. *Now if she is the person who sold the shawl it is not conclusive evidence because it is only like the shawl she sold.*[185]

The third, and most damning piece of circumstantial evidence was a parcel containing Manfred's clothing - found at Brighton station within minutes of Louise meeting her lover there on Saturday afternoon. The clothing had had buttons, cuffs and other identifiable details removed.

A fourth piece of evidence was to become equally contentious. It concerned the testimony of Ellen Rees, a lavatory attendant at London Bridge Station where Louise claimed the hand-over had taken place. Mrs Rees claimed to have spoken to her before 3 o'clock on the 27th, which was not disputed by Louise. However, she also claimed to have spoken to her at 7 o'clock which, if true, meant Louise had lied about which train she had caught and could have committed the murder.[186] After the trial Mrs Rees felt less confident about her positive identification and wrote to jury member Thomas Evans that:

she was not so positive about seeing Prisoner at 7 o'clock as she was earlier in the afternoon. That, although she spoke to her, the witness did not have so full a view of her, but *casually observed to herself* as she passed (while Prisoner was brushing her hair before a glass) that it looked like the person she had seen earlier in the day.[187]

Moreover, Mrs Rees was short-sighted and normally wore glasses, but on this particular day had forgotten them. Another attendant at London Bridge Station, Georgina Worley, failed to recognise Louise but identified

---

[185]HO 144/1540/A61535. Judge Bruce's Summing Up pp.13-14. My emphasis.
[186]*The Telegraph* 18th December 1899. See also Judge's Summing Up pp.22-3 in HO 144/1540/A61535.
[187]HO 144/1540/A61535. Letter from Thos. K. Evans to Home Office dated 6th January 1900. Emphasis in the original.

Manfred from a photo. Mrs Worley testified she had asked Manfred's mother "if she was going by train, and she answered - No, I am waiting for someone to come to me."[188] In short, Mrs Rees' evidence, like the three pieces of circumstantial evidence, was far from conclusive. The prosecution was not deterred by this however, and argued Louise was "a woman of enormous determination, of alarming strength of will. She was not above resorting to falsehood in order to accomplish her object ... and it was obvious that to an iron-nerve that was necessary to commit this crime must be added the tongue of a serpent."[189] Thus, Louise was firmly positioned within the 'bad' category of female criminals during her trial. In the following sections I analyse the discourses mobilised to achieve this categorisation.

The Trial of Louise Masset

As has been argued throughout this book the formal punishment of women cannot be understood outside a gendered perspective. Above I argued that what eventually becomes the dominant 'truth' about individual female defendants depends not only upon what is considered irrefutable evidence about their crimes, but also upon what is 'known' about the defendants as *women.* I argued that such knowledge can, to a certain extent, pass through the criminal justice system unchallenged if the women are members of a muted group. Moreover, it will be apparent that while this mutedness is not dependent upon the defendant's location within the hierarchy of social class, there is nevertheless a strong relationship between membership of the 'lower classes' and muted groups. As has already been noted, those who fail to communicate through dominant modes of expression will become disqualified as speakers. Within the context of the educational and cultural gulf between defendants of the 'lower orders' such as Annie Walters and members of the legal establishment who were (and are) almost exclusively drawn from the white, male middle- and upper-middle classes, and who, with their claim to expert knowledge, exercise the power to define dominant modes of expression, it is inevitable that those who lack the skills to express themselves 'appropriately' are also most likely to become disqualified as speakers.[190] Thus, in Chapter Two I argued that throughout history the labouring poor were most likely to experience punishment in general and execution in particular. As the case-studies unfold it will become apparent that this was as true of the 20th century as of previous centuries. Yet, as always, there were exceptions. Louise was articulate and educated, and her

---

[188]CRIM 1/58/5 Deposition of Georgina Worley dated 16th November 1899.

[189]Mr Matthews's Summing Up for the prosecution in *The Telegraph* 19th December 1899.

[190]See for example Harris's discussion on the class background of legal personnel in Harris, P. (1988) *An Introduction to Law* Weidenfeld & Nicolson, London esp. chapters 12 & 13. See also Chadwick, R. (1992) *Bureaucratic Mercy: The Home Office and the Treatment of Capital Cases in Victorian England* Garland, New York, esp. pp.90-1.

social status was equal to that of legal personnel within the courtroom. As such, she could not be disqualified as a speaker and her account was not muted, either in the courtroom or the media. However, despite these advantages, she could not escape the hangman's noose, for the discourses around her sexual transgressions and immoral behaviour were to take precedence over those around social class. Indeed, as I shall indicate, her conduct came to be viewed as 'doubly' deviant as a *result* of her social class.

Louise Masset: Morality and Sexuality

Smart has identified the late 19th century as a period of "an intense legal gaze on issues of reproduction, mothering and sexuality" which led to a "struggle over the use of law to regulate the feminine body."[191] This regulation was deemed a necessity if the social order was to remain stable. Thus:

> Licit sex ... [was] not merely defined as that between married (heterosexual) couples, but between people within acceptable age brackets, of acceptable 'races' and doing only acceptable things.[192]

According to Smart, the term "acceptable 'races'" not only excluded colonised people who were assumed to be less moral than the British, but also the French and the Belgians who were regarded as being "particularly suspect."[193] With specific reference to women and race we can add Matus's point that:

> Constructions of women of other cultures as wickedly and excessively sexualised persisted in Victorian culture, alongside and in apparent contradiction to arguments about the essential passionlessness of all women.[194]

This was the moral climate, in which Louise - described as a French woman - entered the witness-box, not only to explain that she had an illegitimate child, but also, that at 36 she had a young *French* lover of 19, and that, in order to fulfil her illicit sexual desires, she had told a web of lies to those who loved her and cared about her. Louise's unacceptable sexual attitudes were magnified when she explained it was *her* - not Eudore - who had suggested they go away together:

---

[191] Smart, C. (1992) 'Disruptive bodies and unruly sex: the regulation of reproduction and sexuality in the nineteenth century' in Smart, C. (ed) *Regulating Womanhood* Routledge, London p.13.
[192] Smart 1992:25.
[193] Smart 1992:25.
[194] Matus, J. (1995) *Unstable Bodies: Victorian Representations of Sexuality and Maternity* Manchester University Press, Manchester p.90.

It was I who thought of it owing to the piece of poetry. It was from the 8th Oct. or thereabouts that I thought of spending a night away with him.[195]

As discussed in Chapter Three, the respectable Victorian woman was someone who displayed the qualities of dependency, fragility and delicacy. Louise's display of independence and boldness would have defined her as 'unnatural' and sexually deviant. Not only was she the instigator of this sexual liaison, she also displayed a rather casual attitude towards the relationship which would not have helped her case:

And as from that date of the receipt of the piece of poetry you had determined to go away with him in your own mind.
No, I had not determined upon going away with him in my own mind, I only thought it would be an occasion.
It was your determination.
Determination? It was my thought...
When you formed that intention of going away with Eudor[e] Lucas were you or were you not, in love with Eudor[e] Lucas.
No, I was not in love.
You were going away with him to stay with him, + to stay a night with him.
Yes, Sir, that was simply arranged on the Saturday.
But you were not in love with him.[196]

Louise thus made no attempt to hide that her relationship was based on lust and desire. It was not a statement that either defence or prosecution wanted to hear - the defence because it recognised the moral condemnation her attitude would cause within a culture that defined female sexuality in relation to the male and believed it "to be weak, passive and responsive"[197] - the prosecution because it had failed to establish a motive for the crime and therefore set out to prove Louise had murdered her son because he had become an obstacle to her relationship with Eudore. The prosecution failed to do so, but in destroying this motive Louise had to expose herself further as an 'immoral' woman who readily entered into casual sexual relationships:

Do you represent that in a conversation of this kind [about going away together] there was nothing to be remembered.
I say so certainly.
A man was pressing you to go away with him for the night.
He suggested it, he did not press it.
....

---

[195]HO 144/1540/A61535. Trial transcript p.132. The piece of poetry referred to was passed to Louise over the garden wall by Eudore.
[196]HO 144/1540/A61535. Trial transcript p.64; p.59.
[197]Nead, L. (1988) *Myths of Sexuality* Basil Blackwell, Oxford, p.6.

And you say that that conversation between you and him is not one -
Of importance, no.
Simply in passing, an ordinary conversation in passing.
Yes.
You accept that.
Certainly.[198]

Moreover, this relationship was entered into without thought of or desire for marriage:

> ... You did not say anything about marriage.
> *I never had any idea upon the subject...*
> You never suggested it to him, or he to you.
> *No, it would have been absurd.*[199]

Louise was repeatedly pressed on the subject of marriage and always her response was the same: that she and Eudore had not had "the slightest talk of it in any way."[200] When it was Eudore's turn to give evidence he was questioned no less than five times in the course of nine hand-written pages of testimony about the issue of marriage. On each occasion he confirmed Louise's testimony:

> I did not lead her to believe I intended to marry her ... The subject of marriage was never mentioned between us ... There was never any question of marriage between us ... I never understood from anything she said or did that she hoped I would marry her. She made the arrangement to go to Brighton without any suggestion of marriage ... I slept in the same bed as her - nothing was said about marriage. There was no suggestion of it.[201]

In the previous chapter I introduced the concept of "the double standard of morality" as one of the areas in which women experience social control and regulation. This concept refers to the way in which male sexual activities are tolerated, ignored, condoned or even admired, while similar sexual activities in females signify "deviant and pathological behaviour" and as such are problematised and condemned.[202] Late Victorians were well acquainted with this concept and recognised the importance of female sexual passivity and constraint to the stability of the social order:

> If the passions in women were ready, strong and spontaneous, in a degree even approaching the form they assume in the coarser sex,

[198]HO 144/1540/A61535. Trial transcript p.63.
[199]HO 144/1540/A61535. Trial transcript p.42; p.41.
[200]HO 144/1540/A61535. Trial transcript p.41.
[201]CRIM 1/58/5 Evidence of Eudore Lucas p.46; p.48; pp.52-3; pp.54-5; p.51.
[202]Nead 1988:6.

there can be little doubt that sexual irregularities would reach a height, of which, at present, we have happily no conception.[203]

This double standard of morality was further intensified when applied to the specific category of females to which Louise belonged - those who within Victorian culture fitted the description of 'governess':

The governess, whose task is to supervise the moral growth and education of her charges, must be one whose 'unimpeachable morality' demands that desires and longings of her own be bracketed, sacrificed, thwarted.[204]

That the governess should be expected to comply with such extreme moral demands is indicative of the level of anxiety associated with her perceived unregulated, unstable sexuality as an unmarried, financially independent woman. Yet, Louise - herself a member of the class that exercised the power to define the moral order - refused to contribute towards the stability of that order. Instead her sexual conduct destabilised dominant discourses about women's nature - and epitomised unregulated female sexuality. Together, these aspects were perceived to pose a threat to the moral order that Victorians had worked so vigorously to define for nearly half a century. Louise's sexual conduct alone was more than adequate in ensuring she was perceived as an unruly woman and moral threat. Her threatening propensities were further exacerbated and accentuated by her attitude towards the married status, wherein she defied and undermined one of the most sacred ideologies: that marriage was the crux of family life - an essential union for those who sought personal fulfilment and happiness:

On its own neither sex is complete, together they create a perfect and secure social unit.[205]

Moreover, it was impossible to pretend Louise's liaison with Eudore was an isolated incident, Manfred was proof of a history of sexual relationships outside marriage. Such repeated sexual transgressions ensured she could not be constructed as either a victim or 'fallen woman', betrayed by an unscrupulous man in a superior social position. Exactly the opposite appeared to be the case: it was Louise who was dangerous to *young* men like Eudore. In Chapter Six I analyse the case of Edith Thompson who was executed in 1923. She was 28 and her lover was 19. Filson Young - an observer of this case - argued that this age difference was a crucial factor in

---

[203]W.R. Greg, quoted in Nead 1988:6.
[204]Matus 1995:89.
[205]Nead 1988:34. See also Vicinus, M. (1985) *Independent Women: Work and Community for Single Women 1850-1920* Virago, London p.16, where she writes that "girls were repeatedly reminded that to fulfil their 'natural' destiny they must marry."

presenting Edith as debauched and corrupt, an "experienced woman of the world ... the blackhearted sorceress, weaving her spells, casting her nets, and bringing ruin on everyone connected with her."[206] This perception of an older woman who takes a young lover, would have been intensified with respect to Louise as her case took place during the late Victorian period. The age-gap between Louise and Eudore alone, would have been enough to render their sexual liaison illicit. But, as I shall illustrate, this was only one of many elements in her moral and sexual conduct which together played a crucial role in constructing her as a debauched, morally corrupt and selfish woman, which in turn ensured her case qualifies as a prime example of judicial misogyny.

Louise Masset and Motherhood

I have already discussed the moral and practical difficulties associated with illegitimate motherhood which faced working-class women. Despite her class Louise was not permitted to escape such difficulties. If anything they were exacerbated because she was doubly condemned for her transgression - on the one hand she was condemned for not being ashamed *enough* of her status as an unmarried mother, on the other, she was condemned for her failure to ensure her child's safety. Unlike most Victorian single mothers, Louise did not hide her parental status, and both Miss Gentle and Leonie - Louise's sister - agreed that as Manfred grew older, her affection for him increased as did her visits to him. Miss Gentle testified that she "seemed always fond and proud of the boy."[207] This was confirmed by Leonie who stated that "she used to see the child often and was very fond of him."[208] Yet it was not usual for a single mother of her status to behave as if her child deserved equal status to legitimate children. Leonie, for example had not seen Manfred for over six months prior to his murder and Louise wrote to Manfred's father:

> ... you know as well as I that your son will never be received in my family. They have told me often enough. I ask nothing for myself ... but ... I tell you that your son cannot and must not be thoroughly as dirty linen. ... Your heart is your master but remember my own is a mother's heart and it also speaks.[209]

Louise was thus in a perpetual dilemma - on the one hand her family had made it clear she was expected to hide her status as a single mother, on the other, her feelings for Manfred were not affected by this status - her love for him was as strong as that of a 'respectable' mother, thus she felt pride rather than shame in acknowledging his existence. Within the Victorian

---

206 Young, F. (ed) (1951) *Trial of Frederick Bywaters and Edith Thompson* William Hodge & Company, Glasgow p.xiv.
207 CRIM 1/58/5 Testimony by Eleanor Gentle dated 25th December 1899.
208 CRIM 1/58/5 Testimony by Leonie Cadisch dated 25th December 1899.
209 HO 144/1540/A61535 Letter from Louise to Maurice dated 6th October 1899.

setting described above, such pride was a sign of unruly motherhood - "an affront to the ideal of motherhood ... in the late-nineteenth century."[210] Thus, although Louise was not permitted to express motherhood on equal terms with a married mother, those who sat in judgement upon her still reserved the right to criticise her conduct as a mother as in Manfred's hand-over to the Brownings. In short, while she was not permitted to take full responsibility for Manfred, the court nonetheless reserved the right to deem her an irresponsible mother. Hence, it is difficult to avoid the conclusion that *whatever* action Louise took in relation to her son, she would have been condemned, since ultimately it was his *existence* which destabilised the dominant order, rather than the details of his upbringing.

In order to demonstrate that Louise was a bad mother the prosecutor focused first, on the manner in which she had entrusted Manfred to the care of the Brownings, pointing out that she had requested no references and had not even paid them a visit.[211] Louise argued she had met them in person and interviewed them on three occasions which amounted to far more contact than she had had with Miss Gentle prior to her appointment.[212] In the case of the latter she had simply responded to a newspaper advert, and although Miss Gentle had volunteered several references Louise had only taken up one. Moreover, as observed from previous case-studies, children were often handed over to complete strangers on street-corners or railway stations with far less ceremony than in this case, and when they were found abandoned or dead it was often impossible to trace the biological parents, who in many cases did not wish to have their association with their child known. When seen within its historical context Louise was therefore not unduly flippant when she stated:

> it filled me with no misgiving that I did not know the place where the child had gone ... I did not go to 45 Kings Rd Chelsea - why should I have gone?[213]

The issue of social class should also be considered in this context. It will be remembered that Louise described the Brownings as 'respectable' and 'perfect' ladies, and in view of their social status she may have felt embarrassed to ask for references.[214] In a culture strictly divided by social class this would not have been an issue where Miss Gentle was concerned since she could be clearly identified as working-class and therefore inferior to Louise.

Second, although Louise had testified she was unaware of Manfred's murder until she read the newspaper account on her way home from work, and although his identity was not published until that evening, the prosecutor

---

[210]Smart 1992:16.
[211]*The Telegraph* 18th December 1899.
[212]HO 144/1540/A61535 Trial transcript p.15.
[213]HO 144/1540/A61535 Trial transcript p.145.
[214]This issue has also been discussed by Fiona Mackay in Woodward 1993:172.

questioned her as if she had known earlier and hence maintained she had not acted as one would expect after learning of her child's murder:

> We may take it that at 4 o'clock you had seen a newspaper which contained a description of the child. Did you wait for your pupil and go back with her.
> *Yes.*
> And did you go and see Mrs Haas as well as her daughters.
> *I think so. I could not remember that special occasion.*
> She says she saw you.
> *If she says so then I did.*
> She says further that when she saw you that evening you were in your usual health and spirits ... As between 4 o'clock and 6.55 when you left Loudoun Road no effort was made by you to go and trace your child.
> *But sir, I only had just a kind of feeling 'that seems to be like the child' - that was all.*[215]

The prosecutor also questioned Eudore about Louise's conduct and behaviour during the weekend they had spent together when Manfred was already dead:

> She seemed calm + just the same as usual. During the visit she was in her usual spirits.[216]

The strategy adopted to disqualify Louise as a speaker is easily identified: the prosecutor asked questions which contained a taken-for-granted assumption that Louise was lying. By her own admission she had told lies in the past, the implication was therefore that her current responses were equally untrustworthy. It was this line of questioning, coupled with other references to Louise's conduct after hearing of Manfred's murder, that led Judge Bruce to include the following statement in his summing up:

> Surely the first impulse would have been at once to inform the police that she had given the child over to Brownings ... and to demand that justice should be done, the person arrested, or inquiries made at once. How does she act? ... She does not go home ... [but] sees Mr Simes, her brother-in-law. She said: ... "I am being hunted for murder, but I have not done it" ... One would have thought that the first thing she would said to her brother would have been "my poor child has been murdered, I want you to help me to find out the person and to bring to justice the persons who have taken over the child and deceived me. ... Let not one moment be lost, so that these persons may be traced and

---

[215]HO 144/1540/A61535 Trial transcript pp.8-9. Presumably it would have been equally irresponsible to abandon her pupil and let her go home unaccompanied.
[216]CRIM 1/58/5 Testimony of Eudore Lucas pp.53-4.

not escape justice." But her own thought apparently was first for her own safety: "I am being hunted for murder, I have not done it." ... Therefore ... Gentlemen, I invite you to consider her conduct before, at the time, and after the murder was committed.[217]

Third, Louise herself did nothing to alter her image as an uncaring and callous mother as when questioned about her reasons for moving in with her sister:

In going to Bethume Road I think you said yesterday that it had an attraction, that it would be fairly near your work?
Yes.
Not far from your child?
Yes.
And that, I presume, would be an additional advantage in the going to Bethume Road?
I found it a great advantage in going to my lessons then: so long as the child was not out of London I could always see him.
Do you say that you did not go there because it would be near your child?
No: I do not think so. It was for my lessons.
And the child was secondary?
Yes.
It did not strike you that you would be near your child?
No.
Notwithstanding the increasing affection you had for your child?
You must understand I am -
Will you answer. Did it strike you as an additional advantage or not?
Not at the time. I do not think it did.[218]

Thus, although Louise was not given the opportunity to act like a 'normal' mother as a result of her family's refusal to allow Manfred into their home or acknowledging his existence in public, she was still judged according to the dominant discourses around a conventional *English* mother-child relationship, for her 'foreignness' did not pass unnoticed by the English media, who seized the opportunity to assert racial superiority:

... sympathy ... for this woman ... would be more marked had not the accused herself alienated that womanly feeling which Englishwomen have in their hearts for an unfortunate member of their own sex ... If Miss Masset had been an Englishwoman she would have "faced the music" and have borne her yoke in silence.[219]

---

[217]HO 144/1540/A61535 Trial transcript, Judge's Summing Up, pp. 41-7.
[218]HO 144/1540/A61535 Trial transcript, pp.44-45.
[219]*Weekly Dispatch* 31st December 1899.

It was the combination of these discourses which ensured that despite the testimonies of those who had seen Louise and Manfred together, she entered history as a wicked, selfish and 'unnatural' mother who furthermore was a member of a 'suspect' race.

Louise Masset: Her Presentation of Herself

The final set of discourses in relation to Louise's trial that I wish to explore are those surrounding the presentation of herself. Louise was among the first women defendants on a capital charge to give evidence on her own behalf following the 1898 Criminal Evidence Act. She was described as being "of attractive appearance" and "an uncommonly good witness",[220] no doubt as a result of being a confident and articulate speaker. Yet that confidence also operated to further reinforce the discourses of judicial misogyny, for her lack of deference and humbleness ultimately resulted in her being constructed as a provocative and 'uppity' woman who needed to be 'put in her place'. This point was discussed in Chapter Three where I also noted the difficulties women face in establishing authority in their speech. Louise broke the rules governing authority by ignoring the 'emotive connectedness and compassion' associated with female speech, and instead adopted the confident and self-assertive manner usually associated with male speech, thus signalling her refusal to accept the role of a subordinate in the courtroom.

The trial transcript contains many examples of Louise's confident demeanour, for instance, when cross-examined about her deception regarding the fictional trip to France she did not sound regretful or apologetic about her lies:

[you were] still keeping up the deception.
Yes.
There was no word to Mrs Cadisch on Monday 30th October after your return as to two strange women.
No, of course not because if I deceived her one way I should not have raised her doubts.
....
Upon that morning you wrote to the Norris's [Miss Gentle's parents] - you sent a testimonial.
It was because they asked me.
And you wrote them the details of your voyage to France.
That was again keeping it up. There was no reason to say any different. It was not Mrs Norris's business was it.[221]

When the prosecution pressured Louise to establish a date for Eudore's return to France she appeared to become impatient:

---

[220]*Daily Telegraph* 14th and 18th December 1899.
[221]HO 144/1540/A61535 Trial transcript entitled 'Mr Dalton's portion' p.5.

> *I just now said to you that I knew he was to go back in December.*
> *.... But he did remain?*
> *Certainly, he is here.*[222]

When cross-examined about why she was not worried about the Brownings disappearing with Manfred without saying goodbye she maintained a confident demeanour and was not afraid to 'answer back':

> There was nothing to be alarmed at. I thought they had taken him off while he was in good spirits. You would not have been alarmed if you had seen the women before, either.[223]

Persistent questioning on the same issue did not unnerve Louise, as when she was questioned about the time she first told Eudore about Manfred:

> *I cannot say.*
> He fixes it early in September. Do you accept that date ...?
> *I say I cannot say.*
> It might have been then.
> *It might have been, I do not know.*[224]

Even on less controversial issues Louise did not simply accept statements by her interrogator. When she was shown a newspaper and asked if it was the one in which she had read about Manfred's murder, she replied: "If that is the paper you have just passed me with that description in it it was."[225] Finally, twice during the summing up Louise "corrected and amplified statements made by the Judge."[226]

It was this confident and challenging attitude - hence her refusal to accept the deferential and timid role associated with appropriate feminine conduct - which constructed her as an 'uppity' woman to the point where several newspapers argued she would have been better off "if her mouth had been closed."[227] Not only did she speak with confidence, she also appeared quite unafraid despite the seriousness of her situation and "at no time during the proceedings did she display the least nervous apprehension."[228] On the second day of the trial Louise was still "displaying no signs of emotion until that part of the evidence was reached which had reference to the finding of the child's body ... Any signs, however, of breaking down were quickly dispelled."[229] Louise's calmness and confident demeanour were repeatedly

---

[222] HO 144/1540/A61535 Trial transcript p.56.
[223] *Daily Telegraph* 18th December 1899 quoting from transcript.
[224] HO 144/1540/A61535 Trial transcript p.59.
[225] HO 144/1540/A61535 Trial transcript p.10.
[226] *Daily Telegraph* 19th December 1899.
[227] *Daily News* 19th December 1899; see also *The Standard* 19th December 1899.
[228] *Daily Telegraph* 14th December 1899.
[229] *Daily Telegraph* 15th December 1899.

commented upon in the media who further maintained that "many of the spectators were plainly astonished at her general bearing and the nature of her evidence."[230] The discourses required to categorise Louise as a thoroughly 'bad' woman had thus been mobilised in almost every one of the areas outlined in Chapter Three. That is to say, she had destabilised discourses and challenged ideologies around female self-representation in general, as well as in the four specific areas of marriage, domesticity, motherhood and respectability. Rather than complying with the ideal image of womanhood as dependent, subordinate and respectable, Louise was an independent and promiscuous woman who failed to guard herself against a 'bad' reputation. She was also an 'unnatural' and selfish mother - devoid of the maternal instinct - instead putting her own pleasures before those of her child's, as indicated by the opening quote of this case-study. This condemnation was echoed throughout the media:

> Surely no more cruel or unnatural crime could have been conceived and perpetrated. The weight of circumstances forcibly compels us to regard her as a most wicked and calculating woman, who, for selfish purposes, coldly planned this murder ... For a crime so shocking little or nothing can be pleaded in extenuation.[231]

> It was the cruel murder of a boy by his own mother, who was perfectly sane, and influenced by motives of the basest self-interest.[232]

> It was a very deliberate, callous, and cold-blooded murder.[233]

Moreover, she was a self-confessed liar, a fact which led the Judge of North London Police-Court to state:

> Miss Masset's word goes for nothing. The jury did not believe her. Nobody believes her.[234]

Other court personnel agreed. For example, after her conviction Justice Bruce commented:

> Her story is an absolutely incredible one ... The evidence leaves, I think, no shadow of a doubt of the prisoner's guilt, and if guilty, the circumstances of the crime show a premeditation and cruelty of

---

[230]*Daily Telegraph* 16th December 1899.

[231]*Daily Telegraph* 19th December 1899.

[232]*Daily News* 19th December 1899.

[233]*The Times* 19th December 1899.

[234]Judge Fordham's response to Miss Gentle who claimed that Louise's testimony had defamed her reputation as a child's nurse quoted in *The Daily Chronicle* 4th January 1900.

purpose far beyond the usual features in the ordinary cases of the murder of illegitimate children; and there is a singular absence of mitigating circumstances such as poverty, necessity for concealment of her shame, or unkindness of relatives ... Her extraordinary self-possession was shown by her subsequent conduct; she never falters in her plan of meeting Lucas; she goes to Brighton that night, is calm and self-possessed ... There was no recommendation to mercy and the case is shown by the evidence to be so much worse than the ordinary run of cases ... there is absolutely nothing to be said in (sic) her behalf except that she is a woman.[235]

It was not only court personnel and the media who united in their condemnation of Louise. So hostile was the public reaction to this selfish, callous, unnatural mother and immoral, foreign seductress, that even before her conviction there were:

disgraceful scenes enacted by a crowd of about 500 persons, mostly composed of low class women ... who nearly succeeded in overturning the cab, in which your petitioner was conveyed ... and made use of the most filthy and threatening language towards her.[236]

The process of constructing Louise as a thoroughly 'bad' woman had thus been successful to the point where it transgressed both social class and gender, she appeared to possess no saving graces or redeeming features whatsoever.

Louise Masset and the Issue of Social Class

The hostility, outrage and condemnation directed at Louise Masset can be understood as being in direct proportion to her perceived transgressions. She was the ultimate example of an 'unruly' woman and dangerous mother - her deviant and unregulated womanhood made her appear despicable to both working and middle classes. Her conduct had exposed the hypocrisy surrounding the self-appointed ruling class who considered itself fit to determine standards of morality and to pontificate about those standards to the lower orders. As a role model in Victorian morality Louise turned out to have clay feet. She had enjoyed the privileges associated with her class, she had been regarded with respect by her employers who had placed her in

---

[235]HO 144/1540/A61535. Judge's Notes dated 28th December 1899. See also Higginbotham's discussion of Victorian trials where she notes that "the more unconventional the woman's behaviour and background, the more likely she was to lose the sympathy of the court, a pattern also apparent in outcomes of trials of women whose infants were not newborns" (Higginbotham, A.R. (1992) '"Sin of the Age": Infanticide and Illegitimacy in Victorian London' in Garrigan, K.O. (ed) (1992)*Victorian Scandals* Ohio University Press, Athens, Ohio p.276).
[236]HO 144/1540/A61535. (Quoted from folder entitled 'Petition').

responsible positions and allowed her access to their daughters. As such she stood, not only as a 'traitor' to her class who had failed to maintain the licit (a)sexual identity needed "to define and uphold middle-class claims to social superiority"[237]; but also as a sharp reminder of the fragility of the social and moral order so prized by that class, for in the end, she had turned out to be a most unsuitable person to be in charge of young female pupils:

> the governess was "expected to preside over the contradictions written into the domestic ideal - in the sense both that she was meant to police the emergence of undue assertiveness or sexuality in the maturing charges and that she was expected not to display willfulness or desires herself". The question of the governess' sexuality was anxiously focused in one way on her powers of self-control and denial - in so far as she was useful to middle-class households, could she be trusted to regulate and discipline herself appropriately?[238]

The anxiety over the position of the governess was due to a suspicion that "instead of functioning as a 'bulwark against immorality and class erosion', [she] might be the conduit through which sexual laxity could infect the home",[239] and is an indication of how the middle-class depended on its members sharing "the definition of norms of sexual and moral behaviour" for the creation of class hegemony:

> The middle class was composed of a diverse range of occupational groups and levels of income; what was important, therefore, was the creation of a coherent and distinct class identity which would set the middle class apart from the social and economic classes above and below it. In many ways, this class coherence was established through the formation of shared notions of morality and respectability - domestic ideology and the production of clearly demarcated gender roles were central features in this process of class definition.[240]

Yet despite her respectable credentials Louise was no different from members of the 'lower' order. The definition of female sexuality along class lines - achieved by contrasting the 'respectable' female with "the imagined excess passion and sexual deviancy of the women of the undeserving poor"[241] - had been destroyed. Louise's conduct was perceived as threatening and dangerous in the extreme because it forced the dominant class to recognise that the Victorian passion for categorisation and demarcation was unobtainable.[242] Despite a stringent definition of the moral order, as well as

---

[237]Matus 1995:115
[238]Matus 1995:94, referring to the arguments of Poovey.
[239]Matus 1995:126.
[240]Nead 1990:5.
[241]Nead 1990:7.
[242]See Nead's discussion in Nead 1990:6-7.

the employment of disciplinary and regulatory measures to ensure the protection of that order, women like Louise existed, and there appeared to be no way of knowing how many others like her passed for 'respectable' women while at the same time living a life of lies, lust and debauchery.[243] As succinctly expressed by Matus, "respectable surfaces were shown to be no guarantee against clanking skeletons in a myriad of sordid closets."[244]

It is within this context that discourses around Louise's conduct and behaviour overrode those of her class. In many ways her crime appeared *worse* as a result of her class, as can be seen from the comments by Judge Bruce above. As pointed out in a previous case-study, the Victorians often regarded the 'lower' classes as being synonymous with the 'criminal' classes. They therefore did not display the same level of surprise and outrage when women like Annie Walters stood trial for child murder, since such behaviour only confirmed their suspicions and fears regarding the 'residuum'. Louise Masset, on the other hand, came from a class that considered itself morally superior and above such conduct. She was also quite sane which meant there were no extenuating circumstances or excuses for her conduct. Moreover, her confident attitude suggested she herself saw nothing wrong with her behaviour, and therefore had no reason to humble herself unlike more traditional 'fallen' women such as Leslie James, who at least recognised the evil of her ways and sought forgiveness.[245] Louise, a self-confessed liar and "temptress of young men", appeared to have "suffered no hardship for her past moral lapses"[246] which, if media opinion reflected that of the public, had led many to conclude the time had come for her 'come-uppance'. Seen from this perspective, her punishment can also be interpreted as sending a warning to other 'respectable' women contemplating a similar life-style.

Concluding Remarks

I introduced Louise Masset's case by raising doubts about her guilt. If Louise was innocent it would cast her presentation of herself in an entirely different light. Although her demeanour would have remained unconventional by Victorian standards, it would explain why she saw no need to appear sorry, humble herself or seek redemption. If innocent, she may have taken it for granted the court would not convict her. Space does not permit a full investigation into the available evidence regarding Louise's innocence.[247] However, if she was innocent, we do not need to establish an alternative truth since she had provided one herself. We can however, point to the inability of

---

[243]For a discussion about the anxiety around the difficulty of distinguishing morally and physically corrupt women from respectable women, see Matus 1995:114.

[244]Matus 1995:127, referring to the contents of Victorian sensation novels.

[245]For a discussion of fallen women as the pollutants of men as opposed to being innocent 'victims of male pollution' see Matus 1995:114.

[246]Mackay 1992:168.

[247]See Appendix I.

court personnel to consider an alternative truth. For example, Justice Bruce appeared incapable of stepping outside dominant discourses of illegitimacy, when, despite all the evidence to the contrary, he insisted that "quite independently of Lucas the prisoner might well have found the child to be an embarrassment to her."[248] Here, the judge could only interpret Louise's motherhood according to established discourses, he could not conceive of an unmarried mother being proud of her child. Similarly, although Eudore had testified Louise "was not distressed at all when she told" him about Manfred, that he had been "pleased to know", and considered it "very fair of her" - as far as he was concerned Manfred was not an obstacle "in connection with the fact I was making love to her",[249] Justice Bruce found it inconceivable that illegitimacy could be treated with such indifference and commented: "it seemed to me that neither Lucas nor the prisoner told the whole truth about this conversation respecting the child ..."[250]

These are just two examples of the Judge's attempt to silence Louise's alternative truth and in its place, impose a 'dominant' truth - a truth which is instantly recognisable to its listeners because it speaks the language of established discourses within a particular historical moment. Thus, for Louise - who had already been constructed as someone who paid "no allegiance to the established codes"[251] - the attempt to create new discourses around unmarried motherhood was futile. Instead of being listened to, her speech further reinforced her deviance.

Yet, even in the morally oppressive climate of late Victorian society, Louise's conviction and execution did not pass without opposition. Both concerned individuals and newspapers came to her defence. For example, solicitor Gurney-Winter wrote to the Home Office, offering his services for one week free of charge to investigate the case for "the simple desire to see that no miscarriage of Justice takes place in this case." The Home Secretary was "much obliged but has no need of his services in the matter."[252]

A barrister who wished to remain anonymous, argued Louise had in effect established her innocence by claiming to have eaten in Muttons, a restaurant with only two diners in it that day:

> If she had said that she dined at a large restaurant, where fifty or 100 persons sat down to dinner, it would have been different. Her absence could hardly be proved. But she names a hotel where only

---

[248]HO 144/1540/A61535 Judge's Comments dated 2nd January 1900.

[249]CRIM 1/58/5 Testimony of Eudore Lucas p.46; p.47.

[250]HO 144/1540/A61535 Judge's Comments dated 2nd January 1900.

[251]Mackay 1992:168.

[252]HO 144/1540/A61535 Original letter from Mr Gurney-Winter dated 4th January 1900. He was a respected professional whose clients included the Russian ambassador, Sir Edward Thornton GCB. He also wrote extensively to newspapers, championing Louise Masset's case.

two persons dined on that day, and one of these answered in many respects to the description of the prisoner.[253]

Another anonymous correspondent wrote that the prosecutor's closing statement had been "vindictive, harsh and characterised by the absence of that restraint and judicial fairness which ought to adorn the speeches of all prosecuting counsel."[254]

The Humanitarian League submitted a letter to the Home Secretary:

With regard to the sentence of death passed on Louise Masset, and the fact that she was condemned on purely circumstantial evidence, I am instructed by my committee to express our earnest hope that you will give due weight to the element of doubt that exists in her case.[255]

Yet another correspondent recognised the difficulties facing unmarried mothers:

There is seldom a case but carries the obvious conclusion that if the father had done his duty towards his child the pressure of circumstances upon the mother would not have been so overwhelming as to uproot all vestige of natural maternal affection.[256]

Meanwhile 1200 signatures were collected by staff at the French women's newspaper *La Fronde* who eventually submitted the petition to Queen Victoria.[257]

The day after the execution the *Daily News* wrote "if ever a woman deserved to be hanged, it was this one",[258] but, while sections of the media remained hostile to Louise, other newspapers expressed unease prior to the execution as it became clear the Home Secretary would show no mercy. *The Daily Chronicle* for example, claimed "the police appear to have allowed their bias against the prisoner to influence their action in conducting the case."[259] As for the Home Secretary:

If Sir Matthew White Ridley still refuses to allow this unfortunate woman even a chance of proving her innocence, he will lay himself

---

[253]Letter to *The Chronicle* 6th January 1900.

[254]Letter to *The Chronicle* 6th January 1900.

[255]Letter to *The Chronicle* 6th January 1900, dated 4th January 1900 from Joseph Collinson, Secretary, Prison Reform Department, Humanitarian League.

[256]*The Chronicle* 4th January 1900.

[257]HO 144/1540/A61535 original petition. See also *The Chronicle* 29th December 1899 and 4th January 1900.

[258]*Daily News* 10th January 1900.

[259]*The Chronicle* 8th January 1900.

open to the charge of that unworthy form of official cowardice, which shows itself in obstinately refusing to reopen a *chose jugee*.[260]

This diverse range of resistance to dominant discourses around Louise as a 'bad' woman illustrates that judicial misogyny is never complete despite its monolithic appearance at specific historical moments. Yet, there was one last devastating blow to come before Louise's execution. She was one of only four women throughout these case-studies who was able to pay for her defence, and Lord Coleridge, an experienced barrister, was hired to represent her. The fact her trial lasted five days, almost as long as the trials of the previous four women combined, may well be a reflection of that. Yet, ultimately Lord Coleridge turned out to be a liability rather than a defender of her cause. When he learned, that as a result of the submission of petitions on Louise's behalf, her death-sentence was under review he wrote to the Home Secretary:

> I see that a movement is on foot for a reprieve in this case, and as I was Counsel for the accused, I think I ought to communicate the fact that the prisoner had reason to think that she was abandoned by the father of the child, + I believe she did think so. This state of things naturally I suppressed, as to disclose it would have been to supply a motive for the crime, + I argued that no sufficient motive was disclosed by the prosecution. I think that you should know this, before arriving at a final decision in the case.[261]

Home Office staff could not have wished for a more useful piece of information. Operating from preconceived ideas about women's 'nature' they accepted uncritically that a woman abandoned by her child's father provided a motive for killing that child, despite the fact it was known to the court that Louise had not seen Manfred's father for 18 months, and that she was embroiled in an affair with Eudore until the day of her arrest. Whether Lord Coleridge, despite having been paid to act in Louise's interests, was incapable of separating himself from this case of severe judicial misogyny and therefore believed she ought to hang, or whether he acted from good intentions, assuming the Home Secretary would take a more lenient view of her case because of the disappointment and hardship she had suffered, must remain an open question. Either way, the Home Office response was swift and to the point:

> This letter supplies the missing link of motive ... I fear that Lord Coleridge's letter while tending to clinch the prisoner's guilt by

---

[260]*The Chronicle* 8th January 1900, italics in the original.
[261]HO 144/1540/A61535 Letter to Home Secretary from Lord Coleridge dated 1st January 1900.

supplying the motive does not go further in favour of the prisoner ...262

A second Home Office memo indicates that Coleridge's letter not only provided a motive for the murder, but also did irreparable harm to the credibility of the petition submitted on Louise's behalf by her solicitor:

Lord Coleridge's letter seems to destroy any possible weight the solicitor's petition might possibly have had beforehand.263

If the Home Secretary had any reservations about taking responsibility for Louise's execution, her *defence counsel* had laid them to rest. Executed on 9th January 1900, Louise met her death with dignity and "showed not the slightest symptoms of fear at her approaching fate." She walked to the scaffold unaided and "evinced wonderful firmness and self-control right up to the last."264 According to Edward Milman, governor of Newgate prison, "the execution of Louise Masset went off satisfactorily." He added that during a conversation with the assistant chaplain the evening before she had said: "'What I am about to suffer is just.' This is to some satisfaction to all concerned."265 Home Office staff, always acutely aware of the important role a confession played in maintaining legitimacy in capital cases, insisted this was a 'confession' and ordered an addendum to its prepared response to one of the petitions submitted on Louise's behalf:

Add that before execution the prisoner admitted her guilt and acknowledged her sentence.266

Yet, there is not the slightest evidence that Louise's statement was a confession. An alternative 'truth' about her conversation with the chaplain is equally plausible: that she recognised if she had not rushed off to Brighton in pursuit of her own pleasure, but instead taken time to investigate the Brownings further, Manfred would still be alive. If Louise was not Manfred's killer, she undoubtedly blamed herself for his death; thus within the context of a mother's guilt about her child's death, her statement that her punishment was 'just' would not appear inappropriate. Ironically, she may well have considered herself a 'bad' mother during her last hours, and may further have come to terms with her execution by rationalising it - she 'deserved' to die as a

262HO 144/1540/A61535 Home Office Minutes dated 1st January 1900.
263HO 144/1540/A61535 Letter to Home Secretary, Sir Matthew Ridley, from Home Office personnel dated 1st January 1900.
264*The Echo* 9th January 1900.
265HO 144/1540/A61535 Communication from Edward Milman to Home Office.
266HO 144/1540/A61535 Home Office Memorandum dated 12th January 1900, issued by Charles Murdoch, chief of the Criminal Department, referring to the Home Office reply to a petition from Brussels.

way of atoning for her selfishness which had resulted in the death of her only child.

As argued in Chapter One, it was extremely rare for mothers to be executed for the murder of their own children, and Louise was the last woman to be hanged in England and Wales for this crime. Conversely, it was equally rare for a murdering baby-farmer to have her sentence commuted. Thus, although the case of Louise Masset was as different from the other cases discussed in this chapter as she herself was to the baby-farmers Ada Williams, Annie Walters, Amelia Sach and Leslie James, they nonetheless shared one feature: they all died on the scaffold as a result of representing the ultimate in 'dangerous motherhood.' However, my adoption of the case-study approach in theorising women's experience is not designed to formulate a general or global theory applicable to all women fulfilling certain criteria. Rather it has been adopted to illustrate "the power of a general theoretical principle" such as the power of discourses.[267] The point of placing these case-studies under close examination is therefore one of "analysis rather than enumerative induction."[268] In other words, my claim is not that these women suffered unique injustices or 'rough' justice as a result of displaying the characteristics of 'bad' mothering,[269] nor that all 'bad' mothers found guilty of murder would automatically be executed. Instead I have sought to demonstrate how *particular* discourses around women's conduct and behaviour interact and influence what eventually becomes accepted as the established 'truth' about women defendants. In these particular case-studies it has been the production and reproduction of the ideological construct of motherhood, both in the media and within the courtroom, which has come under scrutiny. I have attempted to illustrate, that despite paying with her life, Louise, however small her individual contribution, did act as an agent of social change, by disrupting the otherwise coherent and seamless 'truth' about women's nature in general and their sexuality in particular. Similarly, Ada, Annie, Amelia and Leslie, despite being members of a muted group and thus disqualified as speakers, did possess a 'negative' power - that is - their mere existence stood as a challenge to dominant ideologies and ideal images of motherhood. Each time a baby-farmer or a single mother stood on the

---

[267]Worrall, A. (1990) *Offending Women* Routledge, London, p.12.

[268]Worall 1990:12.

[269]See for example the cases of a) Thomas Fuller Bacon (1857) whose counsel was "assigned at less than an hour's notice and no attorney had been retained due to poverty"; b) John Allen (1864) who "had no money nor inclination to defend himself and no solicitor to collect extenuating circumstances"; c) William Distin (1880) where the "striking feature of the case was the entirely friendless condition in which the prisoner was left at the trial ... no solicitor, no friend coming forward to say a word"; d) George Durling (1881) whose counsel Charles Gill stated that "my instructions consisted of a copy of the depositions and what I could learn from the prisoner *while he was in the dock*." All quoted in Chadwick, R. (1992) *Bureaucratic Mercy: The Home Office and the Treatment of Capital Cases in Victorian England* Garland, New York pp.98-9. Emphasis in the original.

scaffold, the underlying contradictions between the idealisation of motherhood on the one hand, and the condemnation of illegitimacy on the other, was exposed. Each of these women stood as a challenge to existent knowledge, each of them represented "heterogeneity and contradiction" and in so doing (even if unintentional), momentarily played their part in keeping "open the space within which knowledge is produced."[270] The fact that these women did not succeed in keeping that space open long enough to save their lives, does not detract from their contribution towards creating new knowledge and thus new 'truths' about violent women. If anything, it can be argued their executions emphasised that contribution, since their deaths will forever serve as a stark reminder of the price they paid for underestimating the lengths the early 20th century ruling bloc would go to in order to defend the sexual and moral codes which operated "to regulate both gender and class identities."[271] For disturbing the seamless 'truth', for drawing our attention to the existence of underlying contradictions which usually remain hidden beneath the surface of apparent homogeneity, and thus for having in their own way challenged the 'silencing' of the powerless, these women have earned the right to a place within history.

---

[270]Worrall 1990:10.
[271]Nead 1990:28.

5 Women Killing other Women

Part I: Introduction

When women kill, their victims are most likely to be their own children. This was as true of the first half of the 20th century as it is today. As noted in Chapter One, of the 130 women sentenced to death between 1900-49, 102 were found guilty of murdering their own child. The second largest group of female murderers were those who had killed their husbands/lovers. In total 16 women were sentenced for this crime. The killing of a woman by another female was therefore an unusual crime. Home Office statistics indicate that only nine women were sentenced to death for killing another female between 1900-49, five in connection with robbery, two as a result of revenge or jealousy and two are listed under 'miscellaneous'.[1]

Such statistics reinforce stereotypical ideas about women's violence - that it is invariably connected to tense family situations - taking the form of explosive attacks which lack intent. It also reinforces deep-rooted sexist beliefs about women's proneness to hysteria and incapacity for self-control, and as such, appears to be further proof "of female irrationality and emotional instability."[2] The minority of women killers who do not fit this 'highly-strung' image, but instead appear to plan their crime in the rational and calculated manner usually associated with male criminality, and whose motive is personal gain rather than jealousy or revenge, can expect no mercy, for they have violated the basic traits of women's 'nature' which govern female conduct and behaviour just as the female carers who killed children, discussed previously, came to symbolise 'dangerous' motherhood, as a result of having violated the principle of the 'maternal instinct'. As discussed in Chapter Three, 'the maternal instinct' can be extended to include those who care for the sick or helpless. Therefore, when professional women carers killed those they were supposed to protect, they too came to symbolise dangerous womanhood which in turn lessened their chances of a reprieve.

In recent years feminist scholars have begun to create new discourses through which we can analyse such crimes without reference to women's inherent biological instability or psychological inadequacy. For example,

---

[1] *Royal Commission on Capital Punishment 1949-1953 Report* (1953), Her Majesty's Stationery Office, London pp.304-5. The comparative figures for men between 1900-49 were 93 for child-murder, 31 of which were connected to sexual assault, a crime which no woman was found guilty of; 509 for the murder of wife, sweet-heart or mistress; of women who were not wife, sweetheart, mistress or mother 44 were murdered in connection with sexual assault, 61 as a result of robbery, 27 in quarrels, 30 as a result of revenge or jealousy and 27 in the 'miscellaneous' category. Men murdering other men totalled 263.

[2] Kirsta, A. (1994) *Deadlier Than the Male* HarperCollins, London, p.140.

Bettina Heidkamp's study of nurses who killed their patients indicated they were usually 'ordinary' women, "who day in, day out, did their job, had children and went on holidays like everybody else." Therefore it must be recognised that "murder cannot be consigned to the unknown, dark margins of society; that it is not simply 'evil' or 'mad' people who are capable of killing."[3] In the case of nurses, factors which should be taken into account include the superhuman qualities associated with this profession which may result in "intolerable strains" and "a constant feeling of personal failure." Furthermore, long hours of hard work reap little financial reward and may even result in the death of patients despite every effort made by the carer. The result may be stress and a "permanent sense of frustration ... contribut[ing] to feelings of aggression."[4]

While Heidkamp's study plays an important role in the feminist struggle to de-pathologise women-carers who kill, such killings continue to present a problem for feminist discourse when they are overlaid by a financial motive. Worse still, (and rarer still) how do we go about creating feminist discourses around women who are not carers but who nonetheless kill another woman, for example in the course of a robbery? While feminist activists have had considerable success during recent years in establishing new discourses around women who kill their abusive partners,[5] the premeditative nature of a murder carried out by a woman against another woman for no other motive than to further her own ends, financially or emotionally, has proved more problematic for feminist discourse. The apparent 'cold-blooded' nature of such crimes allows them to fit into pre-existing discourses of women's inherent duplicity and deceptiveness,[6] which so far have eluded the feminist challenge mounted against other reductionist representations and explanations of female criminality. For example, Bell and Fox, in their study of Susan Christie who murdered Penny McAllister, her lover's wife, have argued that feminist writers addressing this case, have failed to challenge the dominant media portrayal of Christie as an 'evil' woman compared to 'good' battered women who kill.[7] Thus it can be argued that feminist theorists have

---

[3]Heidkamp, B. (1993) 'Angels of death' in Birch, H. (ed) *Moving Targets* Virago, London, p.220.

[4]Heidkamp 1993:235; 234; 233.

[5]As can be seen from cases such as those of Emma Humphreys, Kiranjit Ahluwalia and Sara Thornton. A recent discussion of these cases can be found in Ballinger, A. (1996) 'The Guilt of the Innocent and the Innocence of the Guilty' as well as Stanko, E. & Scully, A. (1996) 'Retelling the Tale: The Emma Humphreys Case' both in Myers, A. & Wight, S. (1996) *No Angels* Pandora, London pp.1-28 and 57-71.

[6]See for example Hart, L. (1994) *Fatal Women* Routledge, London, p.6.

[7]Bell, C. & Fox, M. (1996) 'Telling Stories of Women Who Kill' in *Social and Legal Studies* Vol 5, No 4, December 1996 p.485. Lorraine Radford has refined this argument further, stating that within the 'battered women who kill' category a further distinction is made between the deserving victim - a good wife, mother and housekeeper who has tried "against all odds, to make a go of the marriage", and the undeserving battered wife - the virago who generally fights back and is "thus not

not yet been successful in establishing discourses which allow an interpretation of women's violence that recognises it is neither 'worse' nor 'better' than men's violence. While some acts of female violence can be understood as "gendered responses to particular events" it is nonetheless imperative, if women are to achieve equality in all areas of life, for feminist theorists to distance themselves from essentialist notions of womanhood which claim "that women are inherently more peaceable than men."[8] Instead it must be recognised that in this area as in all others, women are equally capable. At the same time, because of pre-existing discourses around women's 'irrationality' it is important to be aware of the difficulties involved in distinguishing between women whose mental illness contributes towards their murderous act, and women who kill in a premeditated, rational manner. In the following case-studies it will become apparent that when feminist theorists move beyond the long-established 'mad or bad' categories we also leave behind neat explanations about women who kill. In establishing new discourses about violent women the stories about women who kill become "pluralistic, fragmented and contingent rather than linear and causal"[9], as I shall now illustrate. As in the previous chapter, this chapter is not organised chronologically, but according to the type of murder committed.

The Case of Louie Calvert

> Louie Calvert was an ugly wizened woman of thirty-three, only five feet tall and without a tooth in her head. A viciously bad-tempered and thieving prostitute ... she was also a murderess, and her behaviour after she had been sentenced to death suggests that she was proud of it.[10]

Of the 15 women executed during the 20th century Louie Calvert and Margaret Allen, whose case is analysed in the following section, can justifiably be considered to be the two most 'invisible' women - their 'muted condition' almost complete. The slimness of these women's case files makes it difficult to comprehend they related to matters of life and death. As the end of their lives drew near their cases attracted barely a comment in the media or the Home Office. The trial of Louie Calvert took place during the General Strike in 1926, hence no national newspapers were published, a factor which compounded the silence surrounding her case.[11] Once again, the unevenness of available data has resulted in unequal sized case-studies.

---

really battered." (Radford, L. (1993) 'Pleading for time' in Birch, H. (ed) *Moving Targets* Virago, London p.195).

[8] Birch, H. (1993) 'Introduction' in Birch 1993:5; 4.

[9] Bell & Fox 1996:487.

[10] Wilson, P. (1971) *Murderess* Michael Joseph, London, p.272.

[11] Renee Huggett and Paul Berry who attempted to investigate this case for their book *Daughters of Cain* (1956) 28 years after Louie's execution were faced with similar

Louie Calvert has been described as belonging to the "criminal type" by two authors who listed the characteristics of criminal women as being those of "vanity; dishonesty; craftiness; sensuality; violent temper; contradictory religious tendencies; a capacity to lead a double life; and the tendency to place themselves in tortuous situations."[12] She had always lived within the Leeds area in extreme poverty, eking out a living as a housekeeper and prostitute. In 1925 Louie became Arthur Calvert's housekeeper, a night-watchman almost as poor as herself. She induced Arthur to marry her by falsely claiming she was pregnant. Several months later when no baby had arrived Louie initiated an elaborate web of lies. Initially, she wrote a note to herself which she showed to Arthur, claiming it was from her sister in Dewsbury who had invited her to stay during her confinement. However, after a brief visit to Dewsbury, Louie returned the same day and took up lodgings with Lily Waterhouse only two miles from her home where Arthur was awaiting her return with their baby.

Lily was a widow living in grinding poverty and squalor in a tiny rented terraced house with wooden boxes serving as tables, bare plaster walls and floorboards except for newspapers under the mattress.[13] She had been in poor health for some time,[14] and the post mortem revealed she had "scabies and perdiculi at the time of death."[15] Despite her ill health she survived mainly by prostitution.[16]

When her few possessions began to disappear Lily suspected Louie was responsible and on 31st March she met with Detective-Sergeant John Holland for the purpose of starting proceedings against her. She was murdered that evening. It had been a brutal killing involving "a prolonged struggle before the knock-out blow" and "a penetrating wound down to the

---

problems and wrote of the case: "The case of Louie Calvert presented peculiar difficulties, which at first seemed insurmountable. Her trial coincided with the General Strike when no national newspapers were published. Although the murder occurred 28 years ago we were fortunate to find people who took part in the case and who remembered this under-sized but physically strong woman. Without their help it would have been impossible to have obtained so much information about an obscure but unique murder." (p.10).

[12]Huggett & Berry 1956:43.

[13]ASSI 45/86/2 Public Record Office, Chancery Lane, London WC2A 1LR. Exhibit 1 - photographs of interior of Lily Waterhouse's bedroom.

[14]ASSI 45/86/2 Testimony of Emily Clayton p.7.

[15]ASSI 45/86/2 Testimony of Dr Hoyland Smith p.29. The Clerk to the Leeds City Justices, could not resist a joke at Lily's expense when he wrote to the Clerk of Assizes: "I have handed the original Exhibits to the Police for safe custody, and for your personal information I might add that many of them are said to be loaded with 'itch' germs!" (ASSI 45/86/2 letter from F. Richards to C. Milton Barber dated 20th April 1926).

[16]ASSI 45/86/2 Testimony of Emily Clayton p.7. See also Wilson 1971:273; Huggett & Berry 1956:56.

bone" at the back of the head, prior to strangulation. Lily had also been tied up.[17]

Meanwhile, Louie returned home on the evening of 31st March with a baby she claimed was hers, but which in fact was illegitimate and had been adopted by her in a similar manner to the baby-farming cases described in the previous chapter.[18] Louie's self-addressed letter was found in Lily's house, and police officers consequently interviewed her. They noticed she was wearing Lily's scarf and boots, and following a search the rest of her missing belongings were found.[19] The boots were the only footwear Lily had owned and apart from a sugar bowl, every piece of crockery belonging to Lily was found in Louie's possession. Unperturbed, Louie maintained Lily had given them all to her.[20]

Upon arrest Louie asked "What is it for? Has she done herself in?" By the time she reached the police station she said: "I wish I had not called there last night."[21] During interrogation Louie claimed "... [Lily] was all right when I left her ... - I'll take my dying oath on that."[22] When questioned about the self-addressed letter and why she had adopted a baby, she simply answered:

> Well its's mine now, because it was given to me. My husband and all the neighbours thought I was pregnant and I left home three weeks ago telling him I was going to Dewsbury to my sister's to be confined.[23]

When asked if she was aware an application for a warrant for her arrest for stealing had been requested by Lily, Louie replied:

> No - all the goods I have pledged have been pledged with her knowledge. She asked me to pledge them for money to keep going on. We parted on very good terms and she kissed me before I came away.[24]

However, eyewitnesses had seen Louie re-enter Lily's house at 5.40am the morning after the murder and leave within minutes with a suitcase.[25] When police officers visited Louie's home they found the suitcase

---

[17]ASSI 45/86/2 Testimony of Dr Hoyland Smith p. 30; p.28; p.29.

[18]See *The Times* 5th April 1926.

[19]ASSI 45/86/2 Testimony of Det. Sgt. Thomas Henry Sabey p.25.

[20]ASSI 45/86/2 Testimony of Det. Sgt. Thomas Henry Sabey p.26 and Det. Sgt. John Holland p.23; p.24.

[21]ASSI 45/86/2 Testimony of Det. Sgt. Thomas Henry Sabey p.25.

[22]ASSI 45/86/2 Det. Supt. Charles Walter Pass, referring to Louie's statement p.31.

[23]ASSI 45/86/2 Det. Supt. Charles Walter Pass, referring to Louie's statement p.32.

[24]ASSI 45/86/2 Det. Supt. Charles Walter Pass, referring to Louie's statement p.32.

[25]ASSI 45/86/2 Testimony of Ida Jackson, Sophia Norris, David Darley, Sarah Ann Dutton, Elizabeth Lumb.

with Lily's possessions still inside, including sheets bearing her initials.[26] Taken together with witness reports about disturbing noises emanating from Lily's bedroom at the estimated time of murder, the evidence against Louie was compelling, and she was subsequently charged, to which she replied: "It's a lie ... I was in my own home at that time."[27]

Louie maintained her innocence to friends and family, but is reported to have admitted murdering Lily Waterhouse to two prison officers.[28] She also confessed to a second murder for which she was never charged, that of John Frobisher, found drowned in 1922. Despite a wound to the back of his head an open verdict was returned, and his death was not investigated further. Like Lily, John Frobisher was found without footwear. Louie attended the inquest, where she identified him, explaining she had been his housekeeper. She subsequently remained in Frobisher's house until her eviction for non-payment of rent.[29]

Until her confession Louie had not been suspected of Frobisher's murder and as the Crown decided not to prosecute her for this murder, her motive for killing him remains unknown. Her motive for killing Lily must also remain within the realms of speculation, but the fact that Lily was due to press charges against her the day following the murder suggests it was a drastic action to silence her. That Louie, in what appeared to be an afterthought, returned to Lily's house the morning after the murder to take possession of whatever items she had not already stolen when Lily was alive, indicated to some observers that she was an extraordinary callous and cruel individual - someone with a "criminal mind".[30] Louie's demeanour immediately after the murder did nothing to challenge this opinion. She showed no signs of stress or nervousness when - leaving Lily's house - she made casual conversation with a neighbour:

> [Neighbour:] I asked her if she was going. She said "Yes". I said, "Are you going for good?" She said, "Yes - she has asked me to stay, but I am leaving". I asked her where Mrs Waterhouse was. She said, "I have left her in bed crying" ... The prisoner said, "There is one [a tram] just past. I have missed it and I shall have to catch the next". I asked her what she had been doing in the little bedroom [referring to the noises caused by Lily's struggles as she was being murdered]. She said, "We have been pulling down the bed chair ready for Mrs Waterhouse moving on Saturday." She said she was coming back on Saturday to see if she had got all the things out.[31]

---

[26]ASSI 45/86/2 Testimony of Det Sgt Thomas Henry Sabey.

[27]ASSI 45/86/2 Testimony of Det Insp Joseph Cunton.

[28]*The Manchester Evening News* 24th June 1926 p.6. See also Huggett & Berry 1956:65.

[29]Huggett & Berry 1956:44-5; 59.

[30]Huggett & Berry 1956:47.

[31]ASSI 45/86/2 Testimony of Emily Clayton p.6.

Similarly, when Louie again was seen leaving Lily's house the following morning after having stolen the remaining possessions she was calm and collected despite having just re-visited the murdered woman:

> [Neighbour:] I said, "My word, tha's up early". She said she had been to the Station to fetch her luggage home. She said her sister had given her the things she had in her basket ... She said her sister had also given her some boots ... The basket was not covered up. The cups and saucers were inside. ... Prisoner did not appear to be hurrying and was walking quite openly and not as if she desired concealment.[32]

Carrying the stolen goods unto the tram Louie met another friend:

> The tram-car set off and pulled up again for her [Louie]. She got on - inside the lower deck. She sat down nearly facing me. She said to me, "It's a grand morning, are you working?" I answered "Yes".[33]

These testimonies suggested Louie was unperturbed by her violent deed and went about her normal business immediately after the killing, and again immediately after having faced Lily's corpse following her second visit. Louie's 'nerves of steel' attitude and her failure to appear frightened, nervous or hysterical following her deed stood in sharp contrast to expected female behaviour in such circumstances and indicated a hardened, callous woman. It was thus not only Louie's criminal activities but also her personal appearance, conduct and general demeanour which contributed towards her classification as a 'criminal type' who deserved little or no sympathy,[34] and out of the 15 executed women, she arguably, most accurately fits Lombroso's conception of the 'degenerate woman'. As well as being violent she was also a woman of "promiscuous habits" who intermittently worked as a prostitute and who "for many years had led a wayward life of deception and dishonesty. She had lived by her wits; in a tight corner she lied and schemed her way out."[35] Moreover, she had two illegitimate children, one of whom was in the care of her sister.[36] Hence, she appeared to encompass virtually all the characteristics Lombroso associated with the "the born female criminal ...: 'excessively erotic, weak in maternal feeling, inclined to dissipation, astute, and audacious ... an excessive desire for revenge, cunning, cruelty, love of

---

[32]ASSi 45/86/2 Testimony of Sophia Morris p.19.

[33]ASSI 45/86/2 Testimony of Elizabeth Lumb p.16.

[34]For example, one author who described Louie as a prostitute, added that she was among the "most unattractive members" of her profession, "foul-mouthed and dishonest." She "was a compulsive liar, acting according to the demands of a world she had imagined and incapable of realistic reasoning" (Wilson 1971:276).

[35]Huggett & Berry 1956:59; 57; 59.

[36]Huggett & Berry 1956:46.

dress, and untruthfulness.'"[37]   Louie had thus transgressed appropriate feminine standards in nearly all the areas discussed in Chapter Three, including that of personal appearance. That is, she had failed to internalise the disciplinary practices in relation to 'feminine' beauty - as outlined by Bartky - which ensure male patronage, and she made no attempt to employ a body language that signalled membership of a subordinate group. In short, she was a woman who ignored "the gaze of patriarchy." The consequent withdrawal of male patronage - even by someone unacquainted with her - can be observed in the quotation heading this section.

For Lombroso the female criminal was much 'worse' than the male criminal because she "was perceived to have all the criminal qualities of the male plus all the worst characteristics of women, namely cunning, spite and deceitfulness."[38] The rarity of violent female offenders led Lombroso and Ferrero to conclude that women's nature is "antithetical to crime"[39] which, as argued throughout this book, has meant criminal women are judged by different standards than criminal men, because they have transgressed not only the law but also the rules governing appropriate female conduct and behaviour. The double standard applied to female criminals is articulated in cast-iron terms by Lombroso:

> As a *double* exception, the criminal woman is consequently a monster.[40]

As a result of nearly three decades of feminist challenges we now recognise that such beliefs and ideas are rooted in biological determinism and hence of no sociological value. While Lombroso and Ferrero treated sex and gender as if they are synonymous, feminist theorists have pointed out that although sex usually (but not always) is determined by biology, it is culture which shapes gender and gender role expectations. Hence the fact that women commit less violent crime than men is not due to their sex but to their gender. Similarly, violent female offenders are not more 'masculine' than their non-violent sisters as Lombroso and Ferrero argued, since biological characteristics do not 'cause' cultural traits. In short, criminal women are considered 'monstrous' not as a result "of their innate qualities but because they are socially defined as such."[41]

However, having exposed these fundamental problems with biological determinism, feminist theorists are still left with the task of establishing discourses through which we can understand female violence without falling into another, related trap - that of biological essentialism. Essentialism has traditionally been associated with radical feminism which

---

[37]Lombroso quoted in Zedner, L. (1991) *Women, Crime and Custody in Victorian England* Clarendon Press p.82.
[38]Smart, C. (1976) *Women, Crime and Criminology* RKP, London p.33.
[39]Smart 1976:33.
[40]Lombroso quoted in Zedner 1991:82. My emphasis.
[41]Smart 1976:35.

has been criticised for embracing the view that women are *in essence* emotionally superior to men and therefore 'better' human beings. While men encompass evil and corruption, women encompass 'goodness' and would live in a "warm, supporting, nurturing [world] ... full of creativity," if freed from men's oppression.[42] This view perceives *all* women to be morally pure and *always* "exploited and oppressed" victims, while men are *always* the victimisers.[43] It is therefore ultimately a reactionary and conservative outlook which retains "the categories that have historically defined each gender" and merely revalues them "so that the female traits are the positive ones and the male traits the negative ones."[44] Supporters of this idealisation of womanhood are therefore as guilty as Lombroso and Ferrero were before them, of perpetuating sexist ideologies which reduce complex social relations and interactions to simplistic and immutable truisms about women's and men's 'nature'. In other words, those who refuse to recognise the existence of a female capacity for violence come dangerously near to conducting their argument on the same terrain as Lombroso and Ferrero: that violence is contrary to women's *nature*, an argument which implies women are not *capable* of experiencing the full range of human emotions. It is also an argument which perceives sex roles as inevitable, which in turn renders the feminist struggle for social change futile.[45] To avoid these pitfalls feminists must dispense with *all* sexist myths, including those we cherish and value, if we are serious about overthrowing "the categories that entrap us in rigid roles."[46] As I shall illustrate, the case of Louie Calvert encompasses many features which illuminate the shortcomings associated with both biological determinism and essentialism.

The Trial and Appeal of Louie Calvert

Louie Calvert's trial took place on 6-7th May 1926. As already noted, details of the trial are almost non-existent. Transcripts have not survived, and there were no newspaper reports after the General Strike ended. However, unlike the women in the previous chapter, Louie's trial took place after the establishment of the Court of Criminal Appeal, and it has been possible to glean some details of proceedings from reports of her Appeal held on 7th June 1926. The appeal was fought on the grounds that she "was not charged until 24 hours after [her arrest] and during that time she was subjected to an amount of questioning by the police which exceeded that which was allowable."[47] Louie's counsel, Mr Chappell, maintained that "a detective

---

[42]Tong, R. (1992) *Feminist Thought* Routledge, London p.134; p.137.
[43]Tong 1992:135.
[44]Tong 1992:135 referring to the arguments of Joan Cocks.
[45]For a discussion of the sex role 'inevitability' thesis see Trebilcot, J. (1982) 'Sex Roles: The Argument From Nature' in Vetterling-Braggin, M. (ed) *"Femininity," "Masculinity," and "Androgyny"* Littlefield, Adams & Co, Totowa, pp.40-48.
[46]Tong 1992:135.
[47]*The Times* 8th June 1926.

superintendent had exceeded his duty in cross-examining [her] to an 'unprecedented degree'" hence evidence obtained under these circumstances should not have been "legally admissible."[48] He further argued that as a weapon was never found, another unknown person could have committed the murder:

> There were ... no signs of a struggle, and the dust in the room had not been disturbed. The accused woman ... began by lying, but although she might have lied or gone to the house of the dead woman to steal, that was a long, long way from murder, and should have been pointed out to the jury.[49]

The Lord Chief Justice responded that "nothing in the present case suggested ... the police had gone beyond their duty," and the summing up had been both "clear" and "fair". Moreover, "Calvert did not give evidence, *although her defence was that she was not the person who killed Mrs Waterhouse*."[50] During my analysis of Louise Masset's case I referred to newspaper reports suggesting she would have been better off had she not given evidence. That the Lord Chief Justice should choose to make the above comment during his rejection of an Appeal suggests, that in his opinion, guilt is at least partially implied by a failure to give evidence. Comparing these cases illustrates the ambivalent impact of the 1898 Criminal Evidence Act. While defendants' right to give evidence on their own behalf should be welcomed and ought to ensure the end of 'muted' accounts, the Act nonetheless created a new set of value-judgements which placed some defendants in a 'no-win' situation. For example, it is likely Louie Calvert was deemed an unsuitable witness - unable to make a positive impression on the jury due to her social class, lack of education, personality and general demeanour. Yet, the Lord Chief Justice failed to maintain a neutral attitude towards the fact that she waived her right to give evidence. He concluded the hearing by dismissing her appeal without calling upon the Crown to argue and without legal obligation to consider the fact that 25 witnesses had appeared for the prosecution while none had appeared for the defence.[51]

Louie Calvert's Presentation of Herself

Louie was suitably attired in black for her trial, yet evidence suggests she was credited with being more familiar with courtroom protocol than was the case. For example, in the middle of proceedings at the Magistrates' Court, she suddenly exchanged her hat for a more fashionable and expensive-looking

---

[48]*Manchester Evening News* 7th June 1926 p.5.
[49]Mr Chappell speaking in the Court of Appeal, reported in *Manchester Evening News* 7th June 1926 p.5.
[50]*The Times* 8th June 1996. My emphasis. See also Huggett & Berry 1956:63.
[51]Huggett & Berry 1956:61.

one brought in by her solicitor.[52]   While such behaviour undoubtedly stemmed from ignorance rather than arrogance, it reinforced the view that she was deliberately disrespectful and indifferent to the formalities of the courtroom:

> When standing her trial for murder her shifting black eyes were a psychological study. She seemed callous and indifferent, and her hard, sharp-featured face was the face of a wicked woman.[53]

Other observers interpreted her behaviour as deliberately manipulative, and likened her demeanour to that of Ada Williams discussed in Chapter Four:

> For two days she sat with her hands in her lap, her eyes appealing to each member of the jury in turn as they moved from man to man, up and down the box.[54]

Thus, Louie was credited with understanding "the importance of creating a good impression", and consequently "simulated the attitude of an inoffensive and hapless woman." Outside the courtroom, however, she was "vain", "abusive" and "had a most vicious temper."[55]

Louie's final act within the courtroom was to tell yet another lie in a last bid to save herself. However, her false claim of being pregnant[56] only served to reaffirm she was of the 'criminal type' - beyond reforming regardless of her circumstances.

Louie Calvert: 'Degeneracy' versus Dignity

While the majority of commentators could not find a single redeeming feature within Louie's personality, there was nonetheless opposition to her hanging. A City Councillor who observed the trial declared he was "full of pity for the poor woman, whether she was guilty or not. She was a thin, wan-looking creature only weighing a few stone. I should never legislate on the lines of hanging for women."[57]

Meanwhile, Dr Watts an MP, felt sufficiently concerned about Louie's supposed pregnancy to raise the issue with the Home Secretary

---

[52]Huggett & Berry 1956:63.

[53]Eye-witness at trial quoted in Huggett & Berry 1956:63.

[54]Huggett & Berry 1956:62.

[55]Huggett & Berry 1956:65; 62; 63.

[56]Huggett & Berry 1956:61.

[57]Mr J. Lambert, Leeds City Councillor, quoted in Huggett & Berry 1956:60.

through a Parliamentary question. Sir Joynson-Hicks however, reassured the House that Louie was not pregnant.[58]

As the date of Louie's execution drew near, "strenuous efforts were made to obtain a reprieve."[59] These included "an extensively signed petition"[60], as well as "a motion for an address praying his Majesty to exercise his Royal Prerogative in the case of Louie Calvert", signed by six Labour MPs.[61] It was to no avail - the execution went ahead as planned on 24th June. She "met death better than many a man" - walking "calmly to the scaffold", giving "no trouble" to her executioner.[62] Her bravery in facing death was equally apparent during the last days of her life when she wrote farewell letters and received visits from family for the last time. She wrote to her sister-in-law:

> I only want to see my son once more to kiss him good-bye. Then I am satisfied, you have all done your best, but God has not answered our prayers in the way we wanted. Still he knows what is best for me.[63]

Another of her letters read:

> I am resigned to my fate. I only want to see my sonny once again, to kiss him good-bye. Tell him to be a good boy and he will see his mother in heaven.[64]

Louie's request to see 6-year-old Kenneth was granted on her last afternoon when Arthur, her husband and Leah, her sister-in-law also came to say goodbye:

> The interview lasted half an hour and at the end, when the boy pathetically appealed to his mother to come home, he was told that she had to go to London to see the Queen.[65]

---

[58]*Parliamentary Debates, Commons, 1926 Vol 197, June 21 to July 9.* Sir Joynson-Hicks stated that: "Any doubt which may have existed as to the prisoner's condition has since been dispelled, and it is now certain that there was no pregnancy" (col.249).
[59]*Manchester Evening News* 22nd June 1926 p.5.
[60]*Manchester Evening News* 23rd June 1926 p.9. According to Huggett & Berry 1956:64 the Labour MP for Consett, Rev Sir Herbert Dunnico organised a petition which was signed by almost 3000 people.
[61]*The Times* 23rd June 1926.
[62]*Manchester Evening News* 24th June 1926 p.6.
[63]Louie Calvert's letter to Leah McDermott quoted in *Liverpool Post and Mercury* 25th June 1926.
[64]Louie Calvert's letter quoted in *The Daily Mirror* 25th June 1926, p.2.
[65]*Liverpool Post and Mercury* 25th June 1926.

Following this last visit Leah said "she could not have believed that any woman could have borne up so well in the circumstances",[66] and Arthur told reporters "this was the fourth occasion he had visited his wife ... and it was the hardest. He had previously found his wife was cheerful in the circumstances, and she spoke highly of the treatment she was receiving at the hands of the prison officials",[67] who agreed she had been "quiet and well-conducted and gave no trouble of any kind" during her imprisonment. She maintained her dignified conduct to the very end, walking "stoically" and "with deliberation to the scaffold," where the execution was carried out "humanely and expeditiously."[68] However, those who had classified Louie as a 'criminal type' did not interpret her lack of hysterical behaviour as dignified bravery, but instead saw it as a further indication of her lack of femininity:

> To most women the sentence of death is a shock which their nervous systems are unable to sustain immediately, and leaves many of them dazed and incapable of coherent speech for many hours afterwards. The effect upon Louie Calvert was the reverse; it merely served to increase her volubility.[69]

Huggett and Berry further considered Louie's attempt to look dignified by dressing in black "grotesque ... as if to publicly proclaim her sorrow and mourning for the death of the woman for whose murder she was being tried," when, in their opinion, she was "the most unmoved person present" within the courtroom.[70] Moreover, her bravery in facing death was dismissed as "that cold attitude to death typical of the criminal ... [who] has no sense of guilt":

> To her there was something glorious and grandiose in dying this way. Like the Christians sacrificed in the lions' den, and the Indian fakir lying on his bed of nails, there was more pleasure than pain in the final atonement ... It is vanity alone which sustains the criminal when all else has failed.[71]

Ultimately, Louie's eventual conformity to established female conduct and obedience to prison rules could not erase the powerful and long-established discourses around the 'born female criminal'.

Meanwhile, outside the prison walls where a crowd of 500 people had gathered, the drama of Louie's execution was manifest in ways reminiscent of the 19th century spectacle of public executions discussed in

---

[66]*Liverpool Post and Mercury* 25th June 1926.

[67]*Manchester Evening News* 23rd June 1926 p.5.

[68]*Manchester Evening News* 24th June 1926 p.6.

[69]Huggett & Berry 1956:61.

[70]Huggett & Berry 1956:63.

[71]Huggett & Berry 1956:65.

Chapter Two - confirming what many had predicted then - that private executions would not bring an end to the public's desire for titillating details:

> Every few minutes as the crowd became more and more under the influence of a suppressed excitement the massive doors of the gaol swung slowly open to allow of the passing of some vehicle concerned in the ordinary business of the prison ... About nine o'clock when a strange hush had fallen on a section of the crowd, a bell in the prison began to toll in faint ghostly tones ... As the minutes sped swiftly on, all eyes were fixed on the massive entrance gates, and presently there was an unseemly rush across the road as a warder emerged and quickly took down the single notice and substituted two others with deft fingers ... For long afterwards the notices were studied again and again ...[72]

Louie's behaviour and conduct towards the end of her life illustrate the complexity of her personality, and thus serves to further discredit theories based on biological reductionism and essentialism. Her existence illustrates that a 'thoroughly bad woman' - a liar, a thief even a murderer - can also be a loving mother and a brave and dignified human being. Yet, while feminists must always challenge stereotypical images of female criminality, we cannot condone violent crimes such as those carried out by Louie Calvert. Her capacity for violence reminds us not to idealise womanhood. While her crimes should not be regarded as 'worse' than those of men simply because of her sex, the absence of gender-specific mitigating circumstances which would help us to explain her antisocial behaviour must be equally recognised. For example, there is no evidence which suggests she was a battered or even intimidated wife, if anything, at least in her relationship with Arthur, the evidence suggests the reverse.[73] Her poverty and deprivation were great, but this did not distinguish her from the vast majority of other women in similar social circumstances who did *not* become criminals. In other words, the existence of women like Louie Calvert forces us to recognise that women's violence cannot always or necessarily be justified or even explained by their victimisation. It reminds us that otherwise sane and 'normal' women, have the *capacity* for heinous violence, even if - compared to men - such incidents are rare as a result of their gender-specific socialisation. There are no gender-specific 'excuses' available which justify Louie Calvert's incessant lies, opportunistic thieving and murderous acts. None of these acts can be reduced

---

[72]*Manchester Evening News* 24th June 1926. p.6.
[73]In the interest of fairness towards Louie Calvert it must be reiterated that *any* evidence - gender specific or otherwise - is extremely sparse in this case. However, even if further evidence had been available, feminist theorists would still be faced with the task of analysing and assessing the exact role of such evidence in relation to Louie Calvert as a rational and social agent. A failure to analyse controversial cases such as Louie's (for example, compared to battered women who kill), would result in the language around violent women remaining inadequate.

to her gender. At the same time it is equally important to recognise that their presence within Louie's personality does not indicate she was more 'masculine' than non-criminal women or that she was 'worse' than her male counterparts as Lombroso would have argued. That these two discourses have been the only ones available so far through which the crimes of Louie Calvert can be understood, demonstrates the limited language in which violent women can currently be discussed. Hence, a new language and new discourses are essential if we are to further our understanding of the complexities of female violence.

While feminist activists have enjoyed considerable success in establishing new discourses around female killers who have themselves been victims of violence, and who, as a result of such discourses, are now able to experience empowerment through regarding themselves as survivors of that violence, we are still faced with the task of creating a new language through which crimes like Louie's can be understood. Her decision to murder a woman as powerless and impoverished as herself, cannot be reduced to female victimisation and oppression within a male dominated society. To do so would be patronising and simplistic, and, as argued in Chapter One, comes dangerously close to arguing on the same terrain as men who have perpetrated sexist myths about women's 'nature' while simultaneously refusing to acknowledge that women, like men, possess both rationality and agency. What we are left with, is a recognition that women, like men, have the capacity to experience the full range of human emotions, including those of aggression, and that in certain situations, they are prepared to act upon them. That such situations occur with less frequency than is the case for men, does not require a biological but a sociological explanation. However, the fact that violent female criminals are comparatively rare, has resulted in such women *automatically* being regarded as extreme and abnormal,[74] thus demonstrating that no discourse is yet available through which female criminality can be understood as routinised and non-pathological in nature. Louie Calvert was a habitual criminal - a recidivist - for whom criminal behaviour had become a way of life (and a means of survival) and hence routinised. Identical behaviour in male criminals is accepted as such, without warranting special attention or pathological explanations.[75]

---

[74]Cameron & Frazer write that "The discourse of our culture ... casts women in only those roles which locate them at extremes: they personify spotless innocence, or else essential wickedness; Snow White or the Wicked Queen" (Cameron, D. & Frazer, E. (1987) *The Lust To Kill* Polity Press, Cambridge, p.147).

[75]This is not to argue that we should merely accept male aggression and criminality as a 'normal' part of masculinity. It has only come to be viewed as such as a result of the frequency with which the two work in tandem. In other words, because violent criminals are overwhelmingly male, masculinity itself has come to be understood as the *cause* of this behaviour. But as in the case for women, sociological rather than biological explanations are required when analysing male violence. Thus, a deconstruction of masculinity within a broader gendered perspective is necessary if we are to understand why violent crime is predominantly a male phenomenon.

Creating a language which can conceptualise and accept women's 'routinised' criminal behaviour, must not however, be done at the *expense* of recently developed feminist discourses which recognise battered women's violence as *exceptional*.[76] Such discourses came about through protracted struggles and in creating a new language which recognises and emphasises female agency and rationality as well as victimisation and oppression, the opportunity exists for a renewed anti-feminist backlash involving the resurrection of old stereotypes of the wicked, scheming and calculating female as discussed in previous chapters. Within this climate women stand to lose the hard-won new terrain on which appeals and retrials have been heard in respect of battered women who kill abusive partners, and who have subsequently been released. In short, a recognition that women's crime may in certain cases be routinised should not cancel out the exceptional and extreme circumstances of some women's crimes. It does not mean that women are 'all the same' or that they are 'really the same as men'.[77] Instead it is a reminder that rash generalisations regarding criminal women must be replaced with a richer, wider and more complex vocabulary which can accommodate the diversity of motivating factors coming into play when women kill.

Unlike the circumstances surrounding women who kill abusive partners, our craving for neat resolutions cannot be easily satisfied in cases like Louie's.[78] Yet, feminism has much to gain from examining these more controversial cases. First, analysing the profusion of motives behind women's violent crime draws attention to its diversity and therefore challenges the limitations of the 'mad/victim or bad' discourse through which almost all women's violence is understood. By challenging this discourse with more controversial female crime, "opportunities for dialogue" emerge which allow for the creation of a new terrain on which these cases can be discussed and understood. On this terrain feminist theorists can build discourses which, as discussed above, emphasise the 'pluralistic, fragmented and contingent' nature of female violence.

We can envisage a second gain for feminism, namely that an expanded understanding of female violence carries with it the opportunity for a fairer treatment of female killers - treating individual defendants according to their specific circumstances as opposed to drawing on the 'mad' discourse as a strategy for obtaining lighter sentences, or being categorised 'bad' -

---

[76]As was the case for example with Kiranjit Ahluwalia who had no history of violence prior to killing her abusive and violent husband, and who has not engaged in violence since his death more than a decade ago (Ahluwalia, K. & Gupta, R. (1997) *Circle of Light* HarperCollins, London).

[77]For discussions of a politics of difference see Di Stefano, C. (1990) 'Dilemmas of Difference: Feminism, Modernity, and Postmodernism' and Hartsock, N. (1990) 'Foucault on Power: A Theory for Women?' both in Nicholson, L.J. (ed) *Feminism/Postmodernism* Routledge, London pp.63-82; pp.157-75.

[78]See Bell & Fox 1996:487 on the subject of resolutions.

resulting in an unduly harsh sentence.[79] Furthermore, undermining the 'mad or bad' discourse would provide an opportunity to "evade dominant knowledges and generate new knowledges from repressed common senses",[80] thus fulfilling an important goal for feminist epistemology in general and for standpoint feminism in particular.

Lastly, deconstructing less 'justifiable' murders may be of direct benefit to the defendants themselves in terms of personal empowerment. A fundamental principle of feminist research is to empower the researched. To achieve this feminists can share newly produced knowledge with the researched, thus creating the possibility not only for personal empowerment at an individual level, but also for making alliances which may eventually result in social and legal changes. The feminist struggle to achieve such changes becomes more powerful each time the life-stories of women like Louie Calvert are excavated because such excavation increases our overall knowledge about women of the past. As feminism generates new ways of describing violent women, and a new language in which they can be understood, the contribution of Louie Calvert and the other women within this chapter to this process will become increasingly apparent. In this way newly generated feminist knowledge can help bring an end to several decades of invisibility and muteness of powerless and dispossessed women like Louie Calvert.

The Case of Margaret Allen

The majority of women's crimes of violence ... almost certainly have their origin in a biological circumstance, possibly aggravated by external factors. Very numerous crimes can be traced to distorted maternal emotion (the murders of many children), the after-effects of the suffering of child-birth (infanticide), menstruation (unpremeditated crime), unsatisfactory sexual relations (the murder of a husband or lover), the menopause (violence by hitherto stable

---

[79]Whilst recognising that women (and men) who are certified clinically insane may receive an indeterminate sentence, the 'mad' discourse has a much wider definition that includes terms such as 'diminished responsibility' and - with specific reference to women - 'Battered Woman Syndrome' which may result in a more lenient sentence. This point is further analysed in the conclusion where I discuss the case of Sara Thornton who had a charge of murder reduced to one of manslaughter after being identified as suffering from a 'personality disorder.' See also Ballinger (1996) where I argue that Marie Fahmy qualified for the 'mad' rather than the 'bad' category, simply by displaying 'appropriate' feminine characteristics such as hysteria, incompetence and irrationality, coupled with a general dazed and confused state which indicated she was a woman "ruled by her emotions" (p.7; p.8).

[80]Cain, M. (1990) 'Realist philosophy and standpoint epistemologies or feminist criminology as a successor science' in Gelsthorpe, L. & Morris, A. (eds) *Feminist Perspectives in Criminology* Open University Press, Milton Keynes p.125.

middle-aged women), pregnancy (a few murders of toddlers by over-worked mothers), and Lesbianism (a few murders of women by other women).[81]

It was largely the effects of being a lesbian that led to the circumstances in which 'Bill' Allen murdered Mrs Chadwick and her masculine nature made it possible for her to use violence. If she had been a woman, with a woman's instincts, she would have lashed Mrs Chadwick with her tongue or thrown the nearest piece of crockery, but she would have struck her with nothing more lethal than the back of her hand.[82]

Throughout this book I have argued against the routinised pathologising of female violence and have suggested instead that those interested in creating a new language through which such violence may be understood should keep issues of rationality and agency at the forefront of analyses. This does not, of course, preclude the possibility that violent behaviour in women may occasionally be connected to aspects of their pathology. Yet, as the cases of Margaret Allen and Styllou Christofi (discussed later in this chapter) illustrate, doubts about or concern over the mental health of female murderers did not result in a commutation of the death sentence. The next two case-studies thus illustrate the ease with which discourses of madness can, under certain circumstances be undermined - leading to an ironic (and tragic) situation where, despite a long history of *over-pathologising* violent women in general, specific women whose mental condition *ought* to cause concern, are in fact declared 'normal' after the most preliminary examination and hence judged fit to suffer the ultimate punishment.

Margaret Allen, the 20th of 22 children, had spent all her life in poverty in a small mill town in Lancashire, living with her mother until her death when Margaret was 37. At that time she was a bus-conductress but by June 1946 she resigned her position owing to frequent spells of dizziness and vertigo.[83] Her poverty was now more acute than ever; at the same time both her mental health and her home surroundings were deteriorating. As Margaret felt herself become depressed, lonely and isolated, her tiny rented house became increasingly dirty and neglected to the point where it was infested with lice. She could no longer cook food as she had sold her stove in a futile attempt to overcome her mounting debts.[84] At the time of her trial in December 1948, Margaret owed £15.4.0 rent and over three years' supply of electricity totalling £8.13.10.[85] She also owed £12 to her local grocer and

---

[81]Wilson 1971:282.

[82]Huggett & Berry 1956:192.

[83]Huggett & Berry 1956:192-4.

[84]Wilson 1971:295.

[85]ASSI 52/629 Testimonies of John Naylor Murgatroyd - Estate Clerk, and Frederick Hall King - Chief Collector of Rawtenstall Corporation p.22. The Margaret Allen case-file is closed to the public until 2024 but is available for inspection by special

had borrowed several small sums of money from family and neighbours.[86] She had no hope of clearing these debts as her entire weekly income consisted of 11 shillings "from the Public Assistance" and 26 shillings "from the National Health Sick."[87]

Apart from the sheer struggle to survive on a daily basis Margaret also experienced social difficulties as a result of her lesbianism or transsexualism. We cannot know for certain whether she was a lesbian or a transsexual for she did not have access to the language which expresses sexuality in those terms.[88] Instead she claimed to have had an operation which "had changed her sex"[89], wore men's clothes, had her hair cut in male style, preferred to be known as 'Bill', "spoke in a deep voice"[90], "and pretended to be a man."[91]

We can only guess at the isolation and alienation Margaret experienced as a middle-aged woman, suffering from "funny moods"[92], and living in abject poverty in a tiny mill-town as a lesbian/transsexual in the 1940s. Annie Cook, her only friend, described her as having "completely let

---

arrangement with staff at The Lord Chancellor's Department, Trevelyan House, 30 Great Peter Street, London SW1 2BY, and will henceforth be quoted as ASSI 52/629.

[86]ASSI 52/629 Testimony of Douglas McLeod Walton p.23.

[87]ASSI 52/629 Statement made by Margaret Allen to Police 31st August 1948.

[88]According to Dekker & van de Pol the concept 'transsexuality' was introduced by D. Cauldwell in 1949, the year Margaret was executed, and was not popularised until the 1960s by Harry Benjamin (Dekker, R.M. & van de Pol, L. (1989) *The Tradition of Female Transvestism in Early Modern Europe* Macmillan, London p.64).

[89]*Liverpool Daily Post* 13th January 1949 p.3. Annie Cook giving evidence at Margaret Allen's trial. It is extremely unlikely Margaret had had an actual sex-change operation. According to Janice Raymond such operations were not available in USA until 1945, and were initially performed exclusively on men (*The Transsexual Empire* (1980) Women's Press, London). Even if British medical professionals had scientific knowledge and hospital facilities to perform such an operation over 50 years ago, Margaret's poverty would have prevented her from taking advantage of this surgery as the National Health Service was not established until after the Second World War. We can only speculate that Margaret may have had another operation, perhaps a hysterectomy, which helped her to make sense of her sexuality. Alternatively, it is possible that no operation took place, instead it was Margaret's way of explaining her sexuality. Dekker and van de Pol write that until the end of the 18th century "sex was seen as an exclusively heterosexual act ... Women who fell in love with other women therefore often doubted their gender, and ... female cross-dressing offered them the solution of 'changing into a man.'" (Dekker & van de Pol 1989:69-70). Although referring to an earlier era, it is strongly reminiscent of Margaret's understanding of her own sexuality.

[90]*Daily Mirror* 2nd September 1948.

[91]*Manchester Evening News* 8th December 1948 front-page. Annie Cook under cross-examination.

[92]ASSI 52/629 Margaret Allen's statement to police 1st September 1948.

herself go."[93] This then, was the context in which she murdered an elderly widow, Nancy Chadwick. The sheer pointlessness of the murder together with Margaret's behaviour immediately after it, reinforces the suspicion that she may not have been fully responsible for her actions.

Nancy Chadwick's body was found outside Margaret's home early in the morning of 29th August 1948. When she was interviewed by police during routine inquiries, she denied all knowledge of the body and was not under suspicion. When police divers dragged the river Irwell Margaret was amongst the locals watching, and it was she who drew a police officer's attention to a bag floating on the surface which turned out be Nancy's.[94] The following day Margaret was asked to make a statement at the police station.[95] She stated she had promised to obtain extra sugar for Nancy for some time but had been unsuccessful.[96] On the morning in question she saw Nancy outside her house, who "asked if she could come in for a look, but I said she couldn't because I was in a hurry ... She has never been right inside my house. That was the last time I saw her."[97] She also gave an account of her movements for the entire day, and claimed she had never had a row with Nancy.

The following day police officers revisited Margaret and searched her house. When questioned about what looked like bloodspots, Margaret made no reply. When they found wet rags and asked what they were:

> The Accused made no reply and walked away to the sofa, picked up her macintosh and said "Come on, I'll tell you all about it". I again cautioned her and she said "Let's get out of here". We then walked to the front door ... and as the Accused passed the coal cellar she said "That's where I put her." ... When in the Office she said "I will now tell you the truth".[98]

When charged with Nancy's murder, Margaret replied "I did",[99] thus becoming one of only two executed women during the 20th century to admit their crime before standing trial. After admitting having lied in previous statements she gave the following account:

> ... Mrs Chadwick came round the corner. She asked me if this was where I lived and could she come in. I told her I was going out. I was in a funny mood and she just seemed to get on my nerves although she hadn't said anything. I told her to go as I was going out

---

[93]Huggett & Berry 1956:197, who interviewed Annie Cook for their book.

[94]ASSI 52/629 Testimony of Detective Police Constable Joseph Blinston.

[95]ASSI 52/629 Testimony of Chief Detective Inspector Robert Stevens.

[96]Rationing was still enforced in 1948.

[97]ASSI 52/629 Exhibit 11. Margaret Allen's first statement to police 31st August 1948.

[98]ASSI 52/629 Testimony of Chief Detective Inspector Robert Stevens pp.14-16.

[99]ASSI 52/629 Charge Form dated 1st September 1948.

and she could see me some time else but she seemed somehow to insist on coming in. I just happened to look round and saw a hammer in the kitchen. By this time we were talking just inside the kitchen with the front door shut. On the spur of the moment I hit her with the hammer. She gave a shout that seemed to start me off more. I hit her a few times but I don't know how many. I then pulled the body in my coal house. It was there all day. I've told you where I was all day ... I went to bed about ten to eleven o'clock. I slept but I couldn't tell you how long. When I woke the thought of what was downstairs made me keep awake. I went downstairs. I couldn't tell you the time because the clocks are broke ... My intention was to try and pull her to the river and dispose of the body but it was too heavy and I just put it on the road. I went back to bed and didn't get up again until the officer came to the door ... I went back to bed and went to sleep. Just before I put the body out I went round the corner and threw the bag in the river ... the hammer head I hit her with I threw some distance up the river ... I looked in the bag but there was no money in there. *I didn't actually kill her for that. I had one of my funny moods ... I had no reason at all. It seemed to come over me.* After she shouted after the first hit that seemed to set me off.[100]

The murder had been extremely violent with Nancy suffering at least ten separate blows to the head resulting in the entire vault of the skull being fractured.[101] Nancy's purse was never found and the prosecution argued the motive for the murder was robbery. As can be seen from Margaret's statement above, she denied this. Instead she claimed to have had "no reason at all", the killing having taken place as a result of one of her "funny moods." Moreover, when arrested Margaret had only 4s 5d on her, and having confessed to the murder there would seem little point in lying about any robbery which may have transpired.[102]

Her demeanour immediately after committing the murder was described by Annie Cook: "She seemed a bit queer to me and kept giggling and staring."[103] Prior to the murder Margaret would often sit "with her head in her hands complaining of severe headaches", and had on one occasion attempted suicide in front of Annie.[104] Such behaviour took place within the

---

[100]ASSI 52/629 Exhibit 14 Statement made by Margaret Allen 1st September 1948. My emphasis.
[101]ASSI 52/629 Testimony of Dr Gilbert Bailey p.8.
[102]Huggett & Berry 1956:196. Huggett & Berry who conducted interviews with the villagers of Rawtenstall who knew Margaret, suggested a possible motive for the killing: that Nancy who was renowned for being miserly, had lent Margaret money which she may have insisted on having returned. However, as Margaret borrowed money from several other individuals, she must have found herself in such situations regularly. Overall, it does not seem an adequate murder motive.
[103]ASSI 52/629 Testimony of Annie Cook p.17.
[104]Huggett & Berry 1956:197 - interview with Annie Cook.

context of Margaret having had to give up work as a result of the "mood-swings" and "giddiness" noted earlier. Indeed, her illness must have been officially recognised as she was receiving "National Health Sick".[105] Yet despite this history of mental anguish no medical report is included in her file. However, the senior medical officer at Strangeways prison felt able to offer an opinion. At her trial he testified "he had had Allen under observation since early in September and had found her quite normal."[106]

It was within this context that Margaret was about to stand the shortest trial of any of the 15 women executed during the 20th century. The entire trial lasted only five hours, which must be recognised as a contributing factor to the slimness of her file and the lack of newspaper reports. *There simply was not very much to report.* Even the trial for her life appeared inadequate and mean, another indication of her poverty and powerlessness as well as how little she was valued as a human being.

Margaret entered the dock dressed in full male attire: a fawn overcoat, dark trousers, a checked shirt and "a brightly striped tie."[107] She therefore made no concessions to conventions of femininity for her court-appearance, as discussed in Chapter One. If anything, Margaret gave every sign of being proud of what she termed her "manhood" and pleased that "she was often mistaken for a man by strangers."[108] The unconventional image she subsequently presented may have been the reason her Counsel decided she should not give evidence, instead her statement was quoted in its entirety. Her defence counsel entered a plea of insanity and invited the jury "to commiserate with an unstable woman passing through the change of life, an abnormal woman who had declared that an operation had 'made her into a man', an unbalanced woman who had committed a 'purposeless, fatuous and mad murder'."[109] Margaret had not claimed provocation, did not express regret or remorse and could not even provide a motive - three factors which in their own right ought to have raised doubts about her state of mind. This was not the view of Mr Justice Sellars who in his summing up "said the defence had invited the jury to bring in a special verdict, that of guilty, but insane. He did not think there was any evidence such as the law required to bring in such a verdict."[110] The jury of three women and nine men appeared to be in agreement with the judge for they took less than 15 minutes to return a guilty verdict with no recommendation to mercy.[111] Margaret did not appeal against her sentence.

---

[105] According to Huggett & Berry 1956:104, Margaret had seen a doctor five times within a 12-day period in 1945 for vertigo.

[106] *Manchester Guardian* 9th December 1948 p.6.

[107] Huggett & Berry 1956:189.

[108] *Daily Mirror* 2nd September 1948.

[109] Mr W. Gorman, Q.C. quoted in Huggett & Berry 1956:189.

[110] *Manchester Guardian* 9th December 1948 p.6.

[111] Huggett & Berry 1956:189-90.

A Woman Called Bill: Punishing the 'Abnormal'

The post-war climate in Britain was extremely hostile to gay men and lesbian women with prosecutions for homosexuality reaching a peak in 1953.[112] Three years before Margaret's trial one sexologist wrote:

> Homosexuality is to a very large extent an acquired abnormality and propagates itself as a morally contagious disease ... The growth of a homosexual society in any country is a menace, more or less serious, to the welfare of the state.[113]

Some 'experts' went further in their condemnation of lesbianism - insisting it was connected to criminal behaviour and mental illness:

> ... lesbians were likely to commit serious crimes or even be psychopaths ... when crimes by women were investigated it was often revealed that "the women were either confirmed lesbians who killed because of jealousy or were latent homosexuals with a strong aggressive masculine drive". Some lesbians ... "manifest pronounced sadistic and psychopathic trends". They were also likely to be kleptomaniacs. The vast majority were "emotionally unstable and neurotic".[114]

Being a lesbian does not of course exclude the possibility of suffering from mental illness or neurosis. This is very different however, from the biologically determinist opinion expressed in the above quote which, despite being written over 60 years after Lombroso and Ferrero's *Female Offender* echoes this work. The stigmatising and pathologising of lesbians thus has a long history and has taken many forms, sometimes emphasising physical abnormality, other times psychological abnormality, but always the implication is the same: a lesbian is a person who is *damaged* in some way - an abnormal person.[115] This abnormality, however, is not of the type likely to activate discourses of the violent woman as 'mad' as is the case, for

---

[112]Jeffreys, S. (1990) *Anticlimax* The Women's Press, London. There were 82 prosecutions in 1938 compared to 3,305 in 1953 (p.56).
[113]Thomas V. Moore quoted in Jeffreys 1990:51.
[114]Jeffreys 1990:55 referring to Frank Caprio's *Female Homosexuality* (1957).
[115]See for example Kelley, J. (1967) *When the Gates Shut* Longmans, London, esp pp.45-6 where she describes lesbians as "psychologically damaged women" who are "immature and unable to face a normal adult man-woman relationship." This damage may have come about as a result of having been raped or having had an incestuous relationship as a child. See also Jeffreys, S. (1985) *The Spinster and Her Enemies* Pandora, London, p.112 where she discusses Freud's theory that homosexuality comes about as a result of childhood trauma. See also Faith 1993:213.

example, with women committing infanticide.[116] Instead the tendency has been to uncritically equate lesbianism with masculinity and masculinity with violence, a point which the above quote exemplifies.[117] A lesbian is therefore caught in a double negative - while her deviant sexuality has resulted in her being pathologised, it is not a 'feminine' pathology such as that of puerperal psychosis for example, associated with infanticide. Instead it is a pathology which reinforces her deviant sexuality and underlines her lack of femininity - her non-womanhood. It is these features which allow the lesbian to be classified as pathological and 'bad' simultaneously. A lesbian is the ultimate 'unruly woman' who stands outside any of the control mechanisms discussed in Chapter Three, which normally operate to ensure appropriate female behaviour. Nothing about Margaret Allen signalled her membership of a subordinate group. On the contrary, she moved about freely and alone in public places such as pubs, smoking and drinking heavily when she could afford it. She was not part of a family whose members could regulate her movements, she had no children and did not cook, indeed she was so utterly undomesticated that her house was infested with lice. Margaret's existence, far from being dominated by the 'patriarchal gaze', was an example of a total failure to internalise any of the disciplinary practices of femininity that Foucauldian feminists have identified. She had stepped so far beyond the boundaries of acceptable female conduct and behaviour that she had abandoned her femininity altogether. In short, she had taken on the identity of a male. She even killed like a man - battering someone to death with a hammer. But she was *not* a man, she was a woman *acting* like a man which made her "more terrible than any man."[118] Margaret Allen thus epitomised the doubly deviant woman, constructed as a result of the double standards applied to female criminals, because, unlike men for whom the essence of their being - masculinity - is presented as the motive for most of their crimes,[119] Margaret's crime was seen as an extension of her dramatic deviation from appropriate feminine conduct.

A further insight into how lesbians are pathologised and yet remain within the 'bad' rather than the 'mad' category may be gained by examining the state's response to lesbianism. Lynda Hart for example, takes issue with historians who claim the state has largely ignored or tolerated lesbianism, and instead sees the state's failure to legislate against it in 1921 as a deliberate

---

[116]See Morris, A. & Wilczynski, A. (1993) 'Rocking the cradle' in Birch, H. (ed) *Moving Targets* Virago, London, where they argue the Infanticide Act is overused in order to pathologise women killing their children, since "such an act cannot be the act of a *normal* woman. She cannot have been fully responsible for her actions; she must need help or treatment" (p.206). Emphasis in the original. This is supported by studies indicating that in England and Hong Kong "about half of the mothers convicted of infanticide could not actually have been described as suffering from any mental disorder" (p.207).

[117]Faith, K. (1993) *Unruly Women* Gang Press, Vancouver, p.98.

[118]Hart 1994:12 quoting Lombroso.

[119]Hart 1994:13 referring to Ngaire Naffine's 'Masculinity Theory'.

strategy employed for the specific purpose of preserving the dominant category of 'woman' as white, middle-class, maternal and passive. This theory is supported by the legislators' concern that the creation of a law banning lesbianism would draw attention to the subject:

> You are going to tell the whole world that there is such an offence, to bring it to the notice of women who have never heard of it, never thought of it, never dreamt of it. I think that is a very great mischief.[120]

In short, creating a new law may have the unwanted consequence of also creating a new discourse through which women can experience their sexual identity. The failure to legislate against lesbianism did not, however, result in its disappearance but meant that it entered discourse as a secret "that could be kept from 'women' - white, middle- and upper-class wives and daughters of the legislators," a process designed "to maintain and construct a category of 'women' that was purified, un-mixed with racial and class differences." Thus, at the very time these women were threatening the category 'woman' by showing an interest in lesbianism, it became displaced unto "women of color and working-class women."[121] The discursive lesbian was now someone opposite to the *normal* woman - an *inverted* woman - someone who is *like a man*, recognised by her male characteristics, particularly those of sexual assertiveness, aggression and violence. This process therefore has a secondary benefit for the stabilisation of the category 'woman' because it also displaces female aggression onto the sexually deviant woman.

It is within this context Margaret Allen had to be turned into a 'non-woman' and thus excluded from discourses of 'madness' available only to women who obey the codes of behaviour surrounding femininity. In proudly proclaiming her deviant sexuality Margaret disrupted not only "the fiction of the gendered conflation of femininity with passivity",[122] but also the illusion of sexual identity as stable. Such disruption, although regarded as a threat to the social order generally, was of particular significance in post-war Britain, the time of Margaret's trial, when the state was struggling to gain control of the social disruption caused by the war. Amidst fears "of an imminent collapse of the family"[123], the task before the state was one of major social reconstruction involving the restoring and strengthening of family life. This was embarked upon by focusing on women and marriage in the belief that a stable family life prevented delinquency and crime whilst preserving the

---

[120]Lord Desart quoted in Hart 1994:3.

[121]Hart 1994:6; 4.

[122]Hart 1994:17.

[123]Smart, C. (1981) 'Law and the Control of Women's Sexuality: The Case of the 1950s' in Hutter, B. & Williams, G. (eds) (1981) *Controlling Women* Croom Helm, London p.47.

social order.[124] Apart from considering the moral implications of homosexuality and lesbianism,[125] the state was therefore already preoccupied with other forms of behaviour deemed threatening to family life such as divorce, illegitimacy and prostitution, which resulted in "legislation on sexual behaviour", the aim being to ensure sexual activity took place within marriage only:

> Such legislation was overtly orientated towards maintaining family stability, reproducing, in some instances, patriarchal relations within the family, and containing and controlling social change that was seen as harmful to the family.[126]

This was the context in which "the recognition of lesbianism as a matrimonial offence was suggested"[127], and although such legislation was never implemented, it nevertheless provides an insight into the social, political and moral climate at the time of Margaret Allen's trial. It also widens our understanding of Margaret's classification as a 'bad' woman despite serious concern about her mental state being expressed, not only by those who knew her and observed her behaviour, but also by her local MP who made a last-minute plea to the Home Secretary to spare her life on the grounds of her mental condition.[128] The discourses around Margaret's deviant sexuality, however, overrode discourses of madness. Margaret had become a monster, demonised through a combination of discourses so unified that they could withstand any challenge made on her behalf - so dominant that it had become impossible to 'hear' her story through any other discourse. Judicial misogyny had been translated into judicial homophobia and during that process the meaning of Margaret's experience was lost as her account became muted.

Her case illustrates that it is only certain types of 'madness' - those that fit the dominant model of female madness - which permit a woman to be heard through the 'mad' discourse. Indeed her Counsel appeared to be aware of this for, as noted above, he attempted to link Margaret's 'madness' to a

---

[124]Wilson, E. (1980) *Only Halfway to Paradise* Tavistock, London, p.88; Smart 1981:47-8.

[125]Wilson writes that although the Wolfenden Report published in 1957, recommended decriminalisation of the *private* practice of homosexuality, it was nevertheless the case that "in the political climate of the fifties to suggest that homosexuality might be a matter of moral indifference was heretical." She adds: "In general sexuality outside marriage belonged to the twilight area of 'unlawful sexual intercourse', and effectively the Wolfenden recommendations in relation to homosexuality meant that homosexual behaviour would also be included within this grey area" (Wilson 1980: 101; 102).

[126]Smart 1981:57.

[127]Wilson 1980:73.

[128]G.H. Walker, Labour MP for Rossendale to Home Secretary Chuter Ede. Reported in *Liverpool Daily Post* 12th January 1949.

more acceptable form of pathology - that of the menopause - when he declared she was 'unstable' as a result of "passing through the change of life." The menopause, like menstruation, childbirth and lactation, are ultra-feminine conditions which have all played a role in categorising women "as labile, unstable, at the mercy of a biology which ... leaves us open to all manner of ailments and adversities."[129] They are also conditions which emphasise a woman's femininity, and hence provide 'legitimate' discourses through which a woman's 'madness' may be articulated. Lesbianism and cross-dressing do not. Lesbianism negates femininity and amplifies perversion. No reference to 'feminine conditions' could undercut the perversion associated with Margaret Allen. Hence, Justice Sellars could not accept a verdict of 'guilty but insane', and the Home Secretary could not accept Mr Walker's plea for clemency:

> I am sorry to say that after having carefully considered all the circumstances of the case and having caused a special inquiry to be made as to Miss Allen's mental condition, I regret that I have not been able to find any grounds which would justify me in advising the King to interfere with the due course of justice.[130]

Public opinion appeared to agree with those of establishment figures, for Annie Cook eventually had to abandon the petition she had instigated because she was unable to obtain more than 100 signatures.[131] The only other person who attempted to influence the Home Secretary's decision to allow the execution to proceed was the Rev Austin Lee, who made no pretence of speaking for Margaret but objected to the hanging on behalf of the prison staff:

> In the name of humanity beg you stop the hanging of Margaret Allen ... because of the terrible effect on the prison officers concerned.[132]

---

[129]Ussher, J. (1991) *Women's Madness* HarvesterWheatsheaf, Hemel Hempstead, p.249. See also Ehrenreich, B. & English, D. (1979) *For Her Own Good* Pluto, London, who refer to medical literature which describes the menopause "as a terminal illness - the 'death of the woman in the woman.'" (p.111); Matus, J. (1995) *Unstable Bodies* Manchester University Press, Manchester. Referring to the Victorian era, she reminds us of the long history of the association between women's reproductive organs and mental instability: "The onset of menses and the process of menopause were equally high risk periods in which minds might become unhinged" (pp.198-9).

[130]*Liverpool Daily Post* 12th January 1949. The special inquiry referred to was a statutory inquiry led by Sir Norman East and took place over a two-day period, 27-28th December 1948. (Information obtained by personal communication with the Planning Directorate, Strangeways Prison, Manchester.)

[131]The Rossendale Labour Party continued the petition and eventually obtained 300 signatures in a town of 26,000 inhabitants (*Manchester Guardian* 12th January 1949; Huggett & Berry 1956:208).

[132]*Liverpool Daily Post* 12th January 1949, telegram to the King.

Beg you to intervene to prevent men and women prison officers being degraded and to prevent possible suicide or insanity, by having to drag Margaret Allen to the scaffold.[133]

As noted earlier, Margaret had not appealed against her sentence which would have delayed her execution. She did however, make two simple requests. On 4th January 1949 she learned the Home Secretary would not be recommending a reprieve and as the execution had been set for 12th January, Margaret requested a four-day postponement which would have enabled her to experience Annie's birthday. She also requested a visit from Annie without prison guards being present. Both requests were denied. In the four and a half months since her arrest Annie Cook had been her only visitor, and on the night before her execution Margaret wrote to her:

Just a few lines to thank you and your family for what you have done for me. I cannot put into writing just how I feel, but, once again, thank you for making my last few hours happy by holding on to me, and don't forget what I told you this afternoon to look after yourself ... I cannot say any more, but God bless you all.[134]

The letter also contained Margaret's will which stated: "I, Margaret Allen, wish to leave all my personal property to Annie Cook." This property consisted of a photo of Margaret's mother, a lighter, cuff links, a crucifix and 4s 5 1/2d.[135] Outside Strangeways prison 300 people had been waiting "in the bitter cold since 7am" for her execution on 12th January, but during Annie's last visit Margaret had requested that she should not be amongst them.[136] Instead she had said:

You know the time tomorrow. I don't want you to wait outside the prison. I want you to be at our old meeting place on the main road outside Rawtenstall. As I walk to the scaffold I will think of you - at the end of the road.[137]

Annie fulfilled her promise and - as the execution took place - stood weeping on the agreed location while approximately "40 people watched

---

[133]*Liverpool Daily Post* 12th January 1949, telegram to the Queen. The Rev Austin Lee, who worked at St Stephen's Hounslow London, may of course have formulated his pleas for clemency in this manner because he believed prison staff would be regarded more sympathetically than Margaret Allen.

[134]Margaret Allen's letter to Annie Cook, reproduced in *Manchester Evening News* 13th January 1949.

[135]*Manchester Evening News* 13th January 1949; Huggett & Berry 1956:196.

[136]*Manchester Evening News* 12th January 1949.

[137]Annie Cook being interviewed by the *Daily Mirror* 12th January 1949.

from the opposite corner."[138]   "Other women jeered at Mrs Cook as she sobbed ..."[139]

In 1956 Huggett and Berry, in an attempt to make sense of Margaret's execution, wrote: "It is as if the case belongs to a harsher age and an earlier civilisation." Commenting on the lack of public interest in the case they suggested that "her peculiarly unhappy life was too far removed from general experience to evoke any response from ordinary people."[140]   Those of us engaged in developing feminist theory would add that Margaret's execution - taking place only eight months after MPs had voted in favour of suspending the death penalty,[141] and murderers such as Donald Thomas were reprieved[142] - was also part of the struggle to preserve the category 'woman' at a time when the social order was perceived as being under threat. In a final twist of irony, after 13 years of wearing male clothing, Margaret was issued with a statutory striped prison dress in which she met her death. During Annie's last visit she said:

> I am going to have chicken for dinner and a few bottles before they put a rope round my neck. I shall be dead on Wednesday. It would help if I could cry but my manhood holds back my tears.[143]

There is no record of Margaret's final moments, but we may assume she would have approved of going down in history as having 'died like a man.'

---

[138]*Liverpool Daily Post* 13th January 1949 p.3.

[139]*Daily Mirror* 13th January 1949 p.5.

[140]Huggett & Berry 1956:208; 205. Huggett & Berry are arguably the only authors until now who have attempted to research her case in depth from a humane and sympathetic perspective.

[141]This motion was tabled in November 1947. The suspension was for a duration of five years. The motion was moved by Labour MP Sidney Silverman on 14th April 1948. It was passed by 245 to 222 votes. For details of the parliamentary debate on capital punishment see *Parliamentary Debates House of Commons* Vol 449 6th-23rd April 1948 cols 979-1094. Consequently all prisoners awaiting execution had their sentences commuted "by means of conditional pardons during the period which would elapse before the Bill became law" (Gattey, C.N. (1972) *The Incredible Mrs van der Elst* Leslie Frewin Publishers, London, pp.201-2). However, in June the House of Lords, reversed the House of Commons' decision by voting 181 to 28 against the Bill and executions were resumed.

[142]Jackson, S. (1978) *The Old Bailey* W.H. Allen, London pp.195-6. See also Huggett & Berry 1956:209 who wrote that Thomas "fired three shots at Police Constable Edgar, and showing no mercy, fired again as the dying policeman lay at his feet."

[143]Huggett & Berry 1956:208.

The Case of Styllou Christofi

> This was a stupid murder by a stupid woman of the illiterate peasant type.[144]

> Here was no murder for money, or intrigue, or petty gain. Here was a full-blooded slaughter for mother-love, vengeance, hatred. It was as simple and primitive as Oedipus, and as cruel.[145]

Throughout this book I have argued that the discourse of motherhood is of paramount importance when women stand trial. A 'bad' mother is likely to be judged for her lack of 'the maternal instinct' *as well* as for her crime. Yet a mother who loves with too much intensity - who is too possessive of her children - is no longer a good mother, for instead of being self-sacrificing she has become greedy and needy - a threatening figure who is out of control. The case of Styllou Christofi is an example of the 'good' mother going out of control - someone incapable of setting boundaries in this role - taking it to the extreme of murdering her daughter-in-law in order to 'protect' her son and grandchildren. Styllou crossed the boundaries of 'good' mothering by abusing her power and control over her children, and failing to accept her son's right to an individual and independent life.[146] Instead of fitting into the role of altruistic mother and loving grandmother, she had become a controlling and manipulating woman, thus fitting into another stereotype - the 'dragon-like' mother-in law.

Styllou Christofi was a Greek-Cypriot who had arrived in England in 1953 to visit her son Stavros and his family. At the time of the murder she had stayed with him, his German wife, Hella and their three children for a year, supposedly to look for work to earn money to buy a plot of land in Cyprus. During that year tension had arisen on several occasions between Hella and Stavros, a modern London couple who both worked outside the home, and Styllou, an illiterate 'peasant' woman who had been married at 14, and whose "basic mental capacity ... [was] not high."[147] This tension had resulted in Styllou moving out on three occasions, although she had been living with the family continuously during the four months prior to the murder.[148]

---

[144]Mr Christmas Humphreys QC prosecuting. Quoted in *Manchester Evening News* 25th October 1954.

[145]Huggett & Berry 1956:228.

[146]See discussion of the 'perverse' mother in Welldon, E.V. (1992) *Mother, Madonna, Whore* Guildford Press, New York.

[147]CRIM 1/2492. Medical Report on Styllou Christofi by PMO Thomas Christie, dated 5th October 1954. She had never received schooling and could not write even her name. Styllou Christofi's file is closed to the public but permission to inspect it may be obtained by arrangement with the Supreme Court Unit Manager, at the Royal Courts of Justice, LondonWC2A 2LL.

[148]CRIM 1/2492. Exhibit 18 - statement of Styllou Christofi dated 29th July 1954.

Styllou was incapable of applying the self-control necessary to prevent herself from interfering in her adult children's lives:

> [She] related that her other son (in Cyprus) had married a wanton woman, not fit to look after the children of the marriage, and that all offers of help from her (Mrs Christofi) were rebuffed, and she had to leave the house, and so her grandchildren had no moral protection.[149]

Now Styllou had repeated this pattern by voicing an identical (and equally unfounded) attitude towards her second daughter-in-law. Consequently the strain was so great that it was agreed Hella should take a holiday with the children, and Styllou was asked to return to Cyprus before they returned. However, two weeks prior to Hella's departure, she was murdered. It was a particularly gruesome murder with Hella first being beaten with a metal ash-plate, then strangled with her eldest son's scarf and finally having paraffin poured over her body and set alight.[150] A neighbour noticed a body "surrounded by a circle of flames" in the Christofis' garden, but he took it "to be a wax model lying in the fire."[151] He also saw Styllou:

> She came right into the area, bent over the body and gave me the impression that she was about to stir the fire up. The fire was dying down. Having recognised the accused, I thought all was in order and I returned to my garden and then my house.[152]

Styllou denied all knowledge of the murder. She claimed to have woken up after having been asleep in bed for several hours. Smelling smoke, she went to investigate, whereupon she found Hella's burning body over which she threw water.[153] She then ran into the street, stopped a car and said "Please come, fire burning, children sleeping." When Mr and Mrs Burstoff, the occupants of the car, asked if the body was that of Styllou's son she replied: "No, my son marry German girl he like, plenty clothes, plenty shoes, babies going to Germany."[154]

The evidence against Styllou however, was compelling, and her failure to acknowledge or respond to this demonstrated a certain naiveté which prompted Mr Humphreys, the prosecutor to call her:

---

[149]CRIM 1/2492 Medical Report dated 5th October 1954. Styllou Christofi related this in a conversation with Holloway PMO Thomas Christie.

[150]CRIM 1/2492 Testimony of pathologist Francis Edward Camps 26th August 1954.

[151]CRIM 1/2492 Testimony of John Byres Young 26th August 1954. Hella was employed in the garment industry and owned a mannequin dummy.

[152]CRIM 1/2492 Testimony of John Byres Young 26th August 1954.

[153]CRIM 1/2492 Exhibit 18 - Styllou Christofi's statement 29th July 1954.

[154]CRIM 1/2492 Testimony of Fanny & Harry Burstoff 26th August 1954.

> ... a stupid woman ... [who] really believed that after washing the floor she could eliminate bloodstains, and that with a small tin of paraffin she could so burn a body that it could not be recognised.[155]

When Mr Humphreys employed such condemnatory tones he may have had some of the following evidence in mind: the clothes that Hella had been wearing when murdered had been washed and were still in the pail when police arrived; the empty Daz packet which would have contained soap for washing the clothes, was found inside an ornament in Styllou's room; Hella's wedding ring which she never removed, had also been hidden in Styllou's room, "wrapped in cellophane paper."[156] Styllou's shoes were soaked in both paraffin and blood and her bed had not been slept in.[157] Her ring and bracelet "gave a general reaction for blood."[158] Moreover, the scarf with which Hella had been strangled, had been cut into four pieces, three of which were found in the dustbin, causing Mr Humphreys to comment: "So this is a murderess who is remarkably tidy in clearing away the evidence of the murder."[159] Finally, there were no signs of forced entry into the house. Altogether, the evidence was so strong that Styllou was always the only suspect.

Styllou could speak almost no English and during her initial police interview in the early hours of the morning Stavros acted as translator. She was arrested the following evening when a professional interpreter had been hired. Yet despite the compelling nature of the evidence Styllou maintained her innocence. When she was told an eyewitness had seen her in the garden she made no comment. Instead, after prolonged interrogation she simply replied: "From this story I know nothing more."[160]

As had been the case with Louie Calvert and Margaret Allen, Styllou Christofi was of fleeting interest to both the public and the media. Compared to the trial of Ruth Ellis, which took place only six months after Styllou's execution, and which still holds the power to fascinate the public imagination, Styllou Christofi is an extremely obscure figure. At 53, she was the oldest woman to hang during the 20th century. Heavy set and unglamorous in appearance, she seemed to have no redeeming features. Her crime appeared to be motivated by jealousy and a desire to dominate her son's household. Instead of displaying the feminine characteristics of altruism, docility and gentleness as discussed in Chapter Three, she seemed ungrateful, callous and

---

[155]Opening speech for prosecution quoted in *Daily Mirror* 26th October 1954 p.3.

[156]CRIM 1/2492 Testimony of Det. Sergeant Albert Evans and Det. Superintendent Leonard Crawford. See also testimony of Stavros Christofis all dated 26th August 1954.

[157]CRIM 1/2492 Testimony of Police-Sergeant Edward Welch 26th August 1954.

[158]CRIM 1/2492 Testimony of Lewis Charles Nickolls, director of Forensic Science Laboratory, Scotland Yard, dated 26th August 1954.

[159]Opening speech for prosecution quoted in *Daily Mirror* 26th October 1954. See also CRIM 1/2492 Testimony of Detective-Constable George Claiden.

[160]CRIM 1/2492 Testimony of Detective-Inspector Robert Fenwick 26th August 1954.

domineering - attacking an attractive, young, defenceless mother in a most gruesome manner, who had shown her hospitality and provided a home for her. Moreover, she was *foreign* - a "stupid woman of the peasant type" according to Mr Humphreys. Apart from the implied racism, this comment also suggested atavistic tendencies, which reinforced the image of an unrefined woman lacking in sophistication and feminine attributes, a lack which set her apart from the feminine ideal. This lack had special significance during the 1950s, for as noted above, this decade was preoccupied with preserving the category 'woman'. Consequently, 'feminine attributes' - skills as a homemaker and mother as well as an appropriate and pleasing demeanour - were of special importance during a decade dominated by debates about the role of women and the preservation of family life.

In keeping with the dominant portrayal of Styllou as a possessive and controlling peasant matriarch, the prosecution alleged during the four-day trial that Styllou had been jealous of Hella's "youth and pretty clothes", and that she had thought she "was not wanted and ... [was] being sent home to Cyprus." Styllou, who spoke through an interpreter from the witness-stand replied "never" to all questions asked by the prosecution, and denied she had ever "had any disagreement of a serious kind with her daughter-in-law."[161] However, the jury of ten men and two women, took less than two hours to find her guilty. After having the verdict translated, she was asked if she had anything to say. She responded that she "would like to say something to the court and go into the witness-box."[162] Her request was denied, and she "showed no apparent emotion" as the judge passed the death sentence.[163]

Insane but Fit to Plead: A Contradiction in Terms?

Two months prior to Styllou Christofi's trial when her case was heard in Hampstead Magistrate's Court newspapers reported she was "absolutely bewildered by the proceedings."[164] The Principal Medical Officer at Holloway, Thomas Christie, had had Styllou under observation for over two months and had "seen her frequently" when he wrote his medical report.[165] He and his colleagues had noted she was "hysterical; very distressed; restless; aggressive; sitting in bed, screaming, with her two stockings twisted in her hands." He recognised the difficulties in assessing her "mental defectiveness" due to the language barrier but nonetheless concluded she was "mentally deranged":

> The clinical picture then, is that of a non-systematised delusional mental disorder. This is a recognised disease of the mind. ... [T]he fear that her grandchildren would not be brought up properly induced

---

[161]*Daily Mirror* 28th October 1954;*Manchester Evening News* 27th October 1954.
[162]*Daily Mirror* 29th October 1954.
[163]*Daily Telegraph* 29th October 1954.
[164]*The Times* 27th August 1954.
[165]CRIM 1/2492 Medical Report dated 5th October 1954 by PMO Thomas Christie.

a defect of reason due to the above disease of the mind, whereby however much she may have been capable of appreciating the nature and quality of the acts she was doing, at the time of the acts the defect of reason was such that she was incapable of knowing that what she was doing was wrong. In my opinion Styllou Pantopiou Christofi is insane, but is medically fit to plead and to stand trial.[166]

Although Dr Christie's report was made available to both prosecution and defence it was not revealed during the trial because Styllou herself refused to plead insanity.[167] As pointed out by *The Lancet* this "raises the question of how far a prisoner as to whose sanity there is some doubt, is the best person to decide his or her defence."[168] Yet, having declared a defendant fit to plead, it would seem contradictory to deny her the right to chose her own defence. Members of the *Royal Commission on Capital Punishment* who reported in 1953, recognised the problematic nature of this issue, but only one member, Sir David Henderson, argued that "mental deficiency of whatsoever degree should be regarded as an adequate defence in bar of trial or sentence." Other members argued that "every person who is certifiable as a mental defective ... [should not] necessarily be regarded as unfit to stand ... trial."[169] Yet, even by the definition of those who supported this ambiguous statement, Styllou was insane because the definition of her mental illness fell within the M'Naghten Rules.[170] In short, a defendant could be declared insane and medically fit to plead *simultaneously* resulting in an officially insane person having full responsibility for deciding the nature of her defence. The Styllou Christofi case exemplifies someone who paid with her life for the contradictory assessment of 'insane but fit to plead', for it was widely agreed at the time that had she pleaded insanity, she would almost certainly have been found 'guilty but insane', resulting in institutionalisation rather than execution.[171]

As a result of Styllou's refusal to plead insanity her medical report only became public knowledge days before the execution date. Several Labour MPs responded to this newly publicised evidence by uniting in a last minute effort to save her. In particular Sir Leslie Plummer pointed out that "the mere fact ... she did not claim insanity shows ... she is not of sound mind."[172] Consequently the delegation of MPs made several attempts to

---

[166]CRIM 1/2492 Medical Report dated 5th October 1954 by PMO Thomas Christie.
[167]*Manchester Guardian* 15th December 1954.
[168]*The Lancet* 8th January 1955 (Vol 1) p.96.
[169]*Royal Commission on Capital Punishment 1949-1953 Report* (1953) Her Majesty's Stationery Office, London p.119.
[170]*The Lancet* 8th January 1955 (Vol 1) p.96. See also *Royal Commission on Capital Punishment 1949-1953 Report*, (1953) Her Majesty's Stationery Office, London p.119.
[171]See for example *Manchester Guardian; Manchester Evening News*, both 15th December 1954;
[172]*Daily Mail* 15th December 1954.

present Dr Christie's report to the Home Secretary during the last 48 hours of Styllou's life. However, he refused to see them on the grounds that he had already received assessments concerning her mental condition, from three medical practitioners who had been appointed in accordance with the 1884 Criminal Lunatics Act.[173] The MPs considered the Home Secretary's refusal "unprecedented" to which he responded:

> I am sure that while it is of course open to Members of Parliament to submit representations to the Secretary of State, the House will agree that a Home Secretary should not be expected to receive oral representations, even from Members, and to discuss the case with them, when he is engaged in the discharge of this onerous and anxious duty.[174]

Yet the members of the panel assessing Styllou's mental condition were not bound by the M'Naghten Rules, nor were they necessarily concerned with her condition at the time of the murder, but at the time of the examination.[175] To clarify these points the Home Secretary was asked to publish both the panel's medical evidence and the advice supplied by the trial judge. He refused both requests, because it would "be contrary to long-established practice and open to considerable objection."[176]

Labour MPs such as Sydney Silverman and Leslie Plummer expressed their "great distress that a woman who may well have been insane and had in fact been declared insane by the prison doctor, had been executed" and consequently tabled their disquiet in a censure motion only 12 hours after her death.[177] Styllou Christofi's file does not contain evidence of anybody else pleading her case, hence these MPs stood alone in their public opposition to her execution. As Edgar Lustgarten wrote many years later:

> Nobody raised a fuss when Mrs Christofi was hanged in 1954. But then who was Mrs Christofi? A dark-skinned foreigner.[178]

The scantiness of the Styllou Christofi file means we do not have enough evidence to form a definite opinion regarding her mental state. It does not, for example, contain the medical evidence of the three experts appointed by the Home Secretary. We do know, however, that immediately

---

[173]*The Lancet* 8th January 1955 (Vol 1) p.96. This Act stipulated that where there is doubt about a prisoner's sanity, the Home Secretary must appoint two or more legally qualified medical practitioners to examine the prisoner.

[174]*Manchester Guardian* 15th December 1954; *The Times* 21st December 1954.

[175]*Manchester Guardian* 15th December 1954; *The Lancet* 8th January 1955 (Vol 1) p.96.

[176]Home Secretary Lloyd George quoted in *The Lancet* 8th January 1955 (Vol 1) p.96.

[177]*The Times* 16th & 17th December 1954; *The Daily Mail* 16th December 1954.

[178]*News of the World* 8th October 1972.

after the verdict the public learned this had been Styllou's second trial for murder. Twenty-nine years earlier, she, her sister-in-law and another woman had been acquitted of murdering her own mother-in-law by forcing a burning piece of wood down her throat.[179] Moreover, her son's impression of his mother when he visited her two weeks prior to the execution, supported Dr Christie's report:

> As usual she would not reason at all. She just shouted 'Innocent, innocent.' She turned around to say she had forgiven me for what I have done for her being in prison, and that she had nothing to do with the whole thing. She blamed me because, she said, I was the main witness.[180]

While in prison Styllou dictated several letters to Stavros, reiterating that he was to blame for her predicament, suggesting at best, a failure to come to terms with reality and take responsibility for her own actions, at worst, severe paranoia coupled with an inability to consider the loss Stavros had suffered, which was about to intensify with the trauma of losing not only his wife but also his mother:

> I hope that you are all right as well as your children. I hope that you will always be with God's help. It doesn't alter what is going to happen to me. You have tried too hard to hang me, to put around my neck the noose, so that you may rest. I am not obliging you to come and see me, my son. For my fortune, there are my family in the streets in Cyprus crying for me. If you saw their letters, you would be moved and cry as we do. My brothers say that if the sea were earth they would come on foot to see me. Kiss the children for me.[181]

Styllou's state of mind coupled with the contrast between an illiterate Cypriot woman who had spent all her life in a remote, rural corner of the island, and the andro- and Northern Euro-centric culture of the criminal justice system in central London, have created a vast gap in our comprehension of this case - obscuring Styllou's motives and reasoning. Instead we are left with a set of tantalising questions to which we will never know the answer, because Styllou's account was muted not only in a symbolic sense but also in a very literal sense due to the language barrier. For example, what did Styllou want to say after the verdict was announced? What were the circumstances of her first trial, and why were she and her co-defendants not found guilty? What were her motives in stripping Hella naked before setting fire to her, and why did she remove and hide her wedding-ring? Did she realise that metal would not burn, or did the removal of the ring symbolise the

---

[179]*Daily Telegraph* 29th October 1954; *Daily Mirror* 29th October 1954.
[180]Stavros Christofi quoted in *The Daily Mail* 15th December 1954.
[181]Styllou Christofi's letter reproduced in Wilson 1971:307.

end of Hella's 'ownership' of Stavros whom Styllou felt she had lost to her? We cannot know the answers to these questions because Styllou had failed to communicate through dominant modes of expression not just at a judicial level but also at a cultural level. Moreover, her failure to display acceptable and appropriate feminine behaviour in the crucial area of motherhood ensured she was perceived as a dangerous woman. This dangerousness was magnified by her capacity for extreme violence and her total failure to display remorse. Her shouting and cursing as well as her attempts to blame her own son for her predicament, ensured she could not be constructed as a 'pathetic' or 'helpless' victim. Furthermore, her "mental defectiveness" was not of the type conducive to sympathy which may have resulted in her being declared 'mad' but instead appeared as negative personality characteristics which led to her being described as "obstinate", "suspicious" and "cunning".[182] Not only did these characteristics stand in sharp contrast to the feminine ideal of the naive, malleable and docile woman, they were also important ingredients in the construction of the 'bad' woman. When this construction became overlaid with her "dark-skinned foreignness" Styllou Christofi found herself located at the receiving end of both judicial and cultural misogyny.

Styllou "walked calm and unassisted to the scaffold at Holloway" thus becoming the first woman in British criminal history whose execution was witnessed by a female prison governor.[183] Meanwhile, those of us attempting to make sense of cases such as Margaret Allen's and Styllou Christofi's, are confronted with the ultimate irony of a criminal justice system which throughout history has attempted to categorise relatively 'normal' women as 'mad', while the mental state of criminal women who may have qualified for this category was ignored, and the women sent to their deaths as a consequence of that system.

Part II: Poison - 'A Woman's Weapon'

> As long as capital punishment remains the law of the country, poisoners ... will never be allowed to escape their just punishment whatever juries may recommend. *There are no extenuating circumstances in murder by poison and none can ever be pleaded.*[184]

In Chapter Two I noted that women poisoners have historically been regarded as particularly loathsome and odious because their crimes could never be construed as being due to temporary loss of control, but always indicated premeditation, suggesting a cool, rational and calculating approach to killing,

---

[182]CRIM 1/2492 Medical Report dated 5th October 1954.

[183]*Daily Mirror* 16th December 1954. This governor was Dr Charity Taylor.

[184]O'Donnell, B. (1956) *Should Women Hang?* W.H. Allen, London, pp.175-6. Emphasis in the original.

which contrasts sharply with expected female conduct and behaviour.
Moreover, as a result of women's traditional responsibility for the preparation
of food and the belief that they were "fitted by nature to cheer the afflicted,
elevate the depressed, minister to the wants of the feeble and diseased"[185], the
woman poisoner was understood as having transgressed this 'law of nature'
when she utilised this role for her own end. She thus came to be seen as an
ultra dangerous inversion of womanhood - someone who to outward
appearances accepted her role as cook and carer, yet secretly used that role to
kill her charges:

> Of all the kinds of Murders, that by Poison is the most dreadful, as it
> takes a Man unguarded, and gives him no Opportunity to defend
> himself; much more so when administered [sic] by ... [someone]
> whom one could least suspect, and from whom one might naturally
> look for Assistance and Comfort.[186]

Such anxiety still surrounded the woman poisoner during the first
half of the 20th century, because, as will become apparent, this type of
murder method was still used with relative frequency and always received
maximum publicity. In the remainder of this chapter I analyse the effect that
the discourse of the 'woman poisoner' had on the cases of two women carers
who poisoned their charges. Both women initially stood trial with male
accomplices who were acquitted due to lack of evidence, a factor which
emphasises the significance of discourses of the 'woman carer' and the 'female
poisoner' as I shall now illustrate.

The Case of Dorothea Waddingham

> Dorothy [sic] was 36, a short, plump, fair woman with protruding
> teeth. No one could have called her attractive, but she looked capable
> and very ordinary. Sullivan was a smart dark-haired man of 41 who
> had won the Military Medal in the Great War.[187]

As was the case with the majority of women executed during the 20th
century, the life of Dorothea Waddingham was one of abject poverty. Born
into a large family in 1902, she worked as a maid in the Burton-on-Trent
Workhouse Infirmary by the time she was in her twenties. Although she
possessed no qualifications it was her experience in the Infirmary which
prompted her to call herself 'nurse' Waddingham when years later she was to

---

[185]Jones, A. (1991) *Women Who Kill* Gollancz, London, p.81.

[186]Quoted from the Mary Blandy trial transcript, reproduced in Gonda, C. (1992)
'"Exactly Them Words": Histories of a Murderous Daughter' in Gonda, C. (ed)*Tea &
Leg-Irons* Open Letters, London, p.72.

[187]Wilson 1971:283-4.

run a nursing-home.[188] In 1933 her husband died, leaving her with three children. Even when he had been alive, the family had existed in dire poverty for he had been a "chronic invalid" who was unable to work.[189] Prior to her widowhood Dorethea had committed several poverty-related offences. For example, she had been imprisoned for stealing a watch from a maid she employed. The exact circumstances of the crime were rather more complex: she had obtained the watch by telling the maid she could "get it regulated free of charge." But in reality Dorothea needed the watch to pawn at a time when she "had no money and scarcely any food in the house."[190]

By 1935 Dorothea was running a nursing home with the father of her two youngest children, Ronald 'Joe' Sullivan, whose official role was that of a domestic help. In January she received two new clients, 87-year-old Louisa Baguley and her daughter Ada Baguley aged 50, who was a "helpless cripple" - suffering from progressive disseminated sclerosis.[191] The initial weekly payment for looking after the women soon proved inadequate, and on 7th May Louisa Baguley signed a will which stipulated that her and Ada's estate, valued at £1600, should be divided equally between Dorothea and Joe after the two women's deaths in exchange for their permanent care at the nursing-home. Five days later Louisa was dead, and four months later Ada too died.[192] The Coroner's suspicion was aroused when Joe - who was organising the funeral - produced a letter which read:

> I desire to be cremated at my death for health's sake. It is my wish to remain with nurse and my last wish is that my relatives shall not know of my death.[193]

The letter had originally ended after the word 'nurse', and the following line concerning Ada's 'last wish' had been squeezed in between the last line and Ada's supposed signature, for the letter was clearly in Joe's handwriting. An investigation was soon underway which resulted in both Dorothea and Joe's arrest and trial for murder. At first glance it appeared to be an 'open and shut' case with the prisoners' guilt obvious. Yet, as the trial progressed and each piece of evidence was tested, Mr Justice Goddard, the trial judge expressed reservations about the strength of the case:

---

[188] ASSI 13/66 XC6872 Public Record Office, Chancery Lane, London WC2A 1LR. Statements by Dorothea Waddingham, 24th September 1935; 16th January 1936; O'Donnell 1956:88-9.

[189] Huggett & Berry 1956:188.

[190] *Manchester Evening News* 16th April 1936. At the time of the crime Dorothea also owed the said maid £9 in back-pay. She received a three-month sentence.

[191] *The Times* 15th February 1936.

[192] ASSI 13/66 XC6872. Death certificates and accompanying details included in this file.

[193] ASSI 13/66 XC6872. Original letter dated 29th August 1935.

there was a great deal which at first appeared to be likely to be important evidence for the prosecution, but it had disappeared, and there were facts "which shout almost in her favour."[194]

Poisoners are invariably convicted as a result of circumstantial evidence and indeed the point of this analysis is not to establish Dorothea's guilt or innocence but to examine how it came about that the evidence against Joe came to be understood as 'more' circumstantial than that against Dorothea, for, like Ada Williams' husband before him, Joe was to leave the court a free man, while Dorothea had to face her executioner alone, just like Ada had done 36 years earlier.

Challenging the Dominant Truth: Separating Evidence from Assumption

Nurse Waddingham['s] ... face was red and her figure swayed slowly as she stepped half a pace forward in the dock. "Guilty," the word echoed ... In the court Sullivan stood at attention while it was stated that no evidence would be offered by the Crown ... A second later he walked away to freedom.[195]

Unlike the case against Joe Sullivan, Dorothea's case was heard mainly through the discourses of 'woman as carer' and 'the woman poisoner'. With respect to the first discourse, I have already discussed how notions of the maternal instinct can be extended to include sick and helpless adults since caring for others and putting herself last is part of women's 'nature' and normal femininity. Such beliefs and expectations help to identify and establish what counts as 'appropriate' female conduct and behaviour and provide the context within which Dorothea was judged. With respect to the second discourse, despite history's exposé of numerous cases of male poisoners, the belief that poison is a woman's weapon persisted, and resulted in women poisoners being considered far more threatening than other murderers including male poisoners, due to the lack of male control over a hand which should be serving food, but was serving poison instead:

Murder by poison was particularly feared because there was no way to see it coming or to defend against it ... "it is usually committed in secret, and so insidiously, that no forecast can prevent it - no manhood resist it."[196]

In other words, unlike male poisoners who at times have been portrayed as 'clever', women poisoners, because of their role as providers of food, love and comfort within the supposed safety of the domestic sphere, came to be seen as 'sneaky' and 'lethal' - "the witch who lurked in woman's

---

[194]*Daily Mirror* 28th February 1936.

[195]*Daily Mirror* 28th February 1936.

[196]Jones 1991:110 quoting the prosecutor at the Ann Simpson trial.

sphere and haunted the minds of men."[197] Thus, unlike Joe Sullivan whose gender excluded him from discourses of 'caring' or 'poisoning' the creation of the dominant 'truth' about Dorothea Waddingham involved a struggle between the discourses of 'woman as carer' and 'woman as poisoner'.

In the previous chapter I questioned the quality of the defence received by some of the women standing trial for their lives. Dorothea, like the majority of women executed, was too poor to pay for her own representation.[198] This however, was not reflected in the quality of her defence, as her very able counsel Mr Eales, skilfully undermined the evidence of several key prosecution witnesses. However, Dorothea did not give a favourable impression either during the initial investigation or in the dock. As a result of her lack of subtlety she appeared cold-hearted and insensitive as can be deduced from her statement about the will made in her and Joe's favour:

> They looked like living 20 years and more than that. I had to take the risk. It was pushed on to me - no one else would have them ... All the members of the family wanted their money but didn't want them. I found I had them on my hands and could not get rid of them.[199]

These are not the words of a committed and dedicated carer attempting to ease the lives of the feeble and sick, but are blunt and harsh expressions, indicating a cynical and mercenary attitude towards the Baguleys whose deaths cannot come soon enough.

When questioned about the hours leading up to Ada's death, Dorothea replied:

> She looked very ill. Her eyes were open and her face was flushed and she was breathing heavily. I spoke to her and got no answer. I put brandy to her lips but she could not take it. I thought she was having a stroke. I did not send for the Doctor. I thought she might rally on for days.[200]

Given Ada's condition according to Dorothea's own evidence, it seems extraordinary if not callous, that a doctor was not called immediately. When she recalled the events surrounding Joe's writing of the letter on Ada's behalf concerning her wish to be cremated, Dorothea's choice of words could not have failed to make an impact:

---

[197] This is not to suggest that such men escaped the death penalty as can be seen from Ellis's discussion of the Seddon case in Ellis, J. (1996) *Diary of a Hangman* Forum Press, London p.76; Jones 1991:81; 82.

[198] *The Times* 6th February 1936.

[199] ASSI 13/66 XC6872 Statement by Dorothea Waddingham, 16th January 1936.

[200] ASSI 13/66 XC6872 Statement by Dorothea Waddingham, 16th January 1996.

> She [Ada] said "It is like signing my death warrant". I replied "In a way it is - don't sign it if you don't want to".[201]

The unfavourable impression that Dorothea's choice of phrases created was not improved by her conduct in court where on two consecutive days, she interrupted witnesses, shouting from the dock: "Don't be such a liar! Don't be such a liar!"[202]

Her credibility as a witness was further tarnished as a result of having to admit certain untruths and 'mistakes', such as the fact that she and Joe "were known as brother and sister", and the letters after her name on her business card were "a mistake", for as noted above, she had no formal qualifications.[203]

Nonetheless, Dorothea persisted with her claim that Dr Manfield who attended all patients at the nursing home, was a liar, when he stated he had never provided her with morphine tablets to give to Ada. She further claimed he had left no instructions concerning the dosage of Ada's medicine, and that empty medicine bottles found on her premises had been given to her children by Dr Manfield to play with. Within the context of the hierarchy of credibility and the disparity of social status between Dorothea and Dr Manfield accusations of such professional lapses were regarded with suspicion. As expressed by two observers: "Nurse Waddingham was an unconvincing witness, as hard to believe as she was hard to hear."[204] This became especially apparent when Dorothea made contradictory statements regarding the type of medicine she had given Ada. The prosecution attached great importance to the fact that initially she had claimed never to have given Ada morphine, but later she changed this statement and claimed she had given her 10 morphia tablets provided by Dr Manfield. The reason why she had not revealed this in her initial statement, was that Dr Manfield had instructed Dorothea not to say anything about the tablets, and that "if it was necessary he would deal with it."[205] As the verdict was to show, the jury did not believe this version of events.

Dorothea further suggested that a mistake had been made by the chemist in preparing Ada's medicine, especially since only his assistant was available at the time she called for the medication.[206] She also argued that visitors may have brought Ada the lethal medicine, and commented that "this is a put-up job."[207] However, she did not shy away from the charges against her, and volunteered that "Miss Baguley made a will in favour of me and Mr

---

[201] ASSI 13/66 XC6872 Statement by Dorothea Waddingham, 16th January 1936.
[202] *The Times* 7th and 8th February 1936.
[203] ASSI 13/66 XC6872 Statement by Dorothea Waddingham, 16th January 1936.
[204] Huggett & Berry 1956:116.
[205] ASSI 13/66 XC6872 Statement by Dorothea Waddingham 16th January 1936.
[206] ASSI 13/66 XC6872 Statement by Detective Inspector Albert Pentland, 6th February 1936.
[207] ASSI 13/66 XC6872 Statement by Detective Inspector Albert Pentland, 6th February 1936.

Sullivan and I wish she hadn't. I think it's the will that is causing all this upset."[208]

Other important factors in the case for the prosecution included the accusation that the defendants had conspired to keep visitors away from Ada,[209] that Dorothea and Joe "had taken control of Ada", that her letters were opened, "and if they were not approved of they were not given to Miss Baguley."[210]

Lacking direct evidence, the prosecution attempted to prove that Dorothea had had a store of morphia tablets left over from prescriptions issued to other patients who had died previously, and that she and Joe had used these tablets to poison Louisa and Ada in order to inherit their estate, although ultimately, the Crown decided to prosecute for the murder of Ada only. Evidence of Joe's involvement in the conspiracy included the following: First, he was solely responsible for contacting and making arrangements with the solicitor who drew up the will.[211] Second, he admitted writing the letter quoted above but claimed it was at Ada's request and that she had said: "I should very much like you to put in if you can get it in that small space 'I do not want any relatives to know of my death.'"[212] Third, he was also responsible for writing a letter to Ada's cousin, which he again claimed had been at her request:

> I do not like you saying what you did about Joe as he is kindness itself to me and my mother. He is the only one who has done anything for us, and is kindness itself ... You need not worry about me as everything is all right.

Underneath, Joe had added his own postscript in the form of a threat:

> I should like to know what you mean about that chap you called Jos Has you call him [sic] if ever you cross my path you will know what that means there is always straight-forwardness carried out here, and mark my word we know what you have been trying to do, but if you are not careful you will regret it, so keep your eyes open in future, and Miss Baguley is quite aware of my writing this.[213]

Fourth, several witnesses testified he often played a dominant part in keeping visitors away from the Baguleys, which was interpreted as stemming

---

[208] ASSI 13/66 XC6872 Statement by Dorothea Waddingham 24th September 1935.

[209] ASSI 13/66 XC6872 Testimony of Laurence Baguley p.5 and of Miss Blagg who testified that she was "first refused admission - then Sullivan said: 'Oh very well but I shall be in the room.'" p.7.

[210] ASSI 13/66 XC6872 Testimony of Edith Eyres, deposition file Vol 2 p.19; p.20.

[211] ASSI 13/66 XC6872 Testimony of Mr Lane, deposition file Vol 1 p.25.

[212] ASSI 13/66 XC6872 Statement of Ronald Joe Sullivan 24th September 1935.

[213] ASSI 13/66 XC6872 Exhibit 4. Original letter to Lawrence Baguley - undated.

from a fear that relatives might interfere with the will.[214] Fifth, Joe collected the rent from the properties belonging to the Baguleys.[215] Sixth, a bank clerk testified that Joe had accompanied Ada when she withdrew *all* her money.[216] Seventh, Joe was with Ada throughout her last night, and it was he who called the doctor in the morning.[217] He had also been present when Louisa died.[218] Finally, it was Joe who was in charge of the funeral arrangements and advised by the undertaker about the necessary legal requirements before a cremation could proceed; he subsequently signed a receipt for the appropriate certificates.[219]

Yet, on the third day of the trial, before he had been called to give evidence, the judge ordered the murder charge against him to be dropped because of lack of evidence. The prosecution argued that "certain letters ... showed that Sullivan was a participant in the matter. There is direct participation in the matters ... such as the writing of letters, visits to the bank - direct and personal participation in the matter."[220] The judge however argued:

> The only evidence at present is that Sullivan was in this house, assisting in taking about the patients, raising them in bed, wheeling them about, and doing household work. There is no evidence that he was interested in the house, no evidence as to the relationship of the prisoner, no evidence except what has been given here that he was in the position of servant ... it could not be said that even if every word of the evidence were accepted it raises a case of more than that Sullivan ... may have been connected with the matter and not that he must have been.[221]

---

[214]ASSI 13/66 XC6872 Testimonies of Mary Bardill deposition file Vol 2 p.15; Louisa Taylor Vol 2 p.4. and Miss Blagg p.7. See also evidence of Lawrence Baguley, to whom Joe had said: "It is no use coming back, they don't want to see you" (*The Times* 6th February 36).

[215]ASSI 13/66 XC6872 Statement of Dorothea Waddington 16th January 1936. According to Dorothea, Ada had instructed Joe to collect the money. The testimony of solicitor's clerk J.K. Lane confirmed Joe's involvement in Ada's financial affairs (Statement of J.K. Lane 16th September 1935 p.8).

[216]ASSI 13/66 XC6872 Statement of Mr Alcock 16th September 1935 p.18.

[217]ASSI 13/66 XC6872 Statement of Dorothea Waddingham 24th September 1935.

[218]ASSI 13/66 XC6872 Death Certificate dated 13th January 1936.

[219]ASSI 13/66 XC6872 Statement of undertaker George Musson dated 16th September 1935 p.26 and in deposition file Vol 2 pp.34-5. See also statement of J.K. Lane who testified that Joe Sullivan signed receipts and collected Ada's bank books and Certificates (16th September 1935 p.8). See also reports in *The Times* 6th and 26th February 1936.

[220]Mr Birkett, prosecuting speaking to the trial judge, Lord Goddard. Trial transcript quoted in *The Times* 27th February 1936.

[221]Lord Goddard to Mr Birkett. Trial transcript quoted in *The Times* 27th February 1936 and *Manchester Evening News* 26th February 1936.

Of course there was no evidence that Dorothea had intended to kill either, for she did not deny having given the tablets to Ada, the dispute arose because she claimed to have acted according to the instructions of Dr Manfield, and because it was suspected that Ada had received more than the 10 tablets that Dorothea claimed responsibility for. This point was not lost on the judge for in dismissing the case against Joe he also stated:

> It must be said in relation to the *woman* and the man that they could not have done anything in regard to the disposition of this property in a more open way if they tried. They send papers to the solicitor, they send to the bank, they tell all the relatives. If it had been a case of the production of a will after death and nobody had heard anything about it ... it would have been a very different matter.[222]

Nonetheless Dorothea was now alone in the dock. However, her solicitor had already discredited some of the most damning evidence against her, during the Magistrates' Court hearing, and under Mr Eales' skilful cross-examination of key prosecution witnesses, a very different picture emerged, with some of the insinuations against her being shown to be false while her other unconvincing explanations and claims were proved to be both correct and truthful. First, the witnesses who claimed they had not been allowed to visit the Baguleys, admitted they had made no complaint about this since they believed the Baguleys were properly looked after. Furthermore, Dr Manfield gave evidence that Ada had "told him she had fallen out with her relatives", and she herself had asked the doctor "not to let Lawrence Baguley come to Devon Drive again." Accordingly, as professional adviser to the Baguleys, he instructed Nurse Waddingham that "Lawrence Baguley ... must not be allowed to come again."[223] Indeed Lawrence was exposed as having attempted to have Ada declared mentally unfit to make a will to prevent the Baguley's estate from leaving the family.[224] Moreover, another relative gave evidence that Ada herself had said to her she did not wish to see Lawrence again.[225] Other relatives admitted conflict had arisen between them and Dorothea and Joe because of concern about the Baguley estate leaving the family, not because they were concerned about the Baguleys or the care they received. On the contrary, numerous witnesses testified the Baguleys received proper care in the hands of Dorothea and Joe.[226] For example, Dr

---

[222]Lord Goddard to Mr Birkett. Trial transcript quoted in *The Times* 27th February 1936. My emphasis.

[223]ASSI 13/66 XC6872 Evidence of Dr Manfield, deposition file Vol 5 p.14.

[224]Trial transcript quoted in *The Times* 25th February 1936.

[225]ASSI 13/66 XC6872 evidence of Mary Eyres, Louisa Baguley's niece. See also evidence of Dr Manfield above.

[226]ASSI 13/66 XC6872 Laurence Baguley himself testified that: "My aunt and cousin appeared to be comfortable and contented." Statement dated 16th September 1935 p.5. See also evidence of Mr Alcock deposition file Vol 1 p.17; Miss Blagg p.6

Jacobs, a friend of the Baguleys who had visited them regularly was satisfied that they "were happy and comfortable at Devon Drive."[227] Dr Manfield testified:

> he had always found that Waddingham was very anxious to do the best she could for every one of her patients. On one occasion, when she had been confined, she got up from her bed and attended to her patients in less than 24 hours from her confinement. He had never had a single complaint to make about her work as nurse ... [but] had always been perfectly satisfied with Nurse Waddingham's treatment of his patients.[228]

The insinuations that Dorothea and Joe had something to hide, were mistreating the Baguleys, or were trying to isolate them, were finally disproved with the evidence of Mrs Briggs who had visited Ada on her last afternoon, spending several hours with her during which Ada seemed happy and content and did not at any point suggest she was unhappy at Devon Drive.[229] Moreover, in his summing up the judge pointed out that Dorothea's nursing home was recommended and "selected by the secretary of the County Nursing Association."[230]

The second important piece of evidence against Dorothea was Dr Manfield's testimony which was in direct conflict with her own. As noted above, Dorothea was suspected of having poisoned Ada with tablets left over from other patients, but she claimed to have received 10 tablets from Dr Manfield to be administered at her discretion, something which he strenuously denied. However, evidence was given both in the Magistrates' Court and at the trial, which cast Dr Manfield's professional credibility into doubt. First, he admitted Dorothea had in fact returned "about a dozen tablets which he had prescribed," and six when another patient died.[231] Second, he admitted he had previously made a mistake regarding the dosage of Ada's medicine:

> I suppose doctor, it would be no exaggeration to call that a blunder, would it? - Well, I suppose the best of us make blunders at times, I am not going to commit myself. It was a blunder in the right direction.

---

and Edith Eyres Vol 2 p.23, who all agreed the Baguleys appeared to be happy and comfortable and were "being perfectly well looked after."
[227] ASSI 13/66 XC6872 Evidence of Dr Jacobs, deposition file Vol 7 p.12.
[228] Evidence of Dr Manfield reproduced in *The Times* 26th and 13th February 1936. See also ASSI 13/66 XC6872 where Dr Manfield testified: "I have never known Waddingham attempt to deceive me." (Deposition file Vol 5 p.32).
[229] *The Times* 6th February 1936; *Manchester Evening News* 24th February 1936.
[230] Summing up speech reproduced in *The Times* 28th February 1936.
[231] Birkett examining Dr Manfield, reproduced in *The Times* 27th February 1936.

Mr Smith repeated his question, and Dr Manfield exclaimed "I am not going to answer that question. Why should I?" ...

In view of the fact that you had given medicine 300% weaker in morphia that day, you left at the same time six morphia tablets?

No, I did not.[232]

When Dr Manfield was asked if he had left dosage instructions on Ada's last bottle of medicine, he replied "I don't know." However, both the chemist and his assistant remembered "that there *were* no instructions on the prescription."[233]

Third, the doctor's professionalism was challenged by Dr Owen-Taylor who "said that there was gross neglect in regard to one of ... [Ada's] bed sores and disagreed with Dr Manfield that proper treatment was given."[234] At a less serious level, but nonetheless one which indicates Dr Manfield's lack of good judgement, he admitted that he had indeed given Dorothea's young son empty medicine bottles to play with.[235] In his summing up Mr Justice Goddard appeared to consider the possibility that Dorothea's version of the truth was the accurate one when he suggested Dr Manfield may have felt "his professional reputation was at stake" if a patient had died from medicine which he had prescribed.[236]

Although Dorothea's defence could not prove her innocence it successfully exposed the incompetence and irregular practices of the professionals whose evidence the prosecution relied on. Thus, prior to the cross-examination of Dr Manfield the work practices of Dr Owen-Taylor and Mr Taylor his assistant, who performed Ada's autopsy, came under scrutiny, which revealed that the organs required for examination had not been put into "stoppered jars"; had not been covered at all; and "were all mixed up together." Moreover the container had not been labelled, and no receipt for the organs had been obtained.[237] Mr Taylor further admitted he had never before carried out an analysis for morphine, while Dr Owen-Taylor stated:

I cannot say that the organs I examined and in which I found 3.192 grains of morphia are the organs of Miss Baguley.[238]

---

[232]Mr Smith, Dorthea's solicitor examining Dr Manfield, quoted in *The Times* 12th February 1936. Dorothea claimed that the 10 tablets had been given to her on two separate occasions - six on one occasion, four on the other.

[233]Evidence of Mr Leader and Mr West, reproduced in *The Times* 12th February 1936 and quoted in *The Times* 13th February 1936. Emphasis in the original.

[234]Evidence of Dr Bernard Owen-Taylor quoted in *The Times* 14th February 1936.

[235]Evidence of Dr Manfield quoted in *The Times* 13th February 1936.

[236]Summing up speech reproduced in *The Times* 28th February 1936.

[237]Evidence of Dr Bernard Owen-Taylor quoted in *The Times* 14th February 1936.

[238]Evidence of Mr W.W. Taylor and Dr Bernard Owen-Taylor quoted in *The Times* 12th and 15th February 1936.

The work practices of the police surgeon and his staff were thrown into further disrepute when Mr Taylor conceded that during the examination of the organs, "there was no representative of Nurse Waddingham there and no opportunity for anybody on her behalf to check whatever results ... [were] arrived at". As the organs were destroyed after the examination this could not be rectified.[239] Finally, when Dorothea's representative asked Dr Roche Lynch - an expert witness for the prosecution - if it was possible his opinion could be wrong, the doctor agreed that such a possibility existed.[240]

It remained for the defence to explain Dorothea's original claim that she had never given morphia to Ada. For this purpose Detective Inspector Pentland was cross-examined:

> I think that when Waddingham said "I have never given Miss Baguley any morphia" she may not have meant it literally. I did not take her statement literally nor did I take her statement literally when she said, "I have never had any morphia in the house". When she made those first few remarks she was in a very agitated condition. She collected herself afterwards. It is quite likely that she meant that she never gave or kept any morphia except on instructions of another person - the Doctor.[241]

Pentland added that Dorothea had been "very upset and very ill" and "was expecting the birth of her child any day" when she made her statement, yet had still been willing to assist him "in every way" and voluntarily made a statement, unlike Joe, who when asked to sign his statement replied: "No".[242]

Ultimately then, after the four-day trial in front of an all-male jury a complex and contradictory picture of Dorothea had emerged, which was reflected in the Judge's summing up:

> There are some things which you would say are consistent with the most innocent facts that one could imagine. There are facts which, if you believe them, are equally grave the other way.[243]

On the one hand, the Baguleys (or any other resident of Devon Drive) had never made a complaint against Dorothea or the quality of care she provided, despite ample opportunities since, as pointed out by the judge: "a procession of witnesses, relatives and friends ... had called at the home without let or hindrance."[244] Furthermore, she was considered to be an "efficient and loving mother" who "worshipped" her children.[245] She

---

[239]Trial transcript quoted in *The Times* 26th February 1936.
[240]Testimony of Dr Roche Lynch quoted in *The Times* 14th February 1936.
[241]ASSI 13/66 XC6872 Testimony of Albert Pentland 6th February 1936.
[242]ASSI 13/66 XC6872 Testimony of Albert Pentland 6th February 1936.
[243]Judge Goddard quoted in *Manchester Evening News* 27th February 1936.
[244]Summing up reproduced in *The Times* 28th February 1936.
[245]Huggett & Berry 1956:138.

therefore appeared to fulfil the ideological expectations of woman as a devoted mother and committed carer.

On the other hand her conduct in court had created an unfavourable impression of a coarse yet hapless woman, her answers barely audible one minute, while the next she was shouting at witnesses and disrupting proceedings.[246] The image Dorothea presented was thus a mixture of negative and positive characteristics associated with femininity: at one level she appeared to conform in every way to the stereotypical image of femininity - someone who was hapless, helpless and naive who also obeyed traditional attitudes to the female role of 'caring'. At another level, she was a deadly poisonous monster, made all the more dangerous because of her appearance as harmless and ordinary.[247] One author described her as an "ordinary, capable-looking woman, with a face like an amiable sheep's",[248] a description which implies her 'deviousness' - the apparent gentle and harmless female who secretly harbours poisonous urges under the guise of her conformity - as discussed in Chapter Two. She represented the kind of woman Adam had in mind when he wrote:

> ... it is not a welcome experience to have those sentiments rudely violated which we have imbibed at the breast, to be called upon to make it clear that some of those creatures whom we have been taught to contemplate as nearly approaching the angelic are, by their own acts, more nearly allied to things hellish than to beings heavenly.[249]

The gender-specific nature of this quotation reminds us not to underestimate the power surrounding the discourses of women as 'devious' and as 'carers', and illustrates the specific and unique way criminal women come to be understood as a result of gender role expectations. For example in relation to child-care, beliefs about appropriate gender roles have been so enduring, that until the 1970s fathers appeared in research "only in response to worries that their total *absence* from the home was a threat to boys' sex-role identity."[250] Indeed the belief that women's 'caring instinct' is innate rather than socially conditioned still holds currency.[251] It is as a result of such beliefs that women like Dorothea come to be regarded as doubly deviant because they have committed a crime not only against their victims but also against their *nature*.

---

[246]Hugget & Berry 1956:116, wrote that "many of her replies which could scarcely be heard in complete silence, were drowned by coughing in the public gallery or a movement in the courtroom."

[247]See for example Wilson's description of Dorothea Waddingham in Wilson 1971:284.

[248]Wilson 1971:288.

[249]Adam, H. (1910) *Women and Crime* T. Werner Laurie, London p.3.

[250]Segal, L. (1990) *Slow Motion* Virago, London, p.34. Emphasis in the original.

[251]See for example Badinter, E. (1981) *The Myth of Motherhood* Souvenir Press, London.

Meanwhile, Joe was described as "five years older than Nurse Waddingham but look[ing] younger, and physically he was still attractive with straight, brushed-back hair and a clean open face."[252] Immediately prior to his dismissal in court he was further described by a police detective as being "a man of first-class character ... [who had] gained the Military Medal for conspicuous bravery in rescuing a wounded officer."[253] This process of distancing Joe from Dorothea was reinforced by emphasising he was in the position of a servant, and merely "mended the fires [and] swept the floors ..."[254] In reality, however, his role within the nursing home was not notably different from hers.[255] As we have seen from Ada's letter, she held Joe in high regard, describing him as "kindness itself". Moreover, Ada was a large woman who could not walk and at times could not feed herself as a result of her illness. Subsequently Joe was constantly involved in caring for her as was confirmed by numerous witnesses. For example, a niece, Mary Bardill, testified that when she went to visit Ada, "Nurse Waddingham and Sullivan were with her the whole time", and another niece, Louisa Taylor, gave evidence that "there was no time when I could have spoken to Ada when Sullivan was not there."[256] Such eyewitness accounts, together with the other circumstantial evidence against him listed earlier, indicate that, just as he had an 'equal' motive in terms of the will, so it was 'equally' possible that he had administered tablets to Ada.

My aim in listing the main pieces of evidence against Dorothea and Joe has been to illustrate, that, as had been the case with Ada and William Williams 36 years earlier, there was not a single piece of direct evidence which irrefutably proved that one of the accused rather than the other had conceived of or carried out the murder. Instead Dorothea's positioning within the established discourses of woman as carer and woman as poisoner became crucial in establishing a dominant 'truth' about her. Conversely, the absence of these discourses in relation to men is equally noteworthy, because as I have indicated, Joe's role as carer was essentially the same as Dorothea's, yet this carried no special significance for the judge, who, while accepting Dorothea's access to the patients as circumstantial evidence, refused to apply the same logic to Joe. At a different level, Joe's transgression of the masculine role in terms of working as a 'domestic' and hence Dorothea's subordinate, carried none of the negative connotations associated with female transgression as discussed for example, in the case of Margaret Allen. Unlike women who transgress their gender role, Joe was not judged more harshly as a result of his

[252]Huggett & Berry 1956:110.

[253]Trial evidence of Detective William Richardson reproduced in *The Times* 27th February 1936.

[254]*The Times* 27th February 1936; Huggett & Berry 1956:119.

[255]See for example Mr Lyons' cross-examination of Mr Ferniough quoted in *The Times* 26th February 1936.

[256]ASSI 13/66 XC6872 Evidence of Mary Bardill and Louisa Taylor, Deposition file Vol 2 p.4. See also evidence of Edith Eyres: "I spoke to Ada [at her mother's funeral] but never except in Sullivan's presence" (Vol 2 p.18).

transgression. On the contrary, his masculinity was emphasised by drawing attention to his army record, his 'conspicuous bravery' and his 'first class character'. This stands in sharp contrast to Dorothea's case which suffered further detriment as a result of her being cast in the role usually reserved for men - as the 'boss' of the establishment, thus making it less likely that she was unaware of and uninvolved in the poisoning. Thus, even Joe's transgression worked in his favour by contributing towards what was to become the dominant 'truth' about Dorothea Waddingham.

An Alternative Truth

As I have indicated, the dominant truth can be challenged by employing the tools of feminist analysis - in this case - by being alert to the discourses surrounding gender role assumptions. However, we can also re-interpret the available data in order to create an alternative truth, and I shall therefore argue that while Joe had received a medal for bravery, Dorothea too displayed "conspicuous bravery" for it was partly as a result of her evidence that Joe was not convicted. The most suggestive piece of evidence of a conspiracy to murder can be found in Dorothea's last letter to Joe:

> ... Now don't be afraid. I shall be alright, don't worry. I shall do my best for all. I have such a lot to remember. You not so much dear. *But I will not shout so don't worry about that* ...[257]

The most obvious interpretation of the last sentence must be that she will not talk of his involvement in the crime. It also suggests that Dorothea fitted Bartky's description of a 'docile body' who has internalised disciplinary practices without the need for prompting by external forces. In short, it was unnecessary to 'mute' Dorothea's account, for muteness was already self-imposed.[258] This was the last of a series of measures she took to protect Joe at a time when she could have attempted to save herself by implicating him. First, in her statement to the police she specifically stated he "has had nothing to do with the nursing ..."[259] Second, she testified that he "could not have given ... [the medicine]: he was not there."[260] Third, when the chemist's assistant said that "he had a distinct recollection that Sullivan fetched the medicine ... Nurse Waddingham jumped to her feet in the dock [and shouted]

---

[257]Letter quoted in Huggett & Berry 1956:139. My emphasis.

[258]In a tantalizing statement the day before her execution, Dorothea told her solicitor "that certain facts were not fully investigated at her trial and that she now desires that they shall be made known to the Home Secretary." Quoted in *The Liverpool Daily Post* 15th April. 1936. Her solicitor requested a respite to allow time for further investigations. It was refused.

[259]ASSI 13/66 XC6872 Statement by Dorothea Waddingham 16th January 1936.

[260]Proceedings from the hearing at the Magistrates' Court, reported in *The Times* 6th February 1936.

'It is a lie, I fetched it.'"[261] Thus, even when witnesses were ready to implicate Joe, she chose to protect him, an act which may well have meant the difference between life and death for Joe.

At another level, it is noticeable that all existing accounts of this case place great emphasis upon the disparity of the physical appearances of Dorothea and Joe. As stated above, commentators considered Joe a handsome man while Dorothea "was a gaunt, sallow-faced woman who obviously cared little about her appearance."[262] Dorothea's husband had been almost double her age, and it was he who had invited Joe to live with them. When he died Joe simply remained in the house.[263] Did Dorothea herself feel inferior to Joe? Was their love for each other equal, or did Dorothea consider herself lucky to have the attention of this "good-looking" man with "a first class character" while she herself was an ex-convict who found it difficult to write even a short letter?[264] Her letters indicate she was deeply in love with Joe, and she appointed him guardian of all her children, requesting they should take his name and be allowed to live together, and receive "private schooling and a comfortable home":

> Tell them of my death ... and that I am innocent. Never let them forget it.[265]

Joe, however, disregarded her wishes, even during the short period of time left before her execution. On the day before the execution the *Manchester Evening News* reported that three of the children were staying with Dorothea's parents, one was "in an institution belonging to the Nottingham Public Assistance Committee", and one was with a friend.[266] Although he temporarily had three of the children returned to him,[267] none of them, including the two youngest whom he had fathered, were to remain with him. He did however, receive his half of Ada's estate.[268]

Dorothea's loyalty towards Joe was not lost on the jury who issued "a strong recommendation to mercy."[269] Moreover, the trial judge was reported to have issued the death sentence in "a quiet and broken voice",[270] reassuring

---

[261]Testimony of Bernard West in Magistrates' Court, reported in *The Times* 8th February 1936.

[262]O'Donnell 1956:88.

[263]Huggett & Berry 1956:117-119.

[264]ASSI 13/66 XC6872. Like most of the women discussed within these case-studies, Dorothea had received little formal education and original letters included in her file indicate difficulty with spelling and grammar.

[265]Letters quoted in Huggett & Berry 1956:139.

[266]*Manchester Evening News* 14th April 1936.

[267]*Daily Mirror* 17th April 1936.

[268]Bresler, F. (1992) 'Suddenly at a Nursing Home ...' in Goodman, J. (1992) *The Medical Murders* Warner Books, London p.230; Wilson 1971:289.

[269]*Manchester Evening News* 27th February 1936.

[270]*Daily Mirror* 28th February 1936.

the prisoner that he had "no doubt" this recommendation would receive "the strongest consideration."[271] Members of *The Royal Commission on Capital Punishment* were to interpret this recommendation as being the result of Joe's acquittal.[272] It is certainly possible that had the judge not ordered the jury to acquit Joe, he too would have been found guilty, hence the jury perceived it to be unjust to execute one and not the other. This argument, however, would carry more weight if the outcome of Dorothea and Joe's trial stood in isolation, but as will become apparent in the following case-study, and as the case of Ada and William Williams illustrated, this outcome was not unique. An alternative interpretation of the trial outcome can be reached by considering the struggle between two conflicting discourses which excluded Joe altogether - those of woman as carer and as evil poisoner. The image Dorothea presented was not as straight-forward as that of other carers discussed in this book. For example, she did not fit the caricature of a 'hopeless alcoholic prostitute' as Leslie James had done. Nor did she fit the image of the 'hypocritical and wicked stepmother' like Ada Williams. Least of all, she could not be likened to the sophisticated, independent, ultra-confident Louise Masset, who selfishly pursued sexual pleasure at the expense of her child. Instead, Dorothea's appearance, her demeanour, her love for as well as loyalty and commitment to her family, all indicated a potential to fit into the 'victim' category rather than the 'bad' category. In other words, whereas the women discussed so far, found themselves firmly located within the 'bad' category with remarkably little conflict or contradiction, Dorothea possessed many characteristics which caused conflict between the discourses of woman as 'bad' and as 'victim'. That conflict became visible not just through the ambivalence expressed by the judge and jury, but also through the public's reaction to her execution which was far more hostile than had been the case with other executed women discussed in this chapter. Thus, over 5,000 people, mainly women and children, gathered outside Winson Green prison on the morning of the execution, singing hymns under the leadership of Mrs Van der Elst, one of the most active anti-hanging campaigners of the 20th century.[273] Meanwhile:

> A line of sandwichmen appeared bearing placards on which were the words "Stop this terrible crime of hanging a mother of five children."[274]

Mrs Van der Elst had also arranged for six aeroplanes to fly over the prison dropping leaflets, but was informed just hours before the execution that the planes "had been held back." Undeterred, she arrived fully equipped

---

[271] *Manchester Evening News* 27th February 1936.

[272] *Royal Commission on Capital Punishment 1949-1953 Report* 1953:320.

[273] *Daily Mirror* 17th April 1936; *Manchester Evening News* 16th April 1936. For a full account of Mrs Van der Elst's life and anti-hanging campaign see Gattey, C.N. (1972) *The Incredible Mrs Van der Elst* Leslie Frewin, London.

[274] *Manchester Evening News* 16th April 1936.

with a radio-car and loudspeakers, and despite the presence of 500 police officers who "had taken strong measures to prevent the development of any serious demonstration," made the following speech:

> Men and women, I appeal to you to prevent the hanging of a mother. This barbaric age would hang the mother of five children.[275]

As police officers pushed her car away with her still at the wheel she was shouting to the crowd "Stop this terrible thing."[276] It was no coincidence that protesters argued their case through the discourse of motherhood. When Dorothea first appeared in court:

> [she] entered the dock with her three months old baby in her arms. It was ... awake and soon its mother realised that she could not nurse it and properly attend to the grim business of court so she handed it over to a wardress beside her. The baby began to cry and Nurse Waddingham took it back and, rocking it gently, tried to quieten it. She was unable to do so and the noise so disturbed the court that a nurse was called in and the baby was taken out of hearing.[277]

The powerful image created by this scene is reminiscent of the tragic case of Mary Jones discussed in Chapter Two, who was still breast-feeding her baby as she was placed on the scaffold and, while Dorothea had sinned against woman's 'nature' by poisoning her charges, the court was now reminded that it too was about to sin against 'natural instincts' by permanently separating a mother from her children.

Ultimately, however, her chosen murder method was of the most despicable kind, and although at odds with the rest of Dorothea's image, it was powerful enough to close down the space on which she may have been heard more sympathetically. Against the discourse of 'the evil woman poisoner', the discourse of 'the good mother and hapless, ordinary, subservient woman' could send no more than a few momentary ruffles.

The Case of Louisa Merrifield

> Mrs Merrifield was a grasping woman who seized every opportunity which was to her advantage. She was also rather a stupid woman and mentally dull her deceptions were obvious, and her lies easily detected. She had none of the guile of the educated and sophisticated woman.[278]

---

[275] Quoted in *Manchester Evening News* 16th April 1936.
[276] *Manchester Evening News* 16th April 1936.
[277] O'Donnell 1956:88.
[278] Huggett & Berry 1956:215.

Louisa Merrifield made the worst possible impression at her trial, for she loved to shock by the coarseness of her words and manners. She talked incessantly and vulgarly, drank when she could, and tried to impress all whom she met.[279]

She was never an attractive woman - plump, with untidy hair, thick woollen stockings, dowdy clothes and spectacles.[280]

Like Dorothea Waddingham before her, Louisa Merrifield was found guilty of poisoning her charge in order to hasten her inheritance. Also like Dorothea, Louisa was to face the gallows alone although her husband Alfred had been her co-defendant throughout the trial. The by now familiar features of grinding poverty and related criminal activity were also applicable to Louisa who had been imprisoned for 84 days in 1946 for non-payment of a £10 fine.[281] This however, is where the similarities ended for where Dorothea was perceived to possess certain redeeming characteristics, Louisa had none. She was repeatedly described as "coarse" and "stupid" - desperate to be the centre of attraction and displaying an obsessive tendency towards self-aggrandisement - making her "one of the most loquacious murderers ever known."[282] Of all the women poisoners discussed here Louisa came closest to resembling the stereotypical psychopathic poisoner described by MacNalty:

The psychology of the poisoner is strange and terrible. It is dictated by egotism pushed to the verge of megalomania; it displays cunning, nerve, resource and refined cruelty.[283]

Even Mrs Van der Elst who submitted a passionate plea to the Home Secretary on behalf of Louisa called her "a fearful bragger."[284]

Louisa was 46 and Alfred was 70 when in March 1953 they were hired by Sarah Ricketts as house-keepers/companions in return for free accommodation. In their two and a half years of married life Louisa and Alfred had lived at more than twenty different addresses as a result of their constant change of employment.[285] The Merrifields therefore had stability

---

[279]Wilson 1971: 298.
[280]Description of Louisa Merrifield in *Daily Mirror* 1st August 1953.
[281]HO 291/330 (p.22) Public Record Office, Kew, Richmond, Surrey TW9 4DU. She had committed rationing offences and was released 18th November 1946.
[282]Huggett & Berry 1956:218.
[283]MacNalty, A. (1929) *A Book of Crimes* Elkin Mathews & Marrot Ltd, London pp.169-170.
[284]HO 29/229 XC2573 Public Record Office, Kew, Richmond, Surrey TW9 4DU. Original letter dated 8th September 1953.
[285]ASSI 52/785 Exhibit 13 - Statement of Louisa Merrifield dated 17th April 1953. This file is closed to the public until 2029 but is available for inspection by special

within their grasp for the first time when less than a fortnight later Sarah said: "If you do justice to me and look after me I will see that you have got a home for life."[286]   Thus, after only 11 days of employment, Louisa made arrangements for a will to be drawn up which would name her sole beneficiary, although when it was signed a week later, Sarah included both Louisa and Alfred as beneficiaries.[287] Within two weeks of signing the will Sarah had died of phosphorous poisoning which is associated with Rodine rat-poison.

There was no direct evidence linking Louisa to Sarah's death and if she had exercised a minimum amount of discretion and caution it is unlikely there would have been enough circumstantial evidence to convict her. Instead, in an attempt to maintain an air of self-importance, she bragged incessantly, sometimes to complete strangers, about her inheritance.   For example, the day after Sarah first promised Louisa her bungalow and over three weeks *before* her death, Louisa told an aquaintance:

> ... I've had a bit of good luck. Where I have been living the old lady has died and left me the bungalow worth about £3,000.[288]

Mrs Lowe who had employed Louisa for only one week earlier that year, received a letter from her two weeks before Sarah's death:

> I got a nice job nursing an old lady and she left me a lovely littl [sic] Bundlow [sic] and thank God for it, so you see love all come right in the end.[289]

When Louisa met Jessie Brewer, also prior to Sarah's death, she told her:

> We are landed. We went to live with an old lady and she died and she's left me a bungalow worth £4,000 ... It was all left to me, until that old bugger got talking to her and then it was left to us jointly ... I made everything all right. It cost me £2.2.0d to get a Doctor to prove she was in her right mind.[290]

During cross-examination Jessie was adamant that Louisa "definitely informed me that the old lady had died. I am positive. All the conversation

---

arrangement with staff at the Lord Chancellor's Department, Trevelyan House, 30 Great Peter Street, London SW1P 2BY.

[286]ASSI 52/785 - Exihibit 14 - Statement of Alfred Merrifield, 17th April 1953.

[287]ASSI 52/785 - Statement of solicitor William Darbyshire who prepared the will, dated 27th May 1953.

[288]ASSI 52/785 - Statement of David Spittal Brindley 28th May 1953.

[289]HO 291/230 27359.   Original letter included in file.   See also ASSI 52/785 Statement of Norah Lowe 28th May 1953.

[290]ASSI 52/785 - Statement of Jessie Brewer 28th May 1953.

was in the past tense."[291] It was as a result of reading that Sarah had died three days *after* this conversation that Jessie contacted the police.

The most dramatic insight into Louisa's personality can be gleaned from the testimony of Elizabeth Barraclough who "was a complete stranger" to her. While waiting in a bus queue she told her "she was very worried because she was looking after an old lady who was very ill," and after returning the previous day she had found "her husband in bed with the old lady, and was messing about with her and this had got her vexed":

If this goes on again, I'll poison the old bugger and him as well ... She's leaving me the bungalow between me and my husband, but he's so greedy he wants it all on his own.[292]

These testimonies alone, suggested Louisa was a scheming poisoner who had planned Sarah's murder for some time, but when taken together with testimonies of trades-people who had visited the bungalow, an even more sinister picture emerged. For example, George Forjan who made weekly deliveries to Sarah, testified that on the morning before her death, she was unable to pay because she "could not find her money," and said "I don't know what they are doing with my money." She subsequently asked Alfred to go to the bank and also requested he contact her solicitor because she wanted to change her will. Alfred refused, saying it "was too far for him":

Mrs Ricketts said 'What can I do'. Then she started to complain about her food. She said that she hadn't had proper food for the last three days. She said 'They are no good to me. They'll have to go out'. She said that Mrs Merrifield had previously called her a bloody fool.[293]

The money owed to his firm had only been outstanding *since* the Merrifields joined the household: "Before they came to live there Mrs Ricketts paid me every week ... and ... did not owe me any money."[294]

His testimony was supported by that of Joseph Malone who delivered groceries:

Mrs Ricketts said to Mrs Merrifield that she didn't think she was getting the right amount of food. Mrs Merrifield said 'You're getting your full entitlement of rations'. Mrs Ricketts used to pay me in cash when I delivered the order. After the Merrifields arrived Mrs

---

[291] ASSI 52/785 - Statement of Jessie Brewer 28th May 1953.

[292] ASSI 52/785 - Statement of Elizabeth Barraclough 28th May 1953.

[293] ASSI 52/785 - Statement of George Forjan 28th May 1953. That Sarah had had no food recently was confirmed by the testimony by Dr George Bernard Manning (29th May 1953) who carried out the post mortem and stated that "there did not appear to me to be any food in the stomach."

[294] ASSI 52/785 - Statement of George Forjan 28th May 1953.

Ricketts did not pay me. Nobody paid me ... Mrs Ricketts said that for the last fortnight she had not had any money.[295]

A third set of testimonies which cast suspicion on Louisa were those provided by three medical doctors. First, Dr Wood testified that Louisa had requested he visit Sarah the day before she died "in case anything happened to her during the night." When Dr Wood asked if it could wait till the morning Louisa said: "What happens if she died during the night?"[296] When he visited Sarah he could find nothing wrong with her:

> I remonstrated with Mrs Merrifield for calling me out, as I thought, under false pretences. She again said she was afraid of something happening during the night ... Mrs Merrifield mentioned something about a will. I said I wasn't interested.[297]

Second, Dr Yule was asked by Louisa to visit Sarah five days before her death "for the express purpose to see if she was mentally fit to sign a will":

> She said the reason why she wanted me to go was that the old lady might die at any moment with a stroke or a disease and she wanted to keep herself all right with the relatives.[298]

Third, when Dr Page visited Sarah as she lay dying he found the dining table pushed up against her bed, so close that he could not gain access to the patient, with Alfred, apparently unperturbed, eating his lunch. Louisa said: "She ... has been dying since we came to the place"[299], a claim which stood in sharp contrast to the evidence of the three doctors and the tradespeople who had seen Sarah within hours of her death.

Finally Louisa repeated the behaviour of Dorothea Waddingham and Joe Sullivan when she visited a funeral director, requesting a cremation, adding that she did not want Sarah's "two daughters to know she was dead or have anything to do with the funeral."[300]

The Merrifield case, like the majority of poisoning cases, received vast media coverage and virtually all the above evidence had been published both locally and nationally during the hearing at the Magistrates' Court two months before the trial.[301] The details reflected badly on the Merrifields, particularly Louisa who appeared to be the more active of the two. Taken together, the testimonies suggested that a helpless 79-year-old woman had

---

[295] ASSI 52/785 - Statement of Joseph Walter Malone 28th May 1953.
[296] ASSI 52/785 - Statement of Dr Albert Victor Wood 16th May 1953.
[297] ASSI 52/785 - Statement of Dr Albert Victor Wood 16th May 1953.
[298] ASSI 52/785 - Statement of Dr Burton Yule 27th May 1953.
[299] ASSI 52/785 - Statement of Dr Ernest Victor Page 27th May 1953.
[300] ASSI 52/785 - Statement of George Henry Johnson 27th May 1953.
[301] See for example *The Manchester Evening News* 27-29th May 1953.

been starved, robbed, perhaps even sexually abused by the couple. Moreover, the murder weapon, phosphorous, had caused a cruel and painful death with symptoms including severe stomach pains and great thirst until the victim finally slipped into a coma.[302] Louisa herself described how Sarah kept moaning until she collapsed on the hall floor, whereupon she lost the power of speech and was only able to put "her tongue out and open ... her mouth for a drink."[303] The impact this harrowing image created - an old woman totally in the power of her unscrupulous tormentors, accepting sips of what was allegedly poison - can be measured by the level of hate-mail received by the Home Office, and by the judge's comment that this was a most "wicked and cruel ... murder ... ."[304]

Louisa, more than anyone else before or after her, fitted the stereotypical image of the devious and hypocritical woman-poisoner. She expounded high moral standards and religious pretensions, claiming to have been an Army Salvationist for many years, and dramatically called upon her "Maker" when asked about the possibility that Sarah had been poisoned:

> If my Maker sends for me now my conscience is clear. There has never been anything in the house to hurt her.[305]

At the same time she made fantastic and dramatic claims, as when police officers found a watch and ring inside Sarah's handbag: "Those are mine. The old lady gave them to me on the day she died."[306] She also claimed that as Sarah collapsed in the hallway and was about to lose the ability to speak, "she thanked both my husband and me for what we had done for her. Those were the last words she spoke."[307] Her lies were so frequent and complex that at times she contradicted her own statements as I indicate below. Moreover, the frequency of her suggestion to several individuals, that Sarah might have a stroke "any time", followed by the same suggestion to both doctors and police officers after her death, was interpreted as an indication that Louisa had been carefully preparing and plotting the murder in advance.[308] At the same time her attempts to gain the moral highground through her indignant claims of innocence and her public display of Christian values meant that even before her trial she was considered an exceptionally

---

[302]HO291/230 27359 Trial transcript. Evidence of Dr G. B. Manning Vol 4 pp.3-4.
[303]ASSI 52/785 Exhibit 13 - Statement of Louisa Merrifield 17th April 1953.
[304]HO 29/229 XC2573 Judge Glyn-Jones quoted in Home Office Minute Sheet dated 4th September 1953. This file also contains several letters from members of the public, urging the execution to go ahead. One such (anonymous) letter read: "hang them up with their tongues if this could be then this would not be bad enough."
[305]ASSI 52/785 Statement of Detective Superintendent Colin McDougall 29th May 1953.
[306]ASSI 52/785 Statement of Detective Sergeant Norman Steadman 29th May 1953.
[307]HO291/230 27359 Trial transcript Vol 5 p.44.
[308]HO29/229 XC2573 Home Office Minutes dated 4th September 1953.

deceitful and hypocritical woman. More than anybody else, Louisa fitted Blyth's definition of the woman poisoner:

> More devious in their outlook and infinitely more complicated in the working of their conscience than the average male, they could even persuade themselves that they were genuinely acting in a Christian manner when devoting themselves to the care of an invalid whose agonised sufferings were being caused by themselves. Again and again, in poison cases involving women, the prisoner on trial for her life would adopt an air of injured innocence, and even of piety and godliness, calling upon her Maker to witness the purity of her soul. In short, women accused of murder often revealed an astonishing facility for telling lies in Court while preserving an outward appearance of absolute honesty.[309]

It will be necessary to analyse the self-presentation of both defendants in order to demonstrate how this image was reinforced rather than challenged during the double trial, and how Louisa came to be constructed as a "wicked" and "vulgar" woman who deserved to hang, while Alfred was considered to be a "tragic simpleton" - too stupid to have participated in the murder - and subsequently walked out of court a free man.

The Trial of the Merrifields

> It is as well we should face the facts without hypocrisy; you may have formed the opinion of Mrs Merrifield that she was a vulgar and stupid woman with a very dirty mind. I do her no injustice by telling you that. You may similarly have formed the impression of Mr Merrifield that he is at times rather stupid.[310]

The Merrifield trial lasted 11 days, longer than any other trial analysed in this book. Louisa spent three days in the witness box, giving evidence for nine and a half hours, with nearly half that time devoted to cross-examination. In a physical sense at least, her account could not be described as muted. Pat Carlen has compared court hearings with "the theatre of the absurd," describing how the "structures of surreality and psychic coercion" within the courtroom are nonetheless authenticated because "judicial personnel systematically present their coercive devices as being nothing more than the traditional, conventional and commonsensical ways of organising and synchronising judicial proceedings."[311]   Thus, apart from the defendant finding herself in a unusual and alienating situation when she initially enters the dock, there are a series of practical difficulties which may prevent her

---

[309]Blyth, H. (1975) *Madeleine Smith: A famous Victorian murder trial* Duckworth, London pp.15-16.
[310]HO 291/230 27359 Trial transcript, summing up Vol 11 p.12.
[311]Carlen, P. (1976) *Magistrates' Justice* Martin Robertson, London p.20.

from participating fully in proceedings. For example, jargon may be employed which means "procedure isn't made sufficiently plain", and the defendant therefore does not understand what is taking place. Difficulties in hearing are also a common problem, as is "placing and spacing" within the courtroom, resulting in a "series of 'pardons' and 'blank stares'" from the defendant.[312] Finally, while the conversational style of the courtroom is taken for granted by judicial personnel it will be alien to many defendants who find they "are often in the position of having to synchronise their answers and stances in a way quite divorced from the conventions of everyday life outside the courtroom."[313]

The Merrifield trial demonstrates the relevance of every one of these points, yet even with these uppermost in mind, the trial was haunted by an overall impression of a tragi-comic caricature, if not parody, of legal proceedings due to the conduct of the defendants. Indeed, the events leading up to the judge calling Louisa "stupid" and "vulgar" and defence counsel calling Alfred "a tragic simpleton" were set in motion immediately upon arrest when Alfred, after being charged with murder, said "Thank you."[314] Similarly, Louisa indicated her lack of knowledge about court etiquette when - seeing her husband during her second court appearance - she attempted to communicate by waving. Moreover, while her intentions were undoubtedly to display good manners in court, it was nevertheless inappropriate when in response to being told she would be held in remand for another week she replied: "Thank you very much my Lordships."[315] Inappropriate conduct was to become a semi-permanent feature of the Merrifield trial as the defendants appeared to behave more like actors in a farce than murder suspects standing trial. Alfred for example, regularly waved and smiled to observers in the public gallery and on one occasion stopped to say "Good Morning, gentlemen" to journalists, while on a different occasion Louisa "gave a 'V' sign to members of the public when she entered the dock."[316]

Constant interruptions were to become another feature of the trial. They were often caused by Alfred who suffered from deafness and therefore had difficulty in hearing proceedings. However, even when he could hear he could not always understand, as was the case when he was told he "could object to any juror before he took the oath. Mr Merrifield put his hand up and said: '... I can hear you but I cannot follow your words.'"[317] He brought proceedings to a halt on numerous other occasions, as when on the third day of the trial, he burst into tears, exclaiming: "It is not fair. Let me go down

---

[312]Carlen 1976:22; 23.

[313]Carlen 1976:24.

[314]HO291/230 27359 Judge's summing-up, trial transcript Vol 11 p.12; *Manchester Evening News* 30th July 1953; ASSI 52/783 - Statement of Detective Inspector John Dunn 29th May 1953.

[315]*Manchester Evening News* 8th May 1953.

[316]*Manchester Evening News* 20th, 27th, 29th May 1953.

[317]HO291/230 27359 Trial transcript Vol 1 p.2.

while you finish. ... I cannot stick this ... I cannot hear."[318] He also burst into tears twice during his three and a half hours on the stand. When the Attorney-General showed him a packet of rat-poison, Alfred turned his head away saying: "Don't let me look at it. I have heard so much about it ... I can see it in my sleep." When he was asked if he had seen something like it before he "bang[ed] his hand on a table" and "almost shouted":

> I have not and do not ask me again. Definitely not. I have not seen it, and that is a fact.[319]

A further insight into the dynamics between Alfred and judicial personnel can be gained from the following extract:

> You have had a new deaf-aid given you during the course of this trial?
> *I have had ---?*
> A new deaf-aid?
> *Yes.*
> ...
> Is it better?
> *This is much better.*
> The other one was a Government one, was it not?
> *Yes. If I talk a bit louder ---*
> Do not bother about that. It is the fault of the hearing. I believe deaf people is [sic] given that way - they shout at you.
> ...
> You can look at me when I am asking the questions, and when you are answering them look towards the Jury.
> [Mr Justice Glyn-Jones:] You might tell him he is doing extremely nicely.
> His Lordship has asked me to tell you that your are doing very well in the way you are giving your evidence because you are keeping your voice up.
> *Thank you, sir.*[320]

When his counsel asked if he had ever done anything to harm Sarah, Alfred "clenched his fists, held them above his head", and said:

> There is a pair of fists there. If they are never open again I did nothing only to succour the old lady, not destroy her.[321]

318HO291/230 27359 Trial transcript Vol 4 p.51. See also report in *Manchester Evening News* 23rd July 1953.
319HO291/230 27359 Trial transcript Vol 8 p.18. See also report in Manchester Evening News 28th July 1953.
320HO291/230 27359 Trial transcript Vol 7 pp.42-43.
321HO291/230 27359 Trial transcript Vol 8 p.6.

When Alfred's testimony was challenged he exclaimed:

Have you got the Bible there?
The Attorney-General: I don't think you need that at the moment.
Yes, I took the oath to tell the truth, and nothing but the truth, and I am telling it.[322]

When Alfred was asked about eating his lunch next to Sarah's dying body he answered:

Where else could I sit? There was nowhere else to sit.
But you need not have been having your lunch at that moment need you?
Was I not entitled to have my lunch?
Perfectly. Were you very upset about the old lady dying, of whom you were so fond?
... If she had been a blood relation I should have been more upset.
It did not interfere with your appetite?
Yes definitely it did. You were not there to see the quantity of food I ate.[323]

Finally, after persistently denying he owned a grey suit, when one such suit was exhibited in court as evidence he immediately said: "Yes, that is mine. Can I put it on?"[324]

The above examples of Alfred's self-presentation indicate how it became possible for his counsel to portray him as "a man wandering", "'guileless' and 'a tragic simpleton' no more capable of concocting or taking part in this fell scheme than a child":

> ... the whole picture you have of him is of a man getting on in years, simple ... and attempting to give you where he could remember it, a true picture of the position so far as he was concerned.[325]

Thus, while Alfred may well have tested the patience of his interrogators, the apparent simplicity of his character gave an overall impression of someone lacking in imagination and hence in possession of a simple honesty, eager to please and happy to cooperate. This stood in sharp contrast to the impression formed about Louisa, who despite being called "stupid" almost as frequently as Alfred, came to be regarded as "the dominant partner ... on any basis."[326] Like Dorothea before her, as a result of the

---

[322]HO291/230 27359 Trial transcript Vol 8 p.9.
[323]HO291/230 27359 Trial transcript Vol 8 p.16.
[324]HO291/230 27359 Trial transcript Vol 8 p.21.
[325]HO291/230 27359 Trial transcript Vol 10 p.19 and p.24 where Mr Nahum further argued that Alfred was "incapable of this cunning, desperate and vile murder."
[326]HO 29/229 XC2573 Home Office Minutes 14th September 1953.

strong association between women and the private sphere generally, and women as carers in particular, it was taken for granted that it was she who was 'in charge' and 'dominant' in the crime.

Like Alfred, Louisa appeared to have difficulty in understanding and following courtroom procedures, and frequently had to have questions repeated and re-phrased. Her response was often inappropriate, as when after being asked about what time she fetched the doctor, she replied: "I cannot properly remember. I have nearly forgotten the woman has died, to tell you the truth."[327] Similarly, her language was inappropriate by courtroom standards, as when she volunteered that: "Mr Merrifield did not break his neck to get up [in the mornings]"[328], and it was to prove almost impossible to obtain concise or direct answers to questions put by either defence or prosecution. Her communication problems within the courtroom were therefore not substantially different from Alfred's. But, unlike him she appeared deliberately obtuse, her frequent evasive responses validating her guilt. For example, when questioned about the inconsistency concerning the time she claimed to have given Sarah drinks, the Attorney-General put the same question to her no less than seven times:

> [Attorney-General] ... you go on in the next sentence: "When she had gone easy again I went back to bed although I never slept. I next heard her moaning in the hall at a quarter past three ...".
> *Just a moment please.*
> [Justice Glyn-Jones] Yes, Mrs Merrifield, what do you want to say?
> *When she got back easy again I went back to bed although I never slept all night - right, carry on, sir.*
> [Attorney-General] ... Now Mrs Merrifield, there is no doubt about it, is there? It is quite untrue to say you only gave her anything after you had picked her up in the hall?
> *When I picked Mrs Ricketts up ... she could not speak. The last words she said was: "I thank you and your husband for what you have done for me." There was always ... [drinks] prepared on the table before Mrs Ricketts went to bed - and they were always prepared by herself, my jury.*
> It is not true to say you only gave her ... anything after you picked her up in the hall?
> *Well, naturally, as woman to woman you would give her a drink if you thought she was ill and was wanting a drink.*
> So it is not true to say the first time you gave her anything was after you picked her up in the hall?
> *I beg your pardon, sir?*
> It is not true to say that you only gave her anything to drink after you picked her up in the hall?
> *Well, I may have misunderstood it.*

---

[327]HO 291/230 27359 Trial transcript Vol 5 p.39.
[328]HO 291/230 27359 Trial transcript Vol 7 p.7.

Will you not agree it is not true?
It is true that I gave her drinks - naturally.
And putting it another way ... it is not true that you never helped her
to a drink except when she was in a coma?
*I know I gave her these drinks, definitely I know I gave her these
drinks, but the drinks was [sic] prepared on the table before the
woman lost her speech and lost her voice. There was only the one
room that we all lived in.*
And of course, even more so it is quite untrue to say that: "From
beginning to end I never gave her anything to drink"?
I never gave her Rodine to drink.
Well, I am not asking that at the moment. Now, I want you to go on
with this statement just at the point where I was ...
Just a moment.
[Justice Glyn-Jones] ... if I may respectfully suggest it, she reads very
much more slowly than you do; if, therefore, you are proposing to
read a passage and put it to her I would suggest you read every word
slowly ...
If your Lordship pleases.
Just a moment - I have lost my place.[329]

It proved equally difficult to obtain an answer regarding a 'mixture'
which Sarah, supposedly drank regularly:

... what do you mean by mixture?
Well, whatever she took it was a mixture. She would mix anything ...
I am sorry, we must get this plain. You have now said that there was
brandy and there was rum, and there was an eggcup?
Yes, sir.
What was the mixture?
*There was no mixture that I know of on the table only what she
prepared herself.*
Yes, but what was that?
The rum and the brandy.
Oh, that was the mixture, was it?
*She used the same cup for rum and brandy. She was not funny about
that.*
Do you say that is what you meant when you spoke of a mixture?
I do not remember her mixing anything together ...
Not during that night?
Well, I cannot count back, but she did all sorts of funny little things.
Yes, well if you take the rum and the brandy together you gave her
well over two tablespoonfuls, did you not?
I would not say.
You would not say you did not?

[329]HO 291/230 27359 Trial transcript Vol 7 pp.3-4.

I do not know.[330]

However, this apparent obtuseness paled into insignificance when Louisa committed the ultimate transgression of speaking ill of the dead and slurring the character of the woman she was accused of murdering by calling Sarah "a very immoral woman":

> What do you mean by saying that?
> *Have I to say it? Is it all right to explain in front of these young men, my Lordship?*
> [Mr Justice Glyn-Jones:] Yes, I am afraid we cannot protect them.
> *When I bathed Mrs Ricketts she asked me to amuse her in an immoral way. At the same time I realised she was a human being and that she had had no husband for ten years ...*
> Yes?
> *I asked why was it if she was in need of a man so much - why she did not marry. She said it was through her private income that came from Mr Ricketts.*
> Well?
> *And he made it if she married her income would have gone away from her. I then explained: "I have had three husbands and I have never had a wage off none of them but have always been provided for."*[331]

The Attorney-General discredited this evidence by pointing out that Sarah "was in her 80th year", and had had "all her sexual organs ... removed."[332] He thus demonstrated that it was Louisa, not Sarah, who was vulgar and immoral. Vulgarity, however, is not proof of murder, and while Louisa had left an unfavourable impression on the jury as a result of her conduct and self-presentation, the trial transcript also contains numerous examples of responses which contradict the dominant truth about her - that she was the "dominant partner" and the "mastermind" behind a crime which Alfred was too "stupid" to carry out. For example, when her evidence that Sarah had not had a cooked meal in two years was challenged, she responded: "Well, what could she have? Because she never had bacon, for a start." Similarly, when she was asked about Sarah's alcohol intake, she asked: "What do you mean by 'alcohol'?"[333] Yet, while Alfred's apparent feeblemindedness was readily accepted, Louisa's equally unorthodox self-presentation in the courtroom was interpreted as further evidence of her deviant personality. Her failure to communicate through dominant modes of expression, especially those of "emotive connectedness" and compassion associated with female speech as discussed in Chapter Three, did not grant her the authority

---

[330]HO 291/230 27359 Trial transcript Vol 7 pp.5-6.
[331]HO 291/230 27359 Trial transcript Vol 7 p.18.
[332]HO 291/230 27359 Trial transcript Vol 7 p.18.
[333]HO 291/230 27359 Trial transcript Vol 7 p.9; p.8.

associated with men's speech, but merely reinforced her deviance. Her inappropriate responses were perceived to be a deliberately obtuse and evasive strategy, which - together with her assertiveness in terms of calling doctors and organising the will - meant she was credited with a rationality denied to Alfred. In contrast, Alfred's deafness reinforced the belief that he was feebleminded, which in turn allowed him to be infantilised, hence casting him in a role usually reserved for women.

Apart from Louisa's behaviour within the courtroom, aspects of her personal history were revealed to the jury that included several of the characteristics which contribute to categorising women as 'bad' rather than 'mad'. For example, the court heard Louisa drank excessively and habitually became severely inebriated.[334] Moreover, she had been married three times within ten months, and had not seen two of her four children "for many years" because they had been taken into care.[335] Louisa not only lacked commitment to marriage and motherhood, but also to domesticity generally:

> The picture has been made of the two of them constantly changing employment and living in furnished accommodation, having no home of their own ...[336]

Louisa was therefore a prime example of a doubly deviant woman. Not only had she abused the carer role, she had also subverted an array of other traditional female roles in relation to marriage, motherhood and domesticity. As discussed above, the post-war period was an era in which women who fell short of acceptable standards in those areas, were greeted with particular concern and anxiety. Together with her failure to limit her alcohol intake, these transgressions totalled an unregulated and undisciplined 'out of control' female in particular and dangerous womanhood generally. The double standards of morality discussed in Chapter Three, became starkly visible when the judge disregarded Alfred's domestic shortcomings. He too had a troubled family history. The father of ten children, he had left his wife and family in 1928 "as a result of domestic differences." Moreover, in 1949, a year before his marriage to Louisa, he was convicted "of indecently assaulting a girl aged 8 years." Eight months after the marriage, Alfred was at the centre of more conflict when the "home was broken up following upon differences between" Alfred and Louisa's son.[337] While the judge quite

---

[334]ASSI 52/785 Testimony of Jessie Jensen 29th May 1953; HO 291/230 27359 Trial transcript, Louisa Merrifield under cross-examination p.21.
[335]Louisa had in fact had nine children, four of whom were still living at the time of the trial, with three of them in care as a result of Louisa "neglecting to provide reasonable education" for them (HO 29/229 XC2573 Blackpool County Borough Police Antecedents 16th June 1953). See also Louisa's medical report issued by Prison Medical Officer Cormack 9th July 1953.
[336]HO 291/230 27359 Trial transcript, summing-up Vol 11, p.12.
[337]HO 29/229 XC2573 Blackpool County Borough Police Antecedents 16th June 1953. As had been the case with Joe Sullivan, Alfred's military record was assessed

properly did not reveal either Louisa's or Alfred's criminal record, he made a notable distinction between the prisoners, when after pointing to Louisa's troubled past, he chose not to refer to Alfred's domestic history - instead commenting to the jury: "I do not know that there is any information you have been given about Mr Merrifield's background."[338] He did however, warn the jury that:

> You must not convict a woman of murder because her character and personality have made an unfavourable impression on you. The fact she may be a vulgar, stupid woman with a dirty mind is not a good ground for convicting her of murder. You must not let any mere dislike for the personality of either of these people prejudice your fair and honest weight of the evidence.[339]

After summing up for nearly four hours the judge ended on a note which emphasised Louisa's dominant role in the crime:

> It is important to draw a distinction between them as best you can in your minds. All the evidence you have heard about the conduct of Mrs Merrifield ... is evidence against her ... It is not evidence against him unless you are satisfied that he did enter into the plot with her ... the evidence of dissension between them ... might point against the fact he was acting in concert, but what you have to consider ... is his personality with the evidence he has given, his own conduct at the time and afterwards. You must make up your minds ... about him and ... her separately.[340]

After almost six hours the all-male jury found Louisa guilty of murder but failed to reach a verdict in Alfred's case.[341] The Attorney-General consequently entered a *nolle prosequi* and he was released from prison a week after the trial had ended.[342]

---

as "very good", thus providing us with a glimpse of the gendered nature of 'relevant' information.

[338]HO 291/230 27359 Trial transcript, summing-up Vol 11, p.12.

[339]HO 291/230 27359 Trial transcript, summing-up Vol 11, p.12.

[340]HO 291/230 27359 Trial transcript, summing-up Vol 11, p.44.

[341]HO 291/230 27359 Trial transcript Vol 11, pp.45-6. Intially two women had been appointed to the jury, but they were successfully challenged by Mr Nahum QC for the defence (*Manchester Evening News* 20th July 1953).

[342]*The Times* 22nd September 1953. A *nolle prosequi* means 'unwilling to prosecute'. Alfred Merrifield was eventually told he would not stand a second trial.

A Fair Hearing?

Space does not permit a full analysis of Louisa's appeal which lasted three days[343]; however, points 6 and 7 of the Appeal Notice are of particular relevance:

> 6. Many of the observations of the learned judge both during the hearing of the evidence and in the summing-up must have indicated to the jury that he himself had come to a conclusion with regard to the case that was adverse to the appellant, and that he regarded the defence as devoid of any foundation.
>
> 7. The whole conduct of the case must have conveyed to the jury that the learned judge was completely convinced of the appellant's guilt and was disparaging the defence.[344]

The Court of Appeal rejected these contentions, stating "that there is no foundation for the criticism of unfairness or prejudice or one-sidedness on the part of the learned Judge."[345] After hearing her Appeal being dismissed Louisa "raised her clenched fist high above her head. She firmly resisted the efforts of two prison officers to pull down her arm."[346]

Now there was only one avenue open to Louisa before she reached the gallows - that of a personal petition for her life. The futility of this action became apparent when *evidence of witnesses not called during the trial*, was taken into account by Home Office staff deciding whether Louisa should live or die. One witness had testified that Alfred "was afraid of his wife and had found a tin of rat poison in one of her cases." A second witness added that Alfred claimed Louisa "was trying to poison him and that he had found some Rodine in his bedroom ..." A third witness stated Louisa "had boasted to her about having done two husbands already."[347] This was yet another example of Louisa's fantastic and dramatic lies for her first husband had undergone a post-mortem which revealed he had died from "sub-acute infective hepatitis", and her second husband had died of a heart attack at the age of 78.[348]

---

[343]Much of the Appeal was concerned with a contestation of medical evidence in relation to the post-mortem carried out on Sarah Ricketts. See Appendix II.

[344]HO 291/230 27359 Particulars of Grounds of Appeal Additional to Those Set Out in the Notice. Dated 26th August 1953.

[345]HO 29/229 XC2573 The Court of Criminal Appeal Judgement no 777 p.19, dated 3rd September 1953.

[346]Huggett & Berry 1956:223.

[347]HO 29/229 XC2573 Home Office Minutes 4th September 1953.

[348]HO 29/229 XC2573 Blackpool County Borough Police Antecedents. With respect to her second husband, Louisa had claimed "that she had set the bed so that when he got into it it would collapse; it did so and the shock killed [him]". Certain newspapers appeared eager to insinuate that these deaths were suspicious. For example the *Daily Mirror* wrote with respect to Louisa's first husband that "a coroner

Finally, a witness testified that the Merrifields "frequently quarrelled, and on a number of occasions ... [Louisa had said] that she had tried to dump her husband in Wigan but that he had traced her again. But, she added, 'I'll do him yet. I'll give him a dose of rat poison.'"[349]

This was not a loving, compliant, altruistic wife who was timid, subordinate or deferential to her husband. Louisa possessed none of the characteristics favoured by the court as described in Chapter Three, but displayed those associated with activating judicial misogyny and came across as an 'uppity' woman needing to be 'put in her place'. Unlike Dorothea, she did not even display loyalty to her husband and children, nor did her remarks suggest Alfred would ever be able to exert a degree of control over her unruliness. Unsurprisingly therefore, the Home Secretary's adviser concluded his consideration of a reprieve with these words: "I am afraid that I can find very little to say in Mrs Merrifield's favour."[350]

Home Office Minutes do not reveal why the above witnesses were not called to give evidence, although we can speculate that had they been called by the prosecution, their testimonies could also have been utilised by the defence to illustrate that Louisa was a proven liar which may have cast doubt on her other claims that were used against her throughout the trial.[351] More, worryingly however, is the revelation that in addressing a question of life and death, Home Office personnel, in their final consideration of her case, took into account evidence that had not been tested in court, but which was highly detrimental to the prisoner. Thus while Louisa had spent three days in the dock talking incessantly, her 'muted' state was total with respect to the most damning evidence against her. As with other women discussed here, judicial misogyny did not end with the trial, but remained a feature of Louisa's existence until her life was extinguished two weeks later.

An Alternative Truth?

Prior to Louisa's execution, one person - Mrs Van der Elst - had constructed an alternative truth about the Merrifields which she presented to the Home Secretary:

> The husband ... posed as a kindly and simple old man, never spoke - and it seemed as if this old man had been made use of by his wife and had been made to do things under her stronger will. This was not true, he was a cunning old man acting a part in court, but if one could

---

said it was difficult to determine the cause of death but after a month of laboratory tests, decided his death was due to natural causes" (1st August 1953).

[349] HO 29/229 XC2573 Home Office Minutes 4th September 1953.

[350] HO 29/229 XC2573 Home Office Minutes 4th September 1953, initialled P.E.

[351] Mr Naham, the Merrifields' QC, in his closing speech said that "much of that mass of suspicion - might we not also call it prejudice? - had been engendered against her by her own foolish talk ..." and her statements were "just vapourings of a woman struggling in difficulties ..." (HO291/230 Trial transcript Vol 9 p.49; 50).

judge of the two people, I would consider that the old man was the most guilty ... He never troubles about his wife being condemned to death. He thinks, to look well he will take her a few flowers, but she can see through him and refused to see him.[352]

The opinion that Alfred was involved in the poisoning was shared by many other correspondents,[353] and evidence had been presented during the trial which strongly suggested he had purchased the rat poison.[354] Louisa herself wrote in her petition that she had:

> had a lot off [sic] Domestic trouble with Mr Merrifield and I had a Black eye ... My husband had both wardrobes locked, and I had No Privacy what so ever ... I had to write [letters] in the toilet bit by bit it was hard on mee [sic], as my husbands [sic] conduct to mee [sic] never been too great. and [sic] he would never let mee [sic] write to anyone not even my oun [sic] children he would rip anything up if he saw mee [sic] writing ... since our marrage [sic] I and Mr Merrifield My husband as [sic] had our domestic troubls [sic], and his fast life, and mine have not been off [sic] the Brightest ...[355]

However, as has been the case with certain contemporary women, Louisa did not fit the role of a battered wife or victim.[356] As a result of what

---

[352]HO 29/229 XC2573 Original letter to Home Secretary from Mrs Van der Elst 8th September 1953. Louisa had refused to see Alfred on two occasions. Unperturbed, he told newspapers: "I shall continue to do what I can for her, and I shall write her a cheery letter every day" (*Liverpool Daily Post* 10th September 1953). Louisa and Alfred appeared to have resolved their differences before her execution, because on her last day, Alfred visited her twice, and according to him, her last words were: "Good-bye Alfie. Look after yourself. God bless you" (*Liverpool Daily Post* 16th September 1953).

[353]HO 29/229 XC2573 includes a file of letters from the public.

[354]The jury was told to ignore evidence relating to an ID parade in which Alfred took part, because a chemist's assistant who "was satisfied at the identification parade that Merrifield was the man", failed to make a positive ID as she "was very nervous" (ASSI 52/785 Testimony of Mavis Atkinson). However, in his summing up, the judge said: "the man who went into the chemist's shop was elderly; he was wearing a hearing-aid; he had ulcers on his legs; he bore ... a general resemblance to the elderly man they saw on the identity parade ... There are many elderly men; there are quite a number of elderly men who wear hearing-aids. Are there so many elderly men wearing hearing-aids with ulcers on their legs, and do you think it an odd coincidence that, in a house in which a woman has died of rat poison, living there is an elderly man wearing a deaf-aid and with ulcers on his legs, who ... bears a resemblance to the man they saw?" (HO 291/230 27359 summing up Vol 11 p.38).

[355]HO 29/229 XC2573 Louisa Merrifield's petition to the Home Secretary. Undated.

[356]See for example Ballinger, A. (1996) 'The Guilt of the Innocent and the Innocence of the Guilty' in Myers, A. & Wight, S. (eds) *No Angels* Pandora, London.

was already known about her character, her version of their relationship was unlikely to be believed. Even if she was believed, her lack of tact in other parts of the petition together with her grandiose religious references ensured that whatever sympathy she may have aroused, would be cancelled out. Thus, she continued to discredit Sarah's character and called her "a very stupid old lady ... [who] would not Sleep ... [but was] Knocking around all night." She also suggested that Sarah and Alfred were having an affair:

> I realised there was the miss-conduct [sic] between Mrs Ricketts and My husband but I could do Nothing about it he denies it, but Mrs Ricketts apoligised [sic] to mee [sic], she New [sic] how conning [sic] he was. and tried to give mee [sic] the understanding he was Not true to mee [sic].[357]

Meanwhile she maintained an air of self-importance and religious fervour which seemed misplaced:

> ... if ever a woman lived to do her best it was I Mrs Louisa Merrifield ... I do Pray to God the Father Almighty that he will Give you Grace and Wisdom to understand that I am Not Gilty [sic] off [sic] this old lady [sic] Death ... I do trust to God Allmighthy [sic]. that He Will Give My Dear Majesty The Queen and you Sir, Grace serfikant [sic] to see from eye to eye ... as I plead to you for my life to be delivered for on my oath off [sic] God The Father Almighty. I did not give Mrs Ricketts rodio [sic].[358]

While Louisa's accounts were not muted, her lack of self-regulation when speaking and writing ensured that her word carried no legitimacy. After repeatedly breaking the rules governing dominant modes of speech she was eventually disqualified as a speaker. Thus, her self-presentation in the courtroom, amongst friends, and in her letters, is perhaps the strongest evidence that she was not the 'mastermind' portrayed by the prosecution. Huggett and Berry wrote that "it was beyond the range of her intellect to see that her coarse conversation turned people against her."[359] Her lack of self-awareness and etiquette reinforced the deep dislike and contempt directed at female poisoners, which in turn enabled a Home Office official to express this view:

> "I cannot think that public opinion would feel that it was wrong that the law should be allowed to take its course in the case of Mrs Merrifield merely because her husband was not convicted ..."[360]

357HO 29/229 XC2573 Louisa Merrifield's petition to Home Secretary. Undated.
358HO 29/229 XC2573 Louisa Merrifield's petition to Home Secretary. Undated.
359Huggett & Berry 1956:217.
360HO 29/229 XC2573 Home Office Minutes dated 4th September 1953. According to the *Royal Commission on Capital Punishment 1949-1953* public opinion was one

Ultimately we can never know the exact relations between the Merrifields, and indeed, the point of examining the case has not been to establish an 'ultimate' truth. Instead my aim has been to illustrate that while there was no direct evidence against either prisoner, established discourses of women's dominance within the domestic sphere, and of the woman poisoner and carer, implied that a female was more likely to attend a sick-bed than a male, and thus cast Louisa in the dominant role. As had been the case with Dorothea Waddingham, this supposed dominance, together with her betrayal of the female caring role, ensured her chances of receiving a 'not guilty' verdict were lower than Alfred's. The judge reminded the jury that "murder by poisoning is a secret and treacherous crime" and "of all forms of death by which human nature may be overcome the most distasteful is that of poison."[361] He specifically instructed members to "take into account not only the evidence which each had actually spoken in the witness-box - the words they have said - but the whole appearance and demeanour and behaviour of each as well in the dock, as in the witness-box."[362] However, the evidence neither proved nor disproved whether Louisa was frightened of Alfred, as she claimed in her petition, or whether she acted under his initiative rather than the other way around. This ambiguity was commented upon by Mr Paget an MP nearly two years later when - after quoting a passage from the summing-up - he concluded that capital punishment was based on no more than "a balance of probabilities."[363] Hence, it was not merely the evidence but also existing discourses of the 'female poisoner' and 'carer', which led the jury to conclude that Alfred was "no more than a stupid old man with the insensitiveness of a stupid old man", while defence counsel's reminder that Louisa was "being tried for murder ... not ... for stupidity", were ignored.[364] It's plea that Louisa was a woman who "left school at ... 14 and had been working in a humble position ... all her life ... had ranged against her all the forces of the Crown" fell on equally deaf ears,[365] and as the judge passed the

consideration when deciding if a reprieve should be granted: "it has occasionally been felt right to commute the sentence in deference to a widely spread or strong local expression of public opinion, on the ground that it would do more harm than good to carry out the sentence if the result was to arouse sympathy for the offender and hostility to the law" (p.12). Unlike the jury who found Dorothea Waddingham guilty, Louisa Merrifield's jury did not recommend mercy.

[361] HO291/230 27359 Trial transcript, Judge's summing up Vol 11 p.2; p.4.

[362] HO291/230 27359 Trial transcript, Judge's summing up Vol 11 p.5.

[363] *Parliamentary Debates (House of Commons)* Vol 536, 25th January-11th February 1955 col 2169. The part of the summing up quoted by Mr Paget was: "Counsel for the defence has said to you more than once that the prosecution must exclude every chance and every possibility that the inferences they ask you to draw are mistaken. That is not the law. You need only deal with such possibilities of error as you think reasonably likely."

[364] *Manchester Evening News* 29th July 1953. Summing up and closing speech for defence.

[365] HO291/230 27359 Trial transcript, closing speech for defence Vol 9 p.50.

death-sentence he told her: "You have been convicted upon plain evidence of as wicked and cruel a murder as I ever heard tell of."[366]

Twenty people had waited outside the court, but "there was no emotion shown when news of the verdict circulated through the crowd."[367] Similarly, on the morning of Louisa's execution, "more than 300 people stood in the rain outside Strangeways Gaol" waiting for the announcement of her death, but when it was made, "no heads were bared and no tears were shed."[368] Two weeks earlier, on hearing Louisa's appeal had failed, Alfred had given an interview to *The Daily Mail*. In it he offered his personal insight into her personality:

> I have learned from bitter experience that she is a wicked woman ... She has absolutely no moral sense and she has done many things to show that she has no feeling for the old man she married ... she dragged my good name in the mud. She ill-treated me so badly and so often that my health broke down ... She showed no pity, not even ordinary womanly kindness ... Not for all the money in the world would I live in the same town, never mind the same house, as Louie again. I would prefer there were thousands of miles between us.[369]

Conclusion

I introduced this chapter by noting the rarity of women killing other women. In every one of the five cases analysed here, the official explanation for the crimes were that of personal gain, although in Styllou Christofi's case, that gain was perceived in emotional rather than financial terms. These killings therefore seem more calculated, 'cold-blooded' and premeditated than the killing of children by an unstable mother or the killing of a partner/husband by an abused, long-suffering wife. In that sense, they also pose a problem for feminist theorists, who, in moving beyond such stereotypically gendered killings, are faced with the difficult task of theorising criminal acts which by their very nature cannot lead to neat resolutions.[370] For example, the gross disparity between Dorothea Waddingham's and Louisa Merrifield's punishment compared to their partners who left court free men, should not be seen as an excuse to detract agency or responsibility away from the two women. In other words, the point of placing their cases within the context of a double trial has not been to excuse the women's part in the crime, nor to

---

[366]HO291/230 27359 Trial transcript, judge's summing up Vol 11, p.46.

[367]*Manchester Evening News* 1st August 1953.

[368]*Liverpool Daily Post* 19th September 1953.

[369]*Daily Mail* 4th September 1953. Front-page interview with Alfred Merrifield, head-lined: "My wife? She had no pity." The contents of this interview suggests the reason why Louisa refused Alfred's visits on at least two occasions, and why Mrs Van der Elst was cynical in her attitude towards him.

[370] See discussion on this point by Bell & Fox 1996:471-494.

portray them as 'helpless victims' being 'led' by their men. Similarly, in the case of Louie Calvert, we cannot justify or empathise with her gruesome act. The cases of Margaret Allen and Styllou Christofi encompassed two women whose deviance appeared so extreme that it could not be typified. Instead they were inappropriately allocated a place within the 'bad' category - thus providing further evidence of the inadequacy of the 'mad/bad' categorising system which frequently deems rational women to be mad whilst failing those whose mental state ought to be further investigated. Nonetheless, the contention outlined in Chapter Three - that it is a certain *type* of woman who is singled out for the most severe punishment - still holds true. Thus, after examining the five cases in this chapter, we have found women with criminal records; who were drinkers; who had children in care; who were prostitutes; who were the mothers of illegitimate children and who were not married to the men they lived with. In short, they were women who had failed in various degrees to attain appropriate standards in the crucial areas of motherhood, domesticity and sexual respectability. Moreover, their offence pattern - committing acts of murderous violence - stood in sharp opposition to sex role expectations, which, as discussed earlier, plays an important part in constructing the 'doubly' deviant woman.

By challenging existing accounts of Dorothea Waddingham and Louisa Merrifield, and by rendering Louie Calvert, Margaret Allen and Styllou Christofi visible, we can end their muted state. By including their cases in the work towards the creation of a more complex language in which to discuss women's violence, we can ensure this language provides even the most powerless of women with a voice. The five women studied in this chapter were never to benefit from the new knowledge generated as a result of 'evading' dominant knowledge in this manner. Due to the historical nature of this book the feminist goal of sharing the research with the researched is not an option. However, these women's histories have been crucial to the principle of generating knowledge from 'below'. In the words of Sawicki, "through the retrieval of subjugated knowledge, one establishes a historical knowledge of resistance and struggle."[371] Hence, in excavating their cases, new spaces are created on which to tell their stories - spaces which in turn are available for the foundation of as yet unopened discourses and unspoken language in relation to violent women of the future.

---

[371] Sawicki, J. (1991) *Disciplining Foucault* Routledge, London, p.57.

6 Women Who Kill their Male Partners

Part I: Introduction

Women who kill their husbands/partners have always been punished more harshly than men who kill their spouses. In Chapter Two I noted that prior to the Enlightenment, women who killed their husbands were guilty of *petit treason* and therefore could be burned at the stake, unlike men who killed their wives who could only be found guilty of murder for which the penalty was hanging. This differential punishment was based on the notion that a woman who killed her husband had "violated the implicit contract between ruler and ruled."[1] She was therefore also guilty of killing her master which was "an affront to God, the King and the entire patriarchal lineage."[2] Beattie has suggested that women who committed *petit treason* may have been battered and subsequently acted in self-defence.[3] However, it is only during the last two decades - as a result of vigorous campaigning by feminist activists - that legal precedents have been set which recognise this alternative truth about women who kill abusive husbands. In this version of the truth such acts are viewed not "as 'cold-calculated killing[s]' but as ... act[s] of self-defence."[4] The legal response to the feminist demand "that the law tell a different story about the same event and the same participants"[5] is still characterised by struggle between a male-dominated criminal justice system steeped in tradition and sheltering behind reactionary views of the social world, and modern women whose everyday experiences have increasingly led to demands for substantive as well as formal justice and equality. While such demands have given rise to a new discourse around violent men - that they 'precipitate' towards their own death by using violence against their partners[6] - no woman is guaranteed leniency when facing the court after having killed an abusive partner. In 1991, two days after Sara Thornton's appeal failed, a case similar to hers, except the defendant was a man and the victim a woman,

---

[1]McLynn, F. (1991) *Crime & Punishment in Eighteenth Century England* Oxford University Press, Oxford, p.120.
[2]Faith, K. (1993) *Unruly Women* Press Gang, Vancouver, p.32.
[3]Faith 1993:33, referring to Beattie (1986).
[4]Stanko, E. & Scully, A. (1996) 'Retelling the Tale: The Emma Humphreys Case' in Myers, A. & Wight, S. (1996) *No Angels* Pandora, London, p.62.
[5]Stanko & Scully 1996:58.
[6]Browne, A. (1987) *When Battered Women Kill* The Free Press, New York, p.10. Browne defines men who precipitate their own death as those who "were the first to use physical force, strike blows, or threaten with a weapon."

had a very different outcome when Joseph McGrail walked free, having received a two-year suspended sentence after murdering his abusive, alcoholic common-law wife.[7] Yet Thornton too is a free woman today, which demonstrates the power of one particular feminist challenge to the legal system with groups such as *Justice for Women* as well as Thornton herself, succeeding in unsettling the legitimacy of the law, a process which also exposed the shifting terrain on which legal hegemony is built. The success of this feminist challenge becomes even more apparent if we compare the present to the first half of this century when the abuse that women suffered was largely ignored. Even when commented upon it did not count as a mitigating circumstance and failed to impact on the execution process in any way.

The Case of Emily Swann

> Emily was ... a confirmed tippler and a slut and her only virtue was that she loved children. She took good care of them but it was her husband, an inoffensive individual, who was left at home to mind the brood while Emily made the round of the local inns.[8]

In previous chapters I have discussed the possibility of spouses being implicated in crimes for which only the woman was executed. This ambiguity did not apply to the 'Wombwell murder' which concluded with a double execution, the second of three to be examined in this book. Emily Swann, who was 42 in 1903, the year of her execution, was hanged four days after Christmas with her lover John Gallagher, for the murder of Emily's husband, William. The case of Emily Swann, like those of Louie Calvert and Margaret Allen, has remained almost invisible throughout this century and merited only a few cursory lines in national newspapers at the time. The main reason for this is likely to be that it appeared utterly unproblematic - an 'open and shut' case of a wicked, scheming and immoral wife plotting with her lover, the murder of her 'innocent', hard-done-by and long-suffering husband. This official version of events ensured the execution of two people was regarded as quite uncontroversial - merely a case of the law taking its rightful course.

The Swann's lived in the tiny mining community of Wombwell when John Gallagher entered their lives, initially as a lodger, later, also as Emily's lover. Neighbours testified "Gallagher slept with her whilst her husband was at work at night",[9] and unsurprisingly, conflict erupted between the two men

---

[7] *The Observer* 4th August 1991.

[8] O'Donnell, B. (1956) *Should Women Hang?* W.H. Allen, London, p.50.

[9] HO144/736/113887 XC2356 Public Record Office, Kew, Richmond, Surrey TW9 4DU. Testimony of Mary Ann Ward included in Judge's Notes dated 11th December 1903. As the name suggests, 'Judge's Notes' are the notes the trial judge makes as witnesses give evidence and the trial unfolds. In cases such as that of Emily Swann,

when William became aware of the affair. John was asked to seek alternative lodgings, but he merely moved into the house of Mary Ann Ward opposite the Swann's and the affair continued. Emily and John were two of the participants at a drinking party in the home of Mary Ann one Saturday afternoon, when Emily took John's clothes - newly released from the pawnbroker - across the road to her own house. She returned almost immediately with a black eye and said: "Look Johnnie what our Bill has done."[10] John replied: "I'll give the b-r something for himself."[11] As they crossed the yard together to see William, Emily was heard to say: "I hope he'll punch him to death."[12] Within 15 minutes John returned alone to the party and said: "I've broken the b-r 4 ribs + I'll break him 4 more."[13] After another drink he left for the Swann's house again saying: "I'll murder the b-y swine before morning." A second violent struggle was overheard which included Emily urging: "Give it to him Johnny - give it to the b-r ... Punch the b-r to death."[14]

After the second struggle John and Emily emerged from the house holding hands.[15] However, within minutes, Emily called for help, perhaps realising William was seriously hurt. John meanwhile went to the local pub, and when told William was dead responded: "'I have not b-y well done it' and at once danced about the floor."[16] To another witness he said: "'I'm not guilty am I?' and started dancing + laughing."[17] He furthermore refused Emily's request to accompany her to the house to face the police and was not captured for two months.[18]

The behaviour of Emily and John before and during the murder allowed for only one interpretation as far as Home Office staff were concerned: it had been a "cruel and deliberate murder" because "the return to the attack shows that they knew what they were about ..."[19] Worse still, it was judged to be a premeditated murder as a result of a witness testifying that a week earlier Mrs Swann had said to Gallagher: "Go and punch his b-y ribs off, and I'll stand and see you do it, and thing [sic] you do no wrong."[20]

---

where no trial transcript exists, the 'Judge's Notes' are therefore the only primary source available which describes in detail - and frequently quotes - evidence given at the trial.

[10]HO144/736113887 XC2356 Statement to the Coroner's Court by Walter Wigglesworth dated 9th June 1903.

[11]HO144/736/113887 XC2356 Testimony of Mary Ann Ward in Judge's Notes.

[12]HO144/736/113887 XC2356 Statement by Walter Wigglesworth 9th June 1903, testimonies by Edward Ward; Alfred Harper and Martha Ward in Judge's Notes.

[13]HO144/736/113887 XC2356 Testimony of Rose Ward in Judge's Notes.

[14]HO144/736/113887 XC2356 Testimony of J.W. Dunn in Judge's Notes.

[15]HO144/736/113887 XC2356 Testimony of J.W. Dunn in Judge's Notes.

[16]HO144/736/113887 XC2356 Testimony of Edward Ward in Judge's Notes.

[17]HO144/736/113887 XC2356 Testimony of Walter Wigglesworth in Judge's Notes.

[18]HO144/736/113887 XC2356 Testimony of Thomas Beard and Detective George Hudson in Judge's Notes.

[19]HO144/736/113887 XC2356 Home Office Minutes 11th December 1903.

[20]HO144/736/113887 XC2356 Testimony of Lavinia Ward in Judge's Notes.

Emily herself agreed she had often heard John tell William "he would make him ready for a coffin"[21], and a third witness appeared to support the Crown's contention that William's murder had been premeditated when she testified: "I have many a time heard Gallagher say 'I'll kill the bugger', meaning deceased."[22] Thus, while one adviser to the Home Secretary conceded "they had evidently some days before contemplated violence though not perhaps actual murder", another was adamant this was "a premeditated + brutal murder. Though they had undoubtedly been drinking they were quite sensible of what they were doing."[23] Even Emily's black eye - the original reason for John's attack on William - was excused as having come about as a result of provocation:

> ... it was his [John's] presence there that provoked Swann to strike his wife.[24]

Events surrounding the murder of William Swann therefore appeared self-explanatory and unproblematic, and the double-trial on which two people's lives depended, lasted less than a day - the jury taking a mere 30 minutes to reach a verdict. At 3.20pm on the opening day of the trial both prisoners had been sentenced to death.[25] No evidence had been presented on behalf of the defence.

Double Standards of Morality - Double Standards of Justice?

In considering whether a reprieve could be justified in the case of death sentence prisoners, it was common practice for the Home Secretary to request a report from the local constabulary concerning the prisoner's background. In Emily's case Superintendent Ouest provided this report, and it is from this document we learn that the violence Emily had suffered at the hands of her husband was not considered a mitigating circumstance. Superintendent Ouest wrote without a hint of irony:

> Swann has undoubtedly thrashed his wife many times but I would not like to say that he has been habitually cruel to her.[26]

---

[21]HO144/736/113887 XC2356 Statement by Emily Swann 9th June 1903.

[22]HO144/736/113887 XC2356 Statement of Mary Ann Ward 24th October 1903.

[23]HO144/736/113887 XC2356 Home Office Minutes 14th & 15th December 1903.

[24]HO144/736/113887 XC2356 Home Office Minutes 23rd December 1903. See also Home Office Minutes dated 24th December 1903 which read that it was "provocation which led Swann to strike his wife."

[25]*The Yorkshire Post* 10th December 1903.

[26]HO144/736/113887 XC2356 Report to Home Secretary supplied by request on Superintendent Arthur C. Ouest dated 22nd December 1903.

Indeed, (and despite the fact William had a conviction for aggravated assault against Emily), the superintendent suggested John had not been violent *enough* towards her:

> ... the wonder is that he has not killed her. He has frequently gone home after leaving work and found his wife drunk in the house and nothing prepared for him in the way of food.[27]

Throughout this book I have discussed the relationship between women and discourses of domesticity. In particular, I described how, as a consequence of the notion that a 'woman's place' is in the home and 'her duty' is to her family, wives can be disciplined by their husbands if they are perceived to fall short of expected standards. Emily was the mother of 11 children and also worked outside the private sphere as a mill-hand. Yet the superintendent appeared to suggest that William would have been justified in beating - if not killing her - for not having dinner prepared on time.

In this book I have also discussed gendered attitudes towards alcohol consumption - that heavy drinking in men is considered 'natural' while women engaging in identical behaviour are believed to be promiscuous and 'disgusting'. The reaction to the Swanns' consumption of alcohol demonstrates how this theoretical point is translated into reality. While both Emily and William were heavy drinkers, William's drinking was excused by his work:

> Glassblowers are a class of men who from the nature of their employment imbibe very freely and the deceased man was no exception to the general description of them ... He was a good workman, attended regularly at his work ... [and] got on very well with his fellow workmen.[28]

Emily's job as a mother of 11 children and a mill-hand was not considered a valid excuse for drinking. Instead she was termed "a drunken, immoral woman" who "was much more to blame than her husband was" for their unhappy existence.[29]

Emily's lack of commitment to domesticity, her drinking and her illicit affair indicated she was the type of woman who ignored gender role expectations and male authority - the 'type' men feel obliged to 'put in their place'. She was therefore also the 'type' of woman likely to be formally judged and punished more severely than a 'good' woman who complies with ideologies around domesticity and respectability. Indeed, prior to the murder,

---

[27]HO144/736/113887 XC2356 Report by Superintendent Ouest 22nd December 1903.

[28]HO144/736/113887 XC2356 Report by Superintendent Ouest 22nd December 1903.

[29]HO144/736/113887 XC2356 Report by Superintendent Ouest 22nd December 1903. Only six of Emily's children were still living at the time of the trial.

she had already experienced double standards of punishment as I shall now illustrate.

Emily and William Swann both had previous convictions against them. William's criminal record was considerably longer with 12 convictions compared to Emily's seven. Included in the 12 convictions was one of common assault against another man as well as the aforementioned aggravated assault against Emily. One of Emily's convictions also included violence when she had unlawfully wounded another woman. Some convictions were identical, for example, they each had three for using "obscene language". Similarly, they had both been found guilty of being "drunk and disorderly". However, William also had two convictions for being "drunk and riotous". The remaining convictions were motivated by financial gain, with William breaking gambling laws, game laws and the Poor Law, while Emily had been convicted of soliciting for prostitution.[30]

Thus, William's criminal record was both more extensive and more serious than Emily's with two convictions of physical violence against Emily's one. Yet, despite his recidivism, William had never received a prison sentence but had instead been ordered to pay fines or costs. Emily, on the other hand, had been sentenced to six months imprisonment for her first and only violent offence until her involvement in William's death. At the time of her sentence, her only previous convictions were for using "obscene language".[31] In Chapter Three, I argued that female criminals are not only judged according to the crime they have committed, but also according to their conduct as *women* - especially in the areas of motherhood, domesticity, respectability and sexuality. For example, the more respectable a woman is, the more lenient her sentence is likely to be, while those considered "to be too free in their behaviour" may be treated more punitively than men.[32] I also argued that women are further judged according to the 'type' of crime they have committed. For example, shoplifting or baby-snatching are crimes considered consistent with sex role expectations of women. Violent physical attacks are not. Ultimately, however, I argued, that women who receive prison sentences are not necessarily punished according to the seriousness of their crimes but according to their performance as women. Those who fail to measure up to 'appropriate' feminine standards are thus deemed to be 'doubly bad', for they are guilty not only of their crime, but also of abandoning their femininity. Finally I presented the hypothesis that all executed women of the 20th century in England and Wales, had stepped beyond the boundary of acceptable female conduct and behaviour. Emily Swann was no exception. As can be gathered from the above, while considering her reprieve, the Home Secretary had in front of him official documentation which showed Emily to

---

[30]HO144/736/113887 XC2356 Previous Conviction Sheets of Emily and William Swann. John Gallagher also had a criminal record but it will not be discussed here since, apart from one 'drunk and disorderly' conviction, his other convictions related to his life in the army i.e. desertion and disobeying orders.

[31]HO144/736/113887 XC2356 Previous Conviction Sheets.

[32]Naffine, N. (1990) *Law & The Sexes* Allen & Unwin, London p.137; p.138.

be a drunken, violent prostitute, a sluttish housewife and unfaithful wife who had a lover 12 years her junior, (which, as I indicated in the case of Louise Masset, always reflects badly on the woman), as well as a foul-mouthed criminal. Emily had thus abandoned every one of the disciplinary practices required to win male patronage - a dangerous 'out of control' woman who needed to be 'put in her place'. Hence, Mr Ouest's comment that thrashing her regularly did not constitute cruelty and that it was a "wonder he had not killed *her*," and hence the Home Office staff's assertion that William had been "provoked" into giving his wife a black eye. In short, Emily *deserved* it. With this information in mind Home Office advisers were united in arguing there was "no ground for interference."[33] The Home Secretary had only one last concern before allowing the execution to proceed - that of public opinion:

> The only reason that remains for considering the question of remission seems to me to be the risk that public feeling might be shocked by the execution of a woman for the murder of a man who had struck her.[34]

Yet, even on this point Superintendent Ouest was able to provide reassurance, claiming that "her own relatives have had little or nothing to do with her for several years now on account of her vicious conduct."[35] Moreover:

> The feeling in the district is very much against the prisoners particularly against the woman, she is undoubtedly a very bad cruel woman.[36]

As a result of Emily's conduct and behaviour, and despite the fact William had been convicted of assaulting *her*, it was he rather than Emily who was perceived as the 'victim' within the relationship even prior to his death. She simply did not fulfil the necessary criteria to qualify for the status of victim. Her failure to be a faithful and domesticated wife, displaying loyalty, compliance and altruism, ensured it was William, not Emily, who deserved sympathy. Even when William's violence against her became

---

[33]HO144/736/113887 XC2356 Home Office Minutes 14-15th December 1903. This document contains the comments of three members of Home Office staff who cannot be named as they merely initialled their notes.
[34]HO144/736/113887 XC2356 Home Office Minutes 23rd December 1903. Official recognition of the importance of public opinion can be gathered from the *Royal Commission on Capital Punishment 1949-1953 Report* para 39: "... it has occasionally been felt right to commute the sentence in deference to a widely spread or strong local expression of public opinion, on the gound that it would do more harm than good to carry out the sentence if the result was to arouse sympathy for the offender and hostility to the law."
[35]HO144/736/113887 XC2356 Report by Superintendent Ouest.
[36]HO144/736/113887 XC2356 Report by Superintendent Ouest.

known, he could still be described as "inoffensive" (see opening quote), because it was not regarded as an important part of her reality, but as the result of a husband's rightful attempt to discipline his wife's wayward behaviour. Thus, even though the evidence needed to provide an alternative account of both Emily and events leading up to the murder, was in existence at the time, it could not be 'heard' because discourses which speak of husbands' violence against their wives as unacceptable had not yet been created.

An Alternative Truth

Unsurprisingly, Emily and John blamed each other for William's death. John claimed Emily had hit William with a poker after which:

> she + Swann ... got up + he sat in a chair between the table + the fire place. I said to him I am going away today + he said good bye Jack. I left the house and went to Mrs Wards [sic] again.[37]

In Emily's version of the truth John struck William:

> knocking him down and punched him a good many times ... I tried to pull Gallagher off him and he (Gallagher) struck me knocking me down - Gallagher then struck deceased more than once with a chair and called him a 'Bloody bastard' and went out of the house ...[38]

The exact truth surrounding William's death could never be known by anyone except Emily and John themselves, and both the trial judge and Home Office staff recognised that:

> it is of course not proved that she struck her husband with the poker - that is merely a statement of Gallagher's ...[39]

Ultimately, however, it was quite irrelevant whether Emily had participated in the physical attack or not, according to the judge:

> If one instigated another to commit murder, and that other committed it, he was guilty of murder, and so was the person who instigated him. If they believed that this woman was standing by encouraging that man to strike him with the poker, or to kick him with his boot, the act was just as much her act as if she had done it herself.[40]

---

[37]HO144/736/113887 XC2356 Statement by John Gallagher 21st December 1903.
[38]HO144/736/113887 XC2356 Statement by Emily Swann 9th June 1903.
[39]HO144/736/113887 XC2356 Home Office Minutes 24th December 1903.
[40]Judge Darling's summing up quoted in *The Yorkshire Post* 10th December 1903.

In other words, Emily could be convicted solely on the evidence of her verbal encouragement. Yet, within the context of having just received a black eye her comments might have indicated an angry and emotional outburst rather than a literal incitement to murder. Judge Darling appeared to have considered this point for in his summing up he stated "that threats might be idle non-sense." However, he then presented a tautological argument:

> when they found that happen which the threats expressed as likely to happen, that was going a long way to prove that they were not mere idle empty words, but that they were the expression of a hope, or possibly of an intention.[41]

In other words, what may have been an idle threat, becomes evidence if and when something happens which matches that threat. At a different level, in a culture and era where the discourse of 'the battered wife' did not exist and where men were perceived as having the right to discipline their wives, Emily could be considered to have provoked William's violence, but that violence could not be considered to have provoked Emily's comments.[42] Rather they were seen as yet another example of Emily's rebelliousness - instead of being submissive to her husband she retaliated. However, the Home Secretary had the opportunity to hear a different truth about Emily before ordering the execution, when her children submitted a petition on behalf of their mother:

> [she] was always a good mother to us ... notwithstanding the drunken habits of our late Father ... who by his drunken habits destroyed our home life and rendered us unhappy causing our Mother ... to go out to work in order to keep the home together although our Father earned good wages which he spent in drink and debauchery and had it not been for his drunken habits and continued illtreatment of our said mother by our Father ... we do not think that our said mother would now have been in the painful position of a Woman condemned to death.[43]

Unlike those in authority, Emily's children considered both William's "continued illtreatment" and his recent assault on their mother to be mitigating factors in subsequent events:

> ... she being at the time under the influence of drink and also suffering acutely from a Brutal Assault just committed upon her by

---

[41]Judge Darling's summing up quoted in *The Yorkshire Post* 10th December 1903.
[42]Feminist writers argue this attitude still holds currency today; for example Susan Edwards writes: "Men have the right to react to provocation, while women do not." (Edwards, S. (1989) *Policing 'Domestic' Violence* Sage, London, p.183).
[43]HO144/736/113887 XC2356 Petition on behalf of Emily Swann 22nd December 1903.

our Father ... consequently she had not the power to resist to the extent she might or would have done ...[44]

The petition was signed not only by Emily's children but also by her sisters and 84-year-old mother "who hopes that her daughter may be reprieved and that the residue of her [Hannah Hinchliffe - Emily's mother] life may not be embittered by the knowledge that one of her children has died on the scaffold."[45] It was further signed by many members of the local community who added:

> Many of us who reside in the Wombwell district and neighbourhood have known the condemned Woman for many years and can and do hereby testify that her general character conduct and disposition has been altogether inconsistent with the unfortunate position in which she is now placed.[46]

These testimonies not only placed William's death within the context of long-term domestic violence unrelated to Emily's affair, but also threw serious doubt upon Superintendent Ouest's claim that Emily's family would have "nothing to do with her" and that "local feelings were against her."[47]

Apart from Emily's family and local community, the prison chaplain at Armley Gaol where she was awaiting execution, was also moved to make an intervention. In Chapter Two I drew attention to the important role played by chaplains historically, in securing a confession from death sentence prisoners, since this added legitimacy to the execution. Chaplain Mausell took this role as seriously as his predecessors, writing to the Home Secretary: "I have spent hours myself in trying to get her to make a confession of her guilt." However, unlike the chaplain discussed in the next case-study, Mausell did not shy away from the possibility of an injustice having been done and added in brackets: "supposing she was guilty." He expressed his doubts thus:

> she persistently denies having touched him with the poker - and says that she did not wish for his death. She had tried to break off her connection with Gallagher, but he had a great power over her because he was kind, when her husband was cruel. [She claims] she has not received justice, because the witness Dunn swore falsely at the Assizes ... While acknowledging other offences [she] denies that she was an accessory to the murder except in so far as she contributed to it by her adultery ... She has not altered her first statement that she is

---

[44]HO144/736/113887 XC2356 Petition on behalf of Emily Swann.
[45]HO144/736/113887 XC2356 Accompanying letter with petition from solicitors Last & Betts 22nd December 1903.
[46]HO144/736/113887 XC2356 Petition on behalf of Emily Swann.
[47]After the Home Secretary refused to grant their mother a reprieve Emily's children sent an appeal to the King via their solicitor (*The Times* 30th December 1903).

innocent ... and that it was Gallagher and Gallagher alone who beat his life out of him.[48]

To emphasise his reservations about Emily's guilt he added: "Sister Sarah, one of the Lady-Visitors ... thinks it is quite possible that Swann took no active part in the murder of her husband."[49] However, it was to no avail, for as indicated above, as far as the judge and the Home Secretary were concerned, it was irrelevant whether Emily had participated in the attack on William - either way she remained guilty of murder.

As stated earlier, we cannot know for certain whether Emily and John conspired to murder in advance. At the very least, four separate factors should be considered before presuming a conspiracy had taken place. First, the killing followed a protracted period of violence, sometimes between the Swanns, sometimes between John and William, at other times between all three of them. John's defence counsel phrased it thus:

> It was the same kind of fight as the prisoner had had again and again with the deceased man. He no more thought of taking Swann's life than he did on several occasions when he had been similarly protecting this woman.[50]

He therefore asked the jury to consider this a case of manslaughter carried out "in a moment of passion" rather than a case of deliberate and calculated murder.[51]

Second, PC Minty found Emily in a state of disbelief when he arrived at the murder scene. She said: "He isn't dead is he - He can't be dead."[52] Another witness testified Emily "seemed upset" when she realised William was dead. It is also known that at one point she "locked door to keep out Gallagher." These details led her defence counsel to conclude that "she was horrified at what was done."[53]

Third, police records indicated that, at least officially, William's history of violence as well as his "drunk and riotous" behaviour spanned a period of 16 years whereas Emily had only been found guilty of similar offences during the last two years of her life.[54]

---

[48]HO144/736/113887 XC2356 Letter to the Home Secretary from Henry Mausell, prison chaplain 22nd December 1903.

[49]HO144/736/113887 XC2356 Letter to the Home Secretary from Henry Mausell.

[50]*Yorkshire Telegraph & Star* 9th December 1903, Mr Michel Innes presenting John Gallagher's defence.

[51]*Yorkshire Telegraph & Star* 9th December 1903, Mr Michel Innes presenting John Gallagher's defence.

[52]HO144/736/113887 XC2356 Statement by PC A.J. Minty in Judge's Notes.

[53]HO144/736/113887 XC2356 Judge Darling's own notes in Judge's Notes. See also *The Times* 10th December 1903.

[54]HO144/736/113887 XC2356 Previous Conviction Sheets. Emily had two convictions for 'obscene language' before this two-year period in 1893 and 1898.

Finally, Emily was a small woman, measuring only 4 feet 10 inches and weighing 122lb, which lends credence to her children's version of events, that it was William who mistreated Emily rather than the other way around as claimed by Superintendent Ouest.[55] Therefore, there appeared to be enough evidence available to situate the killing within the context of a violent relationship in which Emily was often hurt, hence she was 'provoked' into inciting John to give William "nothing more than a good thumping for what he had done."[56] However, because there were no discourses available in which to discuss 'battered' or 'provoked' women, none of the above evidence was utilised to present an alternative truth. Thus, although it was defence counsel's role to present the defendant's version of the truth, it was no more capable of seeing beyond the dominant truth than the prosecution. Indeed, Emily's defence counsel argued on remarkably similar terrain, as I shall now illustrate.

Trial and Judgement

After a tenacious struggle by feminist activists spanning nearly three decades, to make 'visible' the issue of woman-battering, and despite statistics indicating that between 60% and 79% of women who kill their partners have previously been beaten by them, it is still the case today that in so-called 'domestic violence' cases, women are often considered to be "equally to blame" for male violence against them (sometimes even their own murder) while histories of male abuse and female self-defence remain hidden.[57] Thus, in the 1990s, protracted campaigns by groups such as *Justice for Women* and the *Southall Black Sisters*, were necessary before women like Emma Humphreys and Kiranjit Ahluwalia were released on appeal. Both women had been physically and psychologically abused by their partners whom they subsequently killed. No such campaign groups existed during the first half of the 20th century. More particularly, we can gain an insight into the attitude towards marriage and women within Emily's culture from her expression that "my master's dead."[58] Despite her rebelliousness she knew only too well the reality of relationships between husbands and wives. I discussed the subordinate position of women within marriage in Chapter Three, and by having an extra-marital relationship Emily had violated the fundamental belief that a wife *belongs* to her husband. William's *right* to punish his wife for her transgression and to fight with John in order to restore and protect his home-life was so fundamental, that the fact he had a long record of violent behaviour unrelated to the affair, could be overlooked. Indeed neither

[55]Ellis, J. (1996) *Diary of a Hangman* True Crime Library, London, p.161.

[56]*Yorkshire Telegraph & Star* 9th December 1903. Mr Newell presenting Emily's defence.

[57]Campbell, J.C. (1992) '"If I Can't Have You, No One Can": Power and Control in Homicide of Female Partners' in Radford, J. & Russell, D. (eds) (1992) *Femicide* Open University Press, Buckingham, p.110. See also Browne 1987:10 for statistics.

[58]HO144/736/113887 Evidence of Edward Ward in Judge's Notes.

defence counsel put William's violence forward as part of the defence. Instead both *agreed* with the dominant 'truth' that their clients' behaviour had been "sinful" and "immoral". Thus, Emily's *defence* counsel called her conduct "reprehensible, wicked and sinful ... Undoubtedly she used language which she ought not to have used." John's counsel agreed "there was not the slightest doubt that Mrs Swann and Gallagher had ... contracted illicit relations, but ... they were not ... there as a tribunal of morals, neither was it competent for a jury to hang a man because he had committed adultery."[59] However, while Emily appeared to have no saving graces, John's counsel attempted to portray his client as 'gallant' springing to the defence of a woman in distress:

> On May 11th a struggle took place between the husband and wife, and Gallagher then intervened, because such a struggle was unfair ... Whatever, might have been the history of this misdirected affection between the two prisoners, the fact remained that when Mrs Swann was hurt she went to Gallagher as her natural avenger and protector.[60]

Furthermore, a subtle shift towards blaming Emily for 'bewitching' John can be detected:

> It had been said that Gallagher danced about the floor. Could they conceive any fact which spoke more directly to their mind of the besotted condition of the prisoner.[61]

The only other suggestion put forward by defence counsel was that the verdict should be one of manslaughter rather than murder because the attack had come about in "circumstances of passion, excitement and confusion of mind" caused by alcohol.[62] It was a suggestion doomed to failure as a result of John's second visit to the Swann's house, which led Judge Darling to comment:

> Having beaten him, having wounded him, having gone away with time for the *blood to cool* if they had been provoked, they came back and between them they killed him.[63]

---

[59]Closing speech by Mr Newell for Emily Swann and Mr Michel-Innes for John Gallagher, quoted in *Yorkshire Telegraph & Star* 9th December 1903.

[60]Closing speech by Mr Michel-Innes in *Yorkshire Telegraph & Star* 9th December 1903.

[61]Closing speech by Mr Michel-Innes in *Yorkshire Telegraph & Star* 9th December 1903.

[62]Closing speech by Mr Michel-Innes in *Yorkshire Telegraph & Star* 9th December 1903.

[63]Judge Darling quoted in *The Yorkshire Post* 10th December 1903. My emphasis. The issue of 'immediate provocation' will be further discussed in Chapter 7.

After the jury reached a guilty verdict Judge Darling told its members:

> There was a piece of evidence which was not given in evidence before the jury, but which he might now refer to. Counsel for the prosecution thought, and he (his Lordship) thought, it might press unfairly upon Emily Swann if it were given in evidence, but this was the fact that Gallagher, when taken into custody, said that Emily Swann hit the man and beat him with the poker, and that he did not touch him, although he was there. That were not strictly evidence against her, but for all that, from the bruises and wounds, from the position of the poker, he was convinced that that statement which he made was in part true, that she did assault her husband, and did take part in the actual killing of him.[64]

Judge Darling did not indicate what the special feature of the bruises and wounds were which allowed him to conclude they had been inflicted by a woman rather than a man, nor did he explain how the position of the poker made it more likely that it had been used by a woman. However, his comments did indicate his personal belief that even in a situation where two co-defendants were blaming each other in order to save themselves, Emily was less likely to speak the truth. That this should be the case was, at least for one Home Office advisor, due to Emily's "previous character" rather than the position of bruises or pokers.[65] Ironically, the judge's action increased court legitimacy because it "was held to be an example of the even-handedness of the justice system which declined to take unfair advantage of an accused person."[66] In the final section I analyse why - in sharp contrast to the judge - Emily's words held so little credibility.

Authority, Knowledge and Power

In Chapter Three I discussed how women's speech is excluded from authority, arguing that the rules governing authority serve as "a system ... for social control within the context of social hierarchies." The silence surrounding the experiences of the women in these case-studies is another symptom of women's lack of authority - the way in which their "accounts and experiences" are disqualified when faced with one of the highest authorities in our culture - law and the legal system.[67] I also noted that the Enlightenment was characterised by the features of reason, rationality, science and the quest to 'prove' a 'truth' which went "beyond philosophical, theological and

---

[64]Judge Darling's comments to the jury's verdict in *The Yorkshire Post* 10th December 1903.

[65]HO144/736/113887 XC2356 Home Office Minutes 24th December 1903.

[66]Ellis 1996:161.

[67]Smart, C. (1989) *Feminism and the Power of Law* Routledge, London, p.86.

ideological dispute."[68] This movement was made up almost exclusively of men, and Smart has explained how - following the Enlightenment - law although not a science, also became associated and identified with masculinity. This is because both law and men are constituted as *rational*, leading to great similarity in the discourses of law and masculinity. That is to say, both men and law are identified and constituted by rationality, reason, "objectivity and abstract and principled activity."[69] Consequently, when feminists challenge existing accounts about women such as Emily Swann, they "are not simply challenging legal discourse, but also naturalistic assumptions about masculinity. The struggle therefore goes far beyond law."[70]

As a result of the close association between masculinity and law, the knowledge produced within legal discourse "is grounded in patriarchy, as well as in class and ethnic divisions."[71] However, it is not perceived as such but is able to gain access to power by laying "claim to a superior and unified field of knowledge which concedes little to other competing discourses ..."[72] Thus, as a result of law's claim to objectivity and rationality it is able not only to define itself but also the 'truth' about the everyday lives of those who stand in the dock. Other types of knowledges such as those based in experience, hold less status and may be disqualified altogether. They become "'subjugated knowledges' - forms of experience and knowledge that 'have been disqualified as inadequate ... or insufficiently elaborated: naive knowledges, located low down in the hierarchy beneath the required level of cognition or scientificity.'"[73] Subjugated knowledges include the "low-ranking knowledge of ... the housewife and the mother"[74] - the knowledge of women like Emily Swann. Even if those who possess 'low-ranking' knowledge are not disqualified as speakers, their account will be mediated until it can be heard through legal discourse:

> Everyday experiences are of little interest in terms of their meaning for individuals. Rather, these experiences must be translated into another form in order to become 'legal' issues and before they can be processed through the legal system ... the legal process translates everyday experiences into legal relevances, it excludes a great deal that might be relevant to the parties, and it makes its judgement on the scripted or tailored account ... how they are allowed to speak, and how their experience is turned into something that law can digest and

---

[68]Hamilton, P. (1992) 'The Enlightenment and the Birth of Social Science' in Hall, S. and Gieben, B. (eds) (1992) *Formations of Modernity* Polity, Cambridge p.42. See also Ehrenreich, B. & English, D. (1979) *For Her Own Good* Pluto, London p.77.
[69]Smart 1989:86; 87.
[70]Smart 1989:87.
[71]Smart 1989:88.
[72]Smart 1989:4.
[73]Sawicki 1991:87 quoting Foucault.
[74]Sawicki 1991:57.

process, is a demonstration of the power of law to disqualify alternative accounts.[75]

Emily's experience as a battered wife and as a human being was almost totally silenced or 'muted'. In her (and John's) case, every avenue provided for the defendant to speak through was blocked, a factor which exacerbated the already swift trial. First, Emily did not give evidence on her own behalf. Second, no evidence was called on her behalf. Third, there was no appeal.[76] Lastly, Emily, along with many members of her community, was illiterate.[77] Illiteracy within a mainly literate nation, may be understood as another form of 'muteness' since it prevents the non-literate from participating in two major forms of communication. Moreover, in a society divided along rigid class lines, it signals membership of a class at the very bottom of the social hierarchy while members of the legal profession are almost exclusively drawn from the upper and upper-middle classes. Within the setting of the courtroom the gulf between Emily Swann and the legal professionals - including those hired to defend her - appears insurmountable, even for those of us viewing events from the outside almost a century later. To the members of the legal establishment - who take for granted the right to define the 'truth' - Emily's trial must have seemed nothing more than a formality with the outcome a foregone conclusion. For them there was only one truth about Emily Swann, she was a drunken, violent, foul-mouthed, unfaithful wife - a woman who was both out of control and uncontrollable, hence in dire need of discipline. It is within this context Justice Darling considered himself qualified to comment that he believed John's statement which indicated she participated in the actual killing. It is also the context within which the Home Office adviser believed Emily to be guilty because of her "previous character" while William's character escaped scrutiny altogether. As Stanko and Scully have argued, in the absence of "*appropriate femininity*, violent women must be *explained* by their deviance."[78]

On the one occasion when Emily's defence counsel attempted to present an alternative truth about her, the judge advised against it:

> Mr Newell said the only witness he should call was Mrs Swann's daughter, aged 14 years simply as to her mother's character.

---

[75]Smart 1989:11.

[76]The Criminal Appeal Act was introduced in 1907, four years after Emily's execution.

[77]Neither Emily nor many of the local residents who signed her petition could write their own name. The solicitor who prepared the petition on behalf of Emily's children wrote to the Home Secretary: "It must be borne in mind that the Petition has been signed by a class of people - a mining population - many of whom have not had the benefits of education and are therefore unable to write" (HO144/736/113887 XC2356 Letter from solicitors Last & Betts to Home Office 22nd December 1903).

[78]Stanko & Scully 1996:63-4. Emphases in the original.

His Lordship: had you better not? *I don't know whether you know as much about her as I do.*

Mr Newell: The little girl says she has been a good mother, and so on.

His Lordship: Yes, but if you call a witness to prove she has a good character it won't stop there; it cannot.[79]

In other words, as far as Justice Darling was concerned, Emily's one positive feature - that of being 'a good mother' - could not alter the dominant truth about her, so severe were her transgressions of the rules governing appropriate feminine behaviour in all other areas of her life. Not until Emily had died on the scaffold did the public learn she could also be a considerate and sensitive woman. The *Daily Express* reported that "the woman has been much concerned about her ... children," while the *Manchester Evening News* wrote "she has sent numerous kindly messages to her aged mother ... but made a request that the old lady should not visit her, believing that the shock would prove too great for her."[80] Moreover, prison staff reported she was very "worried about the disgrace she was bringing on her family, [a subject] which she talked about continuously." They had become very attached to her and broke down in tears as they led her to the scaffold.[81]

Despite the silence around the 'Wombwell murder' one aspect, especially in relation to Emily was widely reported. Exact details concerning the spiritual support the prisoners had received from the chaplain and priest were published on the three days leading up to the execution, culminating with reports that "both prisoners have expressed contrition for the crime ..."[82], and "Mrs Swann is *said* to have confessed verbally to the chaplain to whom she more than once exclaimed that she had 'made herself right with God.'"[83] As I noted in previous case-studies, such vague references to supposed confessions were common because it was believed to add legitimacy to state executions. However, the detailed references to Emily's and John's religious activities together with the use of the expression 'contrition' is of particular interest, for as Kathy Laster has argued:

---

[79]Trial proceedings quoted in *Yorkshire Telegraph & Star* 9th December 1903. My emphasis.

[80]*Daily Express* 28th December 1903; *Manchester Evening News* 29th December 1903.

[81]Ellis 1996:162; 163.

[82]*Daily Express* 28th December 1903.

[83]*Daily Express* 30th December 1903. My emphasis. See also *Manchester Evening News* 29th December 1903 and *Daily Express* 29th December 1903 which reported that John "attended the Roman Catholic service in the prison yesterday morning, while Mrs Swann was present at the Church of England service. They were in the condemned pews." See also Ellis 1996:161-2 who details the prisoners' attendance "at a special service in the prison chapel on Christmas Day ... Both the condemned displayed religious penitence."

Even without a confession, compliance with Church rituals at least allowed observers to infer that the condemned exhibited, *"the appearance* of sincere *contrition* for their criminal career and patient resignation to their fate."[84]

The prisoners were reported to have "approached the scaffold bravely" although their last moments on this earth were both macabre and dramatic.[85] Ellis who executed the couple wrote of the event:

We were putting the rope round Gallagher's neck when she suddenly cried out: "Good morning, John!" Gallagher started violently under our hands. He had no idea up to that moment that Emily Swann was standing beside him. He answered, "Good morning, love!" By this time the other rope was round her neck, but again she spoke: "Goodbye. God bless you."
This, I had to confess, was an astonishing scene, a dialogue between two people, one of them a woman, standing with pinioned arms and legs, faces blotted out by shapeless white bags, and with ropes fixed round their necks. Then one quick pull of the lever, and their conversation was still for ever.[86]

In line with Home Office instructions, the prison doctor reported that death had been instantaneous and had been "perfectly painless in both cases."[87]

The Case of Edith Thompson

The gulf between the legal cataclysm that destroyed her and her own sense of her position is revealed by her reaction to the sentence. As her family entered her Old Bailey cell after the verdict, Edith rushed towards her father, crying: "Take me home, Dad."[88]

... if only she had been upper class - or working class - or better educated - or even French, there would have been simpler solutions to her problems. If she had been male, of course, her particular problems would not have existed at all.[89]

---

[84]Laster, K. (1994) 'Famous Last Words: Criminals on the Scaffold, Victoria, Australia, 1842-1967' in *International Journal of the Sociology of Law* 1994, 22, 1-18, p.9, quoting from *The Argus*. My emphasis.

[85]*Daily Express* 30th December 1903.

[86]Ellis 1996:163.

[87]Ellis 1996:163. The Home Office instructions to prison personnel concerned with state executions are further discussed in Appendix II.

[88]Weis, R. (1993) 'Not innocent, not guilty' in *The Guardian* 10th November 1993.

[89]Twining, W. (1990) *Rethinking Evidence*, Basil Blackwell, Oxford, p.294.

Edith Thompson and her lover Freddy Bywaters, were executed simultaneously in separate prisons on 9th January 1923, thus constituting the last of three double executions examined in this book. Previously I argued that two of the 15 women executed during the 20th century, may have been innocent of the crime for which they were hanged. The second of these women is Edith Thompson.

The Thompson/Bywaters case is strikingly similar to the Swann/Gallagher case except in one crucial area - that of social class. Edith was a competent business-woman who enjoyed financial independence as a result of an income higher than her husband's, while Emily was part of the late Victorian 'residuum' - unskilled and illiterate. Further, unlike any of the cases discussed so far, the Thompson/Bywaters case has remained controversial to the present day with opinions sharply divided on the issue of Edith's guilt. Thus, while there was little or no attempt to establish an alternative truth in the 11 cases already discussed, with the consequences that the women in question became increasingly invisible and 'mute' until they almost totally disappeared from history, an alternative truth about Edith Thompson was created immediately after her trial which has *gained* credibility with the passing of time.

Whereas in the Swann/Gallagher case the judge had been determined to demonstrate Emily had physically participated in the killing, even though the only evidence in support of this was the word of her co-accused - himself struggling to avoid the gallows - the prosecution in the Thompson/Bywaters case made no attempt to prove that Edith had participated in the actual killing. Instead she was found guilty of having incited Freddy to kill her husband, Percy. Edith and Freddy had been lovers for 14 months, when one October evening, as Edith and Percy were walking home, Freddy suddenly appeared and stabbed Percy. John Webber, a local resident, testified he heard Edith cry: "'Oh, don't; Oh, don't', in a most piteous manner", and reiterated in cross-examination that he "had no doubt whatever" the voice he heard was Edith's.[90] When Edith saw other people in the street she cried: "Oh, my God, will you help me? My husband is dying."[91] Edith herself immediately ran for medical assistance and Dr Maudsley testified that when he arrived at the murder scene she "was in a confused condition, hysterical and agitated." When told Percy was dead she exclaimed: "Why did you not come sooner and

---

[90]Young, F. (1923) *Trial of Frederick Bywaters and Edith Thompson* William Hodge & Co, Edinburgh and London, p.19. This book forms part of the *Notable British Trials Series* and is a *verbatim* transcript of the trial. It will therefore be quoted from extensively in this case-study. The deposition file contained in CRIM 1/206/5 XC6872, Public Record Office, Chancery Lane, London WC2A 1LR also includes witness statements, however the *Transcript* will be utilised in preference to the deposition file as it is more comprehensive. Henceforth the transcript of the *Trial of Frederick Bywaters and Edith Thompson* will be listed as *Transcript* followed by year and page no.

[91]Solicitor-General Sir Thomas Inskip, referring to the evidence of Dora Finch Pittard and Percy Edward Clevely pp.18-19 in his Opening Statement for the Crown.

save him?"[92] When a police officer accompanied Edith to her home, she asked - referring to Percy - "will he come back?"[93] Several witnesses testified Edith did not appear to believe Percy was dead, for example, she said to her lodger: "They have taken him away from me; if they would let me go to him I could make him better."[94]

Edith had in fact recognised Freddy as Percy's assailant, but to shield him as well as to keep their affair secret, lied to the police when she claimed: "I did not see anybody about at the time [of the attack]."[95] She lied again in her written statement when she stated: "I cannot remember whether I saw anyone else there or not."[96] However, at this point Freddy had also been requested to make a statement at the police station, and when Edith was moved into another room, she caught a glimpse of him.[97] Shocked and surprised, she exclaimed: "Oh, God, oh, God, what can I do? Why did he do it? I did not want him to do it. I must tell the truth."[98] Edith then made a third statement:

> ... a man rushed out ... and knocked me away and pushed me away from my husband. I was dazed for a moment. When I recovered I saw my husband scuffling with a man. The man whom I know as Freddy Bywaters was running away.[99]

Until that moment there had been no evidence against Freddy, and there still was none against Edith. However, police searching Freddy's quarters on the ship where he was employed, found 62 letters from Edith, and their relationship was revealed. Every aspect of Edith's behaviour had indicated she was taken by surprise at Freddy's attack on Percy, hence these letters were to remain the only evidence against her, which ensured the conviction was surrounded by controversy from the beginning. Freddy also lied in his initial statement, denying knowledge of the murder and claiming Edith was no more than a family friend.[100] However, with the letters in his

---

[92]Evidence of Dr Noel Maudsley, *Transcript* 1923:20.

[93]Evidence of police sergeant Walter Mew, *Transcript* 1923:21.

[94]Evidence of Fanny Maria Lester, *Transcript* 1923:29; see also evidence of Walter Mew p.21.

[95]Edith Thompson interviewed by detective inspector Richard Sellars 4th October 1922 - evidence for the prosecution in *Transcript* 1923:35.

[96]MEPO 3/1582, Public Record Office, Kew, Richmond, Surrey TW9 4DU, Exhibit 3, statement of Edith Thompson.

[97]This 'chance encounter' has remained a controversial issue as it was believed to have been engineered by police to break the couples' silence. Superintendent Wensley stated in his autobiography that it had been "below the standards appropriate to the justice of which he was the self-dedicated instrument" (Broad, L. (1952) *The Innocence of Edith Thompson* Hutchinson, London, p.79).

[98]Evidence of Dectective-Inspector Richard Sellers, *Transcript* 1923:37.

[99]MEPO 3/1582 exhibit 4, statement by Edith Thompson.

[100]MEPO 3/1582 exhibit 5, statement by Frederick Bywaters.

possession, Detective-Inspector Sellars informed him that he and Edith would be charged "with the wilful murder of Percy Thompson." Freddy responded: "Why her? Mrs Thompson was not aware of my movements."[101] It was time for Freddy to make a second statement:

> I waited for Mrs Thompson and her husband ... I pushed her to one side ... I said to him, "You have got to separate from your wife." He said, "No." ... We struggled. I took my knife from my pocket and we fought and he got the worst of it. Mrs Thompson must have been spellbound for I saw nothing of her during the fight. I ran away ... The reason I fought with Thompson was because he never acted like a man to his wife. He always seemed several degrees lower than a snake. I loved her and I could not go on seeing her leading that life. I did not intend to kill him. I only meant to injure him. I gave him an opportunity of standing up to me as a man but he wouldn't ...[102]

When both prisoners were charged with murder Freddy said: "It is wrong, it is wrong."[103]

The Trial of Edith Thompson and Frederick Bywaters

Trial judge Mr Justice Shearman, told the jury in his summing up that the hearing of the charge "was carried out in an unnatural and unreal atmosphere."[104] A more accurate description is arguably that provided by Edgar Lustgarten who wrote that the trial consisted of "four days of prim sententiousness and virtuous moralising."[105] Similarly, Browne and Tullett wrote that Edith found herself face-to-face with "ridiculous fits of self-righteousness" and a "public, a judge and jury, in its most priggish mood."[106] The sense of drama and scandal surrounding the case ensured immediate and constant media attention and from the very beginning, Edith's seniority (she was 28 and Freddy was 20) ensured she was portrayed as the 'evil seductress':

101 Evidence of Detective-Inspector Richard Sellers in *Transcript* 1923:38; 39.

102 MEPO 3/1582 exhibit 6, statement by Frederick Bywaters.

103 Evidence of Detective-Inspector Richard Sellers, *Transcript* 1923:39.

104 Mr Justice Shearman quoted in a leader article in *The Times* 6th January 1922.

105 Lustgarten, E. (1960) *The Murder and the Trial* Odhams Press, London, p.28.

106 Browne, D.G. & Tullett, T. (1987) *Bernard Spilsbury* Grafton Books London p.286. An example of this pompous self-righteousness can be found in the leading article in *The Daily Telegraph* 12th December 1922: "The Judge['s] ... insistence that the jury and he were investigating a 'vulgar crime' according to the principles of human justice and common sense well expresses the spirit in which English people would have all such cases tried."

She ... had egged him on; he, the poor young fellow, was under the influence of this dominating woman, this unfaithful wife, this wanton, this enchantress, this seductive siren.[107]

Thus, although it was Freddy and not Edith who had killed Percy the perception of the case was that she was 'worse' than him - it was *she* who was ultimately responsible for the crime.[108] This perception was formalised on the prisoners' Indictment Sheets where Freddy was indicted on two counts - murder and conspiracy to murder - while Edith had no less than five indictments against her.[109] As I discuss below, forensic evidence was to prove these additional indictments had no substance whatsoever and they were never proceeded with by the Crown.

Unlike the other women discussed in this book Edith was defended by a KC with a reputation for being one of the best in the country in 1922 - Sir Henry Curtis-Bennett.[110] His first task was to ask for Edith's letters to be rendered inadmissible as evidence, since without them the Crown had no case. As the letters referred to Edith's supposed attempt to poison Percy and to kill him by adding ground glass to his food, Curtis-Bennett argued they could not be used as evidence of a very different type of murder - the stabbing of Percy by Freddy since there was "no nexus between them."[111] Only if the Crown decided to try Edith on the fourth and fifth indictments - administering poison and "a destructive thing with intent to murder" - were the letters admissible.[112] Judge Shearman did not agree, nor did he grant permission for separate trials.

In order to demonstrate that Edith was hanged "for her immorality" rather than murder,[113] I intend to show that the case against her consisted almost solely of insinuation, suspicion and speculation rather than evidence, a

---

[107]Broad 1952:87-8. See also O'Donnell 1956:64 where he writes: "Frederick Bywaters was older than his years but was young enough to be overwhelmed by the personal magnetism of a mature woman."

[108]See for example Sir John Anderson's evidence to the *Select Committee on Capital Punishment Report* (1931) His Majesty's Stationery Office, London, para 129 where Sir John stated: "Probably if Mrs Thompson had been respited and Bywaters executed, there would have been great public indignation because she was *obviously the worst of the two.*" My emphasis.

[109]CRIM 1/206/5 XC6872 Original Charge Sheets included in this file.

[110]Sir Edward Marshall-Hall was considered to be *the* best defence KC by many authors (see for example, Earl of Birkenhead, who was Lord Chancellor at the time of the Thompson/Bywaters trial, in *Famous Trials* (no year) Hutchinson, London p.209). However, according to Fenton Bresler, himself a lawyer, Sir Henry "was renowned for "doing a Curtis" - winning hopeless cases with what his biographers called "a certain combination of honest bluff, cheek, opportunism and a genius in turning a phrase." (Bresler, F. (1965) *Reprieve*, George Harrap London pp.169-70).

[111]*Transcript* 1923:8.

[112]CRIM 1/206/5 XC6872 Charge Sheets.

[113]Sir Henry Curtis-Bennett quoted in Broad 1952:219; see also Twinning 1990:264.

situation that could only be created as a result of her adultery which was utilised by the Crown as 'proof' of her supposed capacity for murder. In other words, motive took the place of evidence. I shall now examine how this was achieved.

The Letters

> [Solicitor-General] I suggest that the phrase "if things are the same again" means "if my husband is still alive ..."[114]

> [Solicitor-General quoting letter] "Don't keep this piece." It is suggested that that was because it might come into her husband's possession. I am bound to say to you that this letter ... is one that deals entirely with this idea now occupying so much of her attention, that her husband must be got rid of. *The passage is full of crime. There is no other interpretation which can fairly be placed upon it ...* I suggest that these letters were being destroyed because his, like hers, referred to the subject of poisoning. In the next letter she has given up something "until you come home." I suggest that this was the idea of administering something to her husband.[115]

> [Solicitor-General quoting letter] "Don't forget what we talked [sic] in the tearoom, I will still risk and try if you will - we have only three and three-quarter years left darlingest." When you review these letters you are driven to the conclusion that right up to the end she was acquiescing in Bywaters' suggestions. She allowed him to think that she was prepared to co-operate with him in poisoning her husband right to the end ... My duty is to suggest that on a fair reading of the letters and a fair construction of the meetings it is only possible to come to a conclusion that the same idea ... resulted in an agreement, the consequence of which was that Mr Thompson was killed.[116]

The prosecution selected only those letters which it regarded as containing incriminating passages,[117] and proceeded to quote these out of context in order to "show that she so worked and preyed on the mind of this young man by her suggestions that although it was his hand that struck the blow, it was her mind that conceived the crime."[118] Moreover, while only one letter referred to poisoning in the five-month period leading up to Percy's murder,

---

[114]Solicitor-General's opening speech to jury referring to a phrase from Edith Thompson's letter in *Transcript* 1923:12.
[115]Solicitor-General's speech to jury in *Transcript* 1923:129-30. My emphasis.
[116]Solicitor-General's speech to jury in *Transcript* 1923:131-2.
[117]Approximately half of those available.
[118]Solicitor-General Inskip's Opening Statement for the Crown in *Transcript* 1923:13.

the Crown presented the letters, not according to dates but according to exhibit numbers, thus presenting a false picture to the jury of "a correspondence that rose to crime in an *accelerando* of incrimination."[119] In reality, however, the majority of references to poison and ground glass occurred in May, five months prior to Percy's death. Numerous repetitions of the same 20 extracts - amounting to approximately 1% of the entire correspondence - helped to establish a second false impression - that the incriminating parts formed the main body of the correspondence.[120] Of the 32 letters selected by the prosecution, only a handful contained unambiguous suggestions that Edith was attempting to kill Percy:

> You said it was enough for an elephant ... But you don't allow for the taste making only a small quantity to be taken. It sounded like a reproach was it meant to be? Darlint I tried hard - you won't know how hard - because you weren't there to see and I can't tell you all - but I did - I do want you to believe I did for both of us ... I was buoyed up with the hope of the "light bulb" and I used a lot - big pieces too - not powdered - and it has no effect - I quite expected to be able to send that cable - but no - nothing has happened from it and now your letter tells me about the bitter taste again ... Wouldn't the stuff make small pills coated together with soap and dipped in liquorice powder ... try, while you're away ... I feel I shall never get him to take a sufficient quantity of anything bitter.[121]

Quoting from a novel she had just read Edith wrote in another letter:

> "It must be remembered that digitalin is a cumulative poison and that the same dose harmless if taken once, yet frequently repeated, becomes deadly". Is it any use?[122]

Once it had been accepted these passages referred to actual murder attempts, a host of other highly ambiguous, and often innocuous passages were *interpreted* as further evidence of murderous intent. Phrases like "You'll never leave me behind again, never, unless things are different"; "I ask you again to think out all the plans and methods for me", "yes, darlint be jealous, so much that you will do something desperate" and "If I do not mind the risk why should you?"[123], were presented as *evidence* of murderous intent. For example the Solicitor-General asked with reference to the first passage: "how

[119]Broad 1952:195.

[120]Broad 1952:195.

[121]Exhibit 19,*Transcript* 1923:13. Copies of all letters exhibited can be found in MEPO 3/1582 *Edith Thompson & Frederick Bywaters* Public Record Office, Kew, Richmond, Surrey TW9 4DU. All 65 letters found amongst Freddie's possessions are reproduced in Appendices I and II in *Transcript* 1923:161-250 (three were his own).

[122]Exhibit 22, *Transcript* 1923:14.

[123]Exhibits 50 p.78; 20 p.12; 28 p.16; 26 p.15.

were things to be different except by the destruction of her husband's life?"
while shortly after quoting the last passage he stated "through the
correspondence it becomes clear that it was Mrs Thompson who was urging
Bywaters on to commit the crime ..."[124]

Several authors have argued that had Edith not given evidence and
hence offered no defence against the charges except a denial, a conviction
would have been virtually impossible. However, in direct conflict with the
advice of her KC, Edith insisted on giving evidence. The consequences were
disastrous with her explanations sounding feeble and unconvincing,
reinforced by the fact she had already been proved a liar as a result of her
early police statements. Her capacity for telling lies was further reinforced
when she was forced to admit she had lied to shield Freddy. This resulted in
irreparable damage to her credibility as a witness and the consequent hopeless
attempts to explain herself can be gathered from the following exchange:

> In your letter ... (exhibit 20) you say - 'Enclosed are some cuttings
> that may be interesting ... The Kempton cutting may be interesting if
> it's to be the same method.'
> What were you referring to there?
> *Our compact of suicide.*
> Look at the letter (exhibit 27) ... 'I had the wrong Porridge to-day, but
> I don't suppose it will matter ...'
> What were you referring to?
> *I really cannot explain.*
> The suggestion here is that you had from time to time put things into
> your husband's porridge, glass, for instance?
> *I had not done so.*
> Can you give us any explanation of what you had in your mind when
> you said you had the wrong porridge?
> *Except we had suggested or talked about that sort of thing and I had
> previously said, 'Oh yes, I will give him something one of these days.'*
> [Mr Justice Shearman] Do you mean that you had talked about
> poison?
> *I did not mean anything in particular.*
> [Examination continued]*We had talked about making my husband ill.*
> How had you come to talk about making your husband ill?
> We were discussing my unhappiness.[125]

Freddy who remained loyal to Edith and tried to protect her
throughout the trial by claiming her letters had had no effect on his mind,[126]
nevertheless did not help their case when he gave evidence:

---

[124]*Transcript* 1923:15.
[125]*Transcript* 1923:75-6.
[126]*Transcript* 1923:52.

[Solicitor-General quotes from Edith's letter] ... he puts great stress on the fact of the tea tasting bitter 'as if something has been put in it' he says. Now I think whatever else I try it in again will taste bitter - he will recognise it and be more suspicious still ...
What do you understand about that passage?
That she had taken the quinine and it tasted bitter.
Look at it again -
[Quoting] he puts great stress on the fact of the tea tasting bitter 'as if something had been put in it' he says.
To whom did it taste bitter?
Mrs Thompson.
Do you suggest that, Bywaters?
I do.
Do you suggest that is how you understood the letter when you received it?
I do.
[Quoting] Now I think whatever else I try it in again will still taste bitter - he will recognise it and be more suspicious still.
Do you still adhere to what you say, that she is speaking of her taste?
Yes.
What did you understand him to be suspicious of?
That she was attempting to commit suicide.
Did you understand her to mean that she would tell him that her tea tasted bitter and she was about to commit suicide?
Possibly she would.
Is that your understanding of that passage?
That is.[127]

The Solicitor-General proceeded to quote a passage from another letter: "I used the 'light bulb' three times but the third time - he found a piece - so I've given it up - until you come home", which resulted in the following exchange:

What did you understand by that passage?
She had been lying to me again.
She had been what?
Lying to me, lying.
What did you understand the lie was?
It was melodrama on her part, trying to persuade me that she had taken broken glass.
[Quoting] 'I used the "light bulb" three times but the third time - he found a piece.'
You understand she meant her husband had detected her in an attempt to commit suicide?
Yes.

---

[127] *Transcript* 1923:63.

[Quoting] 'So I have given it up until you come home.' Do you suggest that she was going to wait for your arrival home in order that you might co-operate with her in committing suicide?
I might give her something more, some quinine.
That would be a strange idea to you, Bywaters, if that is right?
Yes, I do not know her idea.[128]

Freddy was more concerned about Edith's future than his own and gave specific instructions to his counsel that his defence must not harm her defence. This gallant and loyal conduct earned him considerable public sympathy. However, contrary to his intentions, his conduct had the adverse effect of hardening public attitude towards Edith because it seemed to confirm the supposed iron-hold she exercised over him. This hostility towards Edith was reinforced by her own conduct in the witness-box which - in sharp contrast to Freddy's - suggested she was blaming him to save herself:

He [Freddy] suggested giving your husband something to hurt him?
He had given me something.
Given you something to give your husband?
That is so.
Did the suggestion then come from Bywaters?
It did.
...
Did you welcome the suggestion that something should be given to your husband to make him ill?
I did not.
Did you object to it?
I was astonished about it.
Did you object to it?
I did, at the time.
...
You are representing that this young man was seriously suggesting to you that you should poison and kill your husband?
I did not suggest it.
I thought that was the suggestion?
I did not suggest that.
What was your suggestion?
He said he would give him something.
...
You are suggesting now that it was Bywaters who was suggesting that to you?
Yes.
And you did not do it?
No, never.[129]

---

[128]*Transcript* 1923:67.
[129]*Transcript* 1923:93; 94.

The details of the case seemed obvious. Edith was a "corrupt, malignant sorceress" who, having cast her evil spell over an innocent young man, was now prepared to sacrifice him, if it meant saving her own life.[130] Attempts by the defence KCs to place Percy's murder within the context of love, passion and jealousy were swiftly dispelled by Judge Shearman, who interrupted the closing speech on behalf of Edith to remind the jury:

> ... you should not forget that you are in a Court of justice trying a vulgar and common crime. You are not listening to a play from the stalls of a theatre. When you are thinking it over, you should think it over in that way.[131]

Lustgarten wrote that "it is very uncommon - one would have liked to say, unheard of - for a judge to interject antagonistic comment in the middle of a closing speech by counsel for the prisoner."[132] Judge Shearman, however, had not completed his moralising. In his summing up he quoted a passage from one of Edith's letters: "He [Percy] has the right by law to all that you have the right to by nature and love", before telling the jury: "I am certain that you, like any other right-minded persons, will be filled with disgust at such a notion. Let us get rid of all that atmosphere, and try this case in an ordinary common sense way."[133] He also repeated the claim he had made when interrupting the closing speech - that "this charge really is ... a common or ordinary charge of a wife and an adulterer murdering the husband." He referred to Edith's letters as 'gush', claiming they were "the outpourings of a silly but ... wicked affection",[134] and he pompously reprimanded Curtis-Bennett for having used the phrase 'thank God', stating that he did "not like invocations to the Deity."[135] Reinforcing Edith's image as the older 'wicked seductress' he told the jury:

---

[130]Introduction to *Transcript* 1923:xv.

[131]*Transcript* 1923:119. Lewis Broad has written: "Edith Thompson was unlucky in her judge. Of all the Bench, Sir Montague Shearman was the judge least likely to take a tolerant view of the character and lapses of the woman in the dock. A man of strict living and high principles, he had no easy tolerance for loose living and loose loving... This Judge was pre-eminently guided by common sense, limited in his comprehension of the fanciful and fantastic. The romantic was at a minimum in his make-up (Broad 1952:148). This view is supported by Du Cann who wrote: "Strongly prejudiced as he was against immorality, he over-emphasised and over-simplified this aspect of this case, instead of warning the jury against letting moral indignation prejudice them" (Du Cann, C.G.L. (1960) *Miscarriages of Justice* Frederick Muller Ltd, London, p.206. Similarly, Bresler called Shearman "principled and prudish ... a relic from the Victorian era" (Bresler 1965:173).

[132]Lustgarten 1960:29.

[133]*Transcript* 1923:135.

[134]*Transcript* 1923:146.

[135]*Transcript* 1923:134.

You have noticed, I dare say, in the course of the case, that where the woman made statements they are mostly something excusing her and implicating the man, but ... when the man is making statements, they are always exculpating the woman.[136]

This point was reinforced at the end of the summing up when Judge Shearman reminded the jury of Edith's outburst "Why did he do it?" as she caught a glimpse of Freddy when first arrested. As far as the judge was concerned this outburst meant "... she is excusing herself ... again it is noticeable that she is throwing the blame on him."[137] In sum, Judge Shearman failed to notice any ambiguities in the evidence, instead he considered "the facts of this case ... extremely short and simple" the length of the letters being the only reason why the trial had lasted several days.[138] Finally, while Curtis-Bennett reminded the jury that "this is not a Court of morals, because if everybody immoral was brought here I would never be out of it, nor would you"[139], the judge issued no such warning, instead he allowed "the prejudice arising from her immorality ... to operate against her", thus ensuring the case became one of "the erring wife ... most flagrantly disclosed."[140] Another commentator went further and stated that while there was truth in the saying "'She was hanged for immorality'... there was equal truth in saying that the disgust of the trial judge ... for marital infidelity and his unimaginative literal mind hanged this unhappy creature."[141]

The jury, which included one woman, the first ever in a murder trial, took two hours and ten minutes to find both prisoners guilty. There was no recommendation to mercy. Freddy immediately responded: "I say the verdict of the jury is wrong. Edith Thompson is not guilty. I am no murderer, I am not an assassin." Edith was less composed and cried out: "I am not guilty; oh God, I am not guilty!"[142] She had to be carried into the dock to hear the verdict, and was only prevented from total collapse upon hearing the death-sentence being issued, "by the surrounding arms of the wardresses." Several women in the public gallery fainted and Edith's mother collapsed and had to be carried out of the courtroom.[143]

---

[136]*Transcript* 1923:135.

[137]*Transcript* 1923:154. No-one, not even the police inspector who overheard Edith's outburst agreed with Judge Shearman's interpretation of it, but instead regarded it as an outburst taking place when she was "taken off her guard," and therefore more likely to be truthful (HO45/2685 PT2 XC2501).

[138]*Transcript* 1923:135.

[139]*Transcript* 1923:115.

[140]Broad 1952:210.

[141]Du Cann C.G.L. 1960:206.

[142]*Transcript* 1923:156; 157.

[143]*Daily Mirror* 12th December 1922.

An Alternative Truth

Words exist to communicate a meaning. But the meaning inferred by the listener or the reader is not always that intended by the speaker or the writer. There are primary and secondary senses; there are overtones and undertones that are idiosyncratic; there is hyperbole and satire; there is untrammelled fantasy and deliberate make-believe. *It is absurd to suppose that every phrase should be literally construed* ... It is only by reference to the character of their author and to the circumstances in which they were employed that one can hope to extract the true significance of words.[144]

Am I right or wrong in saying that this woman is one of the most extraordinary personalities that you or I have ever met? Bywaters truly described her ... as a woman who lived a sort of life I don't suppose any of you live in - an extraordinary life of make-believe, and in an atmosphere which was created by something which had left its impression on her brain. She reads a book and then imagines herself one of the characters of the book. She is always living an extraordinary life of novels ... This is the woman you have to deal with, not some ordinary woman. She is one of those striking personalities met with from time to time who stand out ...[145]

Fact and reality were no more than a cue for the exuberant fancy of Edith Thompson's mind. When the true story fell short she improved it in her letters, until it was a story worth an artist's while ... relentless poisoning wives, with all the trappings of the novels she had read and all the delirium of the love she had imagined. *This was the driving force behind the famous letters which the prosecution used to get their writer hanged.*[146]

Edith's correspondence to Freddy has been described as "extraordinarily complex human documents ... suggesting a bewildering variety of moods ... motives and manoeuvres." It included:

newsy commentaries, newspaper clippings and emotional outpourings, in various tones and voices ... Edith's style seems to be almost systematically ambiguous. Some of the letters, including some that are central to our enquiry, exhibit a stream of consciousness quality which adds to the difficulties of interpretation.[147]

---

[144]Lustgarten 1960:13-14. My emphasis.
[145]Sir Henry Curtis-Bennett's closing speech in *Transcript* 1923:114.
[146]Lustgarten 1960:18. My emphasis.
[147]Twinning 1990:264-5.

Unlike Professor Twinning, those who sat in judgement on Edith were incapable of noting such ambiguity. Yet, as I shall now illustrate, the evidence presented to prove Edith's guilt was more consistent with her innocence.

Evidence was given during the trial that Edith was in the habit of writing about imaginary incidents - and hence telling untruths - to Freddy. Because of Freddy's job as a ship's writer they had only spent a few weeks together during their 14-month relationship. Hence, during the two to three months between each leave, Edith would immerse herself in a fantasy world of make-believe to relieve the dreary ordinariness of her everyday suburban existence. For example, her father gave evidence that a letter written in June 1922 in which Edith claimed Percy had discussed her affair with him, was untrue. According to her letter, her father Mr Graydon, had said: "it was a disgraceful thing that you should come between husband and wife and I ought to be ashamed." Mr Graydon testified this was "the purest imagination." She further claimed her father was going to talk to her about the affair. Again Mr Graydon testified that: "There is no truth whatever in those two paragraphs. As a matter of fact, I had no idea that my daughter and her husband were not on good terms."[148] Similarly, Edith's sister Avis, testified that the entire incident was "pure imagination on my sister's part."[149] With respect to Edith's statement that she had had "the wrong porridge today", Mrs Lester, the Thompson's lodger, testified it was *she* who prepared Percy's porridge in the mornings, not Edith, thus, lending credence to the claim that any suggestion Edith was attempting to poison Percy was pure fantasy.[150] For those who still doubted that all references to poison and ground glass were pure fiction and imagination, concrete forensic evidence was provided by one of the most famous pathologists of the 20th century - Sir Bernard Spilsbury. Following the discovery of Edith's letters, Percy's body was exhumed for the specific purpose of examining it for evidence of poisoning or scar-tissue caused by ground glass. After the post-mortem Sir Bernard reported:

> I found no indications of poisoning and no changes suggestive of previous attempts at poisoning. I detected no glass in the contents of the intestines.[151]

When Sir Bernard appeared as a witness for the prosecution he repeated: "I did not find any signs of poisoning, nor did I find any scars in the intestines. When pressed further, he reiterated that he "had found no indication of the presence of glass either in large pieces or in powdered particles."[152] For the majority of students of the Thompson/Bywaters case,

---

[148]*Transcript* 1923:26-7.

[149]*Transcript* 1923:104.

[150]*Transcript* 1923:29-30.

[151]CRIM 1/206/5 XC6872 Post-mortem report by Sir Bernard Spilsbury.

[152]*Transcript* 1923:43.

the references to poisoning and ground glass have never been taken seriously. For example, Sir Bernard's biographers asked:

> ... what was Percy Thompson doing about it? Apparently nothing at all. When he was not picking pieces of glass out of his porridge, or complaining because his tea tasted bitter, he was leading his normal domestic life, eating meals prepared by the wife who was trying to kill him, taking her to the theatre ... The letters, in fact, do not make sense, unless they are accepted as nonsense.[153]

Similarly, the Earl of Birkenhead wrote: "It must be admitted that the attempts she describes seem singularly clumsy, and do not ring true."[154] With reference to the extract quoted from Edith's letter "I had the wrong porridge today ..." (f/n 120) Rene Weis has suggested a second alternative truth by arguing that both Edith and Freddy *were* speaking the truth in court when Edith claimed he had "given her something" and Freddy claimed he had given her quinine. The quinine, however, was not meant to poison Percy but to cause Edith to have an abortion:

> As fate would have it, Percy takes the wrong bowl and eats the porridge, before she can intervene. This morning therefore poor Percy has porridge with abortifacient powder in it.[155]

This would explain why, when cross-examined Edith responded "I really cannot explain." Similarly, when Percy complained of the tea "tasting bitter", it was indeed 'drugged' tea, but intended for Edith:

> At the trial the porridge and tea incidents achieved notoriety as corroborative proof of homicidal intent, when even then it was clear that abortion was the real issue at stake. It is an indictment of the skewed moral climate of the time that the woman in the dock did not dare admit in public that she had been trying to abort. The shame of that for herself and her family would have been too unbearable. It almost appeared preferable to be tried as a murderess.[156]

Filson Young, a lawyer who attended the trial, wrote in 1923 that "there is no doubt in my mind" the references to "'daring' and 'risking', of which so much play was made by prosecuting counsel ..." were references to "measures to counteract the results of intercourse ..."[157] At least six letters make unambiguous references to Edith experiencing a miscarriage or

---

[153] Browne & Tullett 1987:293.
[154] Earl of Birkenhead no year:350.
[155] Weis, R. (1990) *Criminal Justice* Penguin, London, p.70.
[156] Weis 1990:70.
[157] Filson Young in the Introduction to *Transcript* 1923:xxv.

abortion.[158] Once we understand this context, phrases quoted in court to prove murderous intent such as ... "think of all the plans and methods for me"; "if I do not mind the risk why should you?" (f/n118); "Why arnt [sic] you sending me something ..." (p.91) and her reference to digitalin (f/n117), acquire a very different meaning. It even explains the apparent pointlessness of Freddy's insistence that it was Edith who had taken quinine and found the taste bitter (f/n 122). Indeed, it helps to explain why Edith and Freddy, who were usually articulate individuals, made such poor witnesses - for in truth - they *did* have something to hide, which their contemporaries - Filson Young and Curtis-Bennett - realised must *remain* hidden:

> Of course, Sir Henry Curtis-Bennett was aware of all these passages and of the value they might have. But there he was in another dilemma, for if he were to introduce them and put the construction adduced as evidence of murderous intention, he would have had to present his client to the jury, not only as an adulteress, but as an abortionist; and he no doubt thought that the prejudice created in their minds by that admission would outweigh any advantage to be gained by such explanation of the poison passages as it might afford.[159]

In other words, Edith's reputation was already shattered by her adultery, to admit to what was a criminal offence in 1922 - procuring an abortion - would further consolidate her image as a dangerous woman. This alternative truth gains yet more credibility when we discover that insinuations and accusations raised by the prosecution could readily be disproved in instances where an alternative truth did not affect Edith's respectability. For example, the prosecution quoted the passage "He's still well ... He's going to gaze all day long at you in your temporary home - after Wednesday", and attempted to convince the jury that 'he' referred to Percy. However, Edith was able to prove that 'he' referred to a brass monkey - a present from Freddy - placed on her desk and 'gazing' at a sketch of the ship where Freddy worked, which Edith was having framed on 'Wednesday' as a present for Freddy.[160] The prosecution's attempt to present such innocuous passages as proof of murder, illustrates how Edith's letters were manipulated against her:

> With a reckless disregard of the processes of logic, by means of a selection of extracts divorced from their context, the prosecution were permitted to advance as proof of her guilt what were no more than smears and suspicions that imposed upon a jury whose minds were inflamed by prejudice.[161]

---

[158]These letters can be found on pp.204; 220; 221; 222; 224; 226 of *Transcript* 1923. Copies of the letters used as exhibits during the trial are available for inspection in MEPO 3/1582 Public Record Office, Kew, Richmond, Surrey TW9 4DU.
[159]Filson Young in Introduction to *Transcript* 1923:xxv-xxvi.
[160]*Transcript* 1923:101.
[161]Broad 1952:213.

Lustgarten agreed:

What did Mrs Thompson mean, "unless things are different"?
Obvious, said the Crown; she meant ways and means of murder.
What did Mrs Thompson mean, "plans and methods"? Obvious, said
the Crown; she meant ways and means of murder ...
What did Mrs Thompson mean, "do something desperate"? Obvious,
said the Crown; she meant, brace yourself for murder.[162]

Not only did the evidence suggest an alternative truth about the
supposed murder attempts by poison and ground glass, it also pointed to an
alternative truth regarding Edith and Freddy's relationship. As indicated
above, she was perceived as "a wicked woman who had led astray a youth of
good character, much younger and more innocent than herself."[163]   Yet
Edith's letters indicated exactly the opposite. She wrote:

I always think about "the difference". Sometimes when I'm happy for
a little while I forget - but I always remember very soon ... Shall I
always be able to keep you? Eight years is such a long time - it's not
now - it's later when I am Joan and you are not grown old enough to
be Darby? ... Don't ever take your love away from me darlint.[164]

This letter indicates that far from Edith being the dominant partner in
the relationship, she was constantly aware "that as the years went by the
chances that she might lose her influence over Bywaters would increase."[165]
Because the letters were not presented in chronological order and because not
all the letters were submitted as evidence, the jury remained unaware that
Freddy had in fact attempted to end the affair during his last voyage. Edith
was very distraught at the prospect of losing Freddy and less than four weeks
before the murder she wrote:

I don't hear from you much, you don't talk to me by letter and help
and I don't even know if I am going to see you ... If you say 'No I
won't see you' then it shall be so.[166]

Only three weeks before Percy's death she wrote again "I felt that you
were not going to come and see me this time and the feeling was awful."[167]
While Freddy's love was renewed immediately he saw Edith again, her letters

---

[162]Lustgarten 1956:21.

[163]Browne & Tullett 1987:291.

[164]Quoted in Lustgarten 1956:19.

[165]HO45/2685 PT2 XC2501. From a 20-page document written by W. Ashley
Brown, a friend of Sir Stephen Demtriadi who delivered the document to the Home
Office, as Brown was a friend of his and had "placed it before him."

[166]Copies of the letters included in MEPO 3/1582. Also quoted in Broad 1952:200.

[167]Quoted in Broad 1952:200.

are nevertheless evidence that while he was absent she often had to struggle hard to retain his affection. Her letters thus demonstrated it was Freddy rather than Edith who was the dominant partner in the relationship, and that he was experiencing a 'cooling off' period immediately prior to his homecoming. Freddy's uncertainty about his feelings for Edith makes it extremely unlikely that he was prepared to enter into a murder plot which involved killing her husband.

The numerous inconsistencies surrounding the Thompson/Bywaters case were analysed by W. Ashley Brown who felt so passionately about the misrepresentation of Edith that he constructed an alternative truth which he presented to the Home Office prior to the execution. Bearing in mind that Edith's struggle to keep Freddy's interest in her alive was well documented he wrote:

> We have ... a woman ... who is dominated by her affection for a man whom she is desperately anxious to persuade to run away with her without further loss of time. In these circumstances the suggestion of poison and murder makes a sudden and unexplained appearance ... Did Bywaters require Mrs Thompson to carry to a successful conclusion the attempts he believed her to be making? Mrs Thompson appeared to think so, how otherwise can we explain the following (written in reply to a letter from Bywaters commenting upon the 'quinine' fiasco) -
> "You said it was enough for an elephant. Perhaps it was. But you do not allow for the taste, making only a small quantity to be taken. It sounded like a reproach - was it meant to be? Darling I tried hard - you won't know how hard."
> We fear that there is no doubt Bywaters believed, <u>as Mrs Thompson intended him to believe</u>, that the attempts were really being made.[168]

In this version of the truth it is not Percy who stands in the way of the two lovers but Freddy who is reluctant to start a new life with Edith. Desperate to demonstrate she will go to any length to keep her lover, Edith *pretends* to be willing to kill her husband. Mr Brown now invites us to "glance at her statements with the presumption that she is, at worst, concerned to deceive Bywaters":

> Now it becomes clear that if in fact there was no attempt to murder, and that there was no intention to murder, Mrs Thompson will be under the necessity, since there will be no evidence to support her, to indulge in an immense number of statements of goodwill ... Mrs Thompson's one ambition is to serve a double purpose, to satisfy Bywaters, firstly - that she had made an attempt and secondly - that she had failed through no fault of her own. [Having 'failed' with the ground glass and the quinine] it is necessary, in her opinion, to convince Bywaters that she has not become less determined, so she

---

[168] HO45/2685 PT2 XC2501 W.A. Brown's document - underlining in the original.

proceeds ... [to write] about poisons of all sorts. Does he know of this poison? Does he remember the case of the man who used that poison? She suggests how easy it would be in all circumstances except those with which she is called upon to deal. There must have been razors in the house, but she does not propose to conceal murder in the cloak of suicide. On the other hand there is no gas, so she writes at length to the tune of how easy it would be if only the gas were there. She is in fact playing a desperate game. She is trying to convince Bywaters that she is preparing to go to any length in order to persuade Bywaters ... [to] tak[e] her away at once.[169]

If we accept Ashley Brown's alternative truth, Edith's answers in cross-examination acquire a very different meaning. Placed within this context her responses (see quotations in text to footnotes 116, 117, 120 and 124 above) indicate, that far from attempting to cast blame on Freddy, she is in fact attempting to *protect* him, just as she had done when first interviewed by police, by being economical with the truth. This alternative truth also explains why Edith repeatedly claimed she participated in talks of poison to please Freddy:

Mr Bywaters had told me he was bringing me something and I suggested to send it to me, to allow him to think I was eager for him to send me something to do what was suggested. *I wanted him to think I was eager to help him, to bind him closer to me, to retain his affections.*[170]

I wanted him to understand that I was willing to do anything he expected me to do or asked me to do - agree with him. *I wanted him to think I would do anything for him to keep him to me.*[171]

I wanted him to feel that I was willing to help him, to keep him to me.[172]

Similarly, we are now able to understand why Freddy's responses sounded unconvincing (see quotations in text to footnotes 122 and 123 above) - it is because they are the result of, not only his attempts to protect Edith, but also himself.

As noted earlier, commentators agreed with Edith's KC that if she did not give evidence she could not be convicted.[173] So why did she go against the advice of both her solicitor and KC? Her action can be interpreted as further evidence of her innocence. Had she been guilty we would expect her

---

169HO45/2685 PT2 XC2501 W.A. Brown's document - underlining in the original.
170*Transcript* 1923:78. My emphasis.
171*Transcript* 1923:81 My emphasis.
172*Transcript* 1923:81.
173See for example Twinning 1990:278.

priority to have been escaping the gallows, *not* to prove her innocence. The fact that Edith chose this far more hazardous - indeed deadly - course of action, demonstrates not just her innocence but also her naiveté:

> The woman herself was not conscious of her peril. She had been overcome by the sight of her lover's deed of violence, she had been prostrated by the shock, horrified by the exposure to her family of the intimacies of her love life, but now she had recovered her composure and she was fortified by her consciousness of innocence. Having had no foreknowledge of her lover's crime, she had no realisation that other persons might take quite the contrary view about her. Her imagination was powerful but her comprehension limited.[174]

Despite having broken her marital vows, Edith was otherwise an obedient daughter, a conventional wife and a conscientious worker, living a rather conservative suburban existence, which placed great emphasis upon appearances and respectability. Because her self-image matched that lifestyle, she failed to grasp that the jury might share the trial judge's view of her as an 'adulteress'. Precisely because she was innocent and as a result of having been brought up to be an honest, law-abiding citizen, she was absolutely certain that all she had to do to clear her name was to enter the witness-box and *tell the truth*. It was her background as a respectable, 'upright' citizen, with no previous experience of law-enforcement agencies, which gave her this blind faith in justice. Far from being a 'scheming, conniving seductress' her behaviour suggests a certain naiveté and lack of awareness of the social climate surrounding her. As I shall now illustrate, this social climate is crucial to an understanding of how a woman - in the words of Curtis-Bennett - came to be executed for immorality rather than murder.

The 1920s

The 1920s was the decade of "the smoking, drinking flapper, freed from corsets and sexual repression."[175] The dominant Victorian portrayal of female sexuality as weak and passive as discussed in the Louise Masset case-study, had been replaced by a new sexual doctrine which recognised women's "erotic rights". Women were now supposed to enjoy sex, indeed, those who failed to do so were encouraged to fake orgasm to ensure their husbands' ego remained intact.[176] Women's fashions began to mirror this supposed sexual liberation, with both short hemlines and hairstyles offering a physical freedom unknown to Victorian women.[177] Edith appeared to fit the image of the 'liberated flapper'. She was elegant and fashionable, smoked cigarettes, had her hair cut in a modern bob, continued to used her maiden name at work

---

[174]Broad 1952:89.

[175]Jones, A. (1991) *Women Who Kill* Gollancz, London, p.256.

[176]Jones 1991:265; 266.

[177]Rowbotham 1977:125.

after her marriage, and, as a result of her earning-power, owned her home on equal terms with Percy. Yet the apparent freedom now enjoyed by women, was strongly resisted by traditionalists. Between 1905-14 Britain had lived through nearly a decade of organised female protests and violence in the form of the suffragette movement which had not achieved full female suffrage at the time of Edith's trial.[178] This first wave of feminism was in itself enough to cause deep concern about the future role of women. However, following de-mobilisation after the First World War, thousands of women protested in support of a different cause - the right to continue to work in the jobs they had originally been drafted into when vast numbers of the male population joined the armed forces. Women who were reluctant to give up 'men's' jobs soon found themselves at the heart of an ideological battle instigated by traditionalists who argued that:

> their first duty was to the soldier - the man who had done his bit for the past 4 years - and who would now be wanting to return to his normal occupation.[179]

At the same time ideologies around motherhood and domesticity were re-mobilised and supported by various scientific experts. The inherent contradictions running through the sexual liberation of the 1920s were personified in one such expert, Havelock Ellis. While his status as a member of the new profession of sexologists ensured he was regarded as a sexual revolutionary, Havelock Ellis's views on women's role were indistinguishable from those of the traditionalists. Thus, he wrote that "'every healthy woman should have ... the exercise at least once in her life of the supreme function of maternity' ... Unless she became a mother, no woman could have a 'complete human life'."[180] The explosion of women's magazines during the 1920s also played a major role in reinforcing and idealising motherhood and domesticity:

> [Editors] expatiated in unison on the sacrificial joys of being a wife and mother ... elevated housewifery into a craft, gave it the status of a profession, and sold it to readers on the most attractive of terms,

---

[178]See for example Hamer, E. (1996) 'Fighting for Freedom: Suffragette Violence Against their State' in Myers, A. & Wight, S. (eds) (1996) *No Angels* Pandora, London pp.72-84; Morley, A. & Stanley, L. (1988) *The Life and Death of Emily Wilding Davison* The Women's Press, London.

[179]Lilian Barker quoted in Braybon, G. & Summerfield, P. (1987) *Out of the Cage: Women's Experiences in Two World Wars* Pandora, London, p.121. By 1919 benefits could be excluded to women who refused domestic or laundry work. By contrast unemployed men "could only be offered jobs in their usual trade" (pp.123-4).

[180]Havelock Ellis quoted in Jones 1991:259. See also Jeffreys S. (1985) *The Spinster and Her Enemies* Pandora, London, pp.128-38; Ehrenreich, B. & English, D. (1979) *For Her Own Good* Pluto, London, Chapter 5 pp.141-81.

thereby nullifying all that had been achieved by the women's rights movement.[181]

Once more, such ideologies were supported by a reality of decreasing opportunities. For example, three years after Edith's execution London County Council enforced a jobs ban on married women,[182] while at the same time, becoming a divorcee could result in dismissal as Edith herself recognised. Divorce rates had reached a new height in 1918 and continued to rise. The year of Edith's execution saw the introduction of the Matrimonial Causes Act, which made adultery grounds for divorce for a wife as well as a husband.[183] Couples who chose to remain childless were increasing and 'flappers' and feminists were quickly identified as being responsible for this supposed threat to family life.[184] The battle to domesticate women's new-found freedom had never seemed more urgent. At specific moments this battle was fought in the law courts. For example, in the year of Edith's trial, Rose Witcop who published Margaret Sanger's *Family Limitation*, a book on birth control, was successfully prosecuted for "producing an obscene work," on the grounds that "'birth control was a danger to the race and against nature's law.'"[185] Meanwhile, the punishment for procuring abortions was penal servitude (potentially for life) with hard labour.[186]

While women's ongoing fight for birth control and legal abortion gradually made these subjects less taboo during the 1920s,[187] it was nevertheless the case that 'flappers' who continued to conduct themselves according to the principles of emancipated female sexuality were soon labelled 'over-sexed' for they had "crossed the fine line between being 'free' and 'loose' ... The bad woman and the 'over-sexed' woman were, as they had always been, one and the same."[188] This new 'liberation' of female sexuality was therefore only legitimate when practised in the marital bed. At other

---

[181]Cynthia White quoted in Oakley, A. (1986) *Subject Women* Fontana London p.21. In 1920 attempts to convince women of the joys of motherhood were sometimes less than subtle: "Do you realise, Mother of Baby - that you can be one of the greatest artists in the world? - Just like every other artist a mother must study her Art - the greatest Art of all - the great Art of creating strong, straight, noble men and women" (Quoted in Oakley 1986:21).

[182]'Past Notes' in *The Guardian* 17th February 1997.

[183]Rowbotham, S. (1977) *Hidden From History* Pluto, London p.123.

[184]Jones 1991:258.

[185]Quoted in Rowbotham 1977:150.

[186]Rowbotham 1977:156.

[187]This fight took many forms, for example Rowbotham has described how a miner's wife, Mrs Lawther, in 1927 "appealed at the Labour Party conference for support from the miners for birth control in return for the women's solidarity with the miners in the lock-out" in Blaydon, Durham (Rowbotham 1977:150).

[188]Jones 1991:257. Jones's analysis appears uncannily accurate, for Edith has been variously described as 'highly-sexed' (Bresler 1965:165) and 'over-sexed' (O'Donnell 1956:52).

times it was accompanied by the belief "that moral standards were in decline ... [and] sexual morality was 'on the brink of complete disintegration.'"[189] Hence it benefited men as much, if not more so, than women - who soon found that the old standards relating to 'keeping one's reputation' sprang into force, when they attempted to practice the new code of sexual liberation outside marriage.

Edith's trial thus took place during a period of intense struggle over women's role, and a pronounced preoccupation with their sexuality. As traditionalists considered the post-war period to be "shallow and decadent"[190], and fought to restore the pre-war social order, the notion of the childless 'career woman' - as Edith was - had not yet become accepted as can be seen from the Solicitor-General's comments in his opening statement that "perhaps because there were no children, or for other reasons, she was carrying on her employment."[191] Within this social context Edith's KC felt unable to suggest that several incriminating passages in the letters referred to abortion rather than murder. She already fulfilled the criteria of a 'sexually insatiable', 'immoral' and 'dangerous' woman without this knowledge being revealed - her adultery proof that an independent woman who is not under her husband's constant supervision soon becomes dangerously out of control. She appeared to be the kind of woman Bloch had in mind when in 1909 he wrote:

> Women are in fact pure sex from knees to neck. We men have concentrated our apparatus in a single place, we have extracted it, separated it from the rest of the body ... They [women] *are* a sexual *surface* or target; we *have* only a sexual arrow ... Properly speaking they procreate unceasingly, they stand continually at the witches' cauldron, boiling and brewing; while we lend a hand merely in passing, and do no more than throw one or two fragments into the vessel.[192]

From the moralists' point of view, at a time when women were forced to either give up paid work entirely or return to the drudgery of domestic service[193], Edith had everything - a highly paid job, her own home, a loyal husband. Unlike most women executed during the 20th century, she could not claim under-privilege, financially or emotionally. Yet she failed to be content and instead broke social conventions repeatedly through adultery - a serious enough misdemeanour in its own right - but amplified considerably by

---

[189]The Bishop of Durham speaking in July 1923, quoted in Rose, A. (1991) *Scandal at the Savoy* Bloomsbury, London, p.9.

[190]Rose 1991:8.

[191]*Transcript* 1923:9.

[192]Iwan Bloch quoted in Jeffreys 1985:138-9.

[193]See Braybon & Summerfield 1987:123-6. See also Rose 1991:9 quoting the *Daily Mail*: "'Thousands upon thousands of women are drawing the dole, when they ought to be in domestic service' ... women capable of such work should have their dole money stopped."

the youth of her lover, her preference for paid work rather than motherhood, her ability to earn *more* than either her husband or father and her decision to remain 'Miss Graydon' at work. It was such conduct and behaviour which ensured Edith's letters were heard through the discourses of a 'dangerous' and 'immoral' woman. Moreover, the lack of mitigating circumstances made her conduct appear 'doubly' deviant and helps to explain the widely held self-righteous opinion that she was "the author of her own deserved misfortunes,"[194] someone who needed to be 'put in her place'.

Throughout this book I have argued that the Crown will employ what is 'known' about female defendants as *women* for the purpose of establishing a dominant truth which is likely to secure a conviction. Once such 'knowledge' has been heard, 'disreputable' discourses are invariably unleashed which operate to reinforce the Crown's case whilst diminishing the case for the defence. As a result of the dubious and ambiguous nature of the evidence against Edith, she has become the ultimate example of a woman judged according to her sexual conduct and behaviour, rather than according to the evidence. This was recognised as early as 1952 when Lewis Broad asked: "Had Mrs Thompson by her immoralities placed herself so far beyond the pale that proof could be dispensed with?[195] Yet Edith was not muted but had a comprehensive understanding of how to communicate through dominant modes of expression. But like Louise Masset 22 years earlier, Edith was a self-confessed liar, and if she could not be disqualified as a speaker, she could be discredited instead. Indeed, she had already done so herself, by mobilising discourses of the 'immoral woman', the disloyal and deceitful wife, the sexually insatiable, predatory adulteress preying on 'innocent' younger boys, the scheming woman-poisoner and liar. Once mobilised, these discourses ensured the jury would hear Edith's letters predominantly through them. In particular, the discourses surrounding an older woman with a young lover were so dominant that evidence indicating Freddy must have committed the murder alone, was ignored. For example, Edith's letter written the day before the murder read: "Until we have funds we can do nothing,"[196] a sentence which indicates, that as far as she was concerned, they were still planning to run away together. Similarly, in a letter written on the very day of the murder, Edith referred to an agreement she had made with Freddy when they first became lovers, that they would wait five years before running away together: "We only have three and three-quarter years left",[197] again not the sort of statement one would expect from a person planning murder that very night. Even though these passages were included in the closing speech on behalf of Edith, it proved impossible to challenge the discourses surrounding Freddy - namely that he was a "manly young fellow ... of spotless reputation and good character" who was "corrupted and debauched by the experienced

---

[194]O'Donnell 1956:53.
[195]Broad 1952:216.
[196]*Transcript* 1923:121.
[197]*Transcript* 1923:122-3.

woman of the world".[198]   So dominant were the discourses surrounding Edith's immoral conduct that the evidence presented for examination became increasingly irrelevant until finally it was ignored altogether.

A final indication of the exceptional condemnation of Edith's sexual transgressions and subversive domesticity is indicated by the fact she was the first woman to be executed since Leslie James in 1907. Until Edith's death sentence, many contemporaries had considered it unthinkable a woman "should ever again be sent to the scaffold."[199] However, even the promise of the resurrection of the scaffold, did not terminate the condemnation of Edith Thompson. Instead the Lord Chief Justice continued to moralise about her behaviour in the Court of Appeal, the hearing of which was to be as unorthodox and controversial as the trial.

The Appeal

Lord Chief Justice Hewart, described by one author as "a horror"[200], presided over the appeal of the Thompson/Bywaters case. He defined the case as one of "lust and adultery", "squalid" and "indecent", possessing "no redeeming feature ... from beginning to the end". It was "a commonplace and unedifying case" involving "deplorable correspondence ... which was full of the most mischievous and perilous stuff":

> Mrs Thompson was, with every sort of ingenuity by precept and by example, actual or simulated, endeavouring to incite Bywaters to the commission of the crime.[201]

Space does not permit an examination of all seven points on which the appeal was fought, however, three major issues should be noted. First, "that the learned Judge was wrong in rejecting an application for ... separate trial[s].[202] By the Lord Chief Justice's own definition separate trials should have been granted:

> No doubt in cases where the defence of one accused person is to incriminate another accused person that is a good reason for not trying the two persons together.[203]

---

[198]*Transcript* 1923:xiv; 109; xiv. See also Twinning 1990:290-3.

[199]Ellis 1996:15; Weis 1990:150.

[200]Devlin, P. (1981) *The Judge* Oxford University Press, Oxford p.24.

[201]*Criminal Appeal Reports* Vol XVII, July to December 1922-23, pp. 66; 74; 72; 73, available for inspection at the Supreme Court Library, Royal Courts of Justice, London. Refering to the appeal Terence Morris wrote of Lord Chief Justice Hewart that he "was arguably one of the rudest incumbents of that office ..." Morris, T. (1991) 'Reviews' in *British Journal of Criminology* vol 31, No 1, Winter 1991 p.88.

[202]HO45/2685 PT2 XC2501, point 5 of Appeal Document.

[203]*Criminal Appeal Report* Vol XVII, July to December 1922-23, dismissal of Frederick Bywater's appeal pp.66-70.

This was exactly the case where Edith and Freddy were concerned, since Edith would have both implicated and incriminated Freddy by presenting what is now widely accepted as the correct explanation - "an unpremeditated attack inspired by a frenzy of jealousy."[204]

Second, the judge had failed "to direct ... [the jury] that there was no evidence that the Appellant was a party to or had knowledge of the attack upon Percy Thompson ..."[205] Fenton Bresler, himself a lawyer, has argued Judge Shearman did in fact include this in his instructions, hence it was the jury rather than the judge, who had acted wrongly in convicting Edith. He further argues that Lord Hewart *realised* she had been wrongly convicted, hence to ensure the verdict fitted the evidence, he used the Appeal Court to *redefine* the case:

> The real case against Edith Thompson was that "the letters were evidence of a protracted continuous incitement to Bywaters to commit the crime which he did in the end commit ... It was not necessary to prove that the knifing occurred by arrangement with her. It was enough that she had continuously incited Bywaters to murder her husband ..."[206]

Lord Hewart went a step further when, dismissing Edith's appeal, he argued it was irrelevant whether Edith's letters had been true or false:

> So far as the persuasive effect of incitement was in issue, it depended not upon the question whether the statements were true, but upon the question what they were intended and likely to cause the reader to believe.[207]

Thus, not only was Edith convicted on evidence for which she was not standing trial (poisoning), but that evidence did not have to be true. That is to say, Edith was never charged with poisoning or "administering a destructive thing" to Percy.[208] However, there was not a single piece of evidence to support the indictment she *was* charged with. Therefore, the only possible reason for presenting evidence relating to poisoning and ground glass, would be to cause suspicion by implying that her letters made it more likely she was involved in Percy's murder. Consequently Curtis-Bennett had spent much of his time during the trial arguing that the letters were fantasy only to be told in the Court of Appeal it was "of little importance whether Mrs Thompson was truly reporting something which she had done or falsely reporting something which she merely pretended she had done."[209]

---

[204] Broad 1952:212.
[205] HO45/2685 PT2 XC2501 Appeal Document point 7h.
[206] Bresler quoting Lord Chief Justice Hewart 1965:174; 175.
[207] *Criminal Appeal Reports* Vol XV II July to December 1922-23 p.71.
[208] CRIM 1/206/5 XC6872 Charge Sheet, charges 4 and 5.
[209] *Criminal Appeal Reports* Vol XV II July to December 1922-23 p.73.

Third, Judge Shearman had failed to make any mention of Sir Bernard Spilsbury's evidence which "supported the evidence of the Appellant."[210] This was an important omission, for as noted above, Sir Bernard's evidence provided conclusive proof that Percy had never been the victim of a poison attempt. Therefore the prosecution's case rested on a fabricated theory designed to cast suspicion upon Edith. In other words, because there was no evidence of Edith's involvement in Percy's murder, the Crown utilised 'evidence' of a crime which *had not been committed* (poisoning) to prove, she was guilty of a crime which *had* been committed:

> It cannot be doubted that it was upon this evidence [of the first indictment] that the verdict upon the second indictment was ultimately secured. It was because the Jury believed that Mrs Thompson was prepared to murder her husband when Bywaters was abroad that they accepted her guilt as an accomplice when Bywaters was at home.[211]

To omit Sir Bernard's evidence therefore involved omitting evidence which proved Edith's innocence on two of the five charges, and which proved the Crown's case to be based on smears and insinuations rather than forensic evidence. However, as indicated above, although the crux of the prosecution's case involved evidence of poisoning, by the time the case reached the Appeal Court, the truth/falsehood of the poison attempts were deemed irrelevant as a result of Lord Hewart's redefinition of the case.

A final point which related to the evidence of Mr Webber, was not included in the Appeal Document, but has been discussed by Rene Weis, and deserves consideration. It will be remembered Webber testified he had heard Edith cry out "'Oh, don't, oh, don't', in a most piteous manner." The judge described this to the jury as a "very curious piece of evidence", claiming Webber had been "some way off" when hearing the cries:

> I am not saying it is true, it is for you to say whether it is accurate, or whether it is imaginary, or whether he has made a mistake.[212]

These comments suggest that because Mr Webber's testimony did not fit the case presented by the prosecution, the judge attempted to discredit him as a witness which raises concern about Mr Justice Shearman's ability to remain impartial.

The three Appeal Court judges took five minutes reaching a decision in Freddy's case and eight minutes considering Edith's case.[213] The manner in which the appeal was conducted confirmed not only the "gross moral bias"

[210]HO45/2685 PT2 XC2501 Appeal Document point 7d.
[211]HO45/2685 PT2 XC2501 Document by Sir Stephen Demetriadi. Underlining in the original.
[212]Judge Shearman's summing-up quoted in Weis 1988:316.
[213]Weis 1988:260; 261.

associated with the case, but also Lord Chief Justice Hewart's reputation for "tak[ing] sides in cases that came before him ... [and] seeing one side of the picture more clearly than the other."[214] Overall, the appeal lent further credence to the claim that Edith was hanged not for murder but for adultery.[215]

Edith Thompson: Formal versus Informal Punishment

The level of moralising directed against Edith was superseded only by the level of punishment imposed on her. This punishment was initiated when she was a remand prisoner, and therefore, technically, still innocent. Following their arrest, Edith and Freddy immediately began to communicate by letter. As remand prisoners they were entitled to copies of letters addressed to them. However, by mid-November, the governor of Brixton prison revealed this correspondence to the Prison Commissioners, stating "this sort of correspondence has been going on between this prisoner and his fellow prisoner in Holloway. The letters are not clear."[216] The Commissioners instantly issued reprimands to the governors of both prisons:

> This letter will not be allowed to go ... He should not be told. No letters from this man to the woman Thompson will be posted. *He will not be told of this.* He may continue to write to her, but the letters will be forwarded to this office ... What do you mean by "this sort of correspondence."? No letters to or from ... Thompson have been submitted by you to the Commissioners. If letters have passed why were they not submitted ... The letters should not have been allowed to go and you should have asked for instructions before allowing correspondence between two prisoners in the same case, particularly in such a grave case.[217]

The governor of Holloway was issued with almost identical instructions:

> Please note that letters written by the woman Thompson to the man Bywaters will not be posted. *She will not, however, be told of this.* If she writes any, they will be sent up to this office, where they will be

---

[214]Pannick, D. (1987) *Judges* Oxford University Press, Oxford p.51. Hewart also used to write "letters while sitting in court, although his biographer reassures us that 'nothing passed over his head'" (Pannick 1987:79).
[215]Weis 1988:316.
[216]PCOM 8/22 XC2663 Public Record Office, Kew, Richmond, Surrey TW9 4DU; dated 21st November 1922.
[217]PCOM 8/22 XC2663 Prison Commissioners' Memo, 21st November 1922. My emphasis.

retained. If she has written to him, or if she has received letters from him why were they not submitted to the Commissioners?218

Following these instructions the couple's letters never again reached their destination. The level of anxiety experienced by the prisoners as a consequence of this silence can be gleaned from a telegram from Freddy to Edith:

Have you received letter? Are you ill. Let me know. Freddy.219

The telegram was not posted. We can only speculate as to why Edith and Freddy were never told of their continuing loyalty to each other. Did the authorities hope that if the couple felt increasingly isolated they would reveal much needed evidence of the so-called plot to kill Percy? Or was it a form of informal punishment?220

While prison rules forbade condemned prisoners to correspond with each other,221 Deputy Governor Clayton attempted to have this rule waived when he wrote to the Commissioners after the trial, to request permission for Freddy's letter to be forwarded to Edith "thinking he might divulge some matter of importance."222 Permission was refused.223 In Edith's case, other evidence suggests the Prison Commissioners aimed to punish her long before she reached the gallows. For example, when a bouquet of flowers was sent anonymously two days before her appeal, bearing the message "best wishes" from a "friendly girl", Edith was not told. Instead the Commissioners ordered the flowers to be destroyed.224

A far more serious example of how Edith suffered whilst awaiting execution can be observed from the Commissioners' handling of her request to receive visits from her local priest Canon Palmer. In previous chapters I discussed the crucial role played by prison chaplains in securing confessions

---

218PCOM 8/436 Public Record Office, Kew, Richmond, Surrey TW9 4DU. Memo dated 18.11.1922. My emphasis.

219PCOM 8/22. Original telegram included in this file. No date.

220Some comfort may be gained from the knowledge that Edith Thompson broke the rules of the court by shouting to Freddy "if he had received 2 letters she had sent this week. Bywaters replied he had not." (PCOM 8/22 XC2663 Prison Commissioners Memo dated 24th November 1922). After this realisation the couple passed verbal messages to each other via relatives.

221Introduction to *Transcript* 1923:xxix-xxx. However, instructions printed on the reverse of the official prison paper which Freddy wrote to Edith suggest prisoners did have a right to communicate: Prisoners are allowed "to receive and to write a letter at intervals, which depends on the stage they attain by industry and good conduct" (144/2685 Pt 2).

222PCOM 8/22 XC2663 Public Record Office, Kew, Richmond, Surrey TW9 4DU. Letter dated 2nd January 1923.

223PCOM 8/22 XC2663 Memo dated 3rd January 1923.

224PCOM 8/436. Memo dated 19th December 1922.

from condemned prisoners and argued that a confession added legitimacy to controversial executions. Holloway's chaplain Granville Murray appeared to follow the pattern of his predecessors for Edith soon found his visits "most objectionable, as he was very pressing for a confession and many times she told him she had nothing to confess being quite innocent of the crime ..."[225] The chaplain's attitude stood in sharp contrast to that of Canon Palmer, a priest attached to Edith's local area:

> His visit to her ... was one of the happiest half hours that she had had while there.[226]

Consequently Edith requested that Canon Palmer rather than Chaplain Murray should become her spiritual adviser, which would have allowed him to administer to her during her last moments before the execution.[227] However, the Prison Commissioners ruled that as Edith did not wish to convert to Catholicism, he would not be allowed to visit her again.[228]

From a humanitarian perspective it seems exceptionally punitive that a woman with only days to live was refused this last request. However, when seen within the context of depriving her of letters and flowers, the denial of her request becomes part of a pattern of depriving her of every source intended to offer her comfort and moral support. In effect it amounted to a series of informal punishments, which, as argued in Chapter Three, is designed to teach a defiant woman a lesson - to put a wife who has failed to recognise male authority 'in her place'. In Percy's absence, the state took over his responsibility for disciplining an 'uppity' wife.

Like Louise Masset before her, Edith's 'dangerousness' lay in her ability to deceive even those closest to her. Outwardly, she conformed unwaveringly to conventional feminine standards and expectations. She took care over her appearance, hence imposed a 'feminine body discipline' as discussed in Chapter Three. She gave the appearance of being a loyal, loving, compliant and altruistic wife and was regarded as a 'respectable' woman. Yet, like Louise Masset, behind the facade of convention and conformity lurked a woman who lived a life of lies, lust and debauchery, deceptions viewed as doubly deviant as a result of her social class. Thus, it was she, rather than

---

[225] HO144/2685 Pt 2 XC2501. Letter from Edith's mother, Mrs Graydon to Home Office 3rd March 1923.

[226] HO144/2685 Pt 2 XC2501 Letter from Mrs Graydon 3rd March 1923.

[227] HO 144/2685 Pt 2 XC2501 Letter from Mrs Graydon 3rd March 1923. Moreover, Canon Palmer told Mr Morton, the prison governor, that he was prepared to cancel all his engagements on the Monday before the execution in order to spend time with Edith.

[228] HO144/2685. This file contains several letters from prominent members of the public, who complained to the Home Secretary about this decision. The letter-writers included the Hon Mrs Philip Nelson Ward; Westminster Catholic Federation Vigilance Committee and Catholic Women's Suffrage Society.

Freddy, who was singled out for derogatory comments by the detective-inspector who had worked on her case:

> Mrs Thompson used her utmost endeavours to deceive by deliberately lying to police as to the identity of the assassin ... She is a consummate actress, and it was only after a searching inquiry that her secret lover was disclosed.[229]

Edith represented the stereotypical wicked and sexually insatiable female, who, in previous centuries was considered to be "the Devil's Gateway."[230] Her perceived powers as a seducer and temptress of young men can be gathered from two members of the professional classes who wrote to the Home Secretary pleading for Freddy's life, and who subscribed to the same double standards as the detective-inspector:

> As a youth of 19, of previous excellent character, he was exposed for many months to the malign influence of a clever and unscrupulous woman 8 years older, who ... wrote him numerous letters, inciting him to help her in getting rid of her husband ... An impressionable youth of that age would need to be of unusual strength of character to resist such solicitations ... Bywaters fell a victim to her machinations ...[231]

Similarly, Freddy's solicitor called him a 'boy' and wrote:

> He has been at a very impressionable age ... and ... had it not been for the unfortunate circumstance that he came under the spell of a woman 8 years older than himself he would not be in his present terrible position.[232]

In short, Edith's transgressions resurrected the age-old image of the temptress Eve, literally down to its poisonous detail. They also resurrected the equally old male fear of female sexuality, which, as indicated in Chapter Two, has resulted in women being perceived in highly threatening terms, as possessing "an all-consuming, all-absorbing passion, an animal lust ... never satisfied."[233] The extent of the threat that Edith posed can be measured by the level of cruelty directed against her and her family. Thus, on the day before the execution, during her family's last visit, a telegram addressed to her

---

[229]MEPO 3/1582 Concluding notes on the case dated 19th December 1922.
[230]Tertullian quoted in Noddings, N. (1989) *Women and Evil* University of California Press, Berkeley p.52.
[231]HO144/2685 Part 2 XC2501 Letter from the Committing Magistrate Eliot Howard, 14th December 1922.
[232]HO144/2685 Part 2 XC2501 Letter from Barrington Matthews, 23rd December 1922.
[233]Jones 1991:274.

father was delivered to the cell, bearing the message: "Am in direct communication with the Home Office. Cheer up. Good news coming. Bethell, Romford."[234] Edith and her family assumed it was from the local MP of that name, and undoubtedly also assumed a last minute reprieve had been secured. The telegram was a hoax. Moreover, given the strict censorship imposed on Edith's correspondence, we can only speculate about the reasons for allowing this telegram to reach its intended recipient.

The excesses of cruelty and lack of humanity engulfing Edith's last days - together with the gradual realisation that she was innocent of the crime for which she was hanged - were later to become the ingredients which ensured future generations' revulsion at her punishment. Thus, while resistance to her execution was far from universal at the time, Edith Thompson was eventually to become the "patron-saint of the abolitionist cause."[235]

Resistance and Opposition to the Execution of Edith Thompson

During the four weeks between the trial and execution public opinion as to whether the death penalty should be carried out appeared to be sharply divided. On the one hand, *The Daily Sketch* carried headlines such as 'Bywaters must not be hanged'. It also launched a petition on Freddy's behalf and claimed to have received 10,000 letters in the first 24 hours alone. This petition was eventually to become the largest ever "in Britain for a convicted prisoner."[236] *The Daily Express* also supported the couple by focusing on their unhappy plight and refraining from moralising.[237] On the other hand, *The Daily Telegraph* threw its support firmly behind the trial judge and wrote:

> his insistence that the jury and he were investigating a 'vulgar crime' according to the principles of human justice and common-sense well expresses the spirit in which English people would have all such cases tried. ... It is idle to attempt by sentimental appeals in the name of love - a word which has no place in this case - to throw some glamour over the man and woman who now lie condemned to death. The jury found, after long deliberation ... no cause to ask for mercy upon either. To their silence there is nothing to add.[238]

---

[234]*Daily Express* 9th January 1923.
[235]Goodman, J. (1993) *The Daily Telegraph Murder File* Mandarin, London, p.144.
[236]Weis 1990:255-6. The first portion alone, delivered to the Home Office on Christmas Eve, contained 832,000 signatures (*The Times* 27th December 1922).
[237]See for example *Daily Express* 6th, 7th and 9th January 1923. At that time its editor was Beverley Baxter, who was opposed to the death penalty, and who, when he later became an MP, was to raise the issue of Edith's execution in an attempt to find out the exact truth. See also Appendix II.
[238]*Daily Telegraph* leading article 12th December 1922.

The Daily Mail had no sympathy for the couple either:

> ... looking back on the crusade of sentimentalism which succeeded the jury's verdict the country may congratulate itself on having a Home Secretary capable of carrying out a very painful duty with due firmness. ... We are satisfied ... that public sympathy is not with the murderers but with the unfortunate and inoffensive husband. ... With the judges' decision ... the vast majority of the public are in full agreement.[239]

This difference of opinion was equally apparent amongst individual members of the public. For example, Sir Evelyn Cecil wrote:

> Perverted sympathy for murderers and such mawkish journalism as 'Move to save the Ilford lovers' ... sap the very moral of a nation. I should deplore the future for a country where morbid sentimentality ever got the upper hand.[240]

However, John Ellis, who was to be Edith's executioner, reported that he had received "lots of ... letters", urging him to refuse to carry out the execution:

> Bywaters is a victim of sympathy, drawn into the crime through that agent in the first place. Mrs Thompson's fall is through vanity which is no credit, and, next to greed, the worst sin in the world. But as she did not actually do the crime, and being a woman, she should be reprieved.[241]

On the morning of the executions 4,000 people gathered outside Holloway and 5,000 assembled outside Pentonville prison. While women demonstrators carried placards with the wording "Murder cannot be abolished by murder" and "If these two are hanged judge & jury are murderers also",[242] *The Daily Mail* claimed that "in the large crowds assembled few questioned the justice of the sentences ..."[243] However, two factors were gradually to change the minds of those who still supported the executions. First, throughout his imprisonment Freddy maintained Edith's innocence. In writing a petition for his own life he spent almost two thirds of the limited

---

[239]*Daily Mail* 8th January 1923.

[240]*The Times* Letters Page 9th January 1923.

[241]Letter quoted in Ellis 1996:18. Other letters took a more threatening form: "Dear Sir, - Be a man and don't hang a woman. You know you have to die yourself in a few years. Just think." Another read: "If you go and pull that lever and take a woman's life, Government ain't going to answer for it, God'll send the bill to you" (Ellis 1996:18).

[242]*Daily Mirror* 10th January 1923; Ellis 1996:29.

[243]*Daily Mail* 10th January 1923.

space available on reiterating and clarifying her innocence. He further asked the Home Secretary:

> to accept my word sir, or perhaps you can show me some way in which I can prove to you that I am speaking the truth.[244]

When this plea had no effect, he made a new confession to his mother and persuaded her to send it to the Home Secretary:

> I swear she is completely innocent. She never knew that I was going to meet them that night ... She didn't commit murder. I did. She never planned it. She never knew about it. She is innocent, innocent, absolutely innocent.[245]

Furthermore, during his final hours, he told the governor: "It was my fault. She is innocent. She never did anything - it was me."[246] Freddy's persistent campaign to clear Edith's name reached newspapers immediately after the execution together with press reports describing Edith's last moments as "Nearly unconscious and unable to walk." Throughout her last night she had been "semi-conscious", asking for Freddy whenever she had a moment of clarity. Eventually she reached a "state of collapse", was "dazed" when the executioner entered her cell, and had to be carried to the scaffold "moaning like an animal", barely conscious. She was unable to hold her head up, which consequently rested on the shoulders of one of the warders. The executioner had to hold her head in position to secure the hood.[247] These reports were followed by others, claiming Edith's 'insides' had fallen out, leading to a suspicion she may have been pregnant.[248]

The distressing circumstances of Edith's execution had caused "women officials ... engaged in watching Mrs Thompson ... [to have] felt the strain acutely, and some of them are prostrated in consequence. Many of them declared that they could never again carry out the duty imposed on them

---

[244]HO45/2685 PT 2 XC2501 Original petition dated 5th December 1922, is included in this file.

[245]Quoted in *Daily Express* 8th January 1923.

[246]From Major Blake's memoirs published in *London Evening News* 27th October 1926; this extract also quoted in Broad 1952:206. See also Appendix II.

[247]*Daily Express* and *Daily Mirror* 10th January 1923; *The Times* 11th January 1923. See also evidence of witnesses to the execution in PCOM 9/1983 XC2662, Public Record Office Kew, Richmond, Surrey TW9 4DU, which confirms the truth of these reports.

[248]This suspicion was largely the result of Governor Morton's report that she had gained 15lbs in a matter of weeks. (HO45/2685 PT2 XC2501 Report entitled 'Conduct & general demeanour of Edith Jessie Thompson from Dec 11th to Jan 9th, dated 9th January 1923.) See also PCOM 9/1983 XC2662 which refers to Mr Baxter's mention in the House of Commons "of a sick woman of 28 whose insides fell out before she vanished through the trap".

yesterday."[249] Moreover, Governor Morton was reported to have visited the editor of the *Daily Mail* requesting it "start a campaign against hanging ..." He "had been so upset about what happened at the execution that morning that he had come to say he would never again take any part in the hanging of a woman ..."[250] At the same time Sir Beverley Baxter reported that "on the evening of the execution two warders who had 'taken part in it' visited his office at the *Daily Express* ... and told him that what had happened was 'too terrible to describe'."[251] While these reports were to remain controversial for decades to come,[252] others remained unchallenged. For example Dr Walker, who also witnessed the execution, stated that Edith "groaned several times just before she went on the drop ... and appeared to hang back with some slight struggling ... and grunted as an animal going to be killed. It could not be described as a human shout or scream." She added that "the executioner was most upset and completely broke down. He came out shouting 'Oh Christ, Oh Christ'."[253]

---

[249]*Daily Express* 19th January 1923.

[250]*Sunday Observer* 18th March 1956.

[251]*Sunday Observer* 18th March 1956. See also PCOM 9/1983 XC2662 in which Mr Baxter is quoted from a House of Commons debate: "After her execution two of the warders who had taken part in that execution came to my office, and their faces were not human. I can assure you, Sir, they were like people of another world. Edith Thompson had disintegrated as a human creature on her way to the gallows, and yet somehow they had to get her there ... Those two warders who took part in that execution said to me, 'Use your influence; never again must a woman be hanged.'"

[252]For example, one of the prison warders, M.H. Young, was to deny in 1948 that he had made the said visit. However, he also pointed out that to have done so would make him "guilty of a Breach of the Secret Act" (PCOM 9/1983 XC2662 Letter from M.H. Young dated 15th April 1948 included in this file). See also Appendix II. Moreover Sir Beverley's statement would have carried substantial authority due to his status as a Conservative MP. At the time of the execution he had been the editor of the *Daily Express*. See also Appendix II.

[253]PCOM 9/1983 XC2662. Edith's executioner, John Ellis, later wrote: "She looked as if she were already dead ... I put the white cap on her head and face and slipped the noose over all. It was agonising just to see her being held up by the four men, her bound feet on the trap-doors. Her head had fallen forward on her chest, and she was completely oblivious to what was going on" (Ellis 1996:28) After a failed suicide attempt in 1924, Ellis, who resigned from his post as Britain's hangman 10 months after he had executed Edith Thompson, eventually committed suicide in 1932 by slashing his throat with a razor. Several commentators believed there was a connection between these events (Ellis 1996:235-8). Commenting on his father's suicide, Mr Ellis's son told *The Daily Express* : "Dad had not had a good night's sleep for many years. We all know what prevented him from sleeping. I do not think it was the memory of the 200 executions he had taken part in, but the recollection of the hanging of two women that drove him to suicide." (Quote included in PCOM 9/1983 XC2662). The two women were Emily Swann and Edith Thompson.

Freddy's oft repeated claim of Edith's innocence together with the horrific details of her execution ensured her case was never forgotten.[254] Instead opposition to her execution gathered momentum *after* the event, with one academic fighting to clear Edith's name as late as 1988.[255] While resistance to Edith Thompson's execution was and is to be commended it is nevertheless important to remember that only 19 years earlier Emily Swann had faced the gallows in almost identical circumstances. Edith's execution resulted, rightly, in protracted controversy lasting almost a century, which included major debates on the death penalty and several parliamentary discussions. Emily's execution warranted only ten lines in *The Times*.[256] This discrepancy is reminiscent of the cases of Ada Williams and Louise Masset discussed earlier. These women's executions took place within eight weeks of each other, but while there was no public outcry, protest or discussion in connection with Ada's death, the publicity surrounding Louise's execution was similar to that of Edith's, both in terms of the moralising surrounding these cases and in terms of the support the two women received.[257] The wide interest in the cases of Louise Masset and Edith Thompson is reflected in Home Office files which are nearly as big as the files of all the remaining 13 women put together. What separates Edith and Louise from Ada and Emily (as well as the remaining 11 women) is social class. This issue was explored in Chapter Four in relation to Louise and her role as governess. Twenty-two years later the issue of social class was still important although in Edith's case it was related to the 'newly sexually liberated' woman rather than to 'the governess'. Nonetheless both women represented 'unruly' and unregulated womanhood - possessing an illicit sexual identity - which, as discussed in Chapter Four, was taken far more seriously when affecting previously 'respectable' women. Thus, as had been the case with Louise, discourses surrounding Edith's transgressions overrode those of social class. While acknowledging the vast difference in the State's handling of Emily's case - an impoverished, unskilled, illiterate woman for whom no-one spoke, and the case of Edith - an articulate, educated, middle-class woman who could afford

---

[254] See Appendix II.

[255] See Dr Weis's letter to the then Home Secretary Douglas Hurd reproduced in Weis 1990:313-16.

[256] Between 12th December 1922 and 18th January 1923 extensive debates took place in *The Times*, both on the Thompson/Bywaters case and on the death penalty in general. The same newpaper spent five lines on reporting the Home Secretary's refusal to interfere in the death sentence of Emily Swann and John Gallagher (*The Times* 29th December 1903), and 10 lines on reporting their executions (*The Times* 30th December 1903). Their trial was not reported.

[257] For example in both Louise Masset's and Edith Thompson's case, solicitors not involved wrote to the Home Office defending the women, and in Louise's case, even offering to work on the case without payment. (HO 144/1540/A61535 communication from Mr Gurney-Winter 4th January 1900). Both women also were part of loving and supportive families who did their utmost to save them from the gallows.

a defence KC of national reputation, and who was part of a loving family who understood how to utilise the media to initiate support for her case, the outcome for the two women were nevertheless identical. In other words, while it is correct to identify a relationship between the lack of opposition to the executions of women such as Emily Swann, Louie Calvert, Margaret Allen and Styllou Christofi, and their powerlessness, it was nevertheless the case that women such as Edith Thompson and Louise Masset who had access to power via high status KCs, were still executed. This fact confirms the inadequacy of traditional, ungendered theoretical perspectives on punishment, for their executions can only be adequately explained by applying a gendered analysis to their cases. This case-study was introduced by a quotation stating that had Edith been working or upper-class there would have been a simpler solution to her problems, and if she had been male, the problem would not have existed at all. While this comment may be considered flippant by some, it is nevertheless the case, that it was the combination of Edith's (and Louise's) social class and *gender* which gave special significance to their conduct and behaviour. Ultimately their allegiance to the respectable classes could not save them, but was undermined by their sexual conduct. While their social class put more pressure on the state to legitimise their executions, it could not save them from the gallows. In short, the discourses surrounding their gender transgressions overrode the privileges associated with higher social classes, thus demonstrating that judicial misogyny is not confined to the impoverished and powerless, but transgresses class barriers to produce the same result - an executed woman's body.

Part II: The Female Poisoner Re-visited

The Case of Ethel Major

> The poison was responsible for her death just as her non-appearance in the witness box was responsible for her conviction. If she had hit her husband with a poker or pushed him into a river, Mrs Major would probably be alive today, but poison suggests something more than extreme provocation, self-defence or mental anguish.[258]

As each case-study is analysed it becomes increasingly apparent that the male fear of the 'woman poisoner' had some basis in fact, for statistically a third of all women executed during the 20th century had employed this method of

---

[258]Huggett, R. & Berry, P. (1956) *Daughters of Cain* George Allen & Unwin, London p.108.

murder.[259] Ethel Major was one of them. She was also - along with four of the five women discussed in this chapter - a battered woman.[260] As different aspects of her husband's cruelty emerged during her trial, the discourses of the 'woman poisoner' and 'woman as victim' were competing in the battle to define what type of woman Ethel was. Thus, as was to be the case with Dorothea Waddingham 16 months later, Ethel's case evoked considerable sympathy. Indeed, as I shall illustrate, an alternative truth about her was constantly on the verge of making itself visible during the trial. Ultimately, however, the period between 1920-1970 which includes the cases of three of the four battered women discussed in this chapter, lacked a strong feminist movement such as that emerging after 1970, which was responsible for organising protests and campaigns to ensure cases similar to Ethel Major's were understood within the general context of male violence against women.[261] However, in 1934, the year of Ethel's execution, the discourse of 'domestic' violence was yet to be opened and articulated, either in the law or in the wider culture.

Ethel's marriage to Arthur Major had been unhappy for several years and reached crisis point in 1934. Ethel described her domestic circumstances thus:

> Over a period of years I have had a very miserable existence with my husband who continually quarrelled with me and threatened to beat me. He was an [sic] habitual drinker and very quarrelsome when in drink. He led me a terrible life and I was terrified to death of him. Of late I was afraid to stay in the house with him as I thought he might kill me. He had threatened to do so several times when in drink. On many occasions my husband has struck me. For a fortnight before my husband died he became very much worse and drank much more heavily.[262]

During the three weeks prior to Arthur's death Ethel engaged in a number of actions originally initiated by her discovery of two letters in the bedroom addressed to Arthur. They were intimate in tone and contained hurtful comments about Ethel:

---

[259] If Amelia Sach is included, whom it will be recalled, was executed with Annie Walters who had administered chlorodyne to a baby that subsequently died from asphyxia, the number of poisoners rises to six out of a total of 15.

[260] Only one incidence of violence was recorded against Edith Thompson by her husband, and it is not known if this was an isolated incident. (See for example Weis 1990:55).

[261] Wilson, E. (1983) *What Is To Be Done About Violence Against Women?* Penguin, London p.88.

[262] ASSI 13/64 XC3601 CL Statement by Ethel Major 3rd July 1934. This file is available for inspection at the Public Record Office, Chancery Lane, London WC2A 1LR.

To my dearest sweetheart.
In answer to your dear letter received this morning, thank you dearest ... Baroness looks as if she could kill me today Wed. I am so afraid she should try to get Rita to go to her but I have told her, if Mrs Major ever gives her cake or sweets she is not to go, she is to come running home. She might think she could hurt me through my child if she did I would force my way in & shoot her on sight. I see her watching you in garden & also Auriel, but I dont care a fig for either of them. I shall be out as long as I think fit. I don't care what they say. They can pick at me if they like. Some day I shall be able to show them something & beg me for a [unreadable]. ... Well now I must close love. You will be fed up with me getting so ratty about things but I expect you get worked up some times. Well now sweetheart I will close with fondest love to you my precious one from your ever loving sweetheart. Rose.263

Ethel assumed 'Rose' was her neighbour and her first response was to tackle Rose's husband about the letters. He did not believe her but said "I am tired ... of you watching and prying about."264 She then presented them to her GP saying: "Now you can understand why I have been ill these last few years." Becoming increasingly agitated she added: "'A man like him is not fit to live' ... then words to this effect ... 'I will do him in.'" Dr Armour considered this "an idle threat, by a woman who was in rather a nervous state" adding that "if nothing had happened afterward I should never have thought it worthwhile to mention it."265 Dr Armour's medical opinion of Ethel was that she was unstable:

I should say the accused is of a very nervous disposition. She has always been excitable and I didn't take as much notice of that statement from her as I would from a more stable person.266

Second, Ethel showed the letters to John Holmes a Sanitary Inspector who repaired a broken window at her home. She complained about Arthur's drinking and about her neighbour Rose and "asked if she could be made tenant of the house in place of her husband. I said 'Not without her husband's consent.'"267 Ethel subsequently wrote to Mr Holmes, in Arthur's name:

I have decided to leave as it is unpleasant for my wife after seeing you. I thought it best giving in my notice today to you.268

263ASSI 13/64 XC3601 CL. Original letter, undated, marked EXHIBIT 5.
264ASSI 13/64 XC3601 CL. Testimony of Joseph Kettleborough p.50.
265ASSI 13/64 XC3601 CL. Testimony of Dr George Armour pp.27-32.
266ASSI 13/64 XC3601 CL. Testimony of Dr George Armour p.32.
267ASSI 13/64 XC3601 CL. Testimony of John Henry Holmes pp.55-6.
268ASSI 13/64 XC3601 CL. Original letter included in this file.

When Arthur was notified of the termination of his tenancy, he cancelled it. Ethel denied all knowledge of the letter.[269]

Third, Ethel visited her husband's employer asking how much Arthur had earned that week. She added:

> People in Kirkby tell me that Major is idle, you ought to be ashamed to employ such a man, you should dismiss him.[270]

Meanwhile, the Chief Constable received a letter, supposedly from two parish constables, but believed to have been written by Ethel, complaining that:

> Arthur Major is allways [sic] Drunk [sic] in charge and is not safe to be on the road Will you Please [sic] inform a dissmille [sic] at once for the safty [sic] of others Drink [sic] being consumed on the works at the Graull [sic] Pits ...[271]

Finally, Ethel instructed a solicitor to send a letter to Rose in Arthur's name, giving him the impression that she was acting on his behalf with his consent:

> I request you to stop hiding any more letters for me and I shall not write to you any more and I don't wish to speak to you or have any more trouble with you in the future. Final Notice. Arthur Major.[272]

When Arthur discovered this "he seemed to be in a very excited and troubled condition." Meanwhile Ethel returned to the solicitor to ask if Arthur was going to take out a summons against her and "appeared most anxious to have the matter stopped."[273]

During this period Ethel herself was the recipient of an anonymous letter:

> Your are slow now. Dont you know how your husband spends his weekends he has got a nice bit of fluff now. Besides he would be done any day at the shop if it was not for Mrs sticking up for him. You could get rid of him easy if you had him watched from one who

---

[269] ASSI 13/64 XC3601 CL. Testimony of John Chatterton, Clerk to Horncastle Justices p.54.

[270] ASSI 13/64 XC3601 CL. Testimony of Cyril Thornley, p.53.

[271] ASSI 13/64 XC3601 CL. Original letter included in this file undated, EXHIBIT 12. It was received on 15th May 1934.

[272] ASSI 13/64 XC3601 CL. Original letter included in this file - EXHIBIT 21.

[273] ASSI 13/64 XC3601 CL. Testimony of Walter Holmes pp.60; 61. Solicitor quoted in Huggett & Berry 1956:96.

knows about him and Mrs B. I hear he has now got a little Majar [sic] to look after.[274]

Yet another piece of correspondence was to figure in this case. It was an announcement by Arthur which he had paid to have published in the local newspaper:

I Arthur Major, of Kirkby-on-Bain, hereby give notice that I shall not be responsible to pay my wife's debts and she has no authority to make any statement or to give or sign any notice on my behalf.[275]

Arthur died the day before the announcement was due to be published, and Tom Brown, Ethel's father cancelled its publication.

Prior to Ethel's letter-writing campaign the Majors were well known to the local police. PC Mitchell testified that since 1931 "Mrs Major made complaints to me about her husband, quite a number of times. She complained that he was always drunk ... when she complained that she could not live with [him] ... any longer, owing to him drinking very heavily, I advised her to consult a solicitor."[276] PC Mitchell interviewed Ethel only five days prior to Arthur's death. She again complained about his drunkenness:

She said that she had been ill in bed about a fortnight previous and her husband had been in the habit of taking her a cup of tea upstairs in the mornings, but she did not drink it, as he had put something in it to get rid of her.[277]

When PC Mitchell called again on the day of Arthur's death, Ethel explained that he was ill: "He will not get better and drive the motor lorry again."[278]

There were no suspicious circumstances immediately after Arthur's death, since it was assumed he had suffered an epileptic fit. Thus, when PC Mitchell - accompanied by Inspector Dodson - called on Ethel two days later to view the body it was merely a routine visit. Ethel however, asked: "'I am not under suspicion am I? I haven't done anything wrong.' Inspector Dodson replied: 'Not that I know of.'"[279]

Ethel provided further evidence of a marital breakdown when she told police officers:

[274]ASSI 13/64 XC3601 CL. Original letter included in this file.
[275]ASSI 13/64 XC3601 CL. Copy of original note included in this file. See also testimonies by Ellen Liney and Thomas Taylor, pp.58-9.
[276]ASSI 13/64 XC3601 CL. Testimony of PC James Mitchell pp.61-2.
[277]ASSI 13/64 XC3601 CL. Testimony of PC James Mitchell p.62.
[278]ASSI 13/64 XC3601 CL. Testimony of PC James Mitchell p.63.
[279]ASSI 13/64 XC3601 CL. Testimonies of PC James Mitchell p.63 and Inspector Albert Dodson p.68.

About three weeks ago before he died my husband would not let me prepare or touch his food or do anything for him. He refused to let me buy anything for him and prepared all his food himself.[280]

This statement fitted neatly with Ethel's oft repeated contention, that it must have been the corned beef which only he ate, that had made him ill. She was to repeat this - even after a death certificate was issued which identified the cause of death as an epileptic fit.

A picture had therefore emerged of Ethel not only as deeply unhappy but also as jealous and vindictive. In other words, negative aspects of Ethel's behaviour were not regarded as a consequence of - but as the reason for - her abuse. Thus she was constructed both outside a general context of male violence against women, and also *against* Arthur in particular, who was not without credibility within the local community. The pillar of that community - Canon Blakiston - testified that Arthur "was a decent sort of fellow, and sober as far as I know. I never saw him otherwise."[281] Similarly Mrs Blakiston testified that Arthur had been a parochical councillor and "she had never seen him the worse for drink."[282] Together, Ethel's doctor and neighbours had thus constucted an image of a highly strung, neurotic woman who was equally to blame for marital disharmony. For example, one neighbour had seen her throw two bricks at Arthur during a fight.[283] Similarly, the various professionals - police officers, solicitors, sanitary officers - whose help Ethel tried to enlist in her endeavours to destroy Arthur's reputation - presumably with the aim of justifying his removal from the family home - soon considered her to be a tiresome and troublesome woman best avoided. Moreover, at least one person felt more than simple annoyance at Ethel's attention-seeking behaviour, for it was as a consequence of yet another piece of correspondence that the true cause of Arthur's death was discovered. An anonymous letter sent to the police alerted them to an incident in which Ethel had scraped "something off a plate, and this was eaten by a dog belonging to a neighbour. The following morning the dog died."[284] Following this letter, a post-mortem was carried out which revealed it had died of strychnine poisoning.

Relatives had gathered for Arthur's funeral in the Major household when police arrived and ordered proceedings to be stopped as a post-mortem was now required. At this point Ethel said to Arthur's brother: "It looks very black against me as if they are suspicioning me."[285] During the following weeks Ethel was interviewed on numerous occasions and made several statements, each time reiterating that Arthur had died as a result of eating corned beef. During an interview which took place six days prior to her arrest

---

[280]ASSI 13/64 XC3601 CL. Statement by Ethel Major.
[281]Quoted from transcript in *The Times* 31st October 1934.
[282]Huggett & Berry 1956:91.
[283]ASSI 13/64 XC3601 CL. Testimony of Joseph Kettleborough p.51.
[284]*The Times* 30th October 1934; 4th July 1934.
[285]ASSI 13/64 XC3601 CL. Testimony of Thomas Major p.39.

she stated: "[I] did not know that my husband died of strychnine poisoning."[286] This statement was to become one of three key pieces of evidence against her, for police officers claimed they had not revealed what type of poison had killed Arthur. During this interview she also became agitated when a CID officer suggested it was her and not Arthur who had sent their son Lawrence to buy corned beef at a local shop:

> She became very angry got up from her chair started waving her arms about and shouted "Everyone in this village is a liar, if any woman said I sent my son she is a liar."[287]

When Lawrence confirmed his mother had sent him, "accused ... hung her head and remained silent."[288]

The following day the same officer visited the home of her father, but found only Ethel present. The officer was about to leave when unprompted she said: "If my husband has had poison, it's Mrs Kettleborough who has done it, I leave the latch of my door up when I go out, and she could get in the back way."[289]

Five days later and six weeks after the cancellation of Arthur's funeral, Ethel was charged with his murder. She responded:

> I didn't do it, I am as innocent as the days are long, if I have given my husband poison, its [sic] Mrs Kettleborough a [sic] someone who came into my house, when we were out and put it there [pointing to the ladder]. It's wicked for people to accuse me. I loved my husband, I am his lawful wedded wife.[290]

Yet only six days earlier during the interview discussed above, she had said:

> He was a detestable man, and I feel very much better in health since he has gone ... I could not sleep with him as he smelt so strongly I could not stand it. I thought by the smell of him he had a venereal disease ... I thought my husband had communicated something to me ...[291]

The discourses which dominated Ethel's trial were thus mobilised weeks before her arrest: on the one hand she was an unsophisticated and

---

[286]ASSI 13/64 XC3601 CL. Statement by Ethel Major 3rd July 1934.

[287]ASSI 13/64 XC3601 CL. Testimony of Chief Inspector Hugh Young p.73.

[288]ASSI 13/64 XC3601 CL. Testimony of Chief Inspector Hugh Young pp.73-4.

[289]ASSI 13/64 XC3601 CL. Testimony of Chief Inspector Hugh Young p.74.

[290]ASSI 13/64 XC3601 CL. Testimony of Chief Inspector Hugh Young, quoting comments by Ethel Major p.75. CI Young's testimony was corroborated by Detective Inspector James Salisbury who was also present at the various interviews (p.76).

[291]ASSI 13/64 XC3601 CL. Statement by Ethel Major 3rd July 1934.

pathetic figure - deeply unhappy, neurotic and lonely - and thus deserving pity. On the other hand, she was a highly suspicious figure - a scheming, jealous and vengeful woman who was almost certainly guilty of poisoning her husband. Thus, rather than being a foregone conclusion, her fate appeared to be in the balance, when the trial opened.

The Trial of Ethel Major

While Ethel had entered a plea of not guilty and denied any involvement in her husband's murder, her KC nevertheless presented her defence on the assumption that if she *had* committed murder, there was plenty of justification. Thus as witnesses gradually revealed the depths of Ethel's suffering at Arthur's hands, it became increasingly clear, that while she may be guilty of murder, that action had been taken within the context of a series of mitigating circumstances. For example, 15-year-old Lawrence confirmed the truth of many of Ethel's allegations:

> They quarrelled when my father got drunk, which was practically every night. My father threatened to hit my mother several times ... My mother and I went to sleep at my Grandfathers nearly ever since we went to the Council House [two years] ... Sometimes we slept in the shed at the back ... My father prepared his own food for about ... three weeks before he died. He used to live chiefly on corned beef. He had tea to drink. He made it himself ... my mother fed herself and me, my father fed himself. Our food was on a different shelf and at the other end of the pantry from my father's food ... The quarrels were worse in the last three weeks before my father was taken ill ... When we went round to Grandfathers to sleep we slept in our clothes and I had Grandfather's top coat for covering and my mother had a top coat of her own ... My father was a heavy drinker and when he was drunk he was quarrelsome, they were one-sided quarrels. The drinking had been going on a long while but got worse the last month before he died. The drink was having effect on my father, he was not the man he had been.[292]

When Mr Justice Charles interrupted to ask: "Why did you not stay with your father [at night]?" Lawrence replied: "If we had been at home father would have turned us out." Lawrence agreed when defending KC asked him:

> Should I be right in saying that your mother all your life has been very kind to you, and your father very wicked?[293]

---

[292] ASSI 13/64 XC3601 CL. Testimony of Lawrence Oswald Major pp.1-8.
[293] Quoted from trial in *Manchester Guardian* 30th October 1934.

Ethel's father confirmed Arthur "often threatened his wife"; moreover, her mother had died while the couple lived with her parents, and while she was lying dead in the house, Arthur came in "very drunk" and made a most "painful scene."[294]

Solicitor's clerk Walter Holmes also testified he had heard Arthur "make very violent threats against ... Ethel ... and gathered that their home life was unhappy."[295] Finally, her daughter, Auriel Brown, testified that Ethel had good reason to be jealous for she (Auriel) had seen Arthur and Rose "making eyes at each other. Mrs Kettleborough was always outside the house when Major came home. She put herself in his way."[296]

Yet, although Ethel's KC Lord Birkett was able to destroy one of the three major pieces of evidence against her, by proving her solicitor had discussed with her the fact that strychnine poisoning was the cause of Arthur's death, thus making her comment about this poison to police officers irrelevant, other evidence against her was compelling. I have already noted a dog had died of strychnine poisoning after being fed by Ethel. However, the most important evidence against her was a key found in her home during a search on the day of her arrest. This key had belonged to her father, who assumed it was lost. It fitted a box which contained strychnine, occasionally used by him while carrying out his duties as a game-keeper.

Apart from this circumstantial evidence, several aspects of Ethel's behaviour suggested she was a deceitful liar and a calculated poisoner who had carried out a premeditated killing. First, despite Arthur's severe illness, she failed to seek medical assistance, and it was her father who eventually ensured a doctor was called. Second, when this doctor asked if Arthur had had fits before, she lied and said "Yes, at intervals for a year or two."[297] She did not then suggest that corned beef had poisoned him.

Third, her attempt to discredit Arthur by suggesting that *he* was trying to poison her as discussed above, was disproved by her own statement that she did not sleep at home. Moreover, the idea of Arthur bringing Ethel morning cups of tea seemed highly implausible in view of the hostilities between the couple which Ethel herself had described. Every other aspect of her testimony was designed to portray Arthur as a selfish and inconsiderate husband whose violence terrorised his family. Similarly, her attempt to blame Rose Kettleborough for Arthur's death only served to further discredit her own character.

Fourth, as soon as Arthur had died, Ethel asked Lawrence to burn the paper on which the corned beef had stood on the pantry shelf. Lastly, she asked Lawrence to go the office of the *Horncastle News* to cancel Arthur's

---

[294]Quoted from trial in *The Times* 31st October 1934.

[295]Quoted from trial in *Daily Express* 1st November 1934.

[296]Quoted from trial in *The Times* 31st October 1934.

[297]ASSI 13/64 XC3601 CL. Testimony of Dr Frederick Hugh Smith. For example Lawrence Major testified that "I had never seen my father in a fit." (p.6).

notice regarding his refusal to support her financially "because mother said it wouldn't be any use having it in the paper when my father was dead."[298]

These aspects of Ethel's behaviour ensured the murder could not be construed as a hysterical act carried out by a highly strung woman consumed by jealousy. Instead many aspects of her conduct appeared to be calculated acts designed to hide her guilt and hence stood in sharp contrast to her attempts to present herself as a hapless and helpless victim. Moreover, the timing of the murder - one day before Arthur was due to publicly disclaim his financial responsibility for Ethel - suggested not only that she was guilty but also that she had a strong motive. In the opinion of the trial judge, this discrepancy between Ethel's attempt to present herself as a long-suffering victim of male violence, whilst simultaneously plotting and calculating Arthur's murder, was never satisfactorily resolved because of her failure to give evidence:

> It is clear that they not only quarrelled with one another, but were capable of violence towards one another. In the statements of Mrs Major there are inconsistencies some of which you may think would have been more satisfactorily explained or elucidated by the evidence of the prisoner herself.[299]

I have already discussed the undesirable side-effects of the 1898 Criminal Evidence Act in previous case-studies, and the case of Ethel Major demonstrates how the prisoner's right to remain silent could be interpreted as evidence of guilt. Thus the judge referred to Ethel's non-appearance in the witness box no less than six times in his summing up. While Mr Justice Charles acknowledged Ethel's unhappy existence, and accepted that "one of the most potent causes of an attack by a woman on a man ... is jealousy", he nonetheless required her to explain herself:

> There is very little doubt that Mrs Major lived in a state of bitter unhappiness with her husband. The jury might think it was a misfortune that they had not had the evidence she might have given upon her oath before them.[300]

In an era which lacked discourses through which the 'battered woman' could speak, the judge made the uncritical and simplistic assumption that a failure to appear in the witness box was an indication of guilt or 'having something to hide.' However, as I noted in the case-study of Emily Swann, following nearly three decades of feminist campaigning in relation to male violence against women, evidence accepted uncritically in earlier decades can now be reinterpreted to "tell a different story about the same events."[301]

---

[298]ASSI 13/64 XC3601 CL. Testimony of Lawrence Major p.7.
[299]Summing up by Mr Justice Charles quoted in *The Times* 2nd November 1934.
[300]Summing up quoted in *The Daily Express* 2nd November 1934.
[301]Stanko & Scully 1996:58.

Thus, when battered women choose not to give evidence today, it is not necessarily interpreted as evidence of guilt but may instead suggest they are "too traumatized to give evidence" about the brutality they have suffered.[302] That this alternative interpretation now exists is an example of the feminist success in "the politics of naming" - a vital first step towards the creation of new discourses through which women's experiences can be understood.[303] In 1934 however, the feelings and experiences of battered women had no name, and therefore could not be put forward as part of a defence in a court of law.

As was to be the case with Dorothea Waddingham 16 months later, both judge and jury had a measure of sympathy for Ethel. At the same time they were also caught up in the discourses surrounding the duplicitous and 'lethal' woman poisoner. The jury which included three women, took just over one hour to reach a guilty verdict, but with the foreman stating: "I want to express the view of the jury that a strong recommendation to mercy should be given."[304] In the following section I analyse why the discourses of the ultra-feminine characteristics of being highly strung, hysterical and consumed with jealousy were undermined by the discourses surrounding the female poisoner and the disloyal wife.

An Alternative Truth

I have already noted that the period between 1920-1970 lacked an active, campaigning feminist movement. I have also discussed how the supposed gains for women's liberation during the 1920s, could equally be mobilised to operate against that liberation as in the case of Edith Thompson. The precariousness of feminism during these decades was intensified by a shift in gender ideology during the 1930s, a decade in which women were increasingly blamed for 'family problems', culminating in the belief that they 'provoked' abusive men.[305] In the words of Linda Gordon, "marital violence became a sign of wifely dysfunction."[306] Her arguments are supported by White who notes that summonses for domestic assault declined during the 1920s and 1930s, and by Wilson who writes that by 1935 the problem had all but 'disappeared' and when it re-emerged following the Second World War, "wife-beating became just part of a general picture of slovenly behaviour, associated with drunkenness, and squalor *of the wife's own making.*" This victim-blaming extended to regarding abused wives as "bad mothers",

---

[302]Lees 1997:151.
[303]Spender, D. (1980) *Man Made Language* Routledge & Kegan Paul, London Chapter Six.
[304]Quoted in *Manchester Guardian* 2nd November 1934.
[305]Gordon, L. (1989) *Heroes of Their Own Lives* Virago, London pp.282-3. See also Maguire's discussion of the common-sensical notion that women 'ask for it' in Maguire, S. (1988) '"Sorry love" - violence against women in the home and the state response' in *CSP* Issue 23, Autumn 1988, p.35.
[306]Gordon 1989:282.

"slatternly" and "nagging and vituperative wives."[307] Wife-beating became couched in gender-neutral terms such as 'marital' violence, a point which is illustrated by the judge's summing up above, when he stated that the couple "were capable of violence towards *one another*." This description presents a false sense of equality between the couple and ignores Ethel's economic dependence on Arthur as well as the fact that physically she was of small stature, making it unlikely that a fight between the couple was a fight between equals.[308]

The ambivalent attitude towards wife-beating during the 1930s was reinforced in Ethel's case by the fact that according to dominant gender ideologies of that decade, she had exposed her husband to an extreme form of provocation. Approximately two years prior to marrying Arthur, she had borne an illegitimate child, Auriel. Auriel was brought up as Ethel's sister, hence had always lived with her grandparents.[309] Ethel kept her true relationship to Auriel secret from Arthur, but he eventually discovered the deception which was subsequently held responsible for the couple's unhappiness:

> It was undoubtedly her decision not to tell her husband of her pre-marital lapse which was responsible for all their troubles.[310]

In the courtroom Arthur's violence was thus placed within the context of his disillusionment and resentment towards Ethel as a result of her failure to guard her reputation and maintain her respectability. In other words, it was Ethel - not Arthur - who was held responsible for his violence, for it was her behaviour that had driven him to drink and other women.[311] The case of Ethel Major can thus be seen to demonstrate the contention by Dobash and Dobash that "the primary roots of victimization [are identified] in the background of the victim and not the offender."[312]

Thus, while defence counsel argued the violence Ethel had experienced at the hands of Arthur constituted mitigating circumstances, the

---

[307]White, J. (1986) *The Worst Street in North London,* RKP, London p.141; Wilson 1983:87. My emphasis.

[308]See for example *Daily Mirror* 2nd November 1934. See also photo of Ethel Major in *Daily Express* 19th December 1934. Ethel was described by Huggett & Berry as "a small, long-nosed, tight-lipped little woman of 45, whose eyes peered short-sightedly from behind large, horn-rimmed spectacles" (1956:72). It is difficult to imagine that a woman who was both small and short-sighted posed an equal threat to that of a man. See also Maguire's discussion on how some explanations of wife-battering "neutralises the power dynamics within any family and addresses all parties as equal" (Maguire 1988:37). My emphasis.

[309]ASSI 13/64 XC3601 CL. Testimony of Auriel Brown.

[310]Huggett & Berry 1956:83.

[311]Huggett & Berry 1956:83.

[312]Dobash, R.E. & Dobash, R.P. (1992) *Women, Violence & Social Change* Routledge, London p.225.

enduring belief that women themselves are responsible for the violence committed against them, meant the prosecutor was equally able to argue there were mitigating circumstances attached to Arthur's violence.[313] Not only had Ethel deceived him, and hence secured a husband under false pretences, but it was also "the general impression that Mrs Major was a bad-tempered woman."[314] In Chapter Two I discussed men's right - throughout history - to discipline a 'nagging' wife, and as late as 1915, "a London judge reiterated that 'the husband of a nagging wife ... could beat her at home provided the stick he used was no thicker than a man's thumb'."[315] This ruling demonstrates with exceptional clarity the double standards confronting violent women, for although the question 'Why don't battered women just leave?' has been asked repeatedly over the last two decades, no-one has asked: "If he can't take her nagging any more why doesn't *he* just leave?"[316] While women's passivity within a violent relationship is not only expected but taken for granted, the above ruling provides a clear example of Lees' contention that "the law provides a legitimation for men to behave violently in the face of insubordination or marriage breakdown."[317]

Ethel's deceit with regard to her pre-marital sexual transgression ensured it was *her* reputation which came under scrutiny during the trial. Thus, even though she had been similarly provoked in terms of the letter indicating Arthur now also had an illegitimate child, the attempt by the defence to damage *his* reputation by pointing to his philandering was doomed to failure - not only because of the double standards attached to female sexual conduct - but also because "it is posited in law that, under provocation, it is *reasonable* for men to behave in a violent or irrational way."[318] Ethel, on the other hand, had defied "the ideological vision of female passivity" by actively defending herself against Arthur's violence, not only by murdering him, but also through the brick-throwing incident described above, and through her letter-writing campaign which she hoped would lead to his arrest. Because this active stance stood in sharp contrast to expectations of female passivity it was regarded negatively - as "evil and vengeful."[319] The case of Ethel Major thus provides another example of the argument outlined in Chapter Three, that women defendants who defy gender role expectations can expect harsh punishment, for they have broken not only the formal criminal law but also the informal 'gender law' governing female behaviour.

---

[313]See Edwards, S. (1989) *Policing 'Domestic' Violence* Sage, London, pp.165-8 for a discussion of this type of victim-blaming.

[314]Huggett & Berry 1956:90.

[315]Quoted in Wilson 1983:84.

[316]Lees 1997:142. My emphasis.

[317]Lees 1997:142.

[318]Lees, S. (1997) *Ruling Passions* Open University Press, Buckingham p.147. My emphasis.

[319]Lees does not discuss the case of Ethel Major but argues that this is applicable to women generally, and that women are still regarded thus today (Lees 1997:134).

While Ethel's behaviour was regarded as "spiteful" and "vengeful" in 1934, discourses are available in the 1990s through which an alternative truth may be told. When Ethel's story is 'heard' through the discourses of the battered woman, her behaviour is recognisable as typical of women who have experienced cumulative abuse and provocation. For example, Sara Thornton who stabbed her abusive husband in 1989 had sought help from "numerous agencies" including her "church, her GP, Alcoholics Anonymous, social services and the police."[320] Similarly, Gordon argues that "few battered women ... [keep] their problems to themselves." She further argues that historically, it was common for women to resist male violence by "fighting back, running away, attempting to embarrass the men before others, calling the police."[321] White agrees that women's resistance to male violence, for example by bringing it to the attention of neighbours, was designed to "shame" the man.[322] As I have illustrated, this was exactly how Ethel reacted to Arthur's violence, but in an era where marriage was considered both "a psychological as well as a social necessity for women"[323], discourses of the 'battered wife' did not exist, and her behaviour could therefore not be described in positive terms as acts of resistance. Instead it was perceived solely in negative terms:

> She embarked on a wild round of revenge and malice that included half the population of the village ... Mrs Major had by now almost exhausted her activities. She had brought into her life police, solicitors, doctors, employers ... The impression left on the jury was that Ethel Major had certainly done her best in those last three weeks to ruin her husband. They could not ignore the fact that there was a great deal that was unpleasant about her.[324]

Apart from being considered hysterical, highly strung, vengeful and malicious, Ethel was also considered to be 'stupid' as a result of her badly planned crime and easily detectable plot. Her KC maintained that what observers interpreted as signs of stupidity, were in fact evidence of her innocence. Thus, with reference to the box containing strychnine, he argued she would "have thrown the key away" rather than allowing police to find it. The judge disagreed and - referring to the poisoned dog - told the jury:

---

[320]Lees 1997:151.

[321]Gordon 1989:276; 256.

[322]White 1989:140.

[323]Oram, A. (1989) "'Embittered, sexless or homosexual': attacks on spinster teachers 1918-39" in Angerman, A. et al (eds) (1989) *Current Issues in Women's History* Routledge, London p.187.

[324]Huggett & Berry 1956:93; 97. The availability of the 'battered wife' discourse has not ensured that such women avoid hostility from the court, the public and the media, as can be seen from the case of Sara Thornton who, despite having stood trial 56 years after Ethel Major was greeted with similar hostility. Her case will be discussed further in the final chapter.

Criminals do amazingly stupid things but you may think that this was transcendental stupidity to go out into a place where every one can see you, where a neighbour is looking at you and scrape the meat off the plate and give it to this dog.[325]

Like the majority of women discussed in these case-studies Ethel was nearly destitute and had received only the most rudimentary education. We have already seen that she told easily detectable lies, and some evidence suggested she had only limited comprehension of her circumstances. For example, after being told her appeal had been dismissed, she commented: "I don't mind a few years in prison."[326] Whether Ethel suffered from mental illness or a mental disability will always remain within the realms of speculation for the medical officer who examined her could spare her only 16 words:

Since reception this woman has been under observation. I consider her sane and fit to plead.[327]

Alternatively, Ethel's daily struggle to survive financially,[328] combined with the stress of living within a long-term violent relationship, may have impaired her judgement.[329] Thus, rather than indicating revenge and malice, the timing of Arthur's murder suggests a last desperate attempt to keep her home together. She had attempted to take over the tenancy of her council house, but was told she needed her husband's consent; she had attempted to have Arthur arrested, in order to free herself from him; she had sought legal and medical advice concerning her marriage - all to no avail. Now Arthur was about to disown her financially and publicly. How was she to survive? In 1934 "women's financial dependence on their husbands" was taken for granted.[330] There were no advice centres for battered women, no refuges, the welfare state had not yet been born and the Poor Law was still in effect.[331] Her son and herself were already reduced to sleeping in an

---

[325] Judge Charles' summing up quoted in *Daily Express* 2nd November 1934.

[326] Quoted in Huggett & Berry 1956:107.

[327] ASSI 13/64 XC3601 CL. Medical report (in its *entirety*) by Prison Medical Officer R.J. Barlee, 8th October 1934.

[328] For example, Ethel stated that Mrs Spiking who ran the local dairy gave her a pint of milk "as I could not afford to buy it" (ASSI 13/64 XC3601 CL Statement by Ethel Major 3rd July 1934).

[329] This is not to suggest Ethel suffered from the controversial 'battered wife syndrome' which supposedly includes 'learned helplessness' (see Dobash & Dobash 1992:223-230). Yet few would argue that a person remains unaffected by living in a constantly threatening situation for several years.

[330] Oram 1989:185.

[331] The Poor Law was abolished in 1948 when it was replaced by the National Assistance Act (Bedarida, F. (1994) *A Social History of England 1851-1990* Routledge, London p.195).

outhouse, with Lawrence sleeping "on a rug on the floor" which Ethel "felt very upset about ... and thought it terrible for my young boy."[332] Ethel's daughter Auriel was only 19, but already the mother of an illegitimate child herself; both lived with Ethel's 75-year-old father in a tiny cottage without electricity.[333] These factors also provided the context for the murder, but while there was some acknowledgement of Ethel's suffering and desperate circumstances, her status as a victim was ultimately undermined by the murder method she had employed, which mobilised the powerful discourses of the woman poisoner described previously. In short, Ethel's murder method did not match her claim to victimhood.

The Appeal of Ethel Major

Unlike some women discussed in this book, Ethel was very ably defended, even though she could not afford to pay for her defence,[334] and the hopelessness of her case is demonstrated by the fact it was the first Norman Birkett had ever lost.[335] Consequently, her appeal was considered to be a "fruitless" exercise from the onset.[336] Nevertheless, Birkett "spoke brilliantly" in the Appeal Court, agreeing the summing up had been fair, except that the judge had failed to suggest the case may have been one of suicide rather than murder.[337] The three judges "got together and whispered" before Lord Hewart, the Lord Chief Justice who had dismissed Edith Thompson's appeal 11 years previously, replied:

> The summing up was perfectly fair and sufficient. There are passages in it which perhaps may be said to be almost unduly favourable to Mrs Major. The jury found Mrs Major guilty but for some reason which is not stated in words, they coupled their verdict with a recommendation to mercy. That is a matter with which this Court cannot deal.[338]

---

[332] ASSI 13/64 XC3601 CL. Statement by Ethel Major 3rd July 1934.

[333] *Daily Express* 18th December 1934, interview with Ethel's father, Tom Brown.

[334] ASSI 13/64 3601 CL. Letter from Justices of Peace, requesting that defence counsel be granted a certificate as "her means are insufficient to enable her to obtain legal aid in the preparation and conduct of her defence at the trial" 2nd August 1934.

[335] *Daily Mirror* 2nd November 1934. Norman Birkett became Liberal MP for East Nottingham in 1923, was knighted in 1941 and became Lord Birkett in 1957. Prior to defending Ethel Major he had turned down the opportunity to become a High Court Judge. His biographer wrote of Birkett's involvement in the Major case: "His task was hopeless from the beginning" (Hyde, M.H. (1964) *Norman Birkett* The Reprint Society, London p.382).

[336] Hyde 1964:383.

[337] *Daily Express* 4th December 1934.

[338] Lord Chief Justice Hewart quoted in *Daily Mirror* 4th December 1934; *Daily Express* 4th December 1934. See also *The Times* 4th December 1934.

There remained only one hope for Ethel - that the Home Secretary would respect the wishes of the jury and grant a reprieve.[339]

Ethel Major: Restoration of the Victim Status

Ethel had already had the 'truth' about her altered once, from the victim to the perpetrator of violence. During her final days that truth was altered again to one where she was perceived as a pathetic creature who deserved pity despite her transgressions. Thus, while "it had hitherto been understood that the general opinion was against a reprieve", strenuous efforts to save her life were made during the last few days prior to the execution.[340] For example, the mayor of Hull, Alderman Stark, wrote to the Home Secretary:

> For the sake of humanity I ... implore you to reconsider your decision, especially having regard to the nearness of Christmas and the message of good will that this season teaches us. The heartfelt pleas contained in this telegram are those of 300,000 inhabitants and particularly those of the women of this great city.[341]

When this plea failed, "messages arrived ... from all over the country begging the Lord Mayor to carry on with his pleading and wishing him success."[342] With only one night left before the execution Alderman Stark wrote to the King and Queen:

> The impending execution is causing grave distress to the women in Hull, and it is respectfully pleaded that Her Majesty will use her endeavours for mercy even at this eleventh hour for a woman and a mother.[343]

Mr Stark regretted not having started his efforts earlier, but explained this was due to the widespread belief that the sentence would not be carried out. There was some justification for this belief for only weeks before *The Daily Express* had asked: "What is the point in sentencing Mrs Major to death. For nobody believes that she will be hanged."[344] However, now that the execution was imminent, the reality of it could not be avoided and Stark claimed:

---

[339]Statistics indicate that jury recommendations for mercy did not go unheeded. "Of the 108 women sentenced to death and recommended to mercy between 1900-49, only four were executed, whilst nine of the 22 not recommended to mercy were executed." See Table I in *Royal Commission on Capital Punishment 1949-1953 Report* (1953) Her Majesty's Stationery Office, London p.9.

[340]*Daily Mirror* 18th December 1934.

[341]Quoted in *Daily Express* 19th December 1934.

[342]*Hull Daily Mail* 19th December 1934.

[343]Quoted in *Hull Daily Mail* 19th December 1934.

[344]*Daily Express* leading article discussing a previous article, 19th December 1934.

Women in the city have come to me and said their sleep has been disturbed by thoughts of the poor woman who seems to have been left without anybody to care about her.[345]

Other more prominent people did not appear to lose sleep over Ethel Major. For example, Mr Stark reported that "the Prime Minister ha[d] not had the courage to reply" to his letter pleading for mercy.[346] Local people however, were more sympathetic and organised a petition in Ethel's village for which signatures were reported to have been "given willingly" with "only four or five people" refusing to sign.[347] Among the petitioners was Rose Kettleborough who - during the trial - had been accused of having an affair with Arthur. She claimed she bore "Mrs Major no malice", and "would be one of the first to sign a petition for reprieve."[348]

Even the Home Secretary was reported to have "explored every avenue to discover adequate reasons for giving effect to the jury's recommendation to mercy" by organising a visit by two medical experts who "spent several hours with Mrs Major in an endeavour to find grounds on which they could certify her mental condition as being responsible for her actions."[349] It was to no avail, and Ethel was executed shortly before Christmas on 19th December. Like Edith Thompson before her, Ethel was reported to have been in a total state of collapse with two wardresses at her bedside and a doctor in constant attendance.[350] Only 200 people waited outside Hull prison at the time of the execution. "They were Hull's poorest - nearly all the men were out-of-work labourers, the women poorly clad, many of them wearing shawls."[351]

In executing Ethel Major the state continued its long tradition of denying clemency to those who had been found guilty of committing what was considered "the most subtle, the most secret and the most pitiless" form of murder.[352] The dominant discourses around female poisoners described here and in the previous chapter, thus suggested that such women were coolly

---

[345] Quoted in *Manchester Guardian* 19th December 1934.

[346] Alderman A. Stark quoted in *Daily Mirror* 20th December 1934.

[347] *Daily Mirror* 18th December 1934.

[348] *Daily Express* 3rd November 1934.

[349] *Manchester Guardian* 20th December 1934. This visit may have indicated that the Home Secretary found the 16-word medical report discussed earlier, a little too concise. At the same time it must be remembered that Ethel stood trial 23 years prior to the introduction of the defence of diminished responsibility. Moreover, 15 years *after* Ethel's trial, Lord Chief Justice Goddard maintained that it was "perfectly proper" to execute prisoners who had been certified insane (Koestler, A. (1956) *Reflections on Hanging* Victor Gollancz, London p.11).

[350] *Hull Daily Mail* 19th December 1934. This doctor was Dr Barlee, the same doctor who had written the 16-word medical report concerning Ethel Major's physical and mental health.

[351] *Daily Express* 20th December 1934.

[352] *Daily Express* 19th December 1934.

and rationally plotting their deeds in an emotionally detached - even sophisticated - manner. The female poisoners were the ultimate dangerous women - so dangerous that they must be put to death regardless of the circumstances of their deed. Yet these same women were also described as:

> Ordinary women, rarely beautiful. Square-faced, thin-mouthed, eyes blinking behind National Health spectacles which I have to take off at the last moment, hair scraped thin by curlers, lumpy ankles above homely shoes, in which they have to slop to the gallows because prison regulations demand that there are no shoelaces.[353]

Pierrepoint, Britain's last executioner, had identified a major contradiction running through the discourses surrounding the female poisoner: on the one hand she was imagined to be an extremely threatening figure - duplicitous, devious and subtle in her conduct. On the other hand - as we have seen from this and previous case-studies - the reality was usually very different, with the women conceiving their crimes in a most rudimentary and simplistic manner, operating from ill-conceived plans which ultimately led to their downfall. Their conduct could hardly be described as either discreet or subtle, as the discovery of their crime indicates. Therefore, rather than considering female poisoners to be the most dangerous women in the country it would arguably be more accurate to describe them as the most desperate.

I introduced this case-study with the quote "poison was responsible for her death". While the female poisoner was considered extremely dangerous, and could not by definition have acted 'in a fit of hysteria' or 'on the spur of the moment', poisoning also implied a desire to 'get away' with the crime. Ethel had not confessed to her crime, yet her entire defence was constructed as if she had, by focusing on the mitigating circumstances involved, and especially on her provocation. Had Ethel stabbed Arthur during a fight, and had she subsequently confessed and shown remorse, her status as a victim would have been more credible. Instead that status was subsumed under her status as a woman poisoner, resulting in her various acts prior to the murder being interpreted through the discourses of the woman poisoner. That is to say, her acts of desperation were understood as a naive and ill-conceived murder plan. The unsuccessful nature of this 'planning' was taken to be evidence of her 'stupidity' rather than the uncoordinated and desperate gestures by a traumatised, victimised and powerless individual fighting for survival. Within a patriarchal legal system Ethel's chosen method of murder suggested a high level of rationality which ensured discourses around the victimised woman were quickly subsumed under those of the 'bad' woman. Her case thus provides a chilling example of the consequences for women of a masculinist definition of the law as discussed by MacKinnon who has examined the way in which the male standpoint is represented as

---

[353] Albert Pierrepoint quoted in *Murder Casebook* Vol 7 Part 5 (1991) Marshall Cavendish Ltd, London p.3761.

universal.354 This is particularly poignant in relation to the defence of provocation which until recently has been wholly defined by how the "reasonable man" would act in a given situation. In particular, "the acceptance of 'heat of the moment' retaliation is based on the perceived credibility of the impulsive side of men, who, presented with certain stimuli, can do no other but act."355 Consequently, 'heat of the moment' violence is usually regarded as justifiable while "planned killing, even after cumulative provocation, is seen as heinous and unjustified and the actor as scheming, cunning and wicked."356 But the fact female murderers mainly fall within the latter category does not indicate "they are any less provoked, or less eager to retaliate immediately," but is a reflection of the fact "that it is the only time when self-defensive action is likely to succeed."357 That this is beginning to be recognised within British courts as I discuss in the final chapter, demonstrates the measure of success that feminist theorists and activists have already achieved in creating new knowledge and a new language through which female violence can be understood.

The case of Ethel Major demonstrates not only misconceptions surrounding the female poisoner, but also misconceptions surrounding the battered wife. Her behaviour exemplifies the length that even those women with extremely limited resources and options available will go to in order to escape a violent spouse. After engaging herself in a protracted struggle for survival, Ethel finally found herself trapped in a desperate situation where access to her already meagre financial resources were about to be cut off completely. Ethel was neither subtle nor sophisticated, she could not even tell a plausible lie; rather she responded to a desperate situation by engaging in desperate behaviour in a futile attempt to stem the dam of disaster confronting her. When she eventually paid the price for her desperate act, the economic reality which had led to her execution, and from which she was finally released, still had to be faced by her surviving family. Thus, while Ethel's last letter to her children contained a plea to her daughter: "Make a home for Laurie"358, the means necessary to carry out her mother's last wishes were not available and the financial prospects of the family remained grim, as can be seen from comments by Ethel's father:

> God only knows how I feel tonight ... Now I must act as father to three children - Iris [Auriel] ... her child and Oswald [Lawrence]. I

354MacKinnon, C.A. (1989) *Towards a Feminist Theory of the State* Harvard University Press, Cambridge, Massachusetts p.221.

355Edwards 1989:183. Edwards argues that the acceptance of the 'heat of the moment' retaliation "is rather like the model of uncontrollable male sexual urges, by which men, once aroused by a female, have no choice but to indulge in immediate phallic sex." .

356Edwards 1989:183.

357Edwards 1989:184.

358Quoted in *The Daily Mirror* 20th December 1934.

do not know which way to turn. I am old, poor, and can only manage to keep myself, but the responsibility is mine.[359]

Quite apart from the financial responsibility falling on the 75-year-old man's shoulders, he also had to deal with the emotional stresses faced by those who lose a much loved family member. Not only did he have to come to terms with losing his only daughter, he also had to console his grandchildren. While Auriel had collapsed upon hearing that her mother's execution would go ahead, Lawrence remained unaware of his mother's fate until the last minute:

> What a Christmas for the boy. He loves his mother dearly [and] ... has talked about what he is going to do - how he means to get a job and then make it his life's work to be ready to meet his mother with a home and comfort if ever she came from prison. He is a good lad. Now what has he to hope for? Nothing.[360]

Tom Brown's comments provide a brief glimpse of how family members, who are innocent bystanders in cases such as Ethel Major's, nonetheless also suffer and are punished by the effects of capital punishment, a subject which I shall explore further in later case-studies. Meanwhile, the case of Ethel Major, which is unlikely ever to receive the exposure, fame or notoriety of cases like Sara Thornton's, nevertheless stands as a sharp reminder to those who attempt to employ a strategy of victim-blaming in cases of battered wives, that such women neither 'ask for it', nor 'deserve' to be beaten. Instead, even the most powerless and dispossessed women have a long tradition of resisting male violence by whatever means available in their specific circumstances.

The Case of Charlotte Bryant

> Charlotte Bryant was an illiterate, slatternly Irishwoman of thirty-three, with black hair and dark eyes ... the cottage was filthy and the children neglected ... her hair was lousy and she had only one tooth left.[361]

> It is open to extreme doubt whether a woman who has had no education at all, and who must live with a large family on thirty-eight-and-sixpence a week, can be expected to have any ideas about how to improve the conditions of her life. Even the most intelligent

---

[359]Tom Brown quoted from an interview with *The Daily Express* 18th December 1934. He referred to his grandchildren by their middle names.

[360]Tom Brown quoted in *The Daily Express* 18th December 1934.

[361]Wilson, P. (1971) *Murderess* Michael Joseph, London, p.289.

of us experience difficulties, and she seems to have had no natural intelligence to guide her.[362]

While Ethel Major had been regarded as a vengeful and malicious poisoner Charlotte Bryant was held in even lower regard. Ethel had at least been honest and forthright about her dislike of her husband and had attempted to have him removed by legal and non-violent means before resorting to murder. Moreover, she had been victimised by him. Fred Bryant, Charlotte's husband, was never given the option of leaving the family home peacefully, instead Charlotte appeared to have considered murder as the first and only method of freeing herself from marriage. Moreover, there was no evidence of Fred mistreating Charlotte, a factor which eliminated the possibility of mitigating circumstances. Taken together with Charlotte's sexual conduct these factors ensured she fulfilled the criteria not only of the ultimate dangerous woman poisoner but also of the duplicitous and deceitful wife.

Charlotte and Fred lived in a tiny farmworker's cottage with their five children. To alleviate their poverty they occasionally took lodgers which added to the already overcrowded conditions of their home.[363] They had been married for 12 years when Fred became severely ill in May, August and December of 1935, showing identical symptoms on each occasion. His last attack resulted in death after 12 days of agony. His doctor was suspicious:

> I refused to give a Death Certificate, as I was uneasy & I feared that his death might possibly be due to arsenical poisoning.[364]

A post mortem revealed Fred had indeed died from arsenic poisoning. Pathologist Roche Lynch ruled out suicide:

> The agony of an attack of acute arsenical poisoning is so great that except in insane persons, I cannot credit a suicide with the attempting of his life a second time with arsenic.[365]

Within five weeks the subsequent murder investigation had provided a motive and enough evidence to ensure Charlotte's arrest. The motive was believed to be rooted in 'the eternal triangle' when Leonard Parsons, a hawker, revealed he had "been intimate with her" for approximately two years.[366] Initially he had been a lodger in the Bryant household, but he became Charlotte's lover "soon after we met for the first time."[367] Charlotte joined Leonard on his hawking trips, often staying away from home overnight, and

---

[362]Huggett & Berry 1956:158 referring to Charlotte Bryant.

[363]ASSI 26/48 XC3601 CL. Photographs of the cottage are included in this file, available for inspection in the Public Record Office, Chancery Lane, London.

[364]ASSI 26/48 XC3601 CL. Testimony of Dr Thomas McCarthy p.20.

[365]ASSI 26/48 XC3601 CL. Testimony of Dr Roche Lynch pp.12-13.

[366]ASSI 26/48 XC3601 CL. Testimony of Leonard Edward Parsons p.18.

[367]ASSI 26/48 XC3601 CL. Testimony of Leonard Edward Parsons p.18.

occasionally accompanied by one or two of her children. Leonard further claimed:

> Lottie (accused) has told me I am the father of her youngest child. She also said her husband had no relations with her for some time.[368]

Further damning evidence was revealed when the jury heard more of Leonard's recollections:

> I remember Fred Bryant being ill last year. I remember Mrs Bryant saying to me she thought before long she would be a widow, and if so would I marry her. She asked me this more than once.[369]

The evidence of a second witness, Lucy Ostler, was equally important in ensuring Charlotte was sent for trial. Lucy was staying with the Bryants at the time of Fred's illness and shared a bedroom with the couple and their baby. During Fred's final night she witnessed Charlotte "try & coax her husband to have a cup of Oxo." He immediately started to vomit.[370] Lucy confirmed Leonard's claim that he was the father of Charlotte's youngest child and added "she was very fond of Parsons ... [but] hated her own husband."[371] Worse still, Lucy recounted a conversation between Charlotte and herself while she was reading a newspaper:

> She asked me what I was reading. I said about a poisoning case. She asked what it was + I said about an Arsenic case. Accused asked me 'what would you give anyone if you wanted to get rid of them.' ... This was a few days after she told me she did not like her husband.[372]

Lucy recalled another conversation taking place following the confiscation of various bottles by police officers after a search of Charlotte's home:

> The accused said: 'What did the sergeant want the bottles for.' I said they were wanted [sic] to see if there was anything in the medicine. She then said she hadn't done anything to the medicine. She said to Ernie [Charlotte's son] that some of the bottles in the back must be cleared away ... Accused then started clearing out the cupboards in the front room ... I saw a ... tin marked 'Weed Killer' ... There was also a smaller tin there ... on the lid of the tin it was marked 'Poison'

---

[368] ASSI 26/48 XC3601 CL. Testimony of Leonard Edward Parsons p.20.
[369] ASSI 26/48 XC3601 CL. Testimony of Leonard Edward Parsons p.19.
[370] ASSI 26/48 XC3601 CL. Testimony of Lucy Malvina Ostler p.10.
[371] ASSI 26/48 XC3601 CL. Testimony of Lucy Ostler pp.15-16.
[372] ASSI 26/48 XC3601 CL. Testimony of Lucy Ostler p.16.

... The accused picked it up + said 'I must get rid of this'... Later ... I found a burnt tin amongst the ashes.[373]

Lucy had been present when Charlotte was refused a death certificate and informed that an inquest would be held. Subsequently she had asked Lucy "what an inquest was":

I said there must have been something found in the body which didn't ought to be there. She said 'I suppose they will go to all the chemists to find if anything has been bought ... If they can't find anything they won't be able to put a rope round my neck.'[374]

When arrested Charlotte commented:

I have never got any poison from anywhere, that people do know. I don't see how they can say I poisoned my husband.[375]

The Trial of Charlotte Bryant

The hopelessness of Charlotte's case can be gathered from the fact it was the prosecutor, rather than the defence counsel who opened her trial by reminding the jury: "You are not in a court of morals ..."[376] This reminder was undoubtedly necessary for Charlotte's reputation worked against her in every one of the areas identified in Chapter Three which play important roles in the final outcome of trials of female defendants. The details of the Magistrates' Court hearing held three months previously, received wide coverage in the press, it was therefore public knowledge at the time of the trial that Charlotte had been unfaithful to her husband and had an illegitimate child. Her reputation suffered further damage during the trial following the evidence of several witnesses which indicated "she was immoral, abusive, and slovenly, a woman capable of violence."[377] Thus, while the prosecutor admitted in his opening statement that "it was only fair to say that he was not in a position to put before the jury any evidence that she ... [had] bought any arsenic", nor could he demonstrate she had administered poison to Fred, he nevertheless maintained "that there is a woman here with the strongest motives for destroying her husband ..."[378]

While evidence was lacking regarding the crime itself, there was plenty available indicating Charlotte's callous attitude towards Fred. For

---

373 ASSI 26/48 XC3601 CL. Testimony of Lucy Ostler pp.13-15.

374 ASSi 26/48 XC3601 CL. Testimony of Lucy Ostler p. 12.

375 ASSI 26/48 XC3601 CL. Testimony of Superintendent Joseph Cherrett p.28.

376 Solicitor General Terence O'Connor quoted in *Manchester Evening News* 27th May 1936.

377 Huggett & Berry 1956:161.

378 Solcitor General Terence O'Connor's opening speech reported in *The Times* 28th May 1936. See also *Manchester Guardian* 28th May 1936.

example, when his employer paid a visit during Fred's illness, she claimed she had been shopping all day, despite the seriousness of his condition:

I said 'You don't Damn well stop home to look after him.'379

Moreover, when Fred suffered another vomiting attack she made no move to assist or comfort him but merely "stood up with her arms folded."380 The evidence of a neighbour, Frederick Staunton, was even more damning for he testified that far from having been shopping, which at least suggested engagement in domesticity despite its inappropriate timing, he had seen Parsons "driving off with Mrs Bryant, about 9 o'c."381 In other words, Charlotte had spent the entire day with her lover, while Fred was lying sick and suffering.

Further evidence of Charlotte's callous attitude and lack of sympathy for her husband came from another neighbour, Ellen Stone, who testified that as Fred told Charlotte he was dying and lay 'shuddering', 'moaning' and 'crouched up' with pain, she responded: "He is a B -y fool for eating bread and cheese for his supper."382 As Fred remained conscious but "in great pain" Charlotte's tactlessness and insensitivity seemed limitless:

I have not got Fred insured, but he could have a military funeral.383

Charlotte's attitude towards her husband seemed particularly abhorrent in view of Fred's own tolerant personality. He was repeatedly described as "a very quiet man" and not a single piece of evidence, not even from Charlotte herself, suggested otherwise.384 Even when she accompanied Leonard for several days he did "not seem to mind."385

Charlotte herself seemed oblivious to the impression she was creating of a bad wife and rather than defending herself she reiterated that "Mrs Ostler had looked after him, and that she - accused - had not been looking after her husband during this last illness."386 This claim served only to emphasise her lack of commitment to her marital responsibilities. It also reinforced the dominant image of the woman poisoner as scheming and duplicitous, for implicit in her claim was the suggestion that it was Lucy, rather than herself, who had had the opportunity to administer the poison. Her credibility was

---

379ASSI 26/48 XC3601 CL. Testimony of A.R. Priddle p.6.
380ASSI 26/48 XC3601 CL. Testimony of A.R. Priddle p.6.
381ASSI 26/48 XC3601 CL. Testimony of Frederick Charles Staunton p.10.
382ASSI 26/48 XC3601 CL. Testimony of Ellen Kate Stone p.12.
383ASSI 26/48 XC3601 CL. Testimony of Ellen Kate Stone p.15.
384ASSI 26/48 XC3601 CL. Testimony of Ellen Kate Stone p.17; A.R. Priddle p.6.
385Charlotte Bryant's KC Mr J.D. Casswell quoted in *Manchester Guardian* 30th May 1936.
386ASSI 26/48 XC3601 CL. Testimony of Dr John Broderick Tracey p.23.

further damaged as a consequence of her 'indignant' and 'very nervous' reaction to the subject of the inquest.[387]

Apart from being exposed as an uncaring and unfaithful wife, witnesses also testified that "the house was very dirty", and neighbours had to provide evening-meals for her children as a result of her absence.[388] Altogether, the available evidence indicated Charlotte had failed in every one of the key areas of womanhood outlined in Chapter Three. Thus, she had been exposed as a slovenly housekeeper, an adulterous and uncaring wife and an indifferent mother, to the point where she had left her husband writhing in agony and her children to fend for themselves while she went away with her lover. Despite this, she maintained "she had never been on intimate terms with Parsons":

> I did not like the man, and I do not like him ... I know there has been a lot of talk about ... Parsons ... being the father of my baby. That is not true ... I have never had anything to do with the man. I have never been the same as a wife to him.[389]

Yet when asked shortly afterwards whether she had told "Mrs Ostler the youngest baby was Parsons', [she replied] Yes."[390] During her three hours in the witness box she further claimed to be "on very good terms with her husband: 'I never had a breath wrong with my husband in my life until Leonard Parsons came along.'" Fred was aware that she was with Leonard when she was away from home, but this had never caused even a quarrel.[391] Moreover, in Charlotte's version of the truth it was Parsons who "was after me and not me after Parsons":

> He wanted me to leave my husband. He wanted me to go away with him ... Leonard Parsons knew I did not want him. I had a husband of my own."[392]

She repeatedly denied all knowledge and possession of weed-killer or poison with these words: "I could not tell you poison."[393]

As can be seen from his comments to the jury before calling on Charlotte to give evidence, her KC recognised that her disreputable character would create a negative impact:

---

387 ASSI 26/48 XC3601 CL. Testimony of Dr John Tracey p.23; Ellen Kate Stone p.16.
388 ASSI 26/48 XC3601 CL. Testimony of Frederick Charles Staunton p.9.
389 Evidence of Charlotte Bryant quoted in *Manchester Evening News* 28th May 1936.
390 Evidence of Charlotte Bryant quoted in *Manchester Guardian* 30th May 1936.
391 Evidence of Charlotte Bryant quoted in *Manchester Guardian* 30th May 1936.
392 Evidence of Charlotte Bryant quoted in *The Times* 30th May 1936.
393 Evidence of Charlotte Bryant quoted in *The Times* 30th May 1936.

The Solicitor-General has told you that this is not a court of morals. I know you are not going to hold that against a woman. A woman may be very immoral. You may think there is nothing to be said for her from the moral point of view, and while she is living with her husband, she is going away for two or three days at a time with another man who was staying at the house. Unfortunately, there are women and men who do this sort of thing, but it does not follow from that that they are guilty of murder. Do not let anything of that sort cloud your minds. Just because she is not a moral woman I know you are not going to say that she is a murderess.[394]

Mr Casswell furthermore attempted to destroy the motive of "the eternal triangle" put forward by the prosecution, by arguing that since Fred did not protest at the arrangement between Charlotte and Leonard, there was no need to murder him:

Mrs Bryant had a good home and a good husband. Would she have left that for no home at all to associate with a man the police were after and who had warrants against him for the maintenance of his illegitimate children?[395]

However, defending Charlotte Bryant remained a hopeless task. Whereas female poisoners Dorothea Waddingham and Ethel Major - whose trials were heard three and 19 months earlier respectively - possessed redeeming features, for example in their role as mothers, Charlotte had none. Instead, her personal conduct and behaviour ensured she was perceived as a sexually unruly and dangerous woman. In an era where - as described earlier - marriage was considered sacrosanct and motherhood the only way through which a woman could feel 'complete', Charlotte failed to respect either role. Instead of embracing the role of a loyal and obedient wife she failed to recognise the authority of her husband. Instead of putting her children first and sacrificing her own interests, she neglected them in favour of pursuing an illicit sexual liaison with Leonard Parsons, himself an undesirable individual in terms of family ideology, who, apart from betraying a friend by engaging in a sexual relationship with his wife, had also left his own common-law wife and four children to fend for themselves.[396] Instead of accepting her domestic responsibilites she allowed the house to become dirty. Instead of guarding her reputation and aspiring to respectability she consumed alcohol

---

[394]Defence KC Mr Casswell quoted in *The Times* 30th May 1936.
[395]Defence KC Mr Casswell quoted in *The Times* 30th May 1936.
[396]According to Leonard Parsons he and Fred "were quite friendly" (*The Times* 29th May 1936). Leonard's common-law wife, Pricilla Loveridge gave evidence that she had lived with him for 11 years. "He was a fancy woman's man, and was a man who would break any man's home up" (Quoted in *The Times* 29th May 1936).

and engaged in prostitution.[397] In short, Charlotte had ignored every one of the moral assumptions and ideological expectations associated with 'normal' womanhood in general and the 'good' woman in particular. As argued in Chapter Three, these assumptions and expectations make important contributions to trial outcomes of female defendants. They were of particular relevance in Charlotte's case for apart from having committed the most feared and despised type of murder, she had also stepped far beyond the boundaries of acceptable female conduct and was thus a 'doubly' deviant woman. None of the usual control mechanisms appeared to be effective in moderating her behaviour. Instead she had failed to internalise any of the commands and disciplinary practices which - in Foucauldian terms - produce the self-controlled and docile body. Yet, despite fitting the image of the 'loose' woman - morally, verbally and in terms of her mobility (with Leonard Parsons) - she continued to enjoy male patronage, not only from her husband, but also from her lover. Far from being under the dominating gaze of patriarchy, it was she who dominated Fred. Despite having made no effort to conform to acceptable standards of motherhood, domesticity, respectability, marital and sexual conduct, Charlotte had not suffered either informal or formal punitive consequences, since Fred had failed to fulfil his obligation to discipline an 'uppity' wife by 'putting her in her place'. However, where Fred had failed, the State was about to succeed as it assumed responsibility for her punishment following the guilty verdict, reached by an all-male jury after an hour's consideration.[398]

An Alternative Truth

The file relating to Charotte Bryant is - like many of the women's case-files examined in this book - extremely slim, and does not include a medical report or any other assessment of the defendant. We will therefore never know whether Charlotte would be considered fully responsible for her criminal action according to the criteria defined in modern law. Mr Casswell, Charlotte's defence counsel is reported to have said she was "not very strong in her mind."[399] Huggett and Berry shared this opinion and questioned her ability to understand courtroom procedures:

> Although she was bright enough to know why she was standing in the dock, undoubtedly the procedure at the Magistrates' Court was a drawn out, meaningless ritual of mumbo jumbo.[400]

We furthermore know that Charlotte, who had grown up in impoverished conditions in Ireland, had not had the benefit of education and

---

[397]Huggett & Berry 1956:150. According to the authors, Fred appreciated the extra income and told a neighbour that "Four pounds a week is better than thirty-bob."
[398]*Daily Express* 14th July 1936.
[399]Quoted in Huggett & Berry 1956:159.
[400]Huggett & Berry 1956:159.

hence was illiterate and could not tell the time, conditions which by definition limit access to knowledge and information within a literate society.[401] I have already indicated that Charlotte's vocabulary was limited, as when she asked what 'inquest' meant, and when she responded 'I could not tell you poison'. Evidence is also available which indicates Charlotte's unfamiliarity with courtroom etiquette, as when she sat in the dock, sucking sweets.[402] Moreover, if it is assumed the jury's verdict of guilty was correct, an examination of the remaining evidence strongly indicates Charlotte was at the very least, an extremely naive person who had not taken even the most rudimentary precautions against being exposed as a murderess, as can be gathered from the following: First, she had made no attempt to hide the murder weapon, for as noted above, the tin of weed-killer was still in its usual place *after* a police search. Second, the prosecution alleged Charlotte had attempted to destroy the weed-killer tin by burning it. Yet when she found herself unable to light the copper fire she called Lucy and asked for her assistance, which resulted in Lucy finding "a burnt tin amongst the ashes."[403] Third, only two days prior to Fred's death, Charlotte told insurance agent Edward Tuck she would like to insure her husband. Tuck testified that "Bryant looked a very sick man" and after seeing his condition, refused to insure him.[404] Fourth, only five days after Fred's death she added credibility to the supposed motive for the murder by embarking on a two-day search for Parsons.[405]

It was actions such as these, coupled with her careless remarks and comments quoted earlier, which led Huggett and Berry to conclude that Charlotte's "ideas were severely circumscribed by ignorance."[406] Moreover, they suggested her ignorance was so great that it was questionable whether she could be considered capable of carrying out the murder by herself. As noted above, Charlotte herself attempted to present an alternative truth during her three hours in the witness box when she claimed it was Leonard who was pursuing her, not the reverse, as claimed by the prosecution. If she was speaking the truth, Leonard would also have had a motive for killing Fred. Furthermore, while there was no evidence that Charlotte had ever purchased arsenic, Leonard admitted he had attempted to buy arsenic from a chemist but had been refused because he "was not known" in Sherbourne.[407] Moreover, the weed-killer which Lucy had noticed in the cupboard while in Charlotte's presence could equally have belonged to Leonard who had only left the cottage two months previously; indeed Lucy herself testified Charlotte had

---

[401] See for example testimony of Lucy Ostler ASSI 26/48 XC3601 CL; Huggett & Berry 1956:169.

[402] Huggett & Berry 1956:159.

[403] ASSI 26/48 XC3601 CL. Testimony of Lucy Ostler p.15.

[404] Trial proceedings reported in *Manchester Evening News* 28th May and *The Times* 29th May 1936.

[405] Huggett & Berry 1956:153.

[406] Huggett & Berry 1956:148.

[407] Quoted from trial transcript in *The Times* 29th May 1936.

commented "that 'Parsons' generally did bring things like that home."[408] Hence, within the context of Charlotte being responsible for five young children, her comment "I must get rid of this" seems perfectly reasonable.

Finally, Charlotte's daughter Lily, testified that she had witnessed Leonard pouring liquid from a bottle "on the stone outside and [he] said to mummy: 'If you don't look out I will ram that down your throat.' The liquid 'fizzled all up.'"[409] Charlotte herself provided a final tantalizing clue to the true circumstances surrounding the poisoning when in a dictated letter from the condemned cell she wrote: "It's all ... fault I'm here ... I listened to the tales I was told. But I have not long now and I will be out of all my troubles."[410] The missing name had been crossed out by the prison authorities.

As reiterated throughout this book, its goal is not to provide excuses for women who have committed murder. Rather, as discussed in Chapter Three, the aim is to demonstrate a close relationship between the delivery and quality of justice and the *type* of woman facing the bench. Fred Bryant was by all accounts, including Charlotte's, a placid and peace-loving individual whose protracted suffering and agonising death cannot be justified or excused. Neither can unsafe convictions, especially in capital cases. The fact that Charlotte had deviated from expected standards in every one of the areas associated with 'normal' womanhood and was consequently found severely lacking in respectability, domesticity and as a wife and mother ensured it did not require much effort to believe she was also capable of murder. Yet, apart from Charlotte's own tactless remarks there was no undisputed evidence against her. 'Expert' evidence concerning the arsenic content of the ashes found by the burnt tin described earlier carried great weight during the trial, since it was assumed to prove Charlotte had attempted to burn the remaining weed-killer. However, when another expert, Professor William Bone, read about this evidence during the trial he contacted the defence, declaring that the natural arsenic content present in coal varied greatly, and the amount found in these particular ashes fell well within the normal range. He was willing to testify accordingly at Charlotte's Appeal hearing.[411] Following this revelation, Charlotte's lawyer applied for a re-trial. Permission was refused. When her KC Mr Trapnell attempted to introduce this new evidence into the Court of Appeal, Lord Hewart - who had also heard the appeals of Edith Thompson and Ethel Major - remained unimpressed and "said sternly" that "the application is of the objectionable kind which we foresaw in a recent case when in very exceptional circumstances we admitted further medical evidence":

---

[408]ASSI 26/48 XL3601 CL. Testimony of Lucy Ostler p.14.

[409]Testimony of Lily Bryant quoted in *Manchester Guardian* 30th May 1936.

[410]Letter quoted in Huggett & Berry 1956:179.

[411]Reported in *Daily Express* 15th July 1936; *Daily Mirror* 30th June 1936; *The Times* 29th June 1936. Professor Bone was employed at the Imperial College of Science and Technology.

The Court is unanimously of opinion that there is no occasion for the further evidence. It would be intolerable if this Court, on the conclusion of a capital charge or other case, were to listen to the after-thoughts of a scientific gentleman who brought his mind controversially to bear on evidence that had been given. We adumbrated that possibility in the recent case and we set our minds like flint against any such attempt. It is clear there was no mistake in the Court below.[412]

While Lord Chief Justice Hewart and his colleagues felt so certain about Charlotte's guilt that their minds 'were set like flint', other observers of the case expressed severe unease about her conviction. Charlotte was so poor she could not afford to buy shoes and had to make do with a pair of slippers. She was refused admittance to a dental surgery due to a major infestation of head-lice.[413] She was illiterate. When her husband died she had to move into the local Poor House.[414] The man Charlotte supposedly killed for, Leonard Parsons, was himself penniless and hiding from the police. Such details, together with the lack of, and disputed evidence, led Huggett and Berry to question the prosecution's motive of illicit passion which they regarded as "extremely shaky."[415] Others shared their unease about the case. Labour MP Sydney Silverman expressed concern about the inequality between defence and prosecution in the case and told the House of Commons that "her defence was in the hands of junior counsel only, whereas the prosecution was undertaken by the Solicitor-General, another King's Counsel, and junior counsel."[416] Did the quality of Charlotte's defence reflect her poverty and powerlessness? Was the jury more likely to find her guilty of murder as a result of her immorality and inadequacies as a wife and mother? Would Lord Hewart have allowed new evidence to be admitted in the Court of Appeal if Charlotte had been a respectable and powerful member of her community? Silverman was concerned enough about these issues to raise them in Parliament where he asked:

is the Right Hon Gentleman aware that there is considerable public uneasiness about this case, and does he not think that when a case of such difficulty as to justify the prosecution by a Law Officer in person is defended by junior counsel only, there is a considerable danger of a miscarriage of justice? ... does he not think that where

---

[412]Lord Chief Justice Hewart's judgement on the Appeal of Charlotte Bryant, quoted in *Daily Mirror* 30th June 1936 and *The Times* 30th June 1936.
[413]Huggett & Berry 1956:156.
[414]This was the Sturminster Newton Institution where her children remained after Charlotte's arrest. See for example *Daily Mirror* 28th May 1936.
[415]Huggett & Berry 1956:181.
[416]*Parliamentary Debates*, House of Commons, 29th June-17th July Session 1935-36 Vol 314 cols 1400-1401.

there is such a heavy battery of legal gentlemen on one side the effect on the mind of a rustic jury may be considerable?[417]

The Home Secretary disagreed and argued the Crown was "engaged in trying to present the facts of the case with complete propriety and with the greatest impartiality."[418] However, another MP Mr Pritt, was also concerned enough to ask a parliamentary question on the same matter which the Home Secretary initially refused to answer because "he was thoroughly convinced of Mrs Bryant's guilt, had refused to advise a reprieve ... [and] considered Mr Pritt's inquiry might cause disquiet in the public mind."[419] By the time the Home Secretary asked to have the question "restored to the order paper" it was too late to save Charlotte from the gallows, but future defendants would have benefited from Mr Pritt's proposal that legislation should be introduced which "secure[s] that verdicts founded on mistaken evidence shall be subject to inquiry on appeal."[420] Astonishingly, the Home Secretary referred to the Bryant case as an example of why such legislation remained unnecessary:

> No such legislation is required as, of course, an allegation of mistaken evidence can be considered on appeal and, as I have said, it was in fact considered and fully allowed for in the present case.[421]

In proposing an alternative truth about Charlotte Bryant it has not been my intention to claim she was innocent of the crime for which she was executed. Rather, I have suggested that the evidence needed for a conviction was absent in this case, and that Charlotte's personal inadequacies, immorality and disreputable behaviour were allowed to replace the missing evidence. In Chapter Three, I referred to Carlen's argument that the majority of women are punished, not according to the seriousness of their crimes, but "primarily according to the court's assesment of them as wives, mothers and daughters." I also referred to Wilson's point that punishment is, in some cases, imposed according to "deviations from the expected form of feminine behaviour" rather than as a result of the offence which has been committed. To those two points, a third may be added: that in cases where a woman has severely transgressed acceptable female standards in a multitude of areas, poor quality evidence is more likely to be accepted. As pointed out by Huggett and Berry twenty years after Charlotte's trial:

417*Parliamentary Debates*, House of Commons, 29th June-17th July Session 1935-36 Vol 314 cols 1400-1401.

418*Parliamentary Debates*, House of Commons, 29th June-17th July Session 1935-36 Vol 314 cols 1400-1401.

419*Daily Express* 16th July 1936.

420*Parliamentary Debates*, House of Commons, 29th June-17th July Session 1935-36 Vol 314 col 2221.

421*Parliamentary Debates*, House of Commons, 29th June-17th July Session 1935-36 Vol 314 col 2222.

Trials in this country are based on evidence, and if incorrect evidence is put forward by the Prosecution then a prisoner should be entitled to a re-trial. It creates a dangerous precedent to admit that false evidence was given but that nevertheless you think a prisoner guilty ... Even if the Appeal Judges and the Home Secretary were convinced of her guilt ... [their] attitude is to be deplored.[422]

Charlotte's solicitor demonstrated a strong commitment to her case both when he fought on her behalf to obtain a re-trial, and when he attempted to have her case heard in the House of Lords.[423] Her solicitor and KC had been appointed under the Poor Prisoner's Law and it is not known how much time was available to prepare her case. We do know that an alternative truth could have been presented in court in a multitude of areas. For example, there was no evidence that Fred had suffered from arsenic poisoning on the previous occasions he had been ill. Indeed two doctors had assumed he had suffered from gastro-enteritis at the time of his illnesses and only suggested arsenic poisoning after the result of his post-mortem became known.[424] No examination was conducted in the gravel pit where Fred worked which was renowned for its high arsenic content.[425] The implausibility of Charlotte poisoning Fred single-handed within the context of her illiteracy was not raised, nor was the possibility that the weed-killer found in the cottage could have belonged to Leonard Parsons, who claimed he used arsenic to treat horses.[426] Had Charlotte's defence arranged for its own expert witness and analysis of the ashes in her house, the prosecution's expert witness could have been challenged in court. Instead this crucial evidence was only discovered as a result of an expert volunteering his knowledge and services. When these issues are considered in the context of the lack of evidence discussed above - that it could not be proved whether Charlotte had either bought or administered arsenic - we begin to gain an insight into the rudimentary nature of Charlotte's defence. It is difficult to avoid the conclusion that far from being blind, justice recognises sexual transgression, immorality, poverty and powerlessness at a glance and acts accordingly. Mary Hartman's sentiment that if women "intended to dispose of somebody" it was wise to be 'respectable', refers to women who killed in the 19th century, but after the examination of 14 case-studies it will have become apparent that this was equally true of the first half of the 20th century.[427]

---

[422]Huggett & Berry 1956:181.
[423]*Manchester Evening News* 15th July 1936.
[424]ASSI 26/48 XC3601 CL. Testimonies of Drs John Brodrick Tracey and Richmond McIntosh pp.23 and 24.
[425]Huggett & Berry 1956:179.
[426]Evidence of Leonard Parsons reported in *The Times* 29th May 1936.
[427]Hartman, M. S. (1985) *Victorian Murderesses* Robson Books, London p.1.

Concluding Remarks - Motherhood Re-visited

Ironically, Charlotte Bryant learned to write whilst awaiting execution. This enabled her to write to the King in a last effort to save her life:

> Mighty King, Have pity on your lowly, afflicted subject. Don't let them kill me on Wednesday. Ask them to give Mrs Van der Elst an opportunity of saying what will prove my innocence. From the brink of the cold, dark grave, I am a poor, helpless woman. I ask you not to let them kill me. I am innocent.[428]

It was sorely needed for no one had initiated a public petition on her behalf. Nor did anyone take the trouble to submit a petition on behalf of her five children aged between 18 months and 12 years. Yet there was plenty of evidence that Charlotte was a much loved mother. For example *The Daily Mirror* published a photocopy of a letter by her 12-year-old son, Ernest:

> Dear Mum, When are you coming back to us. We all want you back. It has ben [sic] such a log [sic] time sins [sic] I had see you [sic]. Lily is ill. Pleas [sic] come back soon. from [sic] your loving son Ernest Bryant.[429]

The day after Charlotte had been sentenced to death, Ernest asked a *Daily Mirror* correspondent where his mum was and whether she would be back soon:

> I cried myself to sleep last night. I could not help it. Only Lily and I know about it. The babies have not been told yet ... Do you think if I wrote to the Judge he would let Mummy come home? She has been away for such a long time. ... I was all right waiting because I thought Mummy would be coming back in the end. I do not know what to do now.[430]

Like her son, Charlotte was tormented by the separation from her children. When her appeal was dismissed she wrote to Ernest: "Think of me as last I was" and "asked him to let his brothers and sisters know that she was thinking of them always."[431] As the end drew near, Charlotte's demeanour was "that of a woman resigned to her fate", never betraying the "slightest emotion. Her only concern has been for the welfare of her children."[432] Mr Arrow, her solicitor, visited her three days before the execution and confirmed that "she talked mainly of her children." She also protested "her

---

[428]Quoted in *Manchester Evening News* 15th July 1936.

[429]*Daily Mirror* 1st June 1936. Lily was Charlotte's 10-year-old daughter.

[430]Ernest Bryant quoted in *Daily Mirror* 1st June 1936.

[431]Quoted in *Daily Mirror* 30th June 1936.

[432]*Daily Express* 15th July 1936.

innocence time and again."[433] In her farewell letter to Mr Arrow she asked him to look after her children and requested that her entire wealth "- five shillings and eight pence, halfpenny, - should be divided among them."[434]

As can be gathered from the above, newspapers did not shy away from exposing the emotional heartache an execution of a mother caused. In addition to the above publications the *Daily Mirror* also published photos of Ernest Bryant and referred to the "tear-stained note" from his mother which he had been carrying "in his pocket for the last two days."[435] The implications of the deliberate killing of a mother of five young children were not lost on the general public who began to express concern about the execution through letters to newspapers. Some also considered the hardship in Charlotte's life a mitigating factor:

> It is indeed a terrible ordeal for the children of Mrs Bryant, as it is for all children connected with such tragedies. Many times I have discussed the plight of such children with other women. The condition of life is enough to unbalance any woman who has no time whatever but to struggle with poverty and bear and rear children.[436]

Another letter read:

> Probably most of us remember what torture it was for us as children to think that the mother we loved might some day die. Now think what is happening to these children.[437]

However, only one member of the public translated such sentiments into direct action - Mrs Van der Elst. Not only did she drive through a rope-barrier errected by police and designed to deter demonstrators on the morning of the execution, she also announced, she was establishing a fund for children of murdered and executed parents, and that she personally would contribute £50,000 towards it.[438] That Mrs Van der Elst's demonstration was greeted with hostility by many of the 1000 crowd outside the prison, demonstrates the ambivalent and contradictory attitude towards motherhood. This attitude can be understood by exposing the contradictions on which the discourse of motherhood itself is built. As I discussed in Chapters Two and Four, this

---

[433]Mr Arrow quoted in *Daily Mirror* 13th July 1936.
[434]*Manchester Evening News* 14th July 1936.
[435]*Daily Mirror* 1st and 30th June 1936.
[436]Letter quoted in Huggett & Berry 1956:173-4.
[437]Letter quoted in Huggett & Berry 1956:174.
[438]Gattey, C.N (1972) *The Incredible Mrs Van der Elst* Leslie Frewin, London, pp.121-2. See also *Manchester Evening News* 15th July 1936 and *Daily Mirror* 16th July 1936. Mrs Van der Elst defended herself against police accusations that she was 'mental' and typical of her flamboyant style, after paying a fine of £5 for breaching the peace, she donated another £5 to the police sports fund. Her fund never came into existence, instead she donated money to Dr Barnardo Homes and the RSPCC.

discourse was not created for the benefit of child-welfare, but "to preserve the ideologically important construct of [the] maternal instinct", which in turn acts as an important mechanism of social control on women.[439] The sentiments attached to motherhood are only applicable to mothers who are married, respectable, chaste and living above the poverty line. Poor mothers, adulterous mothers or mothers of illegitimate children are dangerous mothers and "may find themselves punished for their transgressions."[440] In the same way Smart discusses the creation of the 'normative woman' who imposes "a homogeneity which is all too often cast in our own privileged, white likeness", so sentimental and romantic notions of motherhood apply only to the 'normative mother' who poses no threat to the male dominated social order.[441] Charlotte was not a 'normative' but a dangerous mother and unfaithful wife. Hence, her status as a mother carried no currency with the State, despite the fact she was loved and missed by her children in the same measure as would have been the case if their upbringing had been more privileged. Charlotte's punishment was of a higher priority than compassion for her children, for she had transgressed acceptable female behaviour in a multitude of areas and had finally succumbed to the most dangerous form of violence - murder by poison. In sum, in the case of Charlotte Bryant, as had been the case with Dorothea Waddingham three months previously, the discourses of motherhood were easily subsumed under those of the woman poisoner for as the *Daily Express* reminded its readers:

> No reprieves are ever granted in cases of murder by poisoning; the crime is regarded as the most serious it is possible to commit against the community ... Poisoners must die.[442]

To this we may add that 'suspected poisoners must also die' for just as discourses of the female poisoner easily overruled those of motherhood, so the discourses around Charlotte's immorality and perverse womanhood overruled the need for a safe conviction.

Part III: 'Perhaps after I die the truth will be known'

The Case of Ruth Ellis

Much debate has gone on as to why the Ruth Ellis case captured the interest of the public to such an unprecedented extent. Why is she

---

[439]Matus, J.L. (1995) *Unstable Bodies* Manchester University Press, Manchester p.189.

[440]Naffine, N. (1990) *Law & The Sexes* Allen & Unwin, London p.142; Smart, C. (1992) 'Introduction' in Smart, C. (ed) (1992) *Regulating Womanhood* Routledge, London p.23.

[441]Smart, C. (1995) *Law, Crime and Sexuality* Sage, London p.198.

[442]*Daily Express* 14th July 1936.

still remembered forty years on? She was the last of fifteen women to be hanged this century, a fact that most people whom I encounter appear to know whatever their age. However, I never come across anybody who can name any one of the other fourteen.[443]

This court is not a court of morals. We do not sit here to adjudicate on questions of morality. This is a criminal court and the function of it is solely to determine on the evidence whether a person is or is not guilty of the charge which is made against her. You will not, therefore, allow your judgment to be swayed or your minds to be prejudiced in the least degree against the accused because, according to her own admission, when she was a married woman she committed adultery or because she was having two persons at different times as lovers. Dismiss those matters wholly from your minds.[444]

A member of the public gallery remembers her as being a 'typical West End tart'. If that was the impression she left on the jury then the case was lost before she had said a word in her defence.[445]

Of the 15 cases of executed women analysed in this book only the case of Ruth Ellis has received academic, legal and media attention equal to Edith Thompson's case. The two women were however, very different, indeed Ruth's method of murder was unique compared to the other women executed during the 20th century, for she shot her lover four times in a public place in full view of several witnesses. Hence, she became only the second of the 15 women to confess to her crime, although like Margaret Allen, six years earlier, she was persuaded to plead 'not guilty' at her trial.

As in the case of Edith Thompson 32 years earlier, the intriguing and scandalous features surrounding the Ruth Ellis case ensured its status as a *cause celebre*. Almost immediately after the shooting, and long before the case went to trial, the discourses responsible for placing Ruth firmly within the 'bad' rather than the 'mad' category were activated. She was variously described as 'a model' and a 'club-hostess' - the implication being she was a lower class woman employed in non-respectable professions. This image contrasted sharply with that of her lover David Blakely, who was considered a 'play-boy', came from an upper-class background and enjoyed a private

[443]Ellis, G. (1996) *Ruth Ellis, My Mother: Memoirs of a Murderer's Daughter* Smith Gryphon Publishers, London p.5. The heading 'Perhaps after I die the truth will be known' is a quote from Ruth Ellis, 12th July 1955, the day prior to her execution. It appears on an unnumbered page in her daughter Georgie Ellis's book.
[444]DPP2/2430 23271 Trial transcript of the Ruth Ellis case, summing-up by Mr Justice Havers p.81. This transcript is not available for public inspection but access to it may be gained by contacting Miss Grey, Crown Prosecuton Service Headquarters, 50 Ludgate Hill, London EC4M 7EX.
[445]Marks, L. & Van den Bergh T. (1990) *Ruth Ellis: A Case of Diminished Responsibility?* Penguin, London p.148.

income. To fully appreciate the significance not only of Ruth's lack of respectability, but also of the class difference between the couple, it is necessary to situate this case within the social climate of the 1950s.

The Second World War had left an aftermath of austerity, social disruption and commodity shortage in Britain, conditions which made the country ripe for racketeering, corruption, fraud, gambling and prostitution.[446] Official crime statistics confirmed Britain was in the grip of an "appalling wave of crime."[447] Juvenile convictions which had risen by 250% between 1939 and 1947 were of particular concern to the government, and were thought to be linked to "inadequate early socialisation".[448] This theory was coupled with a recognition that families had been "weakened or broken by the experience of war" hence were now in need of support in the task of reintegrating lawless youth into family life and society.[449] The fear of "an imminent collapse of the family" was further fuelled by the rate of illegitimate births which had risen from 25,942 in 1939 to 64,064 in 1945.[450] By 1955 5% of all children born were illegitimate.[451] Divorce rates also soared between 1946 and 1948.[452] Lastly, prostitution came to be regarded as a serious threat to family life during the 1950s. While it is doubtful there was an actual increase in prostitution during this period, a moral panic was nevertheless "successfully orchestrated" in which the prostitute became the new folk-devil as a result of her increasing visibility.[453] Although 1950s' Britain remained a class-ridden society, class distinctions in the post-war period were in the process of change.[454] Thus, while the majority of

---

[446]See for example Chibnall, S. (1977) *Law and Order News* Tavistock, London p.51.

[447]Pearson, G. (1983) *Hooligan* Macmillan, London p.14. Statistics which concerned the Government included those for fraud which rose from 13,122 in 1945 to 27,415 in 1951, an increase of 108.9% (Taylor, I. (1981) *Law and Order: Arguments for Socialism* Macmillan, p.54). Murder statistics too were rising and by 1948 "a murder was being committed every two days" (Yallop, D. (1990) *To Encourage the Others* Corgi Books, London p.33).

[448]Taylor 1981:62; Yallop 1990:29.

[449]Taylor 1981:48.

[450]Smart, C. (1981) 'Law and the Control of Women's Sexuality: The Case of the 1950s' in Hutter, B. & Williams, G. (1981) *Controlling Women* Croom Helm, London p.47; Taylor 1981:48.

[451]Marwick, A. (1990) *British Society Since 1945* Penguin London p.60.

[452]HMSO Table reproduced in Smart, C. (1984) *The Ties That Bind* RKP London p.33.

[453]Smart 1981:50; 49; 48.

[454]See for example Hall et al: "... social changes unhinged many traditional patterns of class relations in the immediate sphere of social life, reorganising some attitudes and aspirations, dismantling some of the stable forms of working-class consciousness and solidarity, and setting aside some of the familiar landmarks of traditional pre-war society" (Hall, S., Critcher, C., Jefferson, T., Clarke, J., Roberts, B. (1978) *Policing the Crisis* Macmillan, London p.231).

prostitutes were drawn from the working-class, they "could no longer be held as a class apart from respectable women; the separate spheres were merging, and in this way the prostitute became more of a threat to respectable family lifestyles":

> Her proximity, both socially and spatially presented a challenge to all the values embodied in ideologies of family life and motherhood so prevalent in the 1950s.[455]

With such an array of perceived threats to family-life the state's plans for post-war social reconstruction strongly emphasised the centrality of marriage and the nuclear family as a basis for organising society. This focus on family ideology was supported by legislation around issues such as family law and sexual behaviour, the overall aim being to preserve family stability as well as "reproducing, in some instances, patriarchal relations within the family ..."[456]

The role of women came under particular scrutiny as can be gathered from the findings of the *Morton Commission* which sat between 1951-1955. The Commission identified women's social and economic emancipation as being responsible for the increased divorce rate, and emphasised "moral values" and the "duties of married life" in an attempt to stem the rising tide of marital breakdown. At the same time it refused to introduce progressive changes to divorce laws.[457] For Smart, this strategy had the effect of renewing "legitimacy to dominant ideologies concerning the patriarchal family."[458] It is also an example of the state's involvement in maintaining "a particular form of patriarchal relations" by *non-intervention*.[459]

Women were furthermore singled out as being responsible for maintaining the moral standards of their community, as indicated by Lord Denning's comment that "the morality of the race depends on the morality of the women folk."[460] The converse was that 'deviant' women were subverting the morality of the nation. This philosophy was used to justify the differential treatment of adulterous women. While the attitude towards men's adulterous behaviour was largely one of tolerance, the double standards applied to women's morality described in Chapter Three, now received state legitimacy in the form of legislation. Thus while an adulterous husband may have left his wife years ago, she could lose maintenance immediately upon becoming sexually active with another man. Not only did this law encourage separated husbands to keep their wives under surveillance, it could also coerce a woman

---

[455]Smart 1981:50.
[456]Smart 1981:57.
[457]Smart 1984:37; 36. The official title of the Morton Commission was *The Royal Commission on Marriage and Divorce*.
[458]Smart 1984:40.
[459]Smart 1984:40.
[460]Smart 1984:45.

into economic dependence on another man. In this way "the patriarchal marital relationship was reconstituted."[461]

A second strategy mobilised in support of the family and patriarchal relations can be observed in the state's response to the increased rate of illegitimate births noted above. As a result of the ideal female model being that of a wife and mother, those who did not conform - such as unmarried mothers - inevitably found themselves at the receiving end of punitive attitudes, for example in the form of a "meagre means-tested allowance." This legitimised surveillance of lone mothers' sexual behaviour, since - like the deserted wife - the unmarried mother would have her allowance withdrawn if suspected of cohabiting with a man.[462] Another attempt to eliminate families not conforming to the nuclear model involved encouraging unmarried mothers to have their babies adopted, a policy which, "at a period where motherhood was so revered", showed no concern for the feelings a single mother might have for her baby. This lack of concern led one author to conclude that unmarried mothers were regarded as "no more than social deviants" marginalised by the new welfare state, "possibly more than the Poor Law had done."[463]

A final legislative measure by the state to protect the nuclear family can be observed in the form of the Street Offences Act which was introduced as the result of recommendations by the Wolfenden Committee set up in 1953 as a response to the moral panic around prostitution. This legislation justified a tightening of the system of surveillance of prostitutes with the result that street walkers were "surrendered even further into the control of the criminal law."[464]

In summary, the period 1945-1955 was one of profound social change and reconstruction. The perception that the structure of the post-war family was under threat following increased rates of illegitimacy, soaring divorce rates and an increased level of visibility of prostitute women, brought the country close to a moral panic which the State responded to in two inter-related ways: first by presenting the ideal woman as a wife and mother committed to a life of domesticity and caring; second, by identifying this wife and mother as being responsible for the nation's moral standards. These two responses in turn, were reinforced by state legislation designed to 'protect' the nuclear family. For women the material reality of this legislation meant an increase in official surveillance over female sexual behaviour, whether she be separated or divorced, an unmarried mother or a prostitute, for in a culture struggling to maintain the patriarchal ties of the nuclear family, these three types of women represented particularly dangerous forms of womanhood. Ruth Ellis fulfilled the criteria for every one of these categories and it is within this social context she stepped out into a public place and shot David

---

[461]Smart 1984:43.

[462]Spensky, M. (1992) 'Producers of legitimacy: Homes for unmarried mothers in the 1950s' in Smart, C. (1992) *Regulating Motherhood* Routledge London pp. 105-6.

[463]Spensky 1992:116; 117.

[464]Smart 1981:51.

Blakely, her lover, and thus became one of the most 'visibly' deviant women of the 1950s.

In this case-study I shall argue that the discourses and ideologies surrounding women's role in the 1950s, coupled with the moral panic around the breakdown of the family, played a major role in ensuring Ruth received no pity or compassion, either from the legal or political establishment. Instead her status as a 'bad' woman proved impossible to challenge, either by the trial procedures generally or by her own defence counsel in particular, for she was perceived to encompass every strand of the 'moral decay' deemed to be responsible for the decline of family life in post-war Britain. This perception became established as a result of Ruth breaking every one of the social conventions of the era and thus committing transgressions in all the areas identified in Chapter Three - respectability, sexuality, motherhood, domesticity. Her final act of violence provided the ultimate reinforcement of her dangerousness, ensuring that in addition to her 'moral bankruptcy', she now also fitted the image of the stereotypical *femme fatale* - "the blonde with perverse sexuality and social aberration" who executed her lover in cold blood in an act of revenge.[465] Meanwhile, as a result of the double standards discussed in Chapter Three, David never suffered damage to his status as victim either from the media or through the trial proceedings, despite being a promiscuous and violent alcoholic. Below I intend to challenge this clear-cut demarcation between victim and aggressor so readily accepted by both the legal profession and the media at the time of the trial.

Ruth Ellis - A Life

At the age of 16 Ruth was already identified as a 'good-time' girl with a 'reputation' as a result of her association with Allied soldiers stationed in London. At 17 one such association resulted in her becoming a single, teenage mother when her son Andy was born.[466] At 18 she had worked as a nude model and was about to embark on a career as a hostess in a night-club owned by Maury Conley, a vice-racketeer, fraudster and brothel-keeper who had been named by *The People* as "Britain's biggest vice boss", and therefore just the sort of person at the centre of the moral panic about crime in the 1950s.[467] In her capacity as a hostess she met George Ellis whom she married in 1950. She soon learned he was both an alcoholic and wife-beater,

---

[465]Birch, H. (1993) 'If looks could kill' in Birch, H. (ed) (1993) *Moving Targets* Virago, London p.52. See also Hancock, R. (1989) *Ruth Ellis* Weidenfeld, London p.6, who, on this page alone, refers to Ellis as 'the blonde' no less than three times.

[466]Ruth's son was named Clare Andria after his French-Canadian father but was known as Andy.

[467]It was journalist Duncan Webb who wrote in *The People* "I hereby name him as Britain's biggest vice boss and the chief source of the tainted money that nourished the evils of London night life" (11th December 1955 quoted in Hancock 1989:20). See also Goodman, J. & Pringle, P. (1974) *The Trial of Ruth Ellis* David & Charles, London p.15.

and the couple consequently separated within a year, prior to the birth of Ruth's second child.[468] As a single parent, separated, soon-to-be divorcee of questionable reputation and a history of immorality, Ruth epitomised the type of woman guaranteed to fuel the moral panic about the break-down of familylife and moral values in austere, button-lipped post-war Britain.[469] This image was further reinforced when in 1953, after only two weeks of courtship she allowed a club-customer - David Blakely - to move in with her and become her lover.

The ensuing 19 months were taken up with their complex, stormy and intense love-hate relationship. Initially Ruth did not take the affair seriously, and it was she who appeared to be the dominant partner - "confident and self-possessed while [David] was weak and ineffectual."[470] This power balance, however, shifted towards the end of their relationship when "the tables had turned" and David repeatedly left Ruth guessing and uncertain about their future together as he see-sawed from promising marriage one moment to ignoring her the next - sometimes disappearing for several days when he was involved in other sexual relationships.[471] Ruth, in a state of nervous exhaustion and mentally drained from these uncertainties, finally shot him on Easter Monday 1955, following yet another protracted period of contradictory and provocative behaviour by David which had left her in mental agony - seething, furious and powerless - for three days. When David had left Ruth on Good Friday morning he had been loving and attentive - hinting at marriage and promising to return that evening to spend Easter weekend with her. Instead he went into hiding at a friend's house. Ruth guessed where he was and repeatedly attempted to contact him during the weekend by phone and by calling at the house. David however, refused all contact, and would not even come out to return her key. She suffered the additional humiliation of being removed from outside the house by police officers, who had been called by David's hosts. The shooting took place only 10 days after she had suffered a miscarriage following one of David's beatings.[472]

The Trial of Ruth Ellis - The Prosecution

> All eyes turned to the wooden dock as she entered. Many of the public were surprised at what they saw. Instead of a dejected young woman, tired-looking, sombre, and about to stand trial for her life,

[468]Ruth Ellis's biography is outlined in Marks & Van den Bergh (1990); Hancock (1989) and Goodman & Pringle (1974). See also Ellis 1996:47 and Ballinger, A. (1996) 'The Guilt of the Innocent and the Innocence of the Guilty: The cases of Marie Fahmy and Ruth Ellis' in Myers, A. & Wight, S. (eds) (1996) *No Angels* Pandora, London p.12.

[469]Bardsley, B. (1987) *Flowers in Hell* Pandora, London p.139.

[470]Goodman & Pringle 1974:106; 107; Healey, T. (1985) *Crimes of Passion* Hamlyn, London p.34.

[471]DPP2/2430 23271 Trial transcript. Evidence of Ruth Ellis p.45.

[472]DPP2/2430 23271 Trial transcript. Evidence of Ruth Ellis p.45.

she looked like she was attending the premiere of a West End show.[473]

With her newly dyed hair, smart suit and stilettos Ruth made no attempt to activate the discourses of victimhood by looking meek or pathetic, but instead appeared confident and glamorous - "like a film-star." Moreover, rather than signalling sorrow or remorse "she was cool, proud and self-possessed."[474] Thus, Ruth's deviance and dangerousness - already firmly established as a result of her masculine murder method and her blatant disregard for social conventions - was further reinforced by her presentation of herself during the trial, where she failed to show either remorse or 'appropriate' feminine emotions such as tearfulness, nervousness or hysteria. Her appearance, coupled with her attitude, simply did "not match the line of her defence" of provocation but instead ensured the jury felt neither compassion nor sympathy for her.[475] Moreover, just as courts have shown reluctance to accept the rape of prostitutes,[476] so there was reluctance to accept that a sexually experienced, 'immoral' woman could suffer provocation equal to that of an 'innocent' woman:

> Her crime was not that of a sexual innocent suddenly discovering man's inhumanity to woman. It seemed like the vengeance of a cool sophisticate, proud of her lone act of savagery.[477]

The struggle to reconcile Ruth's femininity with what appeared to be a rational determination to seek out her lover for the sole purpose of killing him was encapsulated in this newspaper comment:

> It [the murder] was committed by a woman certainly; but a woman capable of such a crime can hardly expect the leniency traditionally given to her sex.[478]

In short, her composure and calmness were interpreted overwhelmingly in negative terms - confirmation of her dangerousness as a cold, calculating and ruthless killer:

---

[473]Marks & Van den Bergh 1990:134.

[474]Goodman & Pringle 1974:50; 51.

[475]Birch, H. 'Twice unnatural creatures' in *New Statesman* 18th March 1988:25.

[476]Lord Chief Justice Bingham's recent comment that "prostitutes were as much entitled to the protection of the law as anyone else" suggests that the rape of prostitutes is finally being taken seriously - at least in theory (*The Guardian* 22nd January 1997).

[477]*Sunday People* 2nd December 1973.

[478]*Daily Telegraph* (editorial) 14th July 1955.

Ruth describes the shooting of the man with whom she has been living, like a male motorist reporting the running down of a stray dog.[479]

Moreover, Ruth made no attempt to excuse her violent act, but instead set out "to prove that she had been morally justified in killing David" - that he had *deserved* to be shot because of his treatment of her.[480] It was this attitude - this refusal to be sorry - combined with what was considered her sexually provocative conduct, which guaranteed she would fit into the stereotypical mould of a dangerous - and in the event - lethal *femme fatale*.[481] In turn this image, together with the circumstances of the murder, ensured the case came to be regarded as 'open and shut'. Unlike the cases discussed previously, this case did not rely on circumstantial evidence. Ruth had shot David in full public view and never attempted to deny this. Indeed after her arrest she specifically stated:

When I put the gun in my bag I intended to find David and shoot him.[482]

Not only did she freely admit her intention to kill David which alone was enough to send her to the gallows, she made no attempt to excuse the killing by presenting it as a *crime passionel* but instead described it in terms which suggested a cold-blooded assassination:

He turned and saw me and then turned away from me and I took the gun from my bag and I shot him. He turned round and ran a few steps round the car. I thought I had missed him so I fired again. He was still running and I fired a third shot.[483]

Her intention to shoot to kill was further confirmed by the pathologist who testified that one bullet "had been fired at a distance less than 3 inches."[484] Her trial was thus perceived to be a mere formality - the 'facts' speaking for themselves and the outcome a foregone conclusion - as can be gathered from the opening statement by the prosecutor, who after only 20 lines of outlining the case told the jury:

---

[479]Hancock 1989:14.

[480]Goodman & Pringle 1974:42.

[481]See for example *News of the World* 8th October 1972 p.10 which describes Ruth as 'experienced', 'worldly, and 'sexually provocative.'

[482]CRIM 1/2582, Exhibit 10. This file is not available for public inspection but access to it may be gained by contacting Mr Manu, Supreme Court Unit Manager, Royal Courts of Justice, London WC2A 2LL.

[483]CRIM 1/2582, Exhibit 10 - Statement by Ruth Ellis after her arrest.

[484]DPP2/2430 23271 Evidence of Lewis Charles Nickolls p.22

That, in a very few words, is the case for the Crown, and nothing else I say to you in however much detail will add to the stark simplicity of that story.[485]

The implication was that Ruth's guilt was *obvious* as can be seen from his repetition of the *'stark simplicity'* of the case as he concluded his opening speech:

Members of the Jury, there in its stark simplicity is the case for the Crown, and whatever be the background and whatever may have been in her mind up to the time when she took that gun, if you have no doubt that she took that gun with the sole purpose of finding and shooting David Blakely and that she then shot him dead, in my submission to you, subject to my Lord's ruling in law, the only verdict is wilful murder.[486]

If the jury still harboured doubts about her guilt the prosecution's emphasis on her immorality in the opening speech may have assisted them in reaching a decision:

In a word, the story which you are going to hear outlined is this, that in 1954 and 1955 she was having simultaneous love affairs with two men, one of whom was the deceased and the other a man called Cussen ... It would seem that Blakely ... was trying to break off the connection. It would seem that the accused woman was angry at the thought that he should leave her, even although she had another lover at the time. She therefore took a gun which she knew to be fully loaded which she put in her bag. She says in a statement ... : "When I put the gun in my bag I intended to find David and shoot him." She found David and she shot him then by emptying that revolver at him ...[487]

The above paragraph was to become the essence of the dominant truth about Ruth throughout the trial, and was never seriously challenged, even by the defence. In this uncomplicated version of the truth Ruth was portrayed as "the epitome of the 'jealous tart'" who unreasonably and unjustifiably gunned down her lover in cold blood.[488] Moreover, issues such as Ruth's relationship with Desmond Cussen which the prosecution considered to be irrelevant to the murder but which emphasised her immorality, were emphasised. The prosecution further alleged "she was living ... with both men" [David and Desmond] simultaneously, and termed

---

[485]DPP2/2430 23271 Opening speech by prosecutor Christmas Humphreys p.2.
[486]DPP2/2430 23271 Opening speech by prosecutor Humphreys pp.6-7.
[487]DPP2/2430 23271 Opening speech by prosecutor Humphreys p.2.
[488]Bardsley, B. (1987) *Flowers in Hell* Pandora, London p.140.

Desmond "her alternative lover."[489] Reinforcing the discourses that Ruth was a 'loose' woman who lacked moral standards, prosecutor Christmas Humphreys commented:

> At some date, I think early in March, *not that it matters very much*, her decree absolute came through. But ... you are not here in the least concerned with adultery or any sexual misconduct. You are not trying this woman for immorality, but for murder ...[490]

The implication was that Ruth's decree absolute 'did not matter' because she was the 'kind' of woman who slept with other men, regardless of her marital status. Moreover, by instructing the jury to ignore Ruth's immorality and adultery, Humphreys achieved exactly the opposite by drawing attention to it. The fact she and David had lived together was freely described by Ruth and never disputed in court, yet their sexual relationship received constant attention from the prosecution as when Humphreys questioned their landlady:

> During the course of your duties did you take tea to their room and find them occupying the same bed?[491]

Similarly, Humphreys informed the jury "it will be proved that she and Blakely occupied the same room" in a hotel while away for a weekend, another fact never in dispute.[492] Thus, while the prosecutor claimed Ruth's immorality was not an issue for the jury's consideration, he nevertheless emphasised it whenever the opportunity arose.

The Defence

Defence counsel Melford Stevenson barely attempted to challenge the Crown's version of the truth about the case; instead he reinforced it, telling the jury:

> ... the Prosecution's story which has been described as one of stark simplicity, as indeed it is, passes without any challenge or question from those who are concerned to advance the defence.[493]

While the Crown had called 16 witnesses - some of them for no other apparent reason than to 'prove' Ruth and David had shared a bed - the defence called just two, one being Ruth herself. Against her wishes she had been

[489]DPP2/2430 23271 Opening speech by prosecutor Humphreys p.2; p.3.
[490]DPP2/2430 23271 Opening speech by prosecutor Humphreys p.3. My emphasis.
[491]DPP2/2430 23271 Evidence of Joan Winstanley p.9.
[492]DPP2/2430 23271 Opening speech by prosecutor Humphreys p.3.
[493]DPP2/2430 23271 Opening address by Melford Stevenson p.31.

persuaded to plead not guilty on the grounds of provocation.[494] Her evidence did nothing to improve her status as an immoral woman, but confirmed her casual attitude towards sexual relationships and disregard for her marriage vows. Thus, she agreed that while still married, she allowed David to move in with her and become her lover. Yet when asked if she was "very much in love with him", she replied: "Not really."[495] Here, she demonstrated not only her willingness to commit adultery, but also that her attitude to sex was so casual she did not even require the basic ingredient of being "in love" prior to sexual intimacy. Her immorality and vindictiveness were further confirmed during questioning about her affair with Desmond Cussen:

> Why did you ... [have the affair]?
> *Well, David had gone to Le Mans motor racing, and he was away a long time. He should have been back some considerable time before he did arrive back. He stayed away longer than he should have done.*
> ....
> When you had that affair with Cussen, what did you hope or think would happen to your association with Blakely?
> *I thought it might finish it; I thought that Desmond would tell David we had been intimate ...*[496]

Not only was Ruth so faithless and disloyal that she immediately took a lover when her partner failed to return on time, she also appeared to use sex to manipulate his feelings for her, an emotion which - as noted in earlier case-studies - carries special significance in relationships between the 'older woman' and her 'young lover' as was the case between Ruth and David. Furthermore, when Ruth was offered the chance to become 'respectable' when David proposed after discovering she was pregnant, she refused:

> *... he offered to marry me, and he said it seemed unnecessary for me to get rid of the child, but I did not want to take advantage of him.*
> When he offered to marry you, what did you say to that? How did you take it?
> *I was not really in love with him at that time, and it was quite unnecessary to marry me, I thought. I could get out of the mess quite easily.*[497]

In the social climate of the 1950s the jury may well have thought Ruth - a "brassy blonde" - ought to be grateful to David - an upper-middle

---

[494]When her advocate at the committal proceedings, Sir Sebag Shaw entered a plea of not guilty, Ruth "was very angry with him" and proclaimed her guilt stating: "I killed him, and I've got to die for it" (quoted in Goodman & Pringle 1974:48).
[495]DPP2/2430 23271 Evidence of Ruth Ellis p.34.
[496]DPP2/2430 23271 Evidence of Ruth Ellis p.36.
[497]DPP2/2430 23271 Evidence of Ruth Ellis p.34.

class person - for the offer of marriage.[498] Yet, thwarting social expectations as ever, she did not appear interested in becoming 'respectable'. Worse still, her response suggested an off-hand - even callous - attitude towards motherhood. Not only did Ruth describe the foetus as 'the mess', she also apparently preferred abortion to marriage and motherhood, an attitude which would have done nothing to endear her to the jury during an era where abortion was illegal and concern about the nuclear family had reached the level of a moral panic. Yet, apparently unperturbed, the defence QC continued this line of questioning until Ruth revealed she did in fact "get out of the trouble by [her]self" when she had an abortion in 1954.[499] Stevenson's inappropriate questioning led Hancock to comment:

> Neither her answers nor Mr Stevenson's questions made her early association with David in the least human ... He could have stressed that the first abortion she had was her attempt not to involve a young man of good family, who was engaged to be married, in an unpleasant dilemma which might provoke a damaging scandal. Instead all he got from Ruth was matter-of-fact answers which dealt with the abortion as casually as a woman might discuss whether she should have the green, or green-patterned, carpet in the front room.[500]

The defence's line of questioning also resulted in Ruth revealing her decision to give up her baby daughter to her alcoholic husband without a struggle:

> ... *I wanted a divorce, and I decided to not claim any maintenance or defend myself in any way and also give my husband my daughter.*
> Did you do that?
> *I did that on the ground I was going to marry David, or so I thought.*[501]

In sharp contrast to the ideal mother who is driven by maternal instincts and therefore loving and altruistic - always putting the interests of her children before her own - Ruth had not only had an abortion but had also voluntarily given up her baby to a highly unsuitable parent in order to secure more free time with her lover.

The second and last defence witness was psychologist Duncan Whittaker. Once again, it was the defence's questions, rather than the prosecution's, which led to confirmation of Ruth as a 'bad' mother:

---

[498]Goodman & Pringle 1974:57.
[499]DPP2/2430 23271 Evidence of Ruth Ellis pp.34-5.
[500]Hancock 1989:158.
[501]DPP2/2430 23271 Evidence of Ruth Ellis p.38.

Did you ask her any questions with a view to finding out whether she considered the consequences of what she was doing.
I asked her if she thought about her children. She said she did not think of them at all.[502]

The defence had thus reinforced the already existing image of Ruth Ellis as an immoral woman, as well as contributed new information which - in addition - revealed her to be a bad mother and an abortionist. Yet, worse was to come, for while the defence was constructed on the grounds of provocation, the actual effort to prove such behaviour was half-hearted and feeble if not outright negligent. Of the 16 witnesses called by the prosecution, Melford Stevenson cross-examined only two. The first was Anthony Findlater with whom David had been staying prior to the shooting. Ruth was convinced he and his wife Carole had been conspiring to separate her from David and held them partly responsible, not only for his failure to return to her, but also for the shooting itself. This was because of her belief that the Findlaters 'tempted' David with their nanny, in order to hasten the end of his relationship with Ruth. This belief was supported by her claim that when she had kept vigil outside the Findlaters' house, she had observed David and 'the nanny' embracing and giggling - events which caused an intense state of jealousy, which in turn, contributed to her decision to shoot him.[503] She communicated her belief to the defence counsel "that they had deliberately and repeatedly lied to her over David's whereabouts over the Easter weekend, and that they had from the outset, intended to ostracise her from David's friends."[504] Indeed it was not disputed that the Findlaters had played an important role in denying Ruth access to David, had repeatedly hung up on her when she phoned and had called the police when she remained outside their house hoping to speak to him. Yet, Stevenson did not call Carole Findlater, an important witness to the motive of provocation as she could have helped to establish that "Ruth was deliberately fobbed off with a pack of lies all over the Easter weekend and that she became more and more hysterically out of control as her every phone call was refused."[505] Moreover, Carole herself had had an affair with David, just the kind of behaviour which would help to establish a motive of provocation.[506]

Anthony Findlater's cross-examination took a most cursory form with him repeatedly claiming he could not remember events of the Easter weekend despite having appeared as a witness for the Crown in the Magistrates' Court

---

[502]DPP2/2430 23271 Evidence of Duncan Whittaker p.60. Hancock wrote of Ruth's atttitude to motherhood: "In times of upset and disaster a mother's immediate thoughts go to her children. It was only while her statement was being taken down that this woman casually disclosed that she had a son" (Hancock 1989:14).
[503]See for example Hancock 1989:154.
[504]Ellis 1996:177.
[505]Ellis 1996:187.
[506]Hancock 1989:55.

only one week after the shooting.[507] He also denied Ruth had appeared to be "in a considerable emotional disturbance", despite having witnessed her - in a fit of temper and frustration - pushing in the windows of David's car, parked outside his home.[508] Since Findlater claimed not to remember or know about David's friendship with 'the nanny', we might expect her to have been called for the defence. Instead, she was not even identified by name. So inept and half-hearted was Stevenson's attempt to establish reasonable grounds for Ruth's jealousy that *the prosecutor* Mr Humphreys explained to Findlater what Stevenson was attempting to say:

> You will appreciate what is being suggested, that here is some reason for Ruth Ellis being jealous by some reason of some new woman being on the stage.
> *I did not even know that Mrs Ellis knew we had a Nannie. She knew we had one, but this one was quite a new one.*
> What my friend is putting is that Ruth Ellis in hanging about might have seen Blakely in the presence of an entirely new young woman. I am sure you will help if you can if you were fooling about or anything of that sort. Was there any incident with a young woman outside the house that you can remember?[509]

We can only speculate whether Mr Humphreys' sense of 'fair play' was so offended that he decided to intervene. This was the interpretation of one author and observer of the trial who commented: "Perhaps Mr Humphreys felt Mrs Ellis was being unnecessarily deprived of legal assistance."[510] Whatever his reasoning, he deserves credit for this gallant attempt to establish jealousy as a mitigating circumstance to the murder, a task which ought to have been performed by Mr Stevenson.

The second of the two people to be cross-examined by the defence was Desmond Cussen whom the prosecutor had called Ruth's "alternative lover".[511] Like George Ellis and David Blakely, Desmond Cussen had been a customer in the club where Ruth worked. Unlike George and David, Desmond never committed violence against Ruth.[512] While Ruth remained committed to her relationship with David, she maintained her friendship with Desmond who appeared to be her only source of emotional and financial support during her last weeks of freedom when she became increasingly traumatised by David's behaviour. He had witnessed David's treatment of Ruth on several occasions and had defended her when David became physically violent. In establishing a defence of provocation, it would seem

---

[507] See for example Hancock 1989:138.

[508] DPP2/2430 23371 Evidence of Anthony Findlater pp.15-18.

[509] DPP2/2430 23271 Humphreys re-examining Anthony Findlater p.19.

[510] Hancock 1989:154.

[511] DPP2/2430 23271 Opening speech for the prosecution p.3.

[512] He had repeatedly proposed marriage to Ruth and assisted her financially, for example by paying her son's school fees.

essential to highlight evidence of such behaviour. Yet Stevenson neither referred to David's boorish and violent behaviour nor asked who had been responsible for Ruth's injuries:

> Have you ever seen any marks or bruises on her?
> *Yes.*
> How often?
> *On several occasions.*
> Have you sometimes helped her to disguise them with make-up and that sort of thing?
> *Yes. ...*
> Did you help to disguise bruises on her shoulders?
> *Yes.*
> Were they bad bruises?
> *Yes. ...*
> I do not want to press you for details, but how often have you seen that sort of mark on her?
> *It must be on half a dozen occasions.*
> Did you on one occasion take her to Middlesex Hospital?
> *Yes, I did.*
> Why was that?
> *She came back when she was staying at my flat, and when I arrived back I found her in a very bad condition.*
> In what respect?
> *She had definitely been very badly bruised all over the body.*
> And did she receive treatment for that condition at Middlesex Hospital.
> *Yes.*[513]

The cross-examination was thus concluded, without reference to who might have inflicted these injuries, an omission which led two commentators to conclude that defence counsel appeared "more concerned with her treatment at the hospital ... than her treatment at the hands of Blakely.[514] Thus, despite having put forward a defence of provocation, Stevenson made the extraordinary statement that he did not want to "press for details" - the very information which would have been crucial in establishing this type of defence. He also failed to call on the evidence of staff at Middlesex Hospital who had treated the injuries.[515]

---

[513]DPP2/2430 23271. Cross-examination of Desmond Cussen by defence QC p.12.

[514]Marks & Van den Bergh 1990:140.

[515]For example Dr Robert Hunter Hill who had noted "multiple bruises on both arms and legs, the left hip, and around the left eye ... [and] a more severe bruise over her left ankle", asked what had been the cause of the injuries. Ruth replied "that she had been beaten up by a friend who was a racing driver" (Goodman & Pringle 1974:24-5).

The jury was not further enlightened by Ruth's evidence for while she revealed David "was violent on occasions" she immediately added "he *only* used to hit me with his fists and hands, but I bruise very easily", a statement which implied the violence was of little consequence, perhaps even caused by Ruth's skin texture.[516] Moreover, David's violent outbursts were - in his words - caused by Ruth "tarting round the bar" where she worked which made him "very jealous".[517] As discussed in Chapter Three, this type of violence has been widely justified by men who consider it not only their responsibility but their *duty* to keep their women in check.

Ruth raised the issue of violence again when, describing the latter stages of their relationship, she said that "instead of being jealous of the 'bar', he was being jealous of Desmond":

> What did he do to you?
> *He used to hit me.*[518]

Stevenson did not ask for elaboration. Yet, despite his reluctance to "press for details", Ruth testified that ten days prior to his murder, "David got very, very violent" and punched her in the stomach, an act which was "followed by a miscarriage."[519]

The two most common causes of provocation - violence and unfaithfulness - were both present in this case. Yet, when the second issue - unfaithfulness - was raised, Stevenson was equally reluctant to "press for details":

> ... did you have occasion to complain to Blakely about his conduct with any other women. *I do not want you to mention any names, but did you?*[520]

Here was a second opportunity to prove the intense jealousy Ruth had justifiably felt, and which Stevenson had failed to uncover in his cross-examination of Findlater; yet he merely hinted at David's unfaithfulness and repeatedly refused to secure proper evidence of such provocative behaviour:

> Again I do not want to mention any names, but ... was some [sic] some trouble about a young woman?

---

[516]DPP2/2430 23271 Evidence of Ruth Ellis p.39. My emphasis. See also Kelly, L. & Radford, J. (1990) '"Nothing really happened": the invalidation of women's experiences of sexual violence' in Hester, M, Kelly, L. & Radford, J. (eds) (1996) *Women, Violence and Male Power* Open University Press, Milton Keynes, where they argue "that as women we tend, and indeed are systematically encouraged, to minimize the violence that we experience from men" (p.19).

[517]DPP2/2430 23271 Evidence of Ruth Ellis p.39.

[518]DPP2/2430 23271 Evidence of Ruth Ellis p.42.

[519]DPP2/2430 23271 Evidence of Ruth Ellis p.45.

[520]DPP2/2430 23271 Stevenson questioning Ruth Ellis p.43. My emphasis.

Yes.
And again without mentioning names was that a woman down at Penn or Beaconsfield?
Yes.[521]

Mr Stevenson's desire to show tact and remain a 'gentleman' seems rather extreme. Given that his client's life was at stake it would have been more appropriate to call these various women to give evidence for the defence rather than concerning himself with protecting their 'reputation'. Moreover, apart from adding to the inadequacy of Ruth's defence, Stevenson's failure to secure evidence of David's numerous affairs provides a blatant example of the double standards of morality discussed in Chapter Three. David's sexual conduct was far more 'immoral' than Ruth's. Apart from living with Ruth, he was engaged to Linda Dawson, a woman from his own class background.[522] He was also having an affair with "a married woman" in his home town. Like "the nanny" with whom David was alleged to be having an affair simultaneously, "the married woman" remained nameless, and was never called to give evidence.[523] It is not known how many women he had affairs with, however, "when he was working ... at the hotel, David was wonderfully placed to exploit his charm in return for free meals and drinks."[524] When Ruth was engaged in identical work as a hostess, she was called a prostitute. David's behaviour however, was considered to be that of a 'play-boy'.[525] The fact than none of the above women were called to give evidence of his promiscuous and faithless character illustrates how the discourses around the double standards of morality, combined with the discourses around social class generated two results. First, David's status as a victim remained intact. Second, the other women with whom he had had affairs were considered entitled to protection from moral scrutiny, a privilege never extended to Ruth, for apart from being a 'tart' she was also a lower class woman, and thus stood utterly alone against David and his friends and lovers who, without exception, came from a higher social class.[526] This isolation was compounded by the defence team's failure to call the evidence of women from a similar class background to Ruth's. For example other waitresses in the club had witnessed David's boorish and violent behaviour "and could have indicated the stresses and strains endemic in the relationship as well as his

---

[521]DPP2/2430 23271 Stevenson questioning Ruth Ellis p.44.
[522]See for example Hancock 1989:57; Ellis 1996:69.
[523]Farran 1988:42.
[524]Hancock 1989:51. See also Marks & Van den Bergh 1990:188 who wrote: "David was a conceited braggart, living off women and afraid of facing up to the scenes his behaviour inevitably provoked."
[525]See for example Hancock 1989:80.
[526]Farran 1988:85 writes of Linda Dawson, 'the married woman' and 'the nanny': "All three would have been of a different and 'better' class than Ruth Ellis, and there might have been a general reluctance to 'bring shame' on 'respectable' women by calling them."

general attitude and behaviour."[527] As no explanation was offered as to why such witnesses were not called we can only speculate that Ruth's defence team shared the 'culpability' discourse outlined in Chapter Three that women who "tart around bars" are partly responsible for the violence directed against them.[528] From the perspective of this discourse Ruth's failure to police her behaviour in the public sphere legitimised David's violence and provides an example of a man disciplining his 'out of control' or 'uppity' partner.

In sum, the two most common causes of provocation - violence and unfaithfulness - could be found in abundance within Ruth and David's relationship, yet defence counsel made no serious effort to prove either and called no witnesses to support Ruth's testimony about this behaviour. Furthermore, there was "astonishingly little examination of such crucial events as to where and how the intent to kill was formed."[529] Ruth's statement that she "had a peculiar idea [she] wanted to kill David",[530] was simply accepted at face-value, and was never problematized - for example - by linking it to the amount of mental and physical abuse she had suffered, or her mental state following the miscarriage. After close inspection of the trial transcript we cannot fail to agree with Georgie Ellis who, 40 years after her mother's execution wrote of her defence:

> The harm that David Blakely inflicted upon my mother had been but peripherally touched upon and thinly portrayed. Thereafter it had been glossed over by a parade of almost irrelevant trivia that had nothing to do with Ruth's state of mind, nor with that which had driven her to exterminate her perfidious lover.[531]

The only possible excuse for the defence's conduct was that Ruth herself grossly understated her suffering:

> As Ruth stepped down from the witness-box, the jury knew nothing of her background whatsoever. She had deliberately suppressed her hardships, her early poverty, the fact that Andy was illegitimate ... the entire gamut of circumstances that might have incited some degree of sympathetic consideration from the twelve members of the jury.[532]

We are thus left with the question: why did Ruth's defence team not argue her case with more vigour? Why did the defence team not question the mental state of a woman - not yet 30 - who appeared to be totally indifferent

---

[527]Farran 1988:87; Ellis 1996:94.

[528]As noted earlier, this was how David himself both excused and explained his violence against Ruth.

[529]Farran 1988:43.

[530]Quoted in Farran 1988:43.

[531]Ellis 1996:189.

[532]Ellis 1996:187.

to her fate and made no effort whatsoever to save herself, but instead told her junior counsel:

> You will make certain, won't you ... that I shall be hanged? That is the only way that I can join him [David].533

In Chapter One I argued that women who refuse to demonstrate commitment to the conventional female role - particularly in the areas of sexuality, respectability, domesticity and motherhood - may become victims of judicial misogyny. In this case-study I have argued that concern about women's conduct in these four areas was especially intense during the 1950s, as the apparent breakdown of family values and moral decay was responded to by an increase in surveillance, regulation and control of women. The overwhelmingly male-dominated legal establishment did not (and does not) operate in an ideological vacuum but was an integral part of a culture which believed that increased regulation and surveillance of women should form a key aspect of the strategy for stemming the tide of moral decay. Mr Stevenson's superficial style of cross-examination can thus be placed within the context of an era stifled by snobbery and respectability which helps to explain why he called Ruth's story "sordid"534 and appeared to be more concerned with "unnecessary mud-slinging" than with saving her life.535 Even 27 years later after several commentators had questioned the justice of her sentence, Stevenson, when asked if justice was done when Ruth was hanged, replied: "I'm afraid it was. But may I in justice to her say how I revere her memory. She was a splendid girl."536 Rather than exposing the cruelty and violence David had inflicted on her, which might have secured a recommendation for mercy, his concern was with upholding the manners and propriety of his class as when he told the court "it is always an unpleasant thing to say anything disagreeable about someone who is dead."537 After all, David was a member of the upper-middle class like Stevenson himself, while Ruth was a "brassy ... blonde tart" whose attempts to 'better' herself had been regarded with contempt by various commentators prior to the trial.538 In the words of one observer:

533Rawlinson, P. (1989) *A Price Too High* Weidenfeld and Nicolson, London p.61. Despite being the junior counsel for the defence in what was arguably the most notorious murder trial of the 1950s, Sir Peter Rawlinson who was to be appointed Attorney-General in 1970, failed to remember the correct date of Ruth Ellis's execution in his autobiography and wrote she was hanged on 12th July 1955.
534DPP2/2430 23271 Mr Stevenson's opening speech for the defence p.32.
535Stevenson quoted in Hancock 1989:152.
536Sir Melford Stevenson quoted in *Sunday Telegraph* 21st March 1982.
537DPP2/2430 23271 Mr Stevenson's opening speech for the defence p.32.
538Marks & Van den Bergh 1990:134; *The Daily Mail* 22nd April 1955 quoted in Bardsley 1987:140. *The Mail* reported that despite taking elocution lessons "she failed to rid herself of a Manchester accent ... every turn failed, for Blakely was still ashamed of her."

> Again and again Mr Stevenson threw away points ... [which] could have won the jury's sympathy... [because] he appeared to have decided that it was best not to probe the unconventional half-drunk world of Ruth Ellis, or to get behind the 'hostess front' and release to the Court the self-love, jealousy and ambition that was really her.[539]

Ruth fitted the criteria for the 'type' of person responsible for the apparent breakdown of clearly defined class barriers. Her existence and 'visibility' exposed the hypocrisy of a culture which, simultaneously emphasised morality and family values, yet also accommodated the desire of men from the 'respectable' classes, to spend time with women like Ruth in daytime drinking clubs.[540] Gone were the days when an 'unsuitable' relationship could be resolved by a 'gentleman' marrying someone from his own class-background whilst satisfying his less respectable urges by maintaining a mistress.[541] Instead of accepting her place as David's mistress, Ruth was an 'uppity' woman demanding full acknowledgement as David's wife. As such she can be seen to exemplify the shift in 'visibility' of the 'immoral' woman discussed above - an aspect which added yet further reinforcement to her dangerousness.

Apart from disobeying the code relating to social class, that of 'knowing your place', Ruth had also repeatedly disobeyed the gender code of conduct. During her trial she failed to display signs of emotional upset, redemption or remorse, or any other characteristic considered appropriate and typical of the female. Instead the judge and jury saw a woman who appeared extremely capable and rational, characteristics in keeping with the already established image of Ruth as a cool, calculating, ruthless and unemotional *femme fatale*. Most serious of all, these characteristics did not meet the requirements of Ruth's defence of provocation but instead added up to an image of dangerous womanhood. So dangerous, that no-one - including her defence counsel - appeared willing to slow down the speed with which Ruth was hurtling towards her death. Indeed no-one even questioned her adamantine wish to die - it was merely another deviant characteristic in an already deviant personality. Even Duncan Whittaker's expert testimony that "an apparent attitude of indifference or detachment ... [could be] a solution to some intolerable problem", fell on deaf ears, as Mr Justice Havers ruled a defence of provocation inadmissible.[542]

539Hancock 1989:159.

540Hancock 1989:22.

541See for example Ryan, B. with The Rt Hon Lord Havers (1989) *The Poisoned Life of Mrs Maybrick* Penguin, London p.28 which describes the case of Florence Maybrick who in 1889 stood trial for the murder of her husband James Maybrick. As well as being married with two children he also had an entire unacknowledged 'parallel' family consisting of a mistress and five children, two of whom had been born after his marriage to Florence.

542DPP2/2430 23271 Evidence of Dr Duncan Whittaker p.59.

The Judgement

In the Ethel Major case-study I discussed the impact of cumulative abuse and provocation, and the difficulties women have experienced in having this form of defence accepted in a court of law. I noted the law has been defined according to how 'the reasonable man' would act under provocation, which has resulted in the acceptance of 'heat of the moment' retaliation. A planned killing however, even after cumulative and severe provocation, is still largely regarded as a heinous act of revenge, carried out by a scheming and cunning individual. The Ellis case provides a poignant example of the history of this male-defined view of provocation. Stevenson was well aware of the difficulties facing him before a defence of provocation could be accepted. He told the judge:

> We are all very, very familiar with ... the degree of provocation which is required so far as a man is concerned ... but ... one finds ... complete silence in the authorities as to the effect of jealous conduct on the average female's mind ... I know, of course, that one of the elements of provocation is the question whether or not in the particular case there is a reasonable interval between the provocation arising and the act of which complaint is made to allow for cooling of the passion.[543]

Mr Stevenson attempted to introduce the notion of cumulative provocation by reminding Mr Justice Havers:

> Repeatedly during the time that she was in this state of emotional tension about him he went off and consorted with other women; marks upon his body which indicated a love affair with another woman were observed by her from time to time while he received financial support, clothes, food, and other advantages from her.[544]

It was within this context that "provocation derived from jealousy, provocation derived from emotional pressure ... had caused her immense suffering over a long period of time."[545]

Even Mr Humphreys, the prosecutor, agreed she had been provoked beyond the tolerance level of the 'reasonable' human being:

> ... I accept fully that there is evidence before the jury that this woman was disgracefully treated by the man who died, and I accept my learned friend's proposition that it would tend to lead her into an

---

[543]DPP2/2430 23271 Mr Stevenson to Mr Justice Havers pp.62-3.
[544]DPP2/2430 23271 Mr Stevenson to Mr Justice Havers p.63.
[545]DPP2/2430 23271 Mr Stevenson to Mr Justice Havers p.63.

intensely emotional condition, even as that hypothetical person 'the ordinary reasonable human being' ...[546]

It was to no avail. Mr Justice Havers maintained "the whole doctrine relating to provocation depends on the fact that it causes or may cause a sudden and temporary loss of self-control."[547] Neither judge nor defence QC had been able to find a precedent concerning how a 'reasonable woman' might act in the face of severe provocation. Ruth Ellis, like Ethel Major and countless others before and after her, therefore had to be judged according to how the 'reasonable man' would act. Hence, Havers directed the jury "that the evidence in this case does not support a verdict of manslaughter on the grounds of provocation."[548] Mr Stevenson's defence of provocation which had been argued half-heartedly throughout the defence, had thus collapsed completely, as the jury was told that manslaughter on the grounds of provocation was no longer an option. With the judge's ruling Melford Stevenson gave up any pretence of defending Ruth, and announced to the jury that there would be no closing speech on behalf of the defendant since such a speech would invite "the jury to disregard your Lordship's ruling ..."[549] The omission of a closing speech on behalf of the defence resulted in the judge commencing his summing up immediately after Ruth had made a particularly damaging reply. In what has been described as "the shortest cross-examination in a murder trial in the records of Number One Court", Humphreys asked Ruth just one question:

---

[546]DPP2/2430 23271 Mr Humphreys to Mr Justice Havers p.69.

[547]DPP2/2430 23271 Mr Justice Havers to Mr Stevenson p.68.

[548]DPP2/2430 23271 Mr Justice Havers to the jury p.71. Arthur Koestler would not have been surprised by Justice Havers' ruling for while he acknowledged "there always existed humane judges", he also maintained that "as a body, the judges of England have, as far as historical evidence goes, at every crucial juncture exerted their influence in favour of maximum severity as against any humanitarian reform." With specific reference to the concept of precedent, Koestler wrote in 1956, the year following Ruth Ellis's execution: "Their judgments are preserved as records, and 'it is an established rule to abide by former precedents ... The extraordinary deference paid to precedents is the source of the most striking peculiarities of the English Common Law.' ... Since precedent must be their only guidance, by the very nature of their calling [judges] had their minds riveted on the past. They not only administered the law; they made it" (Koestler, A. (1956) *Reflections on Hanging* Victor Gollancz, London pp.27; 28). Cases such as those of Sara Thornton, Emma Humphries and Kiranjit Ahluwalia lend credence to Koestler's contentions, since more than 40 years after Ellis's execution, the issues of cumulative provocation and 'delayed' rather than 'heat of the moment' retaliation to such provocation remain highly controversial. For further discussion on this subject see Edwards (1989); Ballinger (1995); Stanko & Scully (1995).

[549]DPP2/2430 23271. Mr Stevenson's reply to Mr Justice Havers' ruling p.72.

Mrs Ellis, when you fired that revolver at close range into the body of David Blakely, what did you intend to do?
It is obvious that when I shot him I intended to kill him.[550]

With this answer Ruth had practically convicted herself but the judge nonetheless ensured the jury was partial to his personal opinion before he commenced dealing with the evidence for the defence:

> ... even if you accept every word of it, it does not seem to me that it establishes any sort of defence to the charge of murder.[551]

Mr Justice Havers ended his summing up by dismissing the evidence of the only witness for the defence apart from Ruth herself, Duncan Whittaker, claiming it had "no relevance in this case," before telling the jury:

> According to our law ... it is no defence for a woman who is charged with murder of her lover to prove that she was a jealous woman and had been badly treated by her lover and was in ill-health and, after her lover promised to spend the Easter holidays with her, he left her without any warning and refused to communicate with her, or that he spent holidays with his friend or in the company of another woman, or if he was committing misconduct with another woman, and that as a result of that she became furious with him and emotionally upset and formed an intention to kill him which she could not control. None of these facts individually afford any defence, nor do they all collectively afford any defence.[552]

This quote illustrates how - after dismissing a defence of provocation - Havers took the liberty of rewriting the events which had been utilised to demonstrate this behaviour. For example, being "badly treated" became a synonym for mental cruelty and physical violence, and "ill-health" became a synonym for suffering a miscarriage after a beating from the baby's father. We may assume this verbal sanitising of the evidence helped the jury to reach the verdict for it took only 14 minutes to find Ruth guilty. According to one juror, even that short time was not devoted to discussing the evidence:

> ... the thing that sticks out in my mind was that the others were going backwards and forwards to the toilet.[553]

---

[550]DPP2/2430 2371 Trial transcript p.58.
[551]DPP2/2430 23271 Judge Havers' summing up p.81.
[552]DPP2/2430 23271 Judge Havers' summing up p.87.
[553]Quoted in Marks & Van den Bergh 1990:162 who interviewed this juror. In several publications the jury was reported to have been out for 23 minutes. It is recorded in the court transcript however that the jury retired at 11.52am and returned

While some may question the integrity of a jury who could spare only 14 minutes on deciding whether a woman should live or die, others may argue the judge had already decided the verdict when he refused to accept a verdict of manslaughter on the grounds of provocation, hence there was really nothing to discuss as noted by one jury member:

> The fact was the judge didn't direct us towards leniency ... There was really nothing to argue about. I mean, it was Mrs Ellis, herself, who admitted she meant to kill him.[554]

When Ruth was asked if she had anything to say in response to her sentence she did not reply. Her case had remained 'open and shut' from beginning to end.

An Alternative Truth

In this final section I take issue with the dominant truth about Ruth Ellis as a cool, calculating, rational killer carrying out premeditated murder in cold blood. I shall argue, that far from being the lone, vengeful *femme fatale* portrayed in the popular press, Ruth had an accomplice who played a far more active role in the murder than, for example, Edith Thompson had done as Freddy Bywaters' supposed accomplice. However, while Edith paid with her life, Ruth's *male* accomplice was simply ignored despite the authorities' knowledge of his activities. While this book would not wish to argue in favour of a male victim equivalent to Edith Thompson, the comparison nevertheless reinforces the gendered nature of punishment.

Ruth had told the jury about the three days leading up to the shooting - how she had had no sleep, had eaten little but drunk plenty of alcohol and smoked numerous cigarettes, as her pursuit of David intensified. Yet the trial generally, and the defence in particular never captured the passion, turmoil and tension endemic within the relationship which led to Ruth's increasingly desperate pursuits of David at all hours and her obsessive vigil of the house where he was staying, before the final dramatic and violent conclusion to the relationship was drawn. These were all acts which belied the idea that Ruth was cold, unemotional and above all - *rational*. However, a more accurate description of her mental state never emerged because the jury was not given the opportunity to hear the evidence of Dr Rees, Ruth's psychiatrist who had treated her for several months and who was still treating her with

---

at 12.06pm. The entire trial lasted less than a day and a half, making it the third shortest after the trials of Emily Swann and Margaret Allen.

554Quoted in Marks & Van den Bergh 1990:162. For further discussion of the verdict see Farran, D. (1988) *The Trial of Ruth Ellis* Studies in Sexual Politics, Sociology Dept, University of Manchester pp.94-98 where she argued the judge's summing up gave the impression to the jury "that there were no mitigating circumstances."

tranquillisers for "intense emotional distress" at the time of the shooting.[555] Dr Rees' partner, Dr William Sargant, later commented that the combination of tranquillisers and alcohol - the main components of Ruth's diet in the three days before the shooting - "would have made her completely without control."[556] There was therefore a long history of Ruth's troubled emotional state prior to the killing which could have been utilised by the defence as a contributory factor in her inability to deal with the deterioration of her relationship with David. At the same time it is important to note that even a more stable person may have found his behaviour highly provocative. As the relationship deteriorated so the extent of David's exploitation of Ruth increased. He contributed nothing to rent or household expenses and left Ruth to settle his bills at the bar where she worked. He took her out only if she agreed to pay all expenses. He refused to contribute to joint expenses such as hotel bills even when he had the necessary funds.[557] He employed emotional blackmail by saying he would have to sell his much loved racing car because of lack of funds. When Ruth protested he responded: "If you can find me £400 I won't need to sell it."[558] As a result of her relationship with David Ruth had lost her flat, her job, her money and her dignity:

> The woman who once had pounds to waste had six-pence in copper in her bag when she was arrested and nothing in the bank. The poverty that she had always feared was here.[559]

In addition to being increasingly humiliated by this exploitation, David's infidelities added jealousy to her already volatile mental state:

> The fires of her jealous insecurity had been continuously stoked during the last week before the murder. Whatever moments of tenderness there had been ... were obliterated by the realisation that

---

[555]Marks & Van den Bergh 1990:157. Dr Rees would have given the jury a different picture of Ruth's state of mind as he was aware that since George Ellis was at Warlingham Park Mental Hospital, being treated for alcoholism, Ruth had been taking tranquillisers. "She had not only shouted for anyone to hear at the hospital that her husband had been having an affair with a woman doctor, but had gone up and down the bus queue outside demanding to know if anyone had seen him misconducting himself at the hospital with the doctors or nurses."

[556]Quoted in Marks & Van den Bergh 1990:161.

[557]Ruth would give money to David so he could pretend to pay the bills in public. For example, he asked her for £5 to pay for a hotel room. Ruth almost immediately discovered that David was in a financial position to pay the bill himself. Typically, she understated her feelings about the incident when during the trial she said: "I just thought it was a mean way of getting money from me ..." (DPP2/2430 23271 p.46).

[558]DPP2/2430 23271 Evidence of Ruth Ellis p.48.

[559]Hancock 1989:185.

David would never marry her ... All the illusions about 'being somebody' had disappeared.[560]

Thus, far from being cool, calm and unemotional Ruth was overwrought and disturbed to the point of suffering from diminished responsibility:

I believe that Ruth Ellis shot her lover because she was temporarily insane with jealousy and humiliation, and her sense of responsibility was destroyed by alcohol.[561]

Similarly, others have argued Ruth found "herself in something like an emotional prison guarded by this young man, from which there seemed to be no escape"[562]:

It was a case where Ruth Ellis had gone through all the transports of rage and jealousy until I am quite convinced she had got into a very calm state of mind where she was in a sort of stratosphere of emotion, in which she thought everything she did was right and justified.[563]

Indeed several commentators, including Ruth's solicitor, have argued her case was a major factor in establishing the defence of diminished responsibility two years after her execution.[564] Ruth herself gave several clues to her state of mind, for example by refusing to appeal against her conviction and when she wrote: "I was in a terribly depressed state."[565] With reference to the Findlaters she said: "I don't mind hanging, but I don't see why they should get away with it."[566] When her solicitor implored her to tell the whole truth about the killing she responded: "I'll tell you ... if you promise not to use it to try and save me."[567] She asked her mother to smuggle sleeping tablets into the prison because she wished to commit suicide.[568] This determination to die as well as her continued insistence that the Findlaters were responsible for David's death ought to have caused concern about her mental state. But, as a result of Ruth's failure to articulate her femininity through dominant modes of expression - in this case by presenting herself as a

---

[560]Hancock 1989:185.

[561]Hancock 1989:184.

[562]*The Sun* 21st September 1972 quoting Mr Melford Stevenson.

[563]Ruth Ellis's solicitor Mr Bickford quoted years after the trial in Marks & Van den Bergh 1979:158. Ruth was to change her solicitor to Mr Mishcon after the trial.

[564]See for example Marks & Van den Bergh 1990:158; Ellis 1996:2.

[565]Quoted from a statement made the day before Ruth Ellis's execution in Marks & Van den Bergh 1979:205.

[566]Quoted in Hancock 1989:173.

[567]Bresler, F. (1965) *Reprieve* George Harrap, London p.247. Fenton Bresler interviewed Mr Mishcon for this book.

[568]Interview with Ruth's sister Muriel Jakubait in *Daily Express* 14th February 1985.

victim - it was not even questioned. Her failure to fulfil gender-role expectations inside the courtroom fitted only too well with her refusal to demonstrate commitment to conventional female roles in her personal life, especially within the areas most likely to give rise to judicial misogyny - sexuality, respectability, domesticity and motherhood. Instead of seeing a woman who had been repeatedly exploited, betrayed and beaten until both her judgement and responsibility became diminished the jury saw "a mechanical, unfeeling doll," ... a "hard-faced, unemotional woman [who] had been left by a man and because she was jealous, she had shot him in the back, one shot having been fired from a distance of less than three inches."[569] Because of what was 'known' about Ruth as a *woman* there was no need to problematise this 'open and shut' case. Her transgressions of the female role ensured she had become categorised as a 'bad' woman even before the killing. As had been the case with Margaret Allen, these transgressions were so severe they "threatened a crisis of sexual difference" for Ruth had indulged in liberties usually reserved for men.[570] She exercised freedom of movement - entering night-clubs when and where she pleased; she enjoyed economic independence, indeed she was occupying the traditional male role of sole provider; she had sexual relationships when and with whom she pleased without shame; she allowed other family members to take main responsibility for her children's upbringing and allowed the other parent sole custody of her daughter following her divorce - all liberties which, when engaged in by men are hardly considered liberties at all, but normal, taken-for-granted behaviour. But Ruth was 'worse' than Margaret Allen because of her outward conformity to feminine standards. Unlike Margaret whose deviance was obvious from her appearance, Ruth was 'a wolf in sheep's clothing', for she imposed all the disciplinary practices which inscribe femininity on the female body. Her carefully applied make-up, dyed hair, slenderness, smart suits and stilettos indicated acceptance of the "dominating gaze of patriarchy" as argued by Bartky.[571] Yet, underneath that exterior lurked a woman, capable of killing the perpetrator of the patriarchal gaze. Thus, her crime as well as her chosen murder method served to reinforce her dangerousness still further for they made her femininity "appear only as an outrage, as something inappropriate and out of place"[572], which in turn became one of the factors that ensured she came to experience the full force of judicial misogyny.

So far I have indicated there was a deep unwillingness to challenge the dominant truth about David Blakely's murder by those inside the courtroom (including Ruth herself). However, officials working on the case outside the courtroom also demonstrated a singular lack of interest in investigating the full details of the murder. Virtually everybody involved in the case - police officers, lawyers, jury members, defence and prosecuting counsels, even the trial judge - admitted they did not believe Ruth's story that

---

[569]Hancock 1989:159; 167.
[570]Rose, J. (1993) *Why War?* Basil Blackwell, Oxford p.50.
[571]See Chapter Three.
[572]Rose 1993:51.

she had obtained the murder weapon as security for a debt.[573] But as a result of the 'open and shut' nature of her case no effort was made to investigate how she had obtained the gun. It was not even tested for fingerprints. Only after continued pressure from her lawyer Mr Mishcon, did Ruth agree to make a new statement less than 24 hours before her execution:

> ... it is only with the greatest reluctance that I have decided to tell how it was that I got the gun with which I shot David Blakely. I did not do so before because I felt I was needlessly getting someone into possible trouble.
> I had been drinking Pernod ... in Desmond Cussen's flat and Desmond had been drinking too. We had been drinking for some time. I had been telling Desmond of Blakely's treatment of me. I was in a terribly depressed state. All I remember is that Desmond gave me a loaded gun. Desmond was jealous of Blakely as in fact Blakely was of Desmond. I would say that they hated each other. I was in such a dazed state that I cannot remember what was said. I rushed out as soon as he gave me the gun. He stayed in the flat. I rushed back after a second or two and said: "Will you drive me to Hampstead?" He did so, and left me at the top of Tanza Road. I had never seen the gun before ...[574]

Fenton Bresler who interviewed Mishcon about this statement, described events rather more bluntly:

> ... by ... Easter Sunday Ruth Ellis and this man were in a maudlin state: "If I was near David now I'd shoot him!" she said. "Well, I've got a gun," he replied ... That evening when there was still no word from Blakely ... the man drove her to the end of the road where the Findlaters lived, handed her the gun and said: "Go and shoot him!" and as she turned to walk down the street with his gun in her hand he drove off. Minutes later Blakely was dead.[575]

The Home Office and police response to Ruth's final statement is shrouded in mystery and contradiction. Mr Mishcon suggested police officers

---

[573]See for example Marks & Van den Bergh 1990:212.

[574]Statement by Ruth Ellis 12th July 1955 quoted in Marks & Van den Bergh 1990:204-5. This statement was also published by *The People* 2nd December 1973. According to Georgie Ellis, Ruth's son Andy who was ten at the time of the murder "saw Desmond Cussen place a gun in mother's handbag. He was not capable of inventing such a story and was able to describe to me precisely where he was in the flat when Cussen deliberately armed Ruth" (Ellis 1996:75). Writer Laurie Manifold traced Desmond Cussen to Australia in 1973 where he confronted him with Ruth's last statement. He responded: "I won't say she's a liar. But funny things go through people's minds at the 12th hour" (*The Sunday People* 2nd December 1973).

[575]Bresler 1965:248.

were given inadequate time to investigate whether Ruth had an accomplice, hence the Home Secretary should have postponed "the execution so that proper inquiries could be made."[576] The Home Secretary however claimed:

> The police were, in fact, able to make considerable inquiries. But anyway it made no difference. If anything, if Mrs Ellis's final story was true it made her offence all the greater. Instead of a woman merely acting suddenly on impulse here you had an actual plot to commit murder, deliberately thought out and conceived with some little care. Even if a man were also guilty he would only have been an accessory before the fact: she would still have been the principal.[577]

The Home Secretary's opinion about 'the man' stood in sharp contrast to official opinion about Edith Thompson 32 years earlier, whose co-accused - Freddy Bywaters - repeatedly insisted that he was not only the principal but the *sole* participant in the killing of Percy Thompson. Moreover, Tenby's claim that inquiries were 'considerable', was challenged by three journalists:

> At 4.30pm on the day before the execution two detectives ... were detailed to investigate Mr X. The two detectives missed their quarry at his office by a narrow margin - he had left 20 minutes before they arrived. They rushed to his home - to find that he had been seen leaving with two suitcases. The detectives maintained their vigil until what they call "late in the evening," when they were instructed to withdraw by a Deputy Commander at Scotland Yard. Ruth Ellis was hanged early next morning.[578]

Ruth's previous solicitor John Bickford, told *The Sunday People* he could have confirmed the truth of Ruth's statement because "Mr X had confessed his part in the crime to Mr Bickford, even admitting he had shown Ruth how to use the gun." Ruth had forbidden him to use this information during the trial and he had no knowledge that Ruth had now told the whole truth, thus releasing him "from his duty to keep silent":

> The Home Office did not contact me. The police did not come near me. Yet I possessed the evidence they were seeking ... I could have given the facts that would have saved Ruth Ellis.[579]

---

[576]Mr Mishcon quoted in Bresler 1965:250.

[577]The Home Secretary, Lord Tenby interviewed by Fenton Bresler 1965:250.

[578]Report by Laurie Manifold, Harry Warschauer & Alan Ridout in *The Sunday People* 9th December 1973. Goodman & Pringle 1974:72 also challenge Lloyd George's claim that inquiries were 'considerable' and write that he omitted to add "that these inquiries all failed."

[579]John Bickford quoted in *The Sunday People* 9th December 1973. Mr Bickford gave an official statement to the police in 1972 in which he relayed that Desmond

These statements throw severe doubt over Home Secretary Lloyd George's claim that inquiries were "considerable", and instead suggest a lack of interest or desire to discover an alternative truth which would reveal the case to be less 'open and shut' than first believed. It suggests it was the Home Secretary's attitude which was 'open and shut' rather than the case of Ruth Ellis. Lloyd George appeared to confirm this himself when - presumably recognising that if evidence was revealed that Ruth had been encouraged to kill David whilst intoxicated or of unsound mind attitudes would change drastically in her favour - he stated: "If she isn't hanged tomorrow, she never will be."[580]

When the execution was only two days away, Lloyd George went to stay with his sister Lady Megan, where he was observed stroll[ing] out to sniff the roses in the garden ... [and] walk[ing] in sunny Welsh lanes ..."[581] During the last 24 hours of Ruth's life when vital evidence concerning the gun could have been uncovered and a life spared, the Home Secretary refused to see both her lawyers and "a group of socialist M.P.s."[582] Meanwhile, the Home Office Permanent Under Secretary, Sir Frank Newsam, "was in the Royal Enclosure at Ascot racecourse."[583]

The failure to complicate the 'stark simplicity' of the Ruth Ellis case by all those involved, demonstrates the power of judicial misogyny. From the very moment of her arrest when police officials failed to order a blood-test to determine Ruth's alcohol level or to examine the gun for finger-prints, throughout the trial, and through to the last 24 hours of her life, when it became increasingly clear, that far from being an 'open and shut' case, this was in fact a highly complex one involving a second jealous lover, who may have believed he had much to gain by David's death, there was a total failure by law enforcement agencies, legal personnel and state servants to question the 'obviousness' of this case. In short, no-one in a position of power appeared interested in saving this woman's life. Ruth was not the 'type' to invoke sympathy but instead repeatedly displayed the signs of dangerous womanhood. By the time she was awaiting execution she had been revealed as a heavy drinker, an ex-prostitute and a club-hostess, a divorcee, a mother of an illegitimate child, an abortionist and a 'bad' mother living an immoral

---

Cussen had told him that he (Desmond) had oiled the gun, given it to Ruth and taken her to a wood for target practice, after which he drove her to the scene of the murder: "He showed her how it worked, his explanation being that she was so beside herself and so persistent and he was so much in love with her that he eventually gave in." According to Mr Bickford, the statement was passed on to the Director of Public Prosecutions who "propose[d] to do no more in the matter" (*The Sunday People* 2nd December 1973). See also *Daily Express* 13th July 1955 which reported that "a report [concerning the ownership of the gun] was made to the Home Office. But it was decided that it had no direct bearing on the case."

[580]Lloyd George quoted in Goodman & Pringle 1974:73.
[581]*Daily Express* 11th July 1955.
[582]*Daily Express* 13th July 1955.
[583]Ellis 1996:21; Bresler 1965:248-9.

existence with her 'toy-boy' lover. During her trial she had continued her pattern of deviancy by failing to mobilise emotional or hysterical images of femininity or downtrodden and pathetic images of victimhood. Instead she activated yet another discourse associated with dangerous womanhood - that of a glamorous but brittle, jealous and vengeful, immoral woman. Her appearance and demeanour, coupled with her social class, lifestyle and attitude towards sex, marriage, motherhood and domesticity ensured that all those involved in her case, including her defence, perceived her in a negative, condemnatory manner, for she encompassed every one of the characteristics conducive to judicial misogyny, which in turn ensured she was perceived to be less deserving of a reprieve:

> She died because she did not plead for mercy, and because she was not sorry. She died because she made fools of those ... who wanted a soiled, identikit, anti-heroine to take pity on, and were confronted instead with a complex, intelligent human being.[584]

While the prospect of Ruth's execution was met with either indifference or support amongst those with the authority to prevent it, it provoked resistance, hostility and outrage within the public both in Britain and abroad. Over 100,000 Britons signed a petition "to reduce the charge against her from murder to manslaughter."[585] Spontaneous petitions for a reprieve were started throughout the country,[586] with individuals such as Frank Neale - a friend of Ruth's - collecting 5,000 signatures alone.[587] Another petition was signed by 35 members of London City Council.[588] Four days prior to the execution 25,000 signatures had reached the Home Secretary.[589]

The decision to let the execution proceed was also condemned internationally. In France *Le Monde* wrote: "the Englishman ... believes himself to be a creature of *sang-froid*, and the legal system in force supports this fiction in overruling once and for all any emotional troubles or irresistible impulses ... the fundamental argument of the traditionalist rests much less ...

---

[584]Bardsley 1987:143. Similarly, Farran has written: "Ruth Ellis was hanged not just because of her act of killing David Blakely, but also and more particularly because of how that killing was constructed and how she was constructed by the popular press, and then by both the prosecution and defence at her trial" (Farran 1988:12).

[585]Clare Cox in *Police Review* 22nd August 1986.

[586]For example, Frieda Pratt, who herself had been accused of the attempted murder of her abusive husband four years previously, started a petition, arguing "we were both faced with emotionally impossible situations." *Daily Express* 5th July 1955. See also Ellis 1996:209.

[587]*Daily Express* 12th July 1955.

[588]*Daily Express* 13th July 1955.

[589]*Daily Express* 9th July 1955. Ruth Ellis's execution was also met with resistance in leading articles from diverse publications such as *The Daily Mirror* 30th June 1955 and *The Lancet* 23rd July 1955.

on the deterrent effect of the system ... than on the old law of 'an eye for an eye.'"[590]

The American writer Raymond Chandler, who was in London at the time of the execution, presented his own version of an alternative truth:

> The case of Ruth Ellis was no bestial or sadistic killing ... It was a crime of passion committed, I feel certain, under a kind of shock which may have flared up uncontrollably shortly before the man was shot. *The phrase 'cold-blooded' doesn't come into it. This woman was hot-blooded ... Sure she is a woman with a background but that doesn't mean to say she can't fall in love ...*[591]

Large crowds registered their protest by standing outside the prison gates the night beforehand, and, under the leadership of Mrs Van der Elst, chanted "Evans - Bentley - Ellis."[592]

In the aftermath of the execution several Labour MPs and one Ulster Unionist MP voiced their disapproval of capital punishment, while Labour MP Emmanuel Shinwell called for its abolition.[593] This issue maintained a high profile in the media for several weeks after the execution with *The Howard League* renewing its call for abolition and the *National Campaign for the Abolition of Capital Punishment* being launched only weeks later.[594] Seven months later the House of Commons passed a Bill to abolish capital punishment. It was rejected by the House of Lords, however, within two years the defence of diminished responsibility became established in law.[595]

---

[590]Quoted in *The Times* 13th July 1955.

[591]Interview with Raymond Chandler in *Daily Express* 1st July 1955. My emphasis.

[592]*The Times* 13th July 1955. This was a reference to Timothy Evans and Derek Bentley whose executions remained controversial for decades to come. Bentley's conviction was quashed on 30th July 1998, more than 45 years after his execution.

[593]*Parliamentary Debates*, House of Commons 18th-28th July 1955 Session 1955-56 Vol 544 cols 538-543. Astonishingly one MP, Lieut-Colonel Lipton appeared to object to the fact that Ruth Ellis had been given brandy immediately prior to her execution when he asked "what prison regulations govern the supply of alcoholic liquor to persons sentenced to death." When the Home Secretary answered that the allowance was 1 pint of beer per day, Lipton asked: "How does the Home Secretary reconcile that with the evidence disclosed at an inquest last week? Will he also say whether hanging takes place whatever the degree of intoxication might be immediately before the hanging?" To Lloyd George's credit he answered: "I do not think I need to enter into that." In fact *The Royal Commission on Capital Punishment 1949-1953 Report* had recommended that the Prison Medical Officer's discretion "should be indulgently exercised" (col 541).

[594]*The Times* 4th and 26th August 1955. See also debates in the 'Letters' pages of *The Times* throughout June-July 1955.

[595]MPs passed the Abolition Bill on 12th March 1956 with 286 in favour and 262 against abolition. (*Parliamentary Debates*, House of Commons Session 1955-56 12th-29th March 1956 Vol 550 cols 36-151). The defence of diminished

Years later, Labour MP Tony Benn, an active abolition campaigner, commented:

> Undoubtedly the Ruth Ellis case played a large part in developing public opinion against capital punishment.[596]

Her very death had caused her immortalisation. Ruth herself never doubted the existence of an afterlife and remained convinced that by dying she would rejoin David.[597] She continued to defy gender expectations to the very end by remaining calm, composed and dignified. Less than 24 hours before her execution she told a friend:

> Have you heard the big news? I'm not going to be reprieved. Don't worry, it's like having a tooth out and they'll give me a glass of brandy beforehand.[598]

During her last evening she wrote to another friend:

> I must close now, just remember I am quite happy with the verdict but not the way the story was told. There is so much that people don't know about.[599]

Her final letter was to her solicitor and demonstrates that to the very end she remained convinced the Findlaters were partly to blame for David's death. She also referred to a letter from David's brother and sister-in-law in the *Evening Standard* where they wrote they required "a great deal more proof than that provided by the defence at the trial that any of the allegations against his character were founded on fact"[600]:

> I am now content and satisfied that my affairs will be dealt with satisfactorily. I also ask you to make known the true story regarding Mrs Fin[d]later & her plan to break up David & I - she should feel content, now her plan ended so tragically.

---

responsibility became established in law as part of the Homicide Bill which was passed on 6th February 1957 with 217 in favour and 131 against the bill. (*Parliamentary Debates*, House of Commons Session 1956-57 Vol 564 cols 454-567).

[596]Quoted in Goodman & Pringle 1974:76.

[597]See for example interview with Sir Melford Stevenson in *Sunday Telegraph* 21st March 1982 where he stated: "She was deeply convinced that she was going to be reunited in the hereafter with ... [David] ..."

[598]Letter to Jacqueline Dyer quoted in Hancock 1989:183.

[599]Letter reproduced in *Daily Express* 14th July 1955.

[600]Letter to the *London Evening Standard* by Mr & Mrs Derek Blakely 7th July 1955. Given the insipid nature of the defence their comment was entirely fair.

... I would also like to answer David's brother's (newspaper remarks) ... he said he would have to have more proof than he heard in court before he would believe my story.

My reply to Derek is, I am sorry. I cannot give any more proof than I have.

I did not defend myself. I say a Life for a Life. What more proof can he want?

I have spoken the truth, and I want to make the truth known for my family and son's sake.

Well, Mr Simmonds, the time is 9.30. I am quite well and not worrying about anything. Thanks once again.[601]

To the very end Ruth demonstrated the existence of an alternative truth about herself. Thus, during her final hours she was concerned not about herself but with reassuring those she was about to leave behind as this postscript to Mr Simmonds' letter indicates:

Just to let you know, I am still feeling alright. The time is 7 o'clock A.M. - everyone is simply wonderful in (staff) Holloway. This is just for you, to console my family, with the thought, that I did not change my way of thinking at the last moment.

Or break my promise to David's mother.

Well Mr Simmonds, I have told you the truth, that's all I can do.

Thanks once again.

Goodbye.[602]

Her efforts to comfort and reassure others challenge the one-dimensional image of Ruth as an uncaring, selfish and vindictive killer and instead indicate a complex and sensitive character, who even at the moment of death put the feelings of her family and friends before her own. Her dignity and bravery in facing death stood in sharp contrast to her executioner's coarse attempt to pay her a compliment:

She was no trouble. She wobbled a bit, naturally. Any woman can do that. Nothing went wrong with her. She was as good as bloody gold, she was.[603]

For those whom Ruth left behind however, her execution signalled the beginning of their punishment. Thus, less than three years later, her ex-husband George Ellis committed suicide by hanging.[604] Ruth's father Arthur Hornby, died next - "from depression and [a] broken heart ..."[605] The mental

---

[601]Letter reproduced in Goodman & Pringle 1974:69.

[602]Letter reproduced in Goodman & Pringle 1974:71.

[603]Albert Pierrepoint quoted in Ellis 1996:4.

[604]Ellis 1996:58.

[605]Interview with Ruth's sister Muriel Jakubait in *Daily Express* 20th July 1982.

health of Ruth's mother began to deteriorate immediately after the execution, and prior to her death, she spent many years institutionalised in a mental hospital.[606] Ruth's sister Elizabeth "starv[ed] herself to death, her heart broken by Ruth's fate."[607] Arguably, most tragic of all, Ruth's son Andy never recovered from the trauma of his mother's execution:

> ... in a pattern that was repeated throughout his life, he had been left to fend for himself without adequate means, skills or powers of reasoning to do so ... he was a destroyed man, unable to fulfil a useful role in society.[608]

In June 1982 at the age of 38, Andy was found dead in his flat. He had committed suicide. His body had lain undiscovered for three weeks.[609] The coroner reported that he had had "an awful problem with depression."[610] Andy had finally re-established contact with his half-sister Georgie in the latter years of his life. During much of their time together, he believed Georgie was his mother and addressed her as such.[611] Arguably, such trauma was the ultimate consequence of a defence which the trial judge in later years was to call "so weak it was non-existent."[612] Unarguably, it is from such trauma that we learn what the reality of capital punishment means.

---

[606]Marks & Van den Bergh 1990:189.

[607]Ellis 1996:77. See also Marks & Van den Bergh 1990:189. See also *Daily Express* 20th July 1982, where Ruth's sister Muriel Jakubait stated: "All the deaths were directly involved with my sister being hanged for murder."

[608]Ellis 1996:77.

[609]*Daily Telegraph, Daily Mail,* 29th June 1982; *Daily Express* 28th June 1982.

[610]*The Times* 20th July 1982.

[611]Ellis 1996:78.

[612]Mr Justice Havers quoted in *Daily Telegraph* 29th June 1977.

7 Conclusion

> As feminists ...we can resist the prejudices upon which social
> divisions are sustained, and we can resist the institutions and social
> structures of oppressive ideologies. We cannot, however, presume
> now or into the future to have arrived at a definitive set of
> knowledges or understandings. In the social sciences, new
> knowledges have never entirely displaced old ideas, and the authority
> to identify "empirical truths" and to interpret observable, testable
> "facts" is dependent on existing power relations within given social
> contests. But as new materials are produced, ideas can be
> reconstructed in new configurations of "truth" which allow for
> previously silenced groups to name themselves and to describe their
> own experiences.[1]

I introduced this book by pointing out that 91% of women sentenced to death
in the first half of the 20th century had their sentence commuted. Although
this figure had come about mainly as a result of the large proportion of
women who had committed infanticide I quoted the *Royal Commission on
Capital Punishment 1949-1953 Report* to illustrate there was "a natural
reluctance" to carry out the death sentence on women. In view of this
reluctance I posed the question "why were the 15 women whose cases have
now been examined, not worthy of a reprieve?" Without background
information we might presume they represented the ultimate irredeemable
face of criminality - that they were "monsters" or "irretrievables"[2] - the 15
'worst' female criminals of the first half of the 20th century. Yet, in several of
these cases, it seems highly unlikely the women would have committed
further crimes had they lived. Even Miss Cronin - the deputy governor of
Holloway prison at the time of Edith Thompson's execution, who "was not at
all a sensitive or easily moved person" - was of the opinion that "if she had
been spared she could have become a very good woman."[3] Conversely,
Sarah Lloyd - found guilty of beating to death her 86-year-old neighbour
Edith Emsley with a spade - was due to be executed on 7th July 1955, six
days before Ruth Ellis's execution. Prior to the beating "Mrs Lloyd had
poured boiling carrots and onions over her."[4] Witnesses at her trial testified
"that Mrs Lloyd stood chatting casually as the street inhabitants watched

---

[1]Faith, K. (1993) *Unruly Women* Press Gang Publishers, Vancouver p.9.

[2]Koestler, A. (1956) *Reflections on Hanging* Gollancz, London p.150.

[3]PCOM 9/1983 XC2662. Margery Fry quoted by Arthur Koestler in *The Observer*
11th March no year, but quoted and discussed in this document.

[4]Ellis, G. (1996) *Ruth Ellis, My Mother* Smith Gryphon, London, p.208. See also
Goodman, J. & Pringle, P. (1974) *The Trial of Ruth Ellis* David & Charles, London
p.60.

incredulously as Edith Emsley was carried into an ambulance. Cool as they come, that night Mrs Lloyd went out with her daughter to the cinema."[5] Sarah Lloyd was reprieved the week before Ruth Ellis's execution.

Examples and comparisons such as that between Ellis and Lloyd demonstrate that women were not simply executed or reprieved according to "merit" as the Home Secretary who was responsible for deciding the fate of these two women, claimed.[6] No impartial criteria existed which the Home Secretary could apply in order to determine whether Ruth Ellis's crime was 'worse' than that of Sarah Lloyd's. Rather, as I have argued throughout this book, what is known about female defendants as individual women play a considerable role in determining how their crimes are perceived and constructed. In particular, in Chapter One, I set myself the task of applying two questions - devised by Anne Worrall - to the case-studies: "under what conditions do certain people claim to possess knowledge about female law-breakers?" and "what is the process whereby such claims are translated into practices which have particular consequences for female law-breakers?" I further argued that the personal conduct of women plays a crucial role in establishing such knowledge claims, particularly in the areas of sexuality, respectability, domesticity and motherhood. In applying this argument to the 15 case-studies I have repeatedly demonstrated that women who stepped outside patriarchal definitions of acceptable female behaviour in these four areas became constructed as 'dangerous' women which in turn resulted in them experiencing the full force of judicial misogyny. In other words, the discourses of dangerous womanhood were mobilised by the women's personal conduct and sexual behaviour. The consequences for these female law-breakers was initially judicial misogyny and ultimately death by hanging.

A brief reminder of the extent of these 15 women's transgressions will reinforce the central hypothesis of this book - that women who fail to conform to traditional expectations in the areas of sexuality, respectability, domesticity and motherhood are more likely to be the victims of judicial misogyny with the consequent result that they receive harsher punishment than women who conform to conventional models of femininity. Bearing in mind that the total sample consists of 15 women the following statistics apply: five had been prostitutes at some point in their lives; two had abortions; seven had illegitimate children; six had affairs while still married; five had lived with men who were not their husbands; six had children who were in care or otherwise not living with them; three had separated from their husbands when divorce was still extremely rare; five had affairs/relationships

---

[5]Ellis 1996:209.

[6]After the execution of Ruth Ellis Labour MP Emmanuel Shinwell asked Lloyd George, whether, rather than the Home Secretary exercising the prerogative of commuting death sentences, this decision could be transferred to "a panel of persons qualified to judge." Lloyd George replied: "... all these cases are decided on their merits, and I am sure that I need hardly remind him that enormous care is taken in each case" (*Parliamentary Debates*, House of Commons, 18th-28 July Session 1955-56 Vol 544, col 539).

with men several years their junior; six were described as promiscuous or over-sexed; seven had previous criminal records (two more would have had records if their abortions had been discovered); four were repeatedly described as heavy drinkers or alcoholics. Numbers in each category may have been higher since much of the data are unavailable. 13 of the 15 women had committed between two and seven of the above transgressions. One woman had committed all but one of them.

Having uncovered the extent of these women's transgressions and deviations from traditional ideas about women's nature - their supposed "passivity, submissiveness, asexuality and gentleness"[7] - we are in a position to demonstrate two important theoretical contentions. First, the story of executed women in the 20th century confirms the hypothesis outlined in Chapter Three - that those who step furthest beyond the boundary of acceptable female conduct and behaviour also receive the harshest form of punishment. In Foucauldian terms, these women's stories have demonstrated that those who fail to regulate their behaviour and impose appropriate disciplinary practices upon their bodies (and indeed their minds) will come under increased surveillance, discipline and control, which - in extreme cases - extend to the point of extermination.

Second, the women's stories provide a challenge to the traditional portrayal of criminal women as 'mad or bad' as discussed in the Introduction - and instead allow us to tell an alternative truth about them. In that alternative truth we learn that women who kill are not the victims of 'raging hormones' or related biological functions - a portrayal which denies the rationality and agency behind their crimes. Equally, we learn that female murderers are not 'evil' aberrations of womanhood who can be set apart from 'normal' women and 'true' feminine conduct and behaviour. Instead, the behaviour of murderous women is firmly rooted within the social world with the patterns of their crimes reflecting "the changing social conditions of women."[8] Thus, as discussed in Chapter Two, the fact that infanticide was a common crime amongst female servants in the 17th century, was not due to defective personality traits or 'madness', nor was it due to an unusually high concentration of 'bad' women. Instead it was both a desperate and rational response to social conditions which regarded an unmarried mother as immoral, unchaste, 'spoiled' and unemployable; while legal conditions ensured the master was rarely, if ever, punished for impregnating a servant. Nor could fathers be held responsible for maintaining their illegitimate children due to the "bastardy clauses".[9] In such circumstances committing infanticide became a matter of *survival*.

Similarly, the preponderance of 'baby-farmers' could only come into existence in a paternalistic culture dominated by "patriarchal concern for

---

[7] See Chapter One, f/n 31 (Morris, A. & Wilczynski, A. (1993) 'Rocking the Cradle: Mothers who Kill their Children' in Birch, H. (ed) (1993) *Moving Targets* Virago, London, p.199).

[8] Jones, A. (1991) *Women Who Kill* Gollancz, London p.xvi.

[9] Clark, A. (1987) *Women's Silence Men's Violence* Pandora, London p.108; 12.

women's virtue ... which enshrined chastity as the measure of a woman's worth."[10] The fact that virtually all baby-farmers were women reflected an androcentric culture which placed child-care responsibilities almost solely upon the female sex. In order to justify this arrangement motherhood was elevated during the Reformation and the 'maternal instinct' was discovered in the 20th century. Thus, with regard to the women in Chapter Four who had killed children, the gendered nature of their trials can be understood as a result of them being on trial not just for murder but also as *mothers*. Their cases demonstrate the existence of the 'double standards' discussed throughout this book for Ada Williams' husband William did not stand trial as a father. Nor was it ever suggested at Louise Masset's trial that the absence of Manfred's father - and hence his failure to share the responsibility for the boy's welfare - was a contributing factor to his murder.[11] In an ungendered universe where the role of the father is treated equally to that of the mother, we would expect the total absence of a father to count as a mitigating circumstance if and when a mother failed to ensure the welfare of her child. It is frequently a mitigating circumstance where single fathers are concerned.[12]

With reference to the women in Chapter Five who had killed other women, I argued that two of them - Margaret Allen and Styllou Christofi - should have been situated within the 'mad' category - that is - they suffered from mental illness and should not have been considered fit to either plead or hang. The fact they were hanged demonstrates once again the consequences of what was known about them as women. That is to say, their mental illness could not be traced to their biological functions, and their crimes did not fit those usually associated with 'mad' women such as infanticide or baby-snatching. Instead knowledge about these women's past behaviour and conduct reinforced and amplified their current transgressions and final criminal acts.

Meanwhile, Louie Calvert became the ultimate example of the deeply entrenched and gendered belief, that "an evil woman must be more evil than an evil man", a belief which has come about because such a woman "departs more markedly from her ascribed gender role"[13], whereas a comparatively high level of deviance and aggression in men has traditionally been regarded as part of 'normal' masculinity.[14]

---

[10]Clark 1987:109.

[11]This point carries equal weight regardless of whether Louise Masset was guilty or innocent.

[12]As can be seen from the case-study of Emily Swann, even a *partially* absent mother became a mitigating circumstance for William Swann's violence against his wife.

[13]Cameron 1996:25.

[14]Susie Orbach has written: "Men who are violent, men who thieve, men who commit sexual crimes, are still perceived as being an exaggeration of what man is. A man has to be a Fred West to be counted a real transgression from the norm" (*The Guardian* 1st March 1997).

In the remaining two cases - those of Dorothea Waddingham and Louisa Merrifield - we find this belief of women being 'doubly bad' amplified to the point where their two male accomplices were released while the women were hanged. That this should be the case was directly related to the women being judged not only as murderers but also as carers of the sick and helpless, arguably the job most closely associated with women's 'caring instinct' and 'natural' desire to nurture. As had been the case with Ada Williams, the fact that Dorothea and Louisa were executed while their male partners were released was not a result of these women's inherent 'evilness' or maladjustment compared to the men, but was instead tied in with both preconceived ideas about women as carers as well as the reality of that role which meant that - unlike their male partners - they carried out many of the day-to-day care duties almost single-handed, which resulted in them being observed to have a closer relationship to their victims. In turn this relationship generated more evidence against the women than their spouses, for it will be recalled, that neither Joe Sullivan nor Alfred Merrified were found to be innocent; they were released as a result of lack of evidence. Similarly, William Williams, Ada's husband, was not declared innocent, but was found guilty of being an accessory after the fact. Again therefore, it is the social role of women as carers rather than individual pathology, which helps us to make sense of these cases and allows us to understand that it was not simply 'bad luck' or 'chance' but discourses around gender and carers, which resulted in the execution of Ada, Dorothea and Louisa while their men walked free.[15]

Lastly, with reference to women who kill their spouses, I have aimed to demonstrate that in the majority of cases, such killings came about - not as a result of the perpetrators being 'mad' or 'bad' - but as the result of severe crises in their personal relationships and within the context of male domination and female subordination.[16] As I indicated, this domination extended to physical violence in four of the five cases. I also described how that violence was severely understated and on certain occasions was not only excused altogether but also justified. Such excuses and justifications could only take place within a culture which accepts the subordination of women and therefore also accepts the belief "that there are times when every woman needs to be taken in hand":

> Usually these are occasions when a woman challenges a man's authority, fails to fulfil his expectations of service, or neglects to stay in 'her place.'[17]

---

[15]As noted in the case-study of Ruth Ellis in relation to Desmond Cussen, this book does not argue in favour of executing these men; instead this point is made to demonstrate the different standards by which men and women are judged, which in turn results in differential punishment between the sexes.

[16]Beatrix Campbell referring to contemporary women who kill in Jones 1991:xi.

[17]Dobash, R.E. & Dobash, R. (1980) *Violence Against Wives* Open Books, Shepton Mallet p.93.

These case-studies have therefore demonstrated the presence of the 'double standard' by pointing out that a woman who has killed her spouse is not only judged for the murder of which she is accused, but also for her performance as a wife. In that sense the case-studies have provided historical background and context to the modern issue of battered women who kill as exemplified in cases such as those of Kiranjit Ahluwalia, Emma Humphreys and Sara Thornton, who were all given life-sentences after being found guilty of murdering their abusive partners, but who after subsequent appeals and retrials were released, having had their charges reduced to manslaughter.

Current debates around women who kill abusive partners clearly demonstrate that double standards still surround such women during their journey through the criminal justice system. For example, Sara Thornton was given a life-sentence for the murder of her husband Malcolm - an alcoholic who frequently became violent when drunk, and who had threatened to kill Sara's daughter Luise prior to his murder. Yet, as I noted in Chapter Six, only two days after rejecting Sara's appeal, the same court allowed Joseph McGrail to be released immediately after his trial:

> McGrail had kicked to death his common law wife Marion Kennedy. His excuse was he had come home to find her drunk again. The judge said "that woman would have tried the patience of a saint."[18]

The case of Joseph McGrail is not an isolated example, instead many such cases do not even go to trial as a consequence of 'plea-bargaining' involving the prosecution accepting "a plea of manslaughter in return for a guilty plea."[19] While men's most frequent excuse for killing their partners is

---

[18]McNeill, S. (1996) 'Getting Away With Murder' in *Trouble & Strife* 33, Summer 1996 p.7.

[19]Lees, S. (1997) *Ruling Passions* Open University Press, Milton Keynes p.143. Researchers for the Channel 4 programme 'Till Death Us Do Part' found "a worrying discrepancy in the way men who kill their wives are treated by the courts. It seems women's lives are worth a lot less than those of a stranger on the street, or the contents of a security van or Post Office safe." Their sample indicated that "in 46% of domestic killings either a plea of guilty to manslaughter was accepted, or a jury returned a manslaughter verdict; only 32% of non-domestics resulted in manslaughter convictions." (Reported in *The Guardian* 13th September 1995). Susan Edwards has provided an in-depth critique of Home Office figures which indicated that women were nearly "twice as likely" to be indicted for manslaughter compared to men: "The issue is not and never has been about a crude comparison of figures. The debate is about whether certain facts are more or less likely to result in a successful defence of provocation ... Attention should have been directed towards an analysis of any differences in the treatment of the male and female cases according to their facts, rather than the statistical end product of these highly problematic and discretionary processes. Issues of discretion regarding decisions as to appropriate indictments, which shape the numerical outcomes were neither raised nor noted, as being of relevance. Hence, the Home Office's stark conclusion that 'women were nearly twice

infidelity, women are not considered to have the right to be equally provoked by their partners' unfaithfulness as the case of Diane and Alan Hunt demonstrates:

> When she discovered her husband was having an affair she punched him on the nose. (It required hospital treatment.) He told her he had had two other affairs. She kicked him. He strangled her. A jury found him not guilty of murder. He walked free. The judge ... said, 'He had been outrageously provoked.'[20]

This and other cases reinforce Bochnak's point that "a woman's husband simply does not belong to her in the same way that she belongs to him."[21] As such, they lend credence to the theoretical points made in Chapter Three about the differential and hierarchical nature of the relationship between husband and wife which legitimises a husband's right to discipline an 'uppity' wife. They also demonstrate that 17th century perceptions of gender relations which maintained that a husband was also a lord and master - as discussed in Chapter Two - still hold some currency.

Repeatedly, and at several different levels, the criminal justice system indicates that "different criteria are applied to male and female behaviour."[22] *The Guardian* for example, made the following comparison in 1995:

> A man who battered his nagging wife to death was given a sentence of only three years at the Old Bailey. He lost his temper with his wife and hit her over the head with a hammer 13 times. Last month, a woman received a sentence of three and a half years for GBH after cracking a bottle over the head of her pregnant sister's violent boyfriend.[23]

It is not necessary for a woman to have been violent for her partner's defence of provocation to be accepted after he has killed her. Mark Williams, for example, "strangled his wife after eavesdropping on her telephone calls

---

as likely as men' to be indicted for manslaughter ... would only be valid, if at the outset the male/female, and female/male homicide were strictly comparable on the facts. Whilst the circumstances surrounding the killing of male spouses by women are likely to be characterised by the abuse of the defendant over a long period, the killing of female spouses, is by comparison, characterised by an escalating trajectory of violence by the defendant which culminates in the killing. The two distinctly different imprints of circumstances surrounding the homicide are not comparable (Edwards, S. (1996) *Sex and Gender in the Legal Process* Blackstone Press Ltd, London pp.371-2).

[20]This case took place in 1994 and is discussed in McNeill 1996:6-7. Alan Hunt was given an 18-month suspended sentence. See also *The Guardian* 29th October 1994.
[21]Bochnak quoted in Lees 1996:144.
[22]Lees 1996:142.
[23]*The Guardian* 23th October 1995.

and discovering she was having an affair ..."[24] His plea of provocation was accepted and he was sentenced to five years imprisonment for manslaughter. An identical sentence was given to Graham Barrie who also had his defence of provocation accepted after discovering his wife June had an affair:

> June Barrie staggered bleeding on to the pavement outside the couple's butcher shop ... after her husband stabbed her several times. As a number of people gave her first aid Barrie went out and stabbed her another four or five times.[25]

Such cases demonstrate that "for provocation to be argued in aid of a woman who has killed her partner, the man must be persistently violent; in the reverse situation, women need only be insubordinate."[26] As pointed out in the case-study of Ethel Major, whereas women trapped within violent relationships are continually asked why they 'don't just leave', no-one asks why men 'don't just leave' when they find women's behaviour provocative:

> If women have violence used *against* them and *fail* to leave, they lack self-respect. If men are stressed by *non*-violent behaviour (e.g. nagging) their *use* of violence is justified as necessary. This reasoning presupposes the traditional belief that a *man's* self-respect *depends* on the use of violence in such a case.[27]

Similarly, neither Arthur Major or David Blakely, nor Malcolm Thornton or other violent and abusive men who were eventually killed by their victims were considered to have provoked their own deaths or 'asked for it', a reasoning frequently applied to women who have either been perceived to be insubordinate in some way or have failed to adequately police their appearance or behaviour. The concept of women 'asking for trouble' is employed to excuse all types of violence by men - including rape and murder - and is a mechanism which displaces the responsibility for male violence onto their victims - arguably the most common form of victim-blaming in existence. It is a reasoning which accepts men's uncontrollable urges in relation to rape and uncontrollable anger in relation to violence against and murder of their spouses. It is a reasoning which "reflects the victim's conduct rather than that of the offender."[28] It is also a reasoning which "establishes

[24]*The Guardian* 24th November 1993.

[25]*The Guardian* 21st October 1995.

[26]Lees 1996:142.

[27]Hoff, L.A. (1990) *Battered Women as Survivors* Routledge, London p.125. Emphasis in the original. See also *Scotland on Sunday* 13th July 1997 where Sue Lees writes that judges do not ask male defendants "why they do not seek help for marital dis-harmony rather than kill, but instead extend sympathy to them."

[28]Joan Smith writing in *The Guardian* 17th June 1997 p.15. See also Joan Smith in *The Guardian* 19th October 1999 where she discusses the conduct and reputation of murder victims Yvonne O'Brien and Vicky Hall.

that non-compliant women are beyond ... [the law's] effective protection."[29] As indicated in Chapter Three, if women are scantily clad in public, out alone at night, hitchhiking or backpacking, they may be considered to have precipitated in their own violent deaths. Thus it matters not whether a woman is a victim or defendant, it is always *her* reputation which is the focus the trial.[30] In the case of Evelyn Howells, for example, whose husband and two sons were found guilty of her murder, it was her reputation as a wife and mother which became the focus of the trial rather than her husband's failure to remove himself and his sons from her care.[31] Similarly, the case of Sara Thornton increasingly came to resemble a modern version of the Ruth Ellis case - both in terms of the focus on the women's reputations rather than that of their partners - and in the sense that neither woman fitted the role of a 'victim'. Instead Thornton was described as "a violent liar" and a "'victim' ... [who] was mostly drunk."[32] The victim status of women such as Ruth Ellis and Emily Swann (who - like Thornton - were both described as heavy drinkers) was further undermined by the fact they had lovers several years their junior. Similarly, the other women within the 15 case-studies who were not victims of chronic male violence but who had lovers considerably younger than themselves - Louise Masset and Edith Thompson - were soon to find this fact helped to ensure they fitted the stereotypical image of 'the evil temptress' who brings 'innocent' young men to their ruin.[33] The assumption was - especially where the women were considered sexually attractive as in the cases of Louise Masset, Edith Thompson and Ruth Ellis - that *they* rather than the men, took the lead and pursued their 'prey'. The fact they had allowed their sexuality to become visible confirmed the continued existence of the ancient male fear of female sexuality discussed in Chapter Two, which resulted in these women being considered "sexually insatiable and weak in character" and hence out of control.[34] No similar moral judgement was passed on William Williams or Alfred Merrifield despite the fact that William was double the age of Ada when they met, and Alfred was 24 years older than Louisa. Indeed, as I demonstrated, in both cases the women were considered to be the dominant partner. Such portrayals still hold currency in more recent trials, for example in the West case where - despite being a 15-year-old-

---

[29]Lees 1996:143.

[30]Lees 1996:147. This is also the case even before the trial as discussed by Joan Smith in *The Guardian* 19th October 1999.

[31]See for example *The Guardian* 13th February 1997.

[32]*The Guardian* 14th and 15th May 1996.

[33]The 'evil' temptress has her modern equivalent in - for example - Tracy Whalin (33) who eloped to America with her son's best friend - Sean Kinsella (14). See for example Decca Aitkenhead writing in *The Guardian* 1st August 1997.

[34]Barstow, L.A. (1994) *Witchcraze* Pandora, London p.14. See also Decca Aitkenhead in *The Guardian* 1st August 1997 who confirms the existence of such discourses in contemporary culture: "a woman's lust is fine when she's faking it for the boys; when she really means it, we panic."

school-girl when she met Fred - who was 28 and already a multiple killer[35] - Rosemary West has been described as "the more dominant of the two killers":

> She was the mistress, he the slave. He kidnapped for her, presented her with victims like a dog carrying a partridge to its master's feet ... without Rose, it is doubtful he would have been anything more than a would-be Casanova with Jekyll and Hyde tendencies.[36]

The focus on a woman's character and reputation becomes particularly noticeable in cases involving double trials which include a male and female defendant. Thus, while I have argued the reputation of all 15 executed women came under scrutiny, the final outcome of the five male/female double trials analysed adds emphasis to this point. That is, three of the five men walked out of court free individuals while their spouses faced their executioner alone. In the two remaining cases - those of John Gallagher and Freddy Bywaters - I demonstrated that despite indisputable evidence in the Thompson/Bywaters case that it was Bywaters, not Thompson, who had carried out the murder, and despite evidence which - at the very least - pointed to Swann and Gallagher being equally involved in the murder of William Swann, the two women were nonetheless repeatedly considered 'worse' than their male co-defendants. In the Thompson/Bywaters case, this took the extreme form of a woman being executed, who today is almost universally considered to have been innocent.

I further argued that in the cases of Charlotte Bryant and Ruth Ellis, where evidence suggested the women may have had a male accomplice, no serious attempt was made to either establish or disprove the existence of an accomplice.

The portrayal of women in double trials as 'worse' than their male co-defendant indicated yet another manifestation of judicial misogyny and 'double standards'. Moreover, such portrayals did not end with the abolition of capital punishment but have their modern equivalents in double trials such as that of Ian Brady/Myra Hindley and the single trial of Rosemary West, whose name - despite her husband Fred West's suicide prior to their trial - remains inextricably linked to his. Thus, Debbie Cameron has observed that Rosemary West was not only judged for the crimes of which she stood accused, but also as a *mother*. Yet:

---

[35]While we cannot know exactly how many people was murdered by Fred West, it is known that Anne McFall was murdered before he met Rose in 1968. West also told his son that he had murdered Mary Bastholm who disappeared on 6th January 1967 (*Daily Mail* 23rd November 1995). Moreover, Burn writes that "local people would always be suspicious about the official reason given for Robin Holt's death" - a 15-year-old boy who was often found in West's company during 1966-67 and whose death was recorded as suicide following the discovery of his body on 3rd March 1967 (Burn, G. (1998) *Happy Like Murderers* Faber & Faber, London p.131).

[36]Colin Wilson writing in *Daily Mail* 23rd November 1995 p.37; p.39.

Fred West also abused the children of his own household. That fact, however, while it was absolutely obvious, did not occasion the same kind or quantity of comment ... Strangely we hear nothing about Fred West's 'failure of fathering': that phrase has an odd as well as unfamiliar ring. Why do people not talk about men's sexual abuse of children in these terms? Is it because we expect so much of mothers and so little of fathers?[37]

With reference to the Brady/Hindley case, despite this trial taking place more than 30 years ago, the repugnance felt towards Myra Hindley is today as strong as ever and far exceeds that expressed towards Ian Brady. As was the case with Rose West, this repugnance is rooted in Hindley being judged as a mother, even though she was not literally a mother:

> ... because of the unquestioned cultural tendency to conflate femininity and maternity ... Myra Hindley's crimes were placed firmly in the context of women's natural and instinctive propensity to nurture children. The greater repugnance felt then and now towards Myra Hindley than towards Ian Brady arises from a conviction that the abuse of children by a woman is peculiarly heinous because it is against the order of nature.[38]

Hence while the horror of the crimes of Rosemary West and Myra Hindley has resulted in these women becoming regarded as 'monsters' - the most dangerous women of modern times - it is nonetheless the case that their murderous capacities have been constructed in gender-specific ways. This is because such women "threaten a crisis of sexual difference" - they force us to challenge what is *known* about women.[39] The employment of the 'mad/bad' categories to criminal women has endured for so long because it is a mechanism for avoiding a re-examination of femininity - and ultimately for avoiding the creation of new discourses around violent women. Thus it is not only her gender but also her *sanity* which has ensured that Myra Hindley has remained one of the most reviled female criminals in England and Wales. For while Ian Brady "at least had the decency to go mad"[40] and has furthermore stated he does not wish to be released, Myra Hindley appears frighteningly 'normal'. Hindley herself has emphasised her sanity:

> In my 30 years in prison I have met, spoken with and been examined by psychiatrists and, in particular, a senior psychologist with whom I did a series of tests, the results of which ruled out psychopathy,

[37]Cameron, D. (1996) 'Wanted: The Female Serial Killer' in *Trouble & Strife* 33, Summer 1996 p.26; p.27. Emphasis in the original.
[38]Cameron 1996:25.
[39]See Chapter Six, Part 3 f/n 570.
[40]Ann West - the mother of Lesley Ann Downey - quoted in Birch, H. (1993) 'If Looks Could Kill' in Birch, H. (ed) (1993) *Moving Targets* Virago, London p.55.

schizophrenia, manic depression, episodic dyscontrol and any form of psychosis or neurosis. In a word, there was no evidence of a mentally disordered mind. And my EEGs revealed no abnormalities or dysfunctions. Nor was I ever, as a child or teenager, cruel to animals or children.[41]

Her 'normality' is reinforced by the reasonable and articulate tone of her letters and articles which have been published, as well as her desires, hopes and aspirations for the future, so normal that we all recognise them, which is precisely why we are so outraged by them. She is simply not *different enough* from us. This is too much to bear for those who - despite her apparent normality - see Hindley's 'evilness' as her *only* characteristic - immutable and unchanging - and thus persist in situating her in the 'bad' category in an attempt to make her stand apart from the rest of the world generally, and from femininity in particular:

> The woman who kills is exactly what she is supposed *not* to be. Her act is deemed not only unnatural but impossible in a real woman; so she is 'unwomaned' by her violence and seen as the classic aberration, exiled from her community and her gender.[42]

The attempt to 'exile' Hindley - not only from her community but also from humanity - has meant that whatever she has to say is irrelevant because no one is *listening* - instead those who answer her are responding to a stereotypical evil image of womanhood which allows the 'bad' category to remain unchallenged. Yet, Hindley's persistent attempts to be heard exemplify the competition between traditional discourses around 'bad' women and new knowledges and discourses of 'alternative truths' about violent women, for every time she speaks, she is re-opening the space within which such new discourses and new knowledges about violent women can be created. And every time, regardless of what she has to say, the response is always the same - vociferous and swift attempts to close that space - to 'mute' her account. To do otherwise would challenge idealised and traditional beliefs about women's 'nature'. It would mean facing up to the reality that the propensity to commit violent acts affects both men *and* women. It would mean moving beyond 'mad/bad' stereotypes and generalisations about violent women, in order to examine the complex set of relations and interactions which eventually lead to murderous crimes. It would mean an end to the comfort we gain from the 'them and us' mentality which is the product of the exploitation of stereotypical images of violent women as 'mad or bad'. And it would mean a recognition that this exploitation is ultimately designed "to

---

[41]Letter to *The Guardian* 4th October 1995.
[42]Campbell, B. (1991) 'Foreword' in Jones, A. (1991) *Women Who Kill* Gollancz, London p.xi.

highlight and promote the image of a good, desirable woman. The monsters serve as the sick/bad backdrop for her potential normalcy."[43]

I introduced this chapter by asking whether the 15 women who have been executed during the 20th century in England and Wales were 'monsters' or 'irretrievables'. Today such labels are still applied to women like Myra Hindley and Rosemary West by those who believe that a desire to understand what led to these women's involvement in murder demonstrates a lack of sympathy for their victims or a condoning of their crimes. But labelling murderous women 'monsters', 'mad' or 'bad' merely serves to over-simplify their violent acts and does nothing to prevent the death of future victims. Instead it signals our desire for seamless truths and freedom from contradictions. However, in challenging these categories we learn that even criminals like Hindley are not made up solely of monolithic 'evilness' but - like the rest of us - are contradictory human beings who also share emotions and characteristics with so-called 'normal' women. Hence, the danger Myra Hindley presents to society today can be understood as rooted not only - perhaps not even primarily - in a fear she may kill again, but in her ability to be a 'monster' - yet 'normal' simultaneously. Similarly, while the crimes and circumstances of the 15 women who were executed were very different to those of Myra Hindley, they did not possess a unique capacity for violence which set them apart from 'normal' women. Instead it was the ordinariness, 'normality' - and in some cases - even dreariness of their lives which united these women. It is appropriate here to repeat and reiterate the quotation referred to in the Introduction that "the story of women who kill is the story of women."[44]

In recent years the discourses of the mad/bad woman have been increasingly challenged by feminist activists and campaigning groups such as *Justice for Women* and *Southall Black Sisters*. These activists have argued for the creation of a new language which would include terms such as 'self-preservation' as a partial defence, and hence help to create new discourses around women who kill.[45] Some success has been achieved, particularly with reference to battered women who have killed their spouses, and it is now possible to point to cases where a battered and abused woman has escaped a prison sentence altogether.[46] Yet, as noted in this chapter's opening quotation, new knowledges never entirely replace old ideas and the authority to define 'truths' and 'facts' is always linked to "existing power relations

---

[43]Faith, K. (1993) *Unruly Women* Press Gang Publishers, Vancouver p.259.
[44]Introduction f/n 39.
[45]See for example Stanko & Scully 1996:71.
[46]See for example the cases of Marjorie Tooley (*The Guardian* 18th December 1996); Susan Murphy (*The Guardian* 2nd July 1996); Ernestine Smith (*The Guardian* 20th May 1995) and Susan McGrath (*The Guardian* 23th October 1999). However, other cases demonstrate the continued failure to punish men who kill their wives using infidelity as an excuse for their violence. For example, David Swinburne left court a free man despite having stabbed his wife 11 times after she had told him of her intention to leave him for another man (*Scotland on Sunday* 13th July 1997).

within given social contexts."[47] Thus, Zoora Shah, an illiterate and powerless Asian woman who had been subjected to "terrible sexual and other abuse" for 12 years at the hands of her co-habitué Mohammed Azam was given a life sentence for murder after she was found guilty of poisoning him. He had also forced her to have sex with other men and attempted "to coerce her into smuggling heroin" after a visit to Pakistan. She killed him after "he made sexual advances towards her daughters."[48] Her appeal failed in April 1998. In view of the history of the criminal justice system's attitude to and treatment of female poisoners we are entitled to ask whether discourses around 'the female-poisoner' are still active.

At another level, some victories have been rather hollow, for example Sara Thornton's release from prison was only secured after the judge had told her she had a "personality disorder":

> ... your responsibility for killing your husband was diminished by your abnormality of mind.[49]

Here the judge simultaneously acknowledged the existence of an alternative truth about the killing of Malcolm Thornton whilst also placing Sara Thornton firmly within the 'mad' category. Similarly in the case of Susan McGrath who was given a non-custodial sentence "the judge told the defendant: 'The evidence of physical and emotional abuse was compelling and I am satisfied that it occurred over a long period of time.'" At the same time the judge also "accepted that McGrath ... was suffering from a depressive illness at the time of the killing."[50] These rulings exemplify the up-hill struggle facing feminist activists in keeping open the spaces on which to create a new language and new knowledge which in turn will signal the end of the muted state that has traditionally surrounded violent women. In the words of Faith:

> By giving names to lies about women who have been historically denied a forum for speaking in their own voices, we open the doors to the cacophony of dissent and reaction. We also expand our range of vision so as to more clearly see that, through their actions of resistance, unruly women have persistently articulated a refusal to acquiesce.[51]

In their various and individual ways every one of the 15 women analysed in this book refused to acquiesce to their circumstances and took direct action to change those circumstances. Despite their 'ordinary' lives, despite the sometimes threatening, violent and dangerous situations they

---

[47]Faith 1993:9.
[48]*The Guardian* 4th May 1998; 2nd November 1998.
[49]Mr Justice Scott Baker quoted in *The Guardian* 31st May 1995.
[50]*The Guardian* 23rd October 1999.
[51]Faith 1993:9.

found themselves in and - in some cases - despite their destitute and bleak existences - each and every one were to take actions which would eventually cost them their lives. In doing so they exposed the presence of judicial misogyny within the criminal justice system. That their cases remain almost totally unknown is a testimony to the criminal justice system's (and by extension the wider society's) ability to mute those who refuse to speak through dominant modes of expression. The "cacophony of dissent and reaction" which now surround murderous women who have been exposed to judicial misogyny came too late for the 15 women executed during the 20th century. However, that "cacophony" has a history which leads directly to their lives and their deaths. As such they are entitled to be restored to their rightful position in the history of the present.

Appendix I

Louise Masset: Further Evidence in Support of her Innocence

a) Miss Teahan, one of the women who found Manfred's body, informed the police that she had seen two women fitting the description of the Brownings "outside the lavatory when she came out."[1] This was not revealed during the trial, as she was not called as a witness. According to Mr Newton, Louise's solicitor, this information was deliberately kept back.[2]

b) Mr Mutton, the proprietor of the Brighton restaurant Louise claimed to have eaten in, testified "that a person resembling Louise Masset in every particular dined at his hotel at an hour which would have made it impossible for her to commit the murder."[3] This too was withheld during the trial, and Mr Mutton was refused the opportunity to either identify or eliminate Louise as the person he had seen.

c) Following wide coverage of the trial in newspapers several members of the public who identified Manfred from a photo, wrote to the Home Office, confirming they had seen him in the company "of two strange women on the day of the murder."[4]

d) At Thames Police Court the magistrate was asked to help trace another nurse-child, the same age as Manfred, who had been snatched from his school by two women, and had not been seen since.[5]

---

[1]*Daily Chronicle* 8th January 1900.

[2]*The Daily News* 5th January 1900.

[3]*Daily Chronicle* 8th January 1900.

[4]*Daily Chronicle* 8th January 1900. For example, Mr Hughes Ellis, himself a man of social standing, had several communications with the Home Office, pointing out that "the child seemed very uneasy and struggled to get down ... but she held him tight ... He seemed to treat her as a stranger" (HO 144/1540/A61535 Sworn statement by Hughes Ellis dated 6th January 1900).

[5]Mackay, F. (1993) in Woodward, E. (ed) (1993) *In Suspicious Circumstances* Boxtree, London p.171.

Appendix II

Louisa Merrifield: The Controversy Surrounding the Medical Evidence

Dr George Bernard Manning, a consultant pathologist to the Bolton Hospital Group, had carried out the post mortem on Sarah Ricketts. It was therefore as a result of his post mortem report and evidence in the Magistrates' Court that it was established Mrs Ricketts had died from phosphorus poisoning. In other words, without his report and evidence Louisa and Alfred Merrifield could not have been found guilty of murder.[1] His report, however, was strongly criticised by Professor James Webster "who had been chief of the Forensic Laboratory at Birmingham for 20 years."[2] So strongly did Professor Webster feel about the medical evidence in the Merrifield case that he wrote a four-page A4 letter to the Permanent Under Secretary of State, Sir Frank Newsham. Professor Webster's opinion of the medical evidence presented at the trial may be gathered from the following extracts:

> ... I was appalled to see Manning's post-mortem report. If you had seen this document, I think you will agree that in two respects at least no person has ever been condemned to death on a more defective post-mortem report. The two points to which I would address your attention particularly are:
>
> a. There is not a single weight of any organ in that report. This was a poisoning case and therefore the weights of the organs were of paramount importance. Their omission reflects considerably upon the efficiency of this medical investigation.
>
> b. This so-called post-mortem report does not even contain a cause of death. I should like to know of any other murder case where that important detail has been absent from the autopsy report ...
>
> I was amazed to find that he had only sectioned three things - one piece of tissue from the liver and two blocks from the marrow of the sternum. Again I would point out that this was a case of poisoning where the effects of phosphorus on the organs are quite well known and where in particular this Prosecution averred that death was due to the impact of phosphorus on the heart. There was not a single section

---

[1]Dr Manning's evidence to the Magistrate's Court can be found in ASSI 52/785 pp.70-2.

[2]*Parliamentary Debates* (House of Commons) 1954-55 Vol 536 25th January-11th February 1955 col. 2170. Professor Webster was Director of West Midland Forensic Science Laboratory.

of heart, kidneys, thyroid, or brain stem, but despite this, extremely categorical statements were made by Manning and the Prosecution with regard to the cause of death.

What is much more important is that the liver shows undoubted evidence of damage long before death. That is not merely my opinion, but the opinion of a Professor of Pathology at one of the London schools to whom I showed the section, as I really began to think that I was becoming mental when I saw the appearance of this liver through the microscope and remembered that Manning had definitely said there was no damage or fat in this organ ...

No attempt was made to see how far along the alimentary tract the phosphorus had progressed. The whole of the intestinal contents were banged together into a flask and examined in this way. This prevented either the Prosecution or the Defence therefore having any certainty as to when the phosphorus was administered.

In view of the fact that no phosphorus was found in any of the other organs, it is astonishing that no analysis was done of the stomach wall and the intestines themselves ...

There is no chemical or pathological evidence which specifically proves that phosphorus was absorbed from this woman's alimentary canal. There is merely a theory put up by the Prosecution that it was absorbed ...

I shall never believe that the Prosecution proved beyond any reasonable doubt that Mrs Ricketts died from phosphorus poisoning. All they did do was prove there was phosphorus in the stomach contents and intestinal contents. Some day in the future I shall in all probability write up this case. By that time it will probably have been discussed widely, and so far as I am concerned, I have no feeling as to whether Louisa Merrifield hangs or not. All I am concerned with is this: That the principal tenet of British justice, namely, that the prosecution should prove a person guilty and not that a person should prove his innocence, should be maintained. In the Merrifield case I feel that we are back to the days antecedent to the first Infanticide Act when a woman had to prove that the thing she was accused of killing was born dead - a defect which was rectified by the first Infanticide Act which laid upon the prosecution the burden of proving that the thing that she had killed was born alive and had had a separate existence.[3]

---

[3] HO29/229 XC2573 Letter from Professor Webster to Sir Frank Newsham dated 8th September 1953.

Both Dr Manning and Professor Webster gave evidence at the trial, the professor maintaining that Sarah Ricketts had "died from the effects of liver necrosis and not phosphorus poisoning as alleged by the prosecution."[4] Had his explanation been accepted the Merrifields could only have been charged with attempted murder.

Louisa Merrifield's appeal document included criticism of the trial judge for omitting certain aspects of Professor Webster's evidence in his summing up.[5] The Appeal Judges dealt with this criticism in the following manner:

> His [Prof. Webster's] view was that Mrs Ricketts died from natural causes. It is therefore raising the issue: Did phosphorous poisoning kill Mrs Ricketts? This was clearly an issue for the jury. The evidence from Professor Webster was technical. On behalf of the Appellant it is said that the learned Judge should have explained it, and he did not. It is said that the failure on the part of the learned Judge to explain it left the jury to flounder in their room. Is that criticism well founded? This Court says that it is not ...

> [Quoting trial judge] "He [Prof. Webster] has read a number of books and read passages from them in support of his theory - I can call it no more - and a number of books have been read to him by the learned Attorney-General in the opposite sense. You must use your practical commonsense."

> Criticism was offered of this last sentence. Does it amount to any more than inviting the jury to give as reasonable a consideration as they could to the medical evidence on both sides? This Court has arrived at the conclusion that the essentials of the medical evidence was left to the jury, and one question which they took with them on their retirement was, Did [sic] the phosphorous poison kill? Their verdict indicates how they answered it.[6]

Although the Appeal was dismissed the controversy surrounding the medical evidence was raised again during the House of Commons debate on capital punishment in 1955 when MP for Northampton R.T. Paget stated:

> The jury, coming to a conclusion upon an issue between two experts - on an issue upon which, frankly, they were not competent to express an opinion, upon the direction which I have read - found Mrs

---

[4]*The Times* 29th July 1953.

[5]HO291/230 27359 - document entitled 'Particulars of Grounds of Appeal Additional to those set out in the Notice'.

[6]HO29/229 XC2573 Transcript of Appeal before Mr Justices Cassels, Slade and Barry, dated 3rd September 1953.

Merrifield guilty, and she was allowed to hang for a murder which Prof Webster said had never taken place.[7]

Paget further drew attention to Prof Webster's high status within his profession:

Prof Webster who had been chief of the Forensic Laboratory at Birmingham for 20 years; who had been the prosecution's witness in every murder case on the Midland Circuit since, I and, I believe the former Attorney-General came to the Bar, and had been relied upon by the prosecution as the foremost pathologist in the Midlands, gave evidence in the trial that the deceased lady had died a natural death.[8]

---

[7]*Parliamentary Debates* (House of Commons) 1954-55 Vol 536 25th January-11th February 1955 col 2170.
[8]*Parliamentary Debates* (House of Commons) 1954-55 Vol 536 25th January-11th February 1955 col 2170.

Appendix III

Edith Thompson: Elaboration on the State's Response to Contentious Issues Surrounding her Execution

Arthur Koestler, who was a keen anti-hanging campaigner, published a book - *Reflections on Hanging* in 1956 in which he quoted the following passage from a confidential Home Office instruction to Prison Governors dated shortly after Edith Thompson's execution[1]:

> Any reference to the manner in which an execution has been carried out should be confined to as few words as possible, e.g., "it was carried out expeditiously and without a hitch". No record should be taken as to the number of seconds, and if pressed for details of this kind, the Governor should say he cannot give them, and he did not time the proceedings, but "a very short interval elapsed", or some general expression of opinion to the same effect.[2]

Koestler suggested these instructions had been amended as a result of the horrific details that emerged concerning Edith Thompson's execution which he also documented in his book. These instructions were so secret that neither the House of Lords nor the House of Commons knew of their existence.[3] His book together with an article he wrote for *The Observer* (4th March 1956) therefore caused great furore amongst anti-hanging MPs who asked for full details of these instructions in the House of Commons. The secrecy of the instructions meant that answering questions in relation to them became a matter of extreme delicacy as can be seen from a comment by the Permanent Under-Secretary to the Home Office - Sir Frank Newsam: "the subject [is] a particularly difficult one to deal with in the House by way of question and answer, when many people will be looking for every opportunity to trip the S. of S. up on these now highly controversial matters."[4] Home Office staff consequently prepared draft answers for the Home Secretary to assist him in answering MPs' questions, one of which included the following paragraph:

---

[1]Koestler claims this document was dated 10th January 1925, but a document bearing almost identical wording can be found in the Public Record Office (PCOM 9/1983 XC2662) and is dated 28th August 1924.

[2]Quoted in Koestler, A. (1956) *Reflections on Hanging* Gollancz London pp.139-40.

[3]PCOM 9/1983 XC2662. MPs were aware of a document which outlined the practical procedures for executions, but did not realise a second document existed which instructed prison staff in how to respond to the media following executions.

[4]PCOM 9/1983 XC2662 Memo dated 28th March 1956.

Nothing happened at the execution to call for the amendment of the instructions governing executions and no amendment was made in consequence of it. These instructions have always been treated as confidential and I am not prepared to depart from the practice of my predecessors.[5]

Another advisory memo to the Home Secretary read:

It would be impossible to give details of the amendments without revealing to some extent the nature of the instructions which have already been declared to be confidential and it is suggested that the most that should be said is that since the date of the execution the instructions have been amended on six occasions, the first being in 1925 and the last in 1954.[6]

Despite these statements a Prison Commission communication reveals that the document Koestler was quoting from bore the following introductory paragraph:

In view of certain remarks made at inquests on recently executed prisoners, it has been thought desirable to amplify the instructions given to Governors in Circular No. 880 of the 31st March, 1922. That circular is, therefore, cancelled and the following *fresh* instructions will be carefully observed.[7]

The instructions referred to are of interest to the Edith Thompson case in particular and to all other cases of executed women discussed here in general for two reasons. First, throughout this book I have argued the state considered a confession highly desirable because it added legitimacy to the execution. The Edith Thompson case demonstrated this principle also worked in reverse. That is to say, when a prisoner proclaims her innocence incessantly, even on her way to the scaffold, as Edith did, it adds *illegitimacy* to the execution. Thus, coincidentally or not, the 'fresh' instructions dated 28th August 1924, no longer recommended the pursuit of a confession:

It is undesirable that information should be given to the public as to whether, or not, a prisoner under a capital charge, or an executed prisoner, has made a confession. Governors are, therefore, informed that should they, or any other officer of the prison, be questioned on the point at the inquest, or otherwise, the answer will be: "I have no authority to say whether a prisoner has confessed or not" ...

[5]PCOM 9/1983 XC2662. Draft answer for Home Secretary (Undated).
[6]PCOM 9/1983 XC2662 Memo entitled 'Amendments to Instructions' (Undated).
[7]PCOM 9/1983 XC3662 Circular to Prisons from A.J. Wall, Secretary to the Prison Commission 28th August 1924. My emphasis. The word 'fresh' is of course ambivalent but suggests the introduction of new instructions.

Similarly, any reference to any remarks such as prisoner may have made, or not made, on the scaffold, or elsewhere, should be avoided.[8]

It will be remembered that the remark by Louise Masset, executed in 1900, "what I am about to suffer is just" was immediately interpreted as a 'confession'. It will be recalled that Ada Williams's failure to confess was interpreted as "fear of implicating her husband", a totally irrational interpretation since a confession would surely have the opposite effect of exonerating her husband. Leslie James's comment that she was "truly repentant for breaking the law" was interpreted as a confession, even though this statement did not in any way undermine her claim that the baby's death had been accidental. Emily Swann too was reported to have "expressed contrition for the crime", an expression which I argued allowed observers to *infer* the guilt of the prisoner. Yet, by 1926 when Major Blake - who had been governor of Pentonville prison at the time of Freddy Bywaters' execution - published his memoirs which included Freddy's confession to Percy Thompson's murder the night before his execution, Blake was prosecuted for breaching the Official Secrets Act. He also revealed that Freddy had "insisted just before his execution that Mrs Thompson ... was innocent.[9] Major Blake's trial was the first case ever of a "prosecution of an official using information for journalistic purposes."[10] Blake's defence KC argued the information regarding Freddy and Edith "had done nothing but shock and annoy some people at the Home Office ... The authorities had decided upon a glorious prosecution" even though they could have settled the case in the police court, "but they loaded the dice against the defendant by taking him to the Central Criminal Court, where though he was calling no evidence, his counsel was denied the last word" because he was being prosecuted by the Attorney General.[11] The prosecution replied:

> If Major Blake had desired to write history, he should have asked the permission of the Home Secretary who was in a better position than he to judge whether such publication would do harm or not.[12]

Apart from Major Blake's revelations, details about the last moments of condemned prisoners' became almost non-existent after the execution of Edith Thompson. After an extensive search in the PRO and newspaper archives I have located only one comment - that Ruth Ellis died bravely.

The second part of the circular of interest to the case-studies in this thesis is the following paragraph which is almost identical to that quoted by Koestler:

---

[8]PCOM 9/1983 XC2662 Circular from Mr Wall.
[9]*The Times* 16th December 1926 - Report of Major Blake's trial.
[10]*The Times* 16th December 1926. Major Blake had received 300 guineas from the *London Evening News* for the extracts from his memoirs.
[11]*The Times* 16th December 1926 - Report of Major Blake's trial.
[12]*The Times* 16th December 1926 - Report of Major Blake's trial.

Any reference to the manner in which an execution has been carried out should be confined to as few words as possible, e.g. "it was carried out expeditiously and there was no hitch." No record should be taken as to the number of seconds, etc., and if pressed for details of this kind the Governor should say he is not able to give them as he did not time the proceedings but "a very short interval elapsed" or some general expression to the like effect may be used.[13]

With these instructions in mind we are able to fully appreciate statements such as that released at the time of Louie Calvert's execution when the hanging was described as having been carried out "humanely and expeditiously." We may also feel concerned about a comment by the executioner John Ellis, who after stating that "when they hanged Edith Thompson, everybody present was upset to vomiting point" added:

> We don't make mistakes nowadays ... it's all taped and worked out, and even if there should be some slight mishap the whole government machine goes all out to save the hangman's face. They have to.[14]

We may question whether it was coincidence that Mr Young, a prison officer who had been present at Edith's execution should write in 1948: "I performed my duty at the execution which was carried out *without a hitch* ..."[15] As I pointed out in Chapter Six, this letter was written in response to a claim by Beverley Baxter, the editor of the *Daily Express*, that two men had entered his office and given an account of the horrendous circumstances surrounding the execution of Edith Thompson. As Mr Young also stated in the letter, if he had revealed such details, he would have been "guilty of a Breach of the Secret Act."[16] In short, the existence of these instructions entitles us to treat with scepticism statements to the press along the lines that a given execution "was carried out without a hitch." While such glib statements may have been based on truth in some cases, the existence of these instructions demonstrates this was not *necessarily* the case. It demonstrates the state could not be relied upon to tell the truth about actions taken in the name of the nation's people. For example, as I indicated in Chapter Six, we

---

[13]PCOM 9/1983 XC2662 Circular from A.J. Wall.
[14]PCOM 9/1983 XC2662. Underlining in the original. This Home Office document is referring to an interview Ellis gave to *The Observer* 18th March 1956. According to a Prison Commission document Ellis had had first hand experience of having his face 'saved' for the execution of the next woman after Edith Thompson - Susan Newell, a Scottish woman executed 10th October 1923 - did not go smoothly: "Ellis bungled the job to the extent that he did not pinion her wrists securely so that she was able to free her hands and tear off the cap" (PCOM 9/1983 XC2662 Seven-page document, undated).
[15]PCOM 9/1983 XC2662 Letter from M.H. Young to Sir John, 15th April 1948. My emphasis.
[16]PCOM 9/1983 XC2662 Letter from M.H. Young 15th April 1948.

have reason to suspect Ethel Major suffered greatly prior to her execution. But we do not *know* the exact facts since they are not included in her file. By insisting that prison staff adhered closely to the 'fresh' instructions the state ensured supporters of abolition would never again have a martyr on the scale of Edith Thompson. For it is not just due to the fact that Edith was innocent of the crime for which she was executed that she is still remembered today, it is also as a result of the horrific circumstances of her execution, circumstances which Home Office staff did their utmost to deny. Yet despite this recalcitrance various details have emerged which have served to increase sympathy for Edith and which may ultimately have assisted the abolitionist cause. Some of these details have already been discussed in Chapter Six. Others included Prison Commission documents which revealed she had been severely drugged throughout her last night and in the morning had received a hitherto unheard of combination of strychnine, hyoscine and morphia:

> Dr Snell says he has never known such a combination of stimulants and sedative to be given and cannot account for it.[17]

This combination of drugs rendered her incapable of walking. Hence, contrary to Home Office instructions, her wrists and legs were strapped while still in the condemned cell, which led to her being carried to the scaffold:

> The Governor explained to me that the prisoner's <u>feet</u> were pinioned in her cell as well as her wrists (behind back). It was thought best in this case to do it in the cell. Prisoner was therefore unable to walk and had to be carried the few yards to the drop. Governor thought she could have walked with assistance but if she had collapsed on the way the necessary pinioning of the feet before the drop fell would have delayed matters and been awkward.[18]

In view of such details it is not surprising the Prison Commissioners drew the following conclusion:

> It seems impossible to avoid giving a full answer [to MPs]. Since the answer will be written, there is less objection to making it long and it seems imperative to avoid giving ground for suspicion that the Department is trying to conceal some unmentionable part of the story. Whatever the starting point chosen, the account of subsequent events should be fairly full. There would be some advantage in beginning with Mrs Thompson's reception as a convicted prisoner but this would make the reply unconscionably long. Perhaps the best starting

---

[17]PCOM 9/1983 XC2662 Six-page document, undated.
[18]PCOM 9/1983 XC2662 Six-page document, undated. Underlining in the original.

point will be the day before the execution. This will bring out that on her last complete day alive Mrs Thompson remained cheerful.[19]

It is of course this sanitising of events surrounding executions which made the practice acceptable for so long, a fact prison and Home Office staff would have been well aware of, otherwise they would not have been so concerned about being seen to be involved in a cover-up in the execution of Edith Thompson and several draft answers to MPs would not have been necessary. Nor would it have been necessary to devote several files to allegations made by both individuals as well as the press regarding the execution, together with extensive discussions as to how the Home Office ought to deal with such allegations. As Koestler pointed out, the grotesque aspect of executions is not just connected with "the brutality but with the macabre, cold-blooded politeness of the ceremony, in which the person whose neck is going to be broken is supposed to collaborate in a nice, sensible manner, as if it were a matter of a minor surgical operation."[20] In refusing to play her part politely, Edith Thompson not only challenged the state's sanitised accounts of capital punishment, but also succeeded in exposing the secrecy engaged in by both the Home Office and the Prison Commissioners in order to make this form of punishment palatable to the general public.

---

[19]PCOM 9/1983 XC2662 Six-page document, undated.
[20]Koestler 1956:139.

Bibliography

Public Record Office Documents

ASSI 13/64 XC3601 CL
ASSI 13/66 XC6872
ASSI 26/48 XC3601 CL
ASSI/45/86/2
ASSI/52/629
ASSI 52/785
ASSI/72/33/1-4
CRIM 1/58/5
CRIM 1/59/4 XC7025
CRIM 1/83/2
CRIM 1/206/5 XC6872
CRIM 1/2492
CRIM 1/2582
DPP2/2430 23271
FO371/29537 XC17007
HO29/229 XC2573
HO45/2685 PT2 XC2501
HO144/280 XC17335
HO144/280/A61654
HO144/690/104226 XC2622
HO144/736/113887 XC2356
HO144/861/155396
HO144/1540/A61535
HO144/2685 PT2 XC2501
HO291/330 27359
MEPO 3/1582
PCOM 8/22 XC2663
PCOM 8/436
PCOM 9/1983 XC2662

Legal Reports & Parliamentary Papers

Criminal Appeal Reports Vol XVII, July-December 1922-23, Supreme Court Library, Royal Courts of Justice, London.
Parliamentary Debates House of Commons, 3rd series, Vol civ, 1st May 1849.
Parlimanetary Debates House of Commons, 3rd series, Vol 142 6th May-27th June 1856.

Parliamentary Debates House of Commons, Vol 197 21st June-9th July 1926.

Parliamentary Debates House of Commons, Vol 314 29th June-17th July 1936.

Parliamentary Debates House of Commons, Vol 449 6th-23rd April 1948.

Parliamentary Debates House of Commons, Vol 536 25th January-11th February 1955.

Parliamentary Debates House of Commons, Vol 544 18th-28th July 1955.

Parliamentary Debates House of Commons, Vol 550 12th-29th March 1956.

Parliamentary Debates House of Commons, Vol 564 4th-15th February 1957.

Royal Commission on Capital Punishment 1949-1953 Report (1953) Her Majesty's Stationery Office, London.

Select Comittee on Capital Punishment 1929-1930 Report and Minutes of Evidence (1931) His Majesty's Stationery Office, London.

Newspapers

The Daily Chronicle
The Daily Express
The Daily Mirror
The Daily Mail
The Daily News
The Daily Telegraph
The Echo
The Evening Express
The Guardian
The Herald
The Hull Daily Mail
The Liverpool Daily Post
The Liverpool Post and Mercury
The London Evening Standard
The Manchester Evening News
The Manchester Guardian
The News of the World
The Observer
The Pall Mall Gazette
The Sun
The Sunday People
The Sunday Telegraph,
The South Wales Daily News
The Times
The Weekly Dispatch
The Western Mail
The Yorkshire Post
The Yorkshire Telegraph & Star

Theses, Unpublished Papers and Periodicals

Agozino, O. (1994) 'Committed Objectivity: Research on Black Women by a Black Man' (Unpublished Paper).
Birch, H. (1988) 'Twice unnatural creatures' in *New Statesman* 18th March 1988.
Cox, C. (1986) 'Who Gave Ruth Ellis the Gun?' *Police Review* 22nd August 1986.
Ward, A. (1996) *Psychiatry and Criminal Responsibility in England 1843 1939.* Unpublished Ph.D. thesis, Faculty of Law, De Montford University 1996.
The Lancet 24th January 1903.
The Lancet 8th January 1955.
The Lancet 23rd July 1955.
The Lancet 30th July 1955.
The Lancet 20th August 1955.
Murder Casebook (1991) Vol 7 Part 5, Marshall Cavendish Ltd, London.

Books and Journal Articles

Adam, H.L. (1911) *Woman and Crime* T. Werner Laurie, London.
Ahluwalia, K. & Gupta, R. (1997) *Circle of Light* HarperCollins, London.
Anderson, B.S. & Zinsser, J.P. (1988) *A History of Their Own: Women in Europe from Prehistory to the Present Vol. I* Harper & Row, New York.
Anderson, B.S. & Zinsser, J.P. (1990) *A History of Their Own; Women in Europe from Prehistory to the Present Vol II* Penguin, London.
Angerman, A., Binnema, A., Keunen, A., Poels, V. and Zirkzee, J. (eds) (1989) *Current Issues in Women's History* Routledge, London.
Badinter, E. (1981) *The Myth of Motherhood* Souvenir Press, London.
Bailey, B. (1989) *Hangmen of England* W.H. Allen, London.
Ballinger, A. (1996) 'The Guilt of the Innocent and the Innocence of the Guilty' in Myers, A. & Wight, S. (eds) *No Angels* Pandora, London, pp.1-28.
Bardsley, B. (1987) *Flowers in Hell* Pandora, London.
Barstow, L.A. (1994) *Witchcraze* Pandora, London.
Bartky, S.L. (1988) 'Foucault, Femininity, and the Modernization of Patriarchal Power' in Diamond, I. & Quinby, L. (eds) *Feminism & Foucault* Northeastern University Press, Boston, pp.61-86.
Beattie, J.M. (1986) *Crime and the Courts in England 1660-1800* Clarendon Press, Oxford.
Bedarida, F. (1994) *A Social History of England 1851-1990* Routledge, London.
Beier, A.L., Cannadine, D. & Rosenheim, J.M. (eds) (1989) *The First Modern Society* Cambridge University Press, Cambridge.
Bell, C. & Fox, M. (1996) 'Telling Stories of Women Who Kill' in *Social & Legal Studies* Vol 5, no 4, December, pp.471-94.
Birch, H. (ed) (1993) *Moving Targets* Virago, London.

Birch, H. (1993) '"If looks could kill": Myra Hindley and the iconography of evil' in Birch, H. (ed) *Moving Targets* Virago, London, pp.32-61.

Bland, L. (1984) 'The Case of the Yorkshire Ripper: Mad, Bad, Beast or Male?' in Scraton, P. & Gordon, P. (eds) *Causes for Concern* Penguin, Harmondsworth, pp.185-209.

Blyth, H. (1975) *Madeleine Smith: A famous Victorian murder trial* Duckworth, London.

Borowitz, A. (1989) *The Bermondsey Horror* Robson, London.

Box, S. (1983) *Power, Crime and Mystification* Tavistock, London.

Braybon, G. & Summerfield, P. (1987) *Out of the Cage: Women's Experiences in Two World Wars* Pandora, London.

Bresler, F. (1965) *Reprieve* George Harrap, London.

Bresler, F. (1992) 'Suddenly at a Nursing Home ...' in Goodman, J. (ed) *The Medical Murders* Warner Books, London, pp.221-30.

Broad, L. (1952) *The Innocence of Edith Thompson* Hutchinson, London.

Browne, A. (1987) *When Battered Women Kill* The Free Press, New York.

Browne, D.G. & Tullett, T. (1987) *Bernard Spilsbury* Grafton Books, London.

Brownmiller, S. (1976) *Against Our Will* Bantam Books, New York.

Burn, G. (1998) *Happy Like Murderers* Faber & Faber, London.

Byrne, R. (1992) *Prisons and Punishments of London* Grafton, London.

Cain, M. (ed) (1989) *Growing Up Good* Sage, London.

Cain, M. (1990) 'Towards Transgression: New Directions in Feminist Criminology' in *International Journal of the Sociology of Law* 18, pp.1-18.

Cain, M. (1990) 'Realist philosophy and standpoint epistemologies or feminist criminology as a successor science' in Gelsthorpe, L. & Morris, A. (eds) *Feminist Perspectives in Criminology* Open University Press, Milton Keynes, pp.124-40.

Cain, M. (1993) 'Foucault, feminism and feeling: What Foucault can and cannot contribute to feminist epistemology' in Ramazanoglu, C. (ed) *Up Against Foucault* Routledge, London, pp.73-96.

Calvert, E.R. (1927) *Capital Punishment in the Twentieth Century* C.P. Putnam's Sons, London.

Cameron, D. & Frazer, E. (1987) *The Lust to Kill* Polity Press, Cambridge.

Cameron, D. (1996) 'Wanted: The Female Serial Killer' in *Trouble & Strife* 33, Summer, pp.21-8.

Cameron, D. (1996-97) 'Motives and Meanings' in *Trouble & Strife* 34, Winter, pp.44-52.

Campbell, J.C. (1992) '"If I Can't Have You, No One Can": Power and Control in Homicide of Female Partners' in Radford, J. & Russell, D.E.H. (eds) *Femicide* Open University Press, Buckingham pp.99-113.

Caputi, J. (1987) *The Age of Sex Crime* The Women's Press, London.

Carlen, P. (1976) *Magistrates' Justice* Martin Robertson, London.

Carlen, P. (1983) *Women's Imprisonment* Routledge & Kegan Paul, London.

Carlen, P. (ed) (1985) *Criminal Women* Polity, Cambridge.

Carlen, P. (1988) *Women, Crime and Poverty* Open University Press, Milton Keynes.

Chadwick, R. (1992) *Bureaucratic Mercy: The Home Office and the Treatment of Capital Cases in Victorian England* Garland, New York.

Chibnall, S. (1977) *Law and Order News* Tavistock, London.

Christoph, J.B. (1962) *Capital Punishment and British Politics* Allen & Unwin, London.

Clark, A. (1987) *Women's Silence Men's Violence* Pandora, London.

Clark, A. (1992) 'Humanity or justice? Wife beating and the law in the eighteenth and nineteenth centuries' in Smart, C. (ed) *Regulating Womanhood* Routledge, London, pp.187-206.

Cobbe, F. P. (1878) 'Wife Torture in England' in Radford, J. & Russell, D.E.H. (eds) (1992) *Femicide* Open University Press, Buckingham, pp.46-52.

Cockburn, J.S. (ed) (1977) *Crime in England 1550-1800* Methuen, London.

Connell, R.W. (1987) *Gender & Power* Polity, Cambridge.

Crowley, H. & Himmelweit S. (eds) (1992) *Feminism and Knowledge* Polity Press, Cambridge in association with Blackwell Publishers Ltd, Oxford and The Open University.

Dahl, T. & Snare, A. (1978) 'The coercion of privacy: A feminist perspective' in Smart, C. & Smart, B. (eds) *Women, Sexuality and Social Control* Routledge & Kegan Paul, London, pp.8-26.

Daly, M. (1979) *Gyn/Ecology* The Women's Press, London.

Dekker, R.M. & van de Pol, L. (1989) *The Tradition of Female Transvestism in Early Modern Europe* MacMillan, London.

Delmar, R. (1976) 'Looking Again at Engels's "Origin of the Family, Private Property and the State"' in Mitchell, J. & Oakley, A. (eds) *The Rights and Wrongs of Women* Penguin, London, pp.271-87.

de Sousa Santos, B. (1985) 'On Modes of Production of Law and Social Power' in *International Journal of the Sociology of Law* 13, pp.299-336.

Deveaux, M. (1994) 'Feminism and Empowerment: A Critical Reading of Foucault' in *Feminist Studies* Vol. 20, no 2, Summer, pp.223-47.

Devlin, P. (1981) *The Judge* Oxford University Press, Oxford.

Diamond, I. & Quinby, L. (eds) (1988) *Feminism & Foucault* Northeastern University Press, Boston.

Dobash, R.E. & Dobash, R. (1979) *Violence Against Wives* Open Books, Shepton Mallet.

Dobash, R.E. & Dobash, R. (1992) *Women, Violence & Social Change* Routledge, London.

Doyal, L. (1990) 'Wages, Work and Women's Well Being' in *Women's Studies International Forum* Vol 13, no 6, pp.587-604.

Du Cann, C.G.L. (1960) *Miscarriages of Justice* Frederick Muller Ltd, London.

Dworkin, A. (1982) *Our Blood* The Women's Press, London.

Dworkin, A. (1988) *Intercourse* Arrow Books, London.

Earl of Birkenhead, (no year) *Famous Trials* Hutchinson, London.

Edwards, S. (1987) '"Provoking Her Own Demise": From Common Assault to Homicide' in Hanmer J. & Maynard, M. (eds) *Women, Violence and Social Control* MacMillan, London, pp.152-68.

Edwards, S. (1989) *Policing 'Domestic' Violence* Sage, London.

Edwards, S. (1996) *Sex and Gender in the Legal Process* Blackstone Press Ltd, London.

Ellis, G. (1996) *Ruth Ellis, My Mother: Memoirs of a Murderer's Daughter* Smith Gryphon Publishers, London.

Ellis, J. (1996) *Diary of a Hangman* Forum Press, London.

Engels, F. (1985) *The Origin of the Family, Private Property and the State* Penguin, Harmondsworth.

English, D. & Ehrenreich, B. (1979) *For Her Own Good* Pluto, London.

Faith, K. (1993) *Unruly Women: The Politics of Confinement & Resistance* Press Gang Publishers, Vancouver.

Farran, D. (1987-8) 'The Trial of Ruth Ellis' in Stanley, L. & Scott, S. (eds) *Studies in Sexual Politics* Sociology Department, University of Manchester, no 24.

Fitzgerald, M. & Sim, J. (1982) *British Prisons* Basil Blackwell, Oxford.

Forster, M. (1984) *Significant Sisters* Penguin Books, Harmondsworth.

Foucault, M. (1979) *Discipline and Punish* Peregrine Books, Harmondsworth.

French, D. (1991) *Working* Gollancz, London.

French, M. (1986) *Beyond Power: On Women, Men & Morals* Abacus, London.

Garland, D. (1993) *Punishment and Modern Society: A Study in Social Theory* The University of Chicago Press, Chicago.

Garry, A. & Pearsall, M. (eds) (1989) *Women, Knowledge and Reality* Routledge, London.

Gatrell, V.A.C. (1994) *The Hanging Tree* Oxford University Press, Oxford.

Gattey, C.N. (1972) *The Incredible Mrs van der Elst* Leslie Frewin Publishers, London.

Gelsthorpe, L. & Morris, A. (eds) (1990) *Feminist Perspectives in Criminology* Open University Press, Milton Keynes.

Gittings, R. (1975) *Young Thomas Hardy* Heinemans' Educational Books, London.

Goode, E. & Ben-Yehuda, N. (1994) *Moral Panics* Basil Blackwell, Oxford.

Goodman, J. & Pringle, P. (1974) *The Trial of Ruth Ellis* David & Charles, London.

Goodman, J. (1993) *The Daily Telegraph Murder File* Mandarin, London.

Gonda, C. (1992) '"Exactly Them Words": Histories of a Murderous Daughter' in Gonda, C. (ed) *Tea & Leg-Irons* Open Letters, London, pp.63-82.

Gordon, L. (1989) *Heroes of Their Own Lives* Virago, London.

Graham, C. M. (1790) 'Letters on Education' in Jones, V. (ed) (1990) *Women in the Eighteenth Century* Routledge, London, pp.112-16.

Green, E., Hebron, S. & Woodward, D. (1987) 'Women, Leisure and Social Control' in Hanmer, J. & Maynard, M. (eds) *Women, Violence and Social Control* MacMillan, London, pp.75-92.

Greer, G. (1973) *The Female Eunuch* Paladin, St Albans.

Hall, S., Critcher, C., Jefferson, T., Clarke, J., Roberts, B. (1978) *Policing the Crisis* MacMillan, London.

Hall, S. & Scraton, P. (1981) 'Law, class and control' in Fitzgerald, M. McLennan, G. & Pawson, J. (compilers) (1986) *Crime & Society* Routledge & Kegan Paul, London, pp.460-97.

Hall, S. (1988) 'The Toad in the Garden: Thatcherism among the Theorists' in Nelson, C. & Grossberg, L. (eds) *Marxism and the Interpretation of Culture* MacMillan, London, pp.35-73.

Hall, S. & Gieben, B. (eds) (1992) *Formations of Modernity* Polity Press, Cambridge.

Hamer, E. (1996) 'Fighting for Freedom: Suffragette Violence Against Their State' in Myers, A. & Wight, S. (eds) (1996) *No Angels* Pandora, London, pp.72-84.

Hamilton, P. (1992) 'The Enlightenment and the Birth of Social Science' in Hall, S. & Gieben, B. (eds) *Formations of Modernity* Polity, Cambridge, pp.17-58.

Hamilton, R. (1978) *The Liberation of Women* Allen & Unwin, London.

Hancock, R. (1989) *Ruth Ellis* Weidenfeld, London.

Hanmer, J. & Maynard, M. (eds) (1987) *Women, Violence and Social Control* MacMillan, London.

Harding, S. (1986) *The Science Question in Feminism* Open University Press, Milton Keynes.

Harding, S. (ed) (1987) *Feminism & Methodology* Open University Press, Milton Keynes.

Harding, S. (1989) 'Feminist Justificatory Strategies' in Garry, A. & Pearsall, M. (eds) *Women, Knowledge, and Reality* Routledge, London pp.189-201.

Harding, S. (1990) 'Feminism, Science, and the Anti-Enlightenment Critiques' in Nicholson, L.J. (ed) *Feminism/Postmodernism* Routledge, London, pp.83-106.

Harding, S. (1992) 'The Instability of the Analytical Categories of Feminist Theory' in Crowley, H. & Himmelweit, S. (eds) *Knowing Women* Polity and Open University Press, Cambridge and Milton Keynes, pp.338-54.

Harris, P. (1988) *An Introduction to Law* Weidenfeld & Nicolson, London.

Hart, L. (1994) *Fatal Women* Routledge, London.

Hartman, M.S. (1985) *Victorian Murderesses* Robson Books, London.

Hartmann, H. 'The Unhappy Marriage of Marxism and Feminism' in Sargent, L. (ed) (1981) *The Unhappy Marriage of Marxism and Feminism* Pluto, London, pp.1-41.

Hartsock, N. (1987) 'Foucault on Power: A Theory for Women?' in Nicholson, L.J. (ed) (1990) *Feminism/Postmodernism* Routledge, London, pp.157-75.

Hay, D. (1977) 'Property, authority and the criminal law' in Hay, D., Linebaugh, P., Rule, J., Thompson, E.P. & Winslow, C. (eds) *Albion's Fatal Tree* Penguin, Harmondsworth, pp.17-63.

Hay, D., Linebaugh, P., Rule, J., Thompson, E.P. & Winslow, C. (eds) (1977) *Albion's Fatal Tree*, Penguin, Harmondsworth.

Healey, T. (1985) *Crimes of Passion* Hamlyn, London.

Heath, J. (1963) *Eighteenth Century Penal Theory* Oxford University Press, London.

Heidensohn, F. (1986) *Women & Crime* MacMillan, Basingstoke.

Heidkamp, B. (1993) 'Angels of death' in Birch, H. (ed) *Moving Targets* Virago, London, pp.218-40.

Held, D. et al (eds) (1984) *States & Societies* Martin Robertson, Oxford.

Hester, M. (1992) *Lewd Women & Wicked Witches* Routledge, London.

Hibbert, C. (1968) *The Roots of Evil: A Social History of Crime and Punishment* Minerva Press, USA.

Hicks, S. (1939) *Not Guilty, M'Lord* Cassell & Co Ltd, London.

Higginbotham, A.R. (1992) '"Sin of the Age": Infanticide and Illegitimacy in Victorian London', in Garrigan, K.O. (ed) *Victorian Scandals* Ohio University Press, Athens, Ohio pp.257-88.

Hoff, L.A. (1990) *Battered Women as Survivors* Routledge, London.

Hoffer, P. & Hull, N.E.H. (1984) *Murdering Mothers: Infanticide in England and New England 1558-1803* New York University Press, New York.

Howe, A. (1994) *Punish and Critique* Routledge, London.

Hudson, B. (1985) 'Sugar and Spice and all things nice' in *Community Care* 4th April.

Huggett, R & Berry P. (1956) *Daughters of Cain* George Allen & Unwin Ltd, London.

Hutter, B. & Williams, G. (eds) (1981) *Controlling Women* Croom Helm, London.

Ignatieff, M. (1978) *A Just Measure of Pain* Macmillan, London.

Jackson, S. (1978) *The Old Bailey* W.H. Allen, London.

Jeffreys, S. (1985) *The Spinster and Her Enemies* Pandora, London.

Jeffreys, S. (1990) *Anticlimax* The Women's Press, London.

Johnson, P. (1993) 'Feminism, and the Enlightenment' in *Radical Philosophy* 63, Spring, pp.3-12.

Jones, A. (1991) *Women Who Kill* Victor Gollancz Ltd, London.

Jones, K.B. (1987) 'On Authority: Or, Why Women Are Not Entitled to Speak' in Diamond, I. & Quinby, L. (eds) (1988) *Feminism & Foucault* Northeastern University Press, Boston, pp.119-33.

Jones, V. (ed) (1990) *Women in the Eighteenth Century* Routledge, London.

Keane, J. (ed) (1988) *Civil Society and the State* Verso, London.

Kelly, L. & Radford, J. (1990) '"Nothing really happened": the invalidation of women's experiences of sexual violence' in Hester, M. Kelly, L. & Radford, J. (eds) (1996) *Women, Violence and Male Power* Open University Press, Buckingham pp.19-33.

Kelley, J. (1967) *When the Gates Shut* Longmans, London.

Kirsta, A. (1994) *Deadlier Than the Male* HarperCollins, London.

Koestler, A. (1956) *Reflections on Hanging* Gollancz, London.

Kramer, H. & Sprenger, J. (1996) *Malleus Maleficarum* Bracken Books, London.

Kurzmics, H. (1988) 'The Civilizing Process' in Keane, J. (ed) *Civil Society and the State* Verso, London, pp.149-76.

Laster, K. (1994) 'Famous Last Words: Criminals on the Scaffold, Victoria, Australia, 1842-1967' in *International Journal of the Sociology of Law* 22, pp.1-18.

Laurence, J. (1932) *A History of Capital Punishment* Kennika Press, N.Y./London.

Lees, S. (1986) *Losing Out* Hutchinson, London.

Lees, S. (1989) 'Learning to Love: Sexual reputation, morality and the social control of girls' in Cain, M. (ed) *Growing Up Good* Sage, London, pp.19-37.

Lees, S. (1997) *Ruling Passions* Open University Press, Buckingham.

Leonard, E.B. (1982) *Women, Crime & Society* Longman, London.

Linebaugh, P. (1977) 'The Ordinary of Newgate and His Account' in Cockburn, J.S. (ed) *Crime in England 1550-1800* Methuen, London, pp.246-70.

Linebaugh, P. (1991) *The London Hanged* Penguin, Harmondsworth.

Lustgarten, E. (1960) *The Murder and the Trial* Odhams Press, London.

Mackay, F. (1993) 'French Leave' in Woodward, E. (ed) *In Suspicious Circumstances* Boxtree, London, pp.153-73.

MacKinnon, C.A. (1989) *Towards a Feminist Theory of the State* Harvard University Press, Cambridge Massachusetts.

MacNalty, A.S. (1929) *A Book of Crimes* Elkin Mathews & Marrot Ltd, London.

Maguire, S. (1988) '"Sorry love" - violence against women in the home and the state response' in *Critical Social Policy* 23, Autumn, pp.34-47.

Malcolmson, R.W. (1977) 'Infanticide in the Eighteenth Century' in Cockburn, J.S. (ed) *Crime in England 1550-1800* Methuen, London, pp.187-209.

Marks, L. & Van Den Bergh, T. (1990) *Ruth Ellis: A Case of Diminished Responsibility?* Penguin, Harmondsworth.

Marwick, A. (1990) *British Society Since 1945* Penguin, Harmondsworth.

Matus, J. (1995) *Unstable Bodies: Victorian Representantions of Sexuality and Maternity* Manchester University Press, Manchester.

McLynn, F. (1989) *Crime & Punishment in 18th Century England* Oxford University Press, Oxford.

McNay, L. (1992) *Foucault and Feminism* Polity, Cambridge.

McNeil, M. (1993) 'Dancing with Foucault' in Ramazanoglu, C. (ed) (1993) *Up Against Foucault* Routledge, London, pp.147-75.

McNeill, S. (1996) 'Getting Away with Murder' in *Trouble & Strife* 33, Summer pp.3-7.

Miles, R. (1989) *Women's History of the World* Paladin, London.

Mills, J. (1991) *Womanwords* Virago, London.

Millman, M. & Kanter, R. (1987) 'Introduction to Another Voice' in Harding, S. (ed) *Feminism & Methodology* Open University Press, Milton Keynes, pp.29-36.

Mitchell, J. & Oakley, A. (eds) (1976) *The Rights and Wrongs of Women* Penguin, Harmondsworth.

Morgan, R. (1989) *The Demon Lover* Methuen, London.

Morley, A. & Stanley, L. (1988) *The Life and Death of Emily Wilding Davison* The Women's Press, London.

Morris, A. (1987) *Women, Crime and Criminal Justice* Basil Blackwell, Oxford.

Morris, A. & Wilczynski, A. (1993) 'Rocking the cradle: Mothers who kill their children' in Birch, H. (ed) (1993) *Moving Targets* Virago, London, pp.198-217.

Morris, T. (1991) 'Reviews' in *British Journal of Criminology* Vol 31 no 1 Winter, pp.86-92.

Naffine, N. (1990) *Law & The Sexes* Allen & Unwin, London.

Naish, C. (1991) *Death Comes to the Maiden* Routledge, London.

Nead, L. (1990) *Myths of Sexuality* Basil Blackwell, Oxford.

Nelson, C. & Grossberg, L. (eds) (1988) *Marxism and the Interpretation of Culture* MacMillan, London.

Nicholson, L.J. (ed) (1990) *Feminism/Postmodernism* Routledge, London.

Noddings, N. (1989) *Women and Evil* University of California Press, Berkeley.

Oakley, A. (1974) *Housewife* Pelican Books, Harmondsworth.

Oakley, A. (1981) *Subject Women* Fontana Press, London.

Oakley, A. (1981) 'Normal Motherhood: An Exercise in Self-Control?' in Hutter, B. & Williams, G. (eds) *Controlling Women* Croom Helm, London, pp.79-107.

O'Donnell, B. (1956) *Should Women Hang?* W.H. Allen, London.

O'Donovan, K. (1985) *Sexual Divisions in Law* Weidenfeld & Nicolson, London.

Oram, A. (1989) 'Embittered, sexless or homosexual: attacks on spinster teachers 1918-39' in Angerman, A., Binnema, G., Keunen, A., Poels, V., and Zirkzee, J. (eds) *Current Issues in Women's History* Routledge, London.

Orel, H. (1987) *The Unknown Thomas Hardy* Harvester Press, London.

Otto, S. (1981) 'Women, Alcohol and Social Control' in Hutter, B. & Williams, G. (eds) *Controlling Women* Croom Helm London pp.154-67.

Pannick, D. (1987) *Judges* Oxford University Press, Oxford.

Pateman, C. (1988) 'The Fraternal Social Contract' in Keane, J. (ed) *Civil Society and the State* Verso, London, pp.101-27.

Pearson, G. (1983) *Hooligan* MacMillan, London.

Philipson, C. (1981) 'Women in Later Life: Patterns of Control and Subordination' in Hutter,B. & Williams, G. (eds) *Controlling Women* Croom Helm, London, pp.185-201.

Pollak, O. (1950) *The Criminality of Women* University of Pennsylvania Press, Philadelphia.

Potter, H. (1993) *Hanging in Judgment* SCM Press Ltd, London.

Pringle, R. (1988) *Secretaries Talk* Verso, London.

Radford, L. (1993) 'Pleading for time: justice for battered women' in Birch, H. (ed) *Moving Targets* Virago, London pp.172-97.

Ramazanoglu, C. (ed) (1993) *Up Against Foucault* Routledge, London.

Ramazanoglu, C. & Holland, J. (1993) 'Women's sexuality and men's appropriation of desire' in Ramazanoglu, C. (ed) *Up Against Foucault* Routledge, London, pp.239-61.

Ransom, J. (1993) 'Feminism, difference and discourse: The limits of discursive analysis for feminism' in Ramazanoglu, C. (ed) *Up Against Foucault* Routledge, London, pp.123-46.

Rawlinson, P. (1989) *A Price Too High* Weidenfeld and Nicolson, London.

Raymond, J. (1980) *The Transsexual Empire* The Women's Press, London.

Rich, A. (1977) *Of Woman Born* Virago, London.

Roberts, N. (1992) *Whores in History* Grafton, London.

Rose, A. (1991) *Scandal at the Savoy* Bloomsbury, London.

Rose, J. (1993) *Why War?* Basil Blackwell, Oxford.

Rose, L. (1986) *The Massacre of the Innocents: Infanticide 1800-1939* Routledge & Kegan Paul, London.

Rowbotham, S. (1973) *Woman's Consciousness, Man's World* Pelican Books, Harmondsworth.

Rowbotham, S. (1977) *Hidden From History* Pluto, London.

Rusche, G. & Kirchheimer, O. (1939) *Punishment and Social Structure* Columbia University Press, New York.

Ryan, B. with The Rt Hon Lord Havers (1989) *The Poisoned Life of Mrs Maybrick* Penguin, Harmondsworth.

Ryan, M. (1978) *The acceptable pressure group* Saxon House, Farnborough.

Sargent, L. (ed) (1981) *The Unhappy Marriage of Marxism and Feminism* Pluto, London.

Sawicki, J. (1991) *Disciplining Foucault* Routledge, London.

Scraton, P. & Gordon, P. (eds) (1984) *Causes for Concern* Pelican Books, Harmondsworth.

Scully, D. (1991) *Understanding Sexual Violence* HarperCollins, London.

Segal, L. (1990) *Slow Motion* Virago, London.

Segrave, K. (1992) *Women Serial and Mass Murderers* McFarland & Co, North Carolina and London.

Sharpe, J.A. (1985) '"Last Dying Speeches": Religion, Ideology and Public Execution in Seventeenth-Century England' *in Past and Present* (1985) 107, pp.145-67.

Sharpe, J.A. (1990) *Judicial Punishment in England*, Faber & Faber, London.

Sim, J. (1990) *Medical Power in Prisons* Open University Press, Milton Keynes.

Smart, B. (1983) 'On Discipline and Social Regulation: A Review of Foucault's Genealogical Analysis' in Garland, D. & Young, P. (eds) *The Power to Punish* Heinemann, London, pp.62-83.

Smart, C. & Smart, B. (eds) (1978) *Women, Sexuality, and Social Control* Routledge & Kegan Paul, London.

Smart, C. (1978) *Women, Crime and Criminology* Routledge & Kegan Paul, London.

Smart, C. (1981) 'Law and the Control of Women's Sexuality: The Case of the 1950s' in Hutter, B. & Williams, G. (eds) *Controlling Women* Croom Helm, London, pp.40-60.

Smart, C. (1984) *The Ties That Bind* Routledge & Kegan Paul, London.

Smart, C. (1989) *Feminism and the Power of Law* Routledge, London.

Smart, C. (1990) 'Feminist approaches to criminology or postmodern woman meets atavistic man' in Gelsthorpe, L. & Morris, A. (eds) *Feminist Perspectives in Criminology* Open University Press, Milton Keynes, pp.70-84.

Smart, C. (ed) (1992) *Regulating Womanhood* Routledge, London.

Smart, C. (1992) 'The Woman of Legal Discourse' in *Social & Legal Studies*Vol 1, no 1, March, Sage, London, pp.29-44.

Smart, C. (1995) *Law, Crime and Sexuality* Sage, London.

Smith, D.E. (1987) *The Everyday World as Problematic* Open University Press, Milton Keynes.

Smith, L.S. (1978) 'Sexist assumptions and female delinquency' in Smart C. & Smart, B. (eds) *Women, Sexuality and Social Control* Routledge & Kegan Paul, London pp.74-88.

Spender, D. (1980) *Man Made Language* Routledge & Kegan Paul, London.

Spender, D. (1983) *Women of Ideas* Ark, London.

Spensky, M. (1992) 'Producers of legitimacy: Homes for unmarried mothers in the 1950s' in Smart, C. (1992) *Regulating Womanhood* Routledge, London, pp.100-18.

Spierenburg, P. (1984) *The Spectacle of Suffering* Cambridge University Press, Cambridge.

Stanko, E. (1990) *Everyday Violence* Pandora, London.

Stanko, E. (1990) 'When precaution is normal: a feminist critique of crime prevention' in Gelsthorpe, L. & Morris, A. (eds) *Feminist Perspectives in Criminology* Open University Press, Milton Keynes, pp.173-83.

Stanko, E. & Scully, A. (1996) 'Retelling the Tale: The Emma Humphreys Case' in Myers, A. & Wight, S. (eds) *No Angels* Pandora, London, pp.57-71.

Stanley, L. (ed) (1990) *Feminist Praxis* Routledge, London.

Stanley, L. & Wise, S. (1990) 'Method, methodology and epistemology in feminist research processes' in Stanley, L. (ed) *Feminist Praxis* Routledge, London, pp.20-60.

Stanley, L. & Wise, S. (1983) *Breaking Out* Routledge & Kegan Paul, London.

Stanley, L. & Wise, S. (1993) *Breaking Out Again* Routledge, London.

Stefano, C.D. (1988) 'Dilemmas of Difference: Feminism, Modernity, and Postmodernism' in Nicholson, L.J. (ed) (1990) *Feminism/Postmodernism* Routledge, London, pp.63-82.

Sumner, C. (1990) 'Foucault, gender and the censure of deviance' in Gelsthorpe, L. & Morris, A. (eds) *Feminist Perspectives in Criminology* Open University Press, Milton Keynes, pp.26-40.

Sydie, R.A. (1987) *Natural Women Cultured Men* Open University Press, Milton Keynes.

Szasz, T. (1971) *The Manufacture of Madness* Routledge & Kegan Paul, London.

Taylor, I. (1981) *Law and Order: Arguments for Socialism* MacMillan, London.

Tong, R. (1989) *Feminist Thought* Routledge, London.

Trebilcot, J. (1982) 'Sex Roles: The Arguments From Nature' in Vetterling-Braggin, M. (ed) (1982) *"Femininity", "Masculinity", and "Androgyny"* Littlefield, Adams & Co, Totowa.

Tuttle, E.O. (1961) *The Crusade Against Capital Punishment in Great Britain* Stevens & Sons Ltd, London.

Twinning, W. (1990) *Rethinking Evidence* Basil Blackwell, Oxford.

Ussher, J. (1991) *Women's Madness* HarvesterWheatsheaf, Hemel Hempstead.

Vetterling-Braggin, M. (ed) (1982) *"Femininity", Masculinity", and "Androgyny"* Litttlefield, Adams & Co, Totowa.

White, J. (1986) *The Worst Street in North London* Routledge & Kegan Paul, London.

Vicinus, M. (1985) *Independent Women: Work and Community for Single Women 1850-1920* Virago, London.

Weis, R. (1990) *Criminal Justice* Penguin, Harmondsworth.

Welldon, E.V. (1992) *Mother, Madonna, Whore* Guildford Press, New York.

Wilson, D. (1978) 'Sexual codes and conduct' in Smart C. & Smart, B. (eds) *Women, Sexuality and Social Control* Routledge & Kegan Paul, London, pp.65-73.

Wilson, E. (1980) *Only Halfway to Paradise* Tavistock, London.

Wilson, E. (1983) *What Is To Be Done About Violence Against Women?* Penguin, Harmondsworth.

Wilson, P. (1971) *Murderess* Michael Joseph Ltd, London.

Woodhull, W. (1988) 'Sexuality, Power, and the Question of Rape' in Diamond, I & Quinby, L. (eds) *Feminism & Foucault* Northeastern University Press, Boston pp.167-76.

Woodward, E. (ed) (1993) *In Suspicious Circumstances* Boxtree, London.

Worrall, A. (1981) 'Out of Place: Female Offenders in Court' in *Probation Journal* 28, pp.90-3.

Worrall, A. (1990) *Offending Women* Routledge, London.

Yallop, D. (1990) *To Encourage the Others* Corgi Books, London.

Young, F. (ed) (1923) *The Trial of Frederick Bywaters and Edith Thompson* William Hodge & Co Ltd, Edinburgh and London.

Zedner, L. (1991) *Women, Crime and Custody in Victorian England* Clarendon Press, London.

Index

367